Henry Morley

Early Prose Romances

Henry Morley

Early Prose Romances

ISBN/EAN: 9783744674386

Printed in Europe, USA, Canada, Australia, Japan

Cover: Foto ©Thomas Meinert / pixelio.de

More available books at **www.hansebooks.com**

EARLY PROSE ROMANCES.

𝔅𝔞𝔩𝔩𝔞𝔫𝔱𝔶𝔫𝔢 𝔓𝔯𝔢𝔰𝔰
BALLANTYNE, HANSON AND CO.
EDINBURGH AND LONDON

EARLY
PROSE ROMANCES

REYNARD THE FOX   FRIAR BACON

ROBERT THE DEVIL   GUY OF WARWICK   VIRGILIUS

HISTORY OF HAMLET   FRIAR RUSH

EDITED BY

HENRY MORLEY, LL.D.

LONDON
GEORGE ROUTLEDGE AND SONS
BROADWAY, LUDGATE HILL
GLASGOW, MANCHESTER, AND NEW YORK
1889

CONTENTS.

INTRODUCTION.

———⊷———

THIS volume contains seven old stories. The first of them is the old Beast Epic of "Reynard the Fox," in Caxton's translation from the Flemish. Jacob Grimm believed that these fables of beasts applied, with a strong national feeling, to corruption growing among strong men who wronged the poor and used religion only as a cloak for violence and fraud, were from their origin Teutonic. Like fables elsewhere could in great measure be accounted for by the like suggestion of natural resemblance between beasts and men. But it has been observed that the earliest known use of such fabling by a German writer is in Fredegar's Chronicle, quoted under the year 612 as a "*rustica fabula*" of the Lion, the Fox, and the Stag, which distinctly follows Æsop, and undergoes change afterwards from the fancy of narrators. The story also of the remedy suggested by the Fox to the sick Lion (see in this volume a chapter of Caxton's "Reynart ") comes from Æsop. It was developed in the eighth century in a Latin poem ascribed to the Lombard Paulus Diaconus, who may have had it at the court of Charlemagne as matter already familiar among the Franks. Either from Byzantium or through contact with Rome, such fables could readily have passed into the hearing or the reading of Teutonic monks, who cared about God and the people, steeped the fables in minds active for reform, and developed them, as the Teutonic races developed also the Arthurian myths, into forms inseparable from their nationality.

The sick Lion reappears in the tenth century in the oldest poem elaborated as a Beast Epic, the *"Ecbasis cujusdam Captivi."* Its author belonged to the monastery of St. Evre, at Toul. Strict reforms among the brethren, in the year 936, caused his *Ecbasis*— his going out. He was brought back, and as a sign of his regeneration wrote the poem, in which he figured himself *"per tropologiam"* as a calf, who, having gone out from safety, became captive to the wolf. The *"Ecbasis"* has already incidents that become further developed in the myth of "Reynart."

The next stage of growth is marked by the Latin poem *"Ysengrimus,"* which was first named *"Reinardus Vulpes."* It was written about the year 1148 by a Flemish priest, Nivardus of Ghent. Here we have the names that afterwards entered so completely into the speech of Europe that the old French word for a fox, *Goupil*, was replaced by Renard, Reinaert. Reynard or Reginhard means absolutely hard, a hardened evil-doer whom there is no turning from his way. It is altogether out of this old story that the Fox has come by that name. Isegrim, the Wolf's name, is also Flemish—Isengrin meaning the iron helm. The bear they named Bruno, Bruin, for the colour of his coat.

The earliest French version of this national satire is lost. There are traces of it to be found in the later *"Roman de Renard"* which confirm the belief that it was known to and used by the Alsatian Heinrich der Glichezare (the name means simulator), who about the year 1180 wrote the first *"Reinart"* in German. He first called it *"Isengrine's Not:"*—

> Nû vernemet seltsarniu dinc
> und vremdiu maere
> der der Glichesaere
> inkünde gît, si sint gewaerlich
> Er ist geheizen Heinrich,
> der hât diu buoch zesamene geleit
> von Isengrînes arbeit.

The poem was afterwards entitled *"Reinhart Fuhs."* There remain two MSS. of it, one at Heidelberg, the other in the Bishop's Library at Kalocsa, in Hungary. Its vigorous author was one of the poets who lived of old by voice as well as pen, themselves reciting what they wrote.

From a French poem on the same subject, written in the beginning of the thirteenth century by a priest, Pierre de St. Cloud, came the Flemish poem of "Reinhart," by Willem, at the beginning of the thirteenth century. This was continued by another poet of less mark about the year 1380. A prose commentary on this appeared in 1480, and a Low German translation of it was printed and published at Lübeck in 1498. In the earliest form of the story, in the tenth century, the Fox triumphed. Willem's "Reinaert" ended with the exile of the Fox from court. It was the continuer of Willem in 1380 who brought the Fox back, and told of his judicial combat with Isegrim, and showed hypocrisy again triumphant.

Willem's Low German poem of "Reinaert" was followed by a prose "Hystorie van Regnaert die Vos," printed at Gouda, in Holland, by Gerard Leeu, in 1479. Caxton's translation was made from the Low German, and retains many Teutonic words in their Dutch form, which was also the form most nearly allied to English. Caxton's long residence at Bruges made the language as familiar to him as his own, and sometimes his English includes a word from the other side of the boundary between English and Dutch. The first edition of Caxton's translation was finished at Westminster in June 1481. There was a second edition in 1489, of which the only known copy is in the Pepys Library at Cambridge.

Caxton's translation is, as the reader will find, free, vigorous, and lively; but, as printed by himself, it is not only without breaks of paragraph, but there is a punctuation in which the end of one sentence is now and then detached from its own connection and joined to the beginning of another, and in various ways the pleasant features of the story are seen dimly sometimes as through a veil. I have, therefore, corrected absolute mistakes, and broken the story into paragraphs that mark the briskness of its dialogue and of its homely wit. Old words and grammatical forms have been left, but I have preferred to print familiar words that remain

to us in modern English in the spelling that now brings their
sense most quickly to the reader's mind. An exact transcript of
Caxton's "History of Reynard the Fox" is easily to be had. It
was published in 1880 by Professor Arber, of Mason's College,
Birmingham, in his "English Scholar's Library," and can be
received from him through the post for eighteenpence.

This old story, said Thomas Carlyle, "comes before us with a
character such as can belong only to very few—that of being a
true world's Book, which, through centuries, was everywhere at
home, the spirit of which diffused itself into all languages and all
minds. The quaint Æsopic figures have painted themselves in
innumerable heads; that rough, deep-lying humour has been the
laughter of many generations."

"Reynard the Fox" was German in its origin; "Robert the
Devil," French. In each tale there was the mediæval popular sense
of cruel oppression by the strong. In "Reinaert," as first written,
fraud and cruelty were banished with the Fox out of the Lion's
court; but the old continuer of the story brought them back, and
left them, as they were in the world, or as they seemed to be,
triumphant over earthly opposition. In "Robert the Devil" force
of cruelty was exaggerated to the utmost, for the purpose of insist-
ing on the higher spiritual force that was alone able to triumph
over it, and for the purpose of teaching that no sinner, however
great, can be beyond the reach of rescue by a true repentance.

The legend of "Robert the Devil" was developed first in
France out of elements that are to be found in the early tales
of widely separated peoples. From France the developed story
spread into Spain. It scarcely passed into Italy. In Germany
it never was acclimatised, though adopted into modern German
romance literature. In the Netherlands the romance of "Ro-
brecht den Duyvel" was forbidden by the Bishop of Antwerp on
the 11th of April 1621.

The oldest known version of the story of "Robert the Devil"
was one in Latin prose by Etienne de Bourbon, a Dominican
Friar who died soon after the middle of the thirteenth century.

It was part of a work that he left unfinished, a collection of historical anecdotes, legends, and apologues, and is there given as a story which he had heard from two of his brethren, and from one who said that he had read it. The story must, therefore, have been contained, earlier than the year 1250, in some monastic writing which is now unknown. The tale is given by Etienne de Bourbon as a religious history to enforce the manifold use of penitence. " *De multiplici utilitate penitencie. Penitentia vincit et superat hostes, et a casu et a miseria elevat.*"

To the thirteenth century belongs also the first version of the tale in French, as a romance in octosyllabic rhyming couplets. Of this there are two MSS. at Paris in the National Library, one of the thirteenth century, and one of the fourteenth. The earlier of these was edited in 1837, in an edition limited to 130 copies, by G. S. Trébutien.

There is also a thirteenth-century prose version of the tale in French prefixed to the old "Croniques de Normandie." The writer of this, whom Littré believes to have lived at the close of the century, also refers to written authority for what he tells, "*selon ce quil mest appareu par aucunes escriptures.*" The two oldest printed copies of the "Croniques de Normandie," with the prefixed tale of "Robert the Devil," differing much in arrangement, both appeared at Rouen in the same year, 1487.

In 1496 the story first appeared, printed at Lyon, as a distinct prose tale, "The Terrible and Marvellous Life of Robert the Devil who was named afterwards the Man of God." It was followed, as it has since often been followed, by "The Romance of Richard, son of Robert the Devil, who was Duke of Normandy." This prose life—differing in some main features from that prefixed to the "Chronicles of Normandy"—was reprinted at Paris in 1497, and has from that time to this been frequently reprinted. It is the accepted French prose version of the tale.

The accepted verse form was that of a "*Dit de Robert le Deable,*" which exists in three MSS. at Paris, and was a recasting in the fourteenth century of preceding versions. The *Dit* is in strophes

of four alexandrines, rhymed together, and it alters the old close
of the story.

Between the romance and the *Dit* there was produced also a
dramatic version, "*Miracle de Nostre Dame de Robert-le-Diable.*"
This was first edited and printed at Rouen in 1836, with Introduction by C. Deville, Paulin Paris, and others.

Reference has also been made to an unpublished metrical
version of the legend made in the sixteenth century by Jacques
de la Hogue.

From the French prose book the story was first translated into
English for the edition twice printed, without date, by Wynkyn
de Worde, Caxton's most energetic assistant and successor, who
printed as many as four hundred and ten books, and was the
introducer of Roman type into England. Wynkyn de Worde's
version—that which is here given—of the "Lyfe of Robert the
Devyll" was printed by William J. Thoms in 1827 in "Ancient
English Fictions, a Collection of Early Prose Romances," of
which there was a second enlarged edition published in 1858,
in three volumes, as "Early English Prose Romances." Except
"Reynard the Fox," the "Historie of Hamlet," and "Guy of
Warwick," the stories in this volume have been chosen from the
collection made by that acute and genial student of the past.

In the earliest known form of the tale of "Robert the Devil"
there is no place named as the scene of it, and we are not told
that the wicked man who was to repent was, as a child, called
Devil by his playfellows. Normandy first appears as his home in
the metrical romance, with Rome for the scene of the penance.
There are variations in the matter of the tale as it is found in
Etienne de Bourbon, in the romance, in the *Dit*, in the *Chronique*, and in the first French prose version of the "Life of
Robert the Devil" as a distinct book for the use of the people.

The prose story in the *Chronique* gives five or six more incidents of Robert's evil-doing, and omits only the blinding of his
father's messengers. It says nothing of his wonderful birth
and the discovery of it from his mother. It ascribes Robert's
conversion to the teaching of a holy man, a hermit who took

charge of him when he was wounded. There is no war with the Saracens at the end of this version of the tale; no marriage with the Emperor's daughter.

The romance, like the separate prose life of 1496, which is in general accord with the romance and the *Dit*, brought the fierce impulse to repentance out of the storm of Robert's own nature. This puts more force into the hero's character, more life into the passion of the tale. The romance and the prose life of 1496 tell of the war with the Saracens and the love of the Emperor's daughter; but in the romance Robert refuses marriage, and passes the rest of his life as a holy anchorite. In the popular prose life his refusal to marry is overcome by the express command of God. Robert marries the Emperor's daughter, succeeds his father in Normandy, and passes the rest of his life as a just and religious ruler of his people.

It is not to be supposed that there was any historical foundation for the legend. Robert the Devil has been identified with the Norman Robert I. the Magnificent, who died in 1035; also with Robert II., Courte-Heuse, son of William the Conqueror, who died in 1134. Le Héricher has found him in the Norman Rollo. Trébutien says that there is nothing to hinder us from believing that he was, not Duke but Dux, son of an Aubert who in the eighth century ruled over the future Normandy. There is nothing to hinder us from so believing, because faith is free; and there is nothing that will help to such belief. It is a Church legend shaped from popular ideas to enforce the efficacy of repentance. It was told first of a nameless person in an unnamed place; it was then furnished with name and place to give it more solidity, and made emphatic by exaggerations of the pictures that set forth on one side the greatness of the sin, and on the other side showed the completeness of the penance and the pardon. The sinner's violence is that of a devil. In his repentance he abases himself below humanity. This is shown vividly by his putting away the use of speech and of intellect; he takes on himself the actions of a fool, and does not sit at the same table with his fellow-men, but eats and sleeps with the dogs. Full pardon comes of full repentance, tested by long resistance of temptation to reveal the secret of his self-abasement.

This volume contains also two tales of conjurors, Virgilius and Friar Bacon.

The story of Virgilius is chiefly of Italian origin. From early days among his countrymen, Vergil was half a god. Silius Italicus, Pliny tells us, kept Vergil's birthday by a religious visit to his monument in Naples as to a temple. Martial counted the Ides of October as sacred to Vergil, " *Octobres Maro consecravit Idus ;* " and Statius also made a temple of the tomb—

> " Maroneique sedens in margine templi
> Sumo animum."

A vague sense of divine greatness in Vergil led to the use of his works as an oracle. By opening his book at random and letting the eye fall on a passage, there was to be found in that passage an oracular solution for any difficulty. This use of the *sortes Virgilianæ* was familiar to the Emperor Hadrian, and is not yet dead. No other books have been so used except Homer and the Bible ; but there were few readers of Homer in the Middle Ages, among followers of the Western Church.

Then came *centoni* of Vergilian verse, in which lines and phrases were rearranged to make Vergilian poems upon subjects not treated by Vergil. The most famous of these, made by the Emperor Valentinian with aid of Ausonius, is a nuptial cento, in which the pure Vergil was made to speak immodestly.

The Christians found in Vergil's fourth eclogue—*Pollio*—a prophecy of Christ. Pope afterwards, following that idea, mixed up in his " Messiah " Vergil's Pollio with the prophecies of Isaiah. This prophecy of the birth of a child with whom there should come a new and happy age of justice, love, and peace, was fastened upon by the Christians as early as the fourth century. To Lactantius the prophecy was of Christ's second coming.

The description of magical charms in the eighth eclogue— *Pharmaceutria*—and the visit to the unknown world in the sixth book of the Æneid, contributed, no doubt, to the growth of the idea that Vergil was a great magician; but there is no definite speaking of him in that character before the twelfth century. At the close of the thirteenth century, when the genius of Dante first breathed the spirit of the artist into modern literature, Dante's great master was Vergil, greatest of the poets known to him, and gifted beyond all men with the poet's insight, which is clearest use of human wisdom.

In the popular literature of the thirteenth century there was in French verse by a monk of Hauteseille, in Lorraine, a variation on "The Seven Sages" called "Dolopathos." Dolopathos was an imagined king of Sicily who lived in the time of Augustus, and sent his son Lucinianus to be taught at Rome by Vergil. Before the son returned to Sicily his mother had died and his father married again. Vergil saw in the stars great danger threatening him, and Lucinianus was bidden to keep strict silence until Vergil himself told him to speak. The stepmother caused the son to be condemned to death by his father. The day of execution was delayed by story-telling until the seventh day, when Vergil came and bade his pupil speak. In consequence of what he told, the stepmother was burnt alive.

Among the people of Naples, apt at story-telling, in the twelfth century, tales of Vergil the magician began to multiply. Naples had been a favourite place of residence with the poet, and after his death at Brundusium, B.C. 19, his remains were taken to Naples and entombed by the Via Puteolana, on the road from Naples to Puteoli. Conrad of Querfurt, in a letter from Italy, dated 1194, describing his travels, tells of Naples provided by Vergil with a palladium in the form of a small model of the city enclosed in a bottle with a narrow neck; also of a magical bronze horse, and a bronze fly that kept flies out of the city, and other wonders that we find woven into the tale of Vergil the Enchanter. Gervase of Tilbury, about eighteen years later, in his "*Otia Imperialia*," tells more such tales, and there are more references to Vergil's magic in Alexander Neckham's book "*De Naturis Rerum.*" The people of Naples adopted Vergil as the protecting genius of

the city, and some of their tales were clearly based on legends
and traditions from the East.   Vergil's releasing of the Devil re-
calls the tale of the Fisherman and Genie in the " Arabian Nights."
Apollonius Tyaneus also was said to have made a bronze fly that
kept flies out of Byzantium.   Professor Domenico Comparetti, in
his two volumes published at Leghorn in 1872—"*Virgilio nel Medio
Evo*"—gives many interesting details of the growth of the tradition,
and finds in many of the tales of Vergil a popular association of
ideas with objects familiar to the people of Naples.   When the
palladium had been transformed from a model of Naples to an egg,
the old castle built in 1154 changed its name in the fourteenth
century from *Castello di mare* to *Castel dell' uovo.*   In the statutes
of a religious house it is described as *Castellum ovi incantati.*
Meanwhile the tales spread over Italy and beyond Italy, from lip
to lip through the story-tellers, and became more and more
familiar in books.   But there have been no manuscripts found of
the French story-book, "*Les Faits Merveilleux de Virgille,*" which
come down to us in rare printed copies of the earlier part of the
sixteenth century.   It was translated into English, into Dutch,
and into German ; there is also at Copenhagen a MS. translation
of it into Icelandic through the Dutch.

The English translation is that given in this volume, as printed,
with woodcuts, in Gothic letter, at Antwerp, without date, by
John Doesborcke.   " This boke treatethe of the lyfe of Virgilius
and of his death, and many maravyles, that he dyd in his lyfe
tyme by witchcraft and nigromansy, thorough the help of the
devylls of hell."   From the one known copy Utterson reproduced
in 1812 an edition of sixty copies, from one of which it was
reprinted in 1828 by W. J. Thoms in the collection already
named, of which a translation into German, with additional matter
by R. O. Spazier, was published at Brunswick in 1830.

" The Historie of Hamlet," that next follows, is from a book
printed by Richard Bradocke for Thomas Pavier in 1608, of
which there is only one known copy.   Nash's " Epistle," prefixed
to Greene's " Menaphon," published in 1589, refers to a play of

"Hamlet" then existing, which was earlier than Shakespeare's. This may have been founded upon the tale as told in the " *Histoires Tragiques*" of Belleforest, together with tales from the Italian of Bandello, whose novels Belleforest and his fellow-translator, Boiastuau, adopted. If it was taken from the English book, which is translated from Belleforest, then the first edition of the English translation was of earlier date than 1589.

The tale of "Hamlet" first appears in the third book of the Danish history of Saxo Grammaticus. And who was he? He was a Danish historian, of noble family, who lived in the latter half of the twelfth century, and died soon after the year 1203. He began life as a monastic writer, who for his Latinity was called "*Grammaticus.*" Upon the suggestion of his patron, Absalon, Archbishop of Lund, he wrote a history of Danish kings and heroes, which, till the tenth century, is legendary. The historian delighted in the legends of the people, and reported them with evident fidelity. This gives especial interest to ten books of his Danish history; in the remaining six he is more simply historian. A translation of Saxo Grammaticus into Danish is a popular book among the Danes. A translation of it into English will some day, I hope, become current in England. I know where there is a translation of it to be had, which should be made accessible to many readers.

In Saxo's third book we are told how, when Rörik Slyngebond, towards the close of the seventh century, was king of Denmark, Gervendill was chief in Jutland. After the death of Gervendill, his two sons, Horvendill and Fengo, succeeded him. Horvendill won to himself glory as a vikingr, that stirred envy in Koller, king of Norway. Koller hunted the seas for Horvendill, and at last met him, and was killed by him on an island in the spring-time, and fought with him the kind of island-duel known as "*Holmgang.*" Horvendill's rich gifts from his booty won the favour of his king, Rörik; so he married Rörik's daughter, Gerutha, and became by her the father of Amleth—Hamlet. All this prosperity of Horvendill stirred envy in his brother Fengo. Fengo fell on Horvendill with open force, slew him, succeeded to his rule, and reigned tyrannically.

He also beguiled the mind of his brother's wife, Gerutha, and married her. Amleth, her son, then simulated madness. It is to be noted also that *Amloda* signified a foolish person. He soiled himself by daily lying in the ashes. He cut little sticks to points and hardened them in fire, and made men laugh by saying that he got them ready to avenge his father. Shrewd minds and guilty minds suspected him. They sought to make him betray himself to a fair woman in a wood, and to certain youths, but a foster-brother took care that he should not be beguiled. Amleth understood the devices, and when offered a horse, mounted with his face looking hindward and took the tail for a bridle. His answers of feigned insanity were always witty. When he was told that the sand by the seashore was meal, he said, "Yes, ground by the storms and the white-crested waves." In the younger Edda there is a fragment of verse which gives Amlodi's Mill as one of the poetical names for the sea. In other ways Amleth contrived so to tell truth as to seem a fool. But Fengo saw the underlying wit, and as he could not make away with him in Denmark for fear of King Rörik, sent him to England with companions who carried lines which Amleth searched for, found, and altered so that they asked for the killing of their bearers, and that Amleth should be married to the king of England's daughter. So the tale goes on, very much as we have it in the English prose history. There was no place in Danish history for a real Hamlet. His adventures were those of a fable current among the people, which owed its permanence to the fact that Saxo thought it worth recording. It seems to have been a tradition of Jutland, for in Saxo's time Amleth's grave was said to be south of the town of Hald, in the district of Randers.

The story of "Hamlet" passed from Saxo into the Danish Chronicle rhymed by a monk, Niel of Sorö, about the year 1480, and first printed at Copenhagen in 1495. Fengo is there said to have been slain in his own house at Viborg in Jutland.

Belleforest took his story from the Latin of Saxo, with rhetorical and moral elaborations, and some variation. Thus in the tale as it was told by Saxo, the spy who was to overhear Hamlet's discourse with his mother was hidden under the straw that in old times was strewn upon the floor. Amleth went about crowing like a cock, and stabbed when his feet came upon somebody concealed under the straw. Belleforest, unaccustomed to such carpeting of royal chambers, translated the word *stramentum* into tapestry; for Belleforest was a *protégé* of Margaret of Navarre, familiar with the houses of French nobles in a time of growing luxury. He died in 1583, aged fifty-three. Margaret of Navarre began her care for him when he was seven years old, and had just lost his father. He was educated by her and bred for the bar, but turned poet and man of letters. Outliving his better days, he wrote much prose of any kind that would earn bread, and among other works the collection of tales which included that showing, " Avec quelle ruse Amleth, qui depuis fut roy de Danne-marck, vengea la mort de son père Horvendille, occis par Fengon son frère, et autre occurrence de son histoire."

The English version of Hamlet is followed in this volume by the old story of Friar Bacon, the Franciscan friar whose clear study of Nature gave him fame as a magician in the stories of the people. The real Roger Bacon, born in 1214, was in his cradle in Somersetshire when the Barons obtained from King John his signature to Magna Charta. He belonged to a rich family, sought knowledge from childhood, and avoided the strife of the day. He studied at Oxford and Paris, and the death of his father may have placed his share of the paternal estate in his hands. He spared no cost for instructors and transcribers, books and experiments; mastered not only Latin thoroughly, but also Hebrew and Greek, which not more than five men in England then understood grammatically, although there were more who could loosely read and speak those tongues. He was made Doctor in Paris, and had the degree confirmed in his own University of Oxford. Then he withdrew entirely from the civil strife that was arising, and joined the house of the Franciscans in Oxford, having spent all his time in the world and two thousand pounds of money in the search for knowledge. Roger

Bacon's family committed itself to the king's side in the civil war which Henry's III.'s greed, his corruption of justice, and violation of the defined rights of his subjects, brought upon him. The success of the Barons ruined Bacon's family, and sent his mother, brothers, and whole kindred into exile. Meanwhile the philosopher, as one of the Oxford Franciscans, had come under Grosseteste's care, and joined an Order which prided itself on the checks put by it on the vanity of learning. But, in spite of their self-denials, the Franciscans, at Oxford and elsewhere, included many learned men, who, by the daily habit of their minds, were impelled to give to scholarship a wholesome practical direction. They were already beginning to supply the men who raised the character of teaching at the University of Oxford till it rivalled that of Paris. Friar Bacon was among the earliest of these teachers; so was Friar Bungay, who lives with him in popular tradition.

Roger Bacon saw how the clergy were entangled in subtleties of a logic far parted from all natural laws out of which it sprang. He believed that the use of all his knowledge, if he could but make free use of it, would be to show how strength and peace were to be given to the Church. And then the Pope, who had been told of his rare acquirements and his philosophic mind, bade Roger Bacon, disregarding any rule of his Order to the contrary, write for him what was in his mind. Within his mind were the first principles of a true and fruitful philosophy. But to commit to parchment all that he had been pining to say would cost him sixty pounds in materials, transcribers, necessary references, and experiments. He was a Franciscan, vowed to poverty, and the Pope had sent no money with the command to write. Bacon's exiled mother and brothers had spent all they were worth upon their ransoms. Poor friends furnished the necessary money, some of them by pawning goods, upon the understanding that their loans would be made known to his Holiness. There was a difficulty between the philosopher and his immediate superiors, because the Pope's command was private, and only a relief to Bacon's private conscience. His immediate rulers had received no orders to relax the discipline which deprived Franciscans of the luxury of pen and ink. But obstacles were overcome, and then Roger Bacon produced within a year and a half, 1268–69, his "*Opus Majus*" (Greater Work), which now forms a large closely-printed folio; his "*Opus Minus*" (Lesser Work), which was sent after the "Opus Majus" to Pope Clement, to recapitulate its arguments and strengthen some of its parts; and his "*Opus Tertium*" (Third Work), which followed as a summary and introduction to the whole, enriched with further novelty, and prefaced with a detail of the difficulties against which its author had contended—details necessary to be given, because, he said, that he might obey the Pope's command the friar had pawned to poor men the credit of the Holy See. These books, produced by Roger Bacon at the close of Henry III.'s reign, and when he was himself fifty-three years old, rejected nearly all that was profitless, and fastened upon all that there was with life and power of growth in the knowledge of his time. They set out with a principle in which Bacon the Friar first laid the foundations of the philosophy of Bacon the Chancellor of later time. He said that there were four grounds of human ignorance : trust in inadequate authority ; the force of custom ; the opinion of the inexperienced crowd ; and the hiding of one's own ignorance with the parading of a super-ficial wisdom. Roger Bacon advocated the free honest question-ing of Nature ; and where books were requisite authorities, warned men against the errors that arose from reading them in bad translations. He would have had all true students endeavour to read the original text of the Bible and of Aristotle. He dwelt on the importance of a study of mathematics, adding a particular consideration of optics, and ending with the study of Nature by experiment, which, he said, is at the root of all other sciences, and a basis of religion. Roger Bacon lived into the reign of Edward I., and died in the year 1292. Friar Bacon's optics appear in that chapter of the popular tale which tells how he took a town by use of a great burning-glass, focussing a chief building in the middle of it, and when he had so set it on fire, and drawn off to it the defenders on the walls, giving the sign for an attack upon the walls. The Brazen Head was an old friend with the

popular story-teller.   William of Malmesbury, who died about
1142, says that Pope Sylvester the Second had one.   Gower,
in the third book of his "Confessio Amantis," tells the story
of Grosteste, who was Roger Bacon's teacher.

> "For of the greté clerk Grostest
> I rede how busy that he was
> Upon the clergie and heved of bras
> To forge, and make it for to telle
> Of suché thingés as befelle.
> And seven yerés besinesse
> He laidé, but for the lachesse
> Of half a minute of an houre
> Fro firsté he began laboure
> He lost all that he haddé do."

Albertus Magnus is said to have made a brazen man, who
answered questions truly, but grew to be so loquacious that the
master's pupil, Thomas Aquinas, whose studies were disturbed
by the incessant talking, about the year 1240, broke his head to
silence him.

The Friar Bungay who was joined with Roger Bacon in
popular fiction was another learned Franciscan, Thomas (called
also John) of Bungay in Suffolk.   He is said to have taught both
at Oxford and Cambridge, and to have been buried at North-
ampton.

The prose "History of Friar Bacon" here given may probably
have been first published before Robert Greene's play of the
"Honorable History of Frier Bacon and Frier Bongay, as it
was plaied by her Majesties servants," and printed in 1594.   But
there were frequent slightly differing editions of the popular prose
book upon which the play was founded.

William J. Thoms, in his preface to "The Tale of Friar Bacon,"
illustrates the popular taste for conjuring-matches, of which Friar
Bungay's contest with Vandermast is an example, by a citation,
through Flögel's "History of Court Fools," from a "History of
Bohemia," by Dubravius.   This tells us that when Charles IV.
married the Bavarian Princess Sophia, the bride's father brought

into Prague, as an agreeable addition to the wedding festival, a waggon-load of magicians. Two of the chief of them were selected to contend together. One was the great Bohemian sorcerer Zytho, who, after desperate trials of skill, at last opened his mouth from ear to ear, seized his opponent, the Bavarian master Gouin, and crammed him down his throat, head, shoulders, body, legs, but stopped at his boots, which he spat out as not eatable because they had not been cleaned. He then disgorged his rival safe and sound. The reader who is gifted with a proper mediæval spirit should have no difficulty in swallowing both these conjurors, with Friar Bacon, Friar Bungay, Vergil, and as many more.

The next story in our collection is a comic specimen of popular heroics, a tall copy of the widely popular tale of "Guy of War-wick." Its writer towered above common men with eloquence raised high upon the stilts of blank verse that was printed like to prose. Prose has its music, but is always bad when it so runs into successive lines of metre that the artifice is obvious. Such artifice of manner weakens faith in the sincerity of what is said.

As a metrical romance, "Guy of Warwick" is as old as the thir-teenth century, and has been doubtfully ascribed to a Franciscan friar, Walter of Exeter. The story of Guy is laid in days before the Norman conquest, and associated with the days of King Athel-stane and the battle of Brunanburh. Guy is said to have been the son of Siward, Baron of Wallingford, to have married Felice, only daughter of the Saxon warrior Rohand, to have lived as a hermit after overcoming Colbrond the Dane, and to have died in the year 929. The romance sprang from the life of the twelfth century. In the prose form here given its mediæval spirit is not wholly lost under the fine rhetoric of clothes with which its body is overlaid. - The earliest edition of the romance in French prose was printed at Paris in 1525. The earliest edition in English prose was printed by William Copland, who died before 1570.

The old Danish tale of " Friar Rush," a satire on the monks, is found in Low German verse of the end of the fifteenth or beginning of the sixteenth century. It was printed also in High German verse at Strasburg in 1515. It was printed again at Nürnberg soon after the middle of the sixteenth century, and again at Magdeburg in 1587. Both in the Low German and the High German versions the Devil Russche or Rausch was received as cook in a Danish monastery to the north of the Lake of Esrom, where there is now, by its wooded shore, a village of that name, about eleven miles from Elsineur, in Seeland. Pontoppidan, in his " *Theatrum Daniæ,*" says that before the Monastery of Esserum was made into a dwelling-house, Brother Rush's effigy was to be seen there, with an epitaph in lines each beginning with Latin words and ending with Danish. They showed also for a long time in the same monastery Brother Rush's cauldron and gridiron. There is a Danish poem on the subject, and also this popular tradition, translated by W. J. Thom from Thiele's " *Danske Folksagn.*"

"BROTHER RUSH.

" It is related that when the Devil once upon a time saw how piously and virtuously the Monks lived in the Monastery of Esrom, he took upon himself the shape of a man, and went to the gate and knocked at it, for to be let in, saying that his name was Rush. Then he gave himself out that he was a Cook's-boy, and was received as such by the Abbot. But when he was once by himself with the Master Cook, he set himself up against him, and got himself therefore punishment. At this he was sore displeased ; and as he had previously a cauldron with water over the fire, and he now perceived that it boiled, he took with all his might the Master Cook, and placing him head downwards in it, began thereupon to run about and to cry, lamenting the misfortune as if it had happened to his master in cooking. Thus he cheated in this manner with falsehood all the brothers in the cloister, that they thought him altogether free, and he was now appointed by them the Master Cook. But it was what he had strived after, in order that he might afterwards deprave them altogether; for now he cooked the meat so unctuously and lickerishly, that the monks neglected fasts and prayers, and gave themselves to feasting. Nay, it is said also that he brought women into the Monastery, and came thereby much in the Abbot's favour, so that he at last caused him to become a Brother, because he well desired constantly to have such a cook at hand. From that time strife and malice prevailed so severely in the Monastery that it had surely come in the power of the Evil One, if none of the Brethren had repented in time. For instance, once Brother Rush was in the wood, and having there seen a beautiful fat cow, he slew it, and took himself one quarter with him to the Monastery, but hung up the rest on a tree in the forest. Then presently came by the countryman who owned the cow; and when he perceived how the three quarters hung in the tree, he hid himself in the other trees to watch until the thief fetched away the remainder. Then he saw, as he sat there, how the Devils had their sport in the forest, and heard much talking about Rush, how he would invite the Abbot and Monks to the banquet with him in Hell. This caused the countryman great alarm, and the next day he went to the Abbot and related to him all that he had seen and heard in the forest.

"When the Abbot heard this he caused all the monks to come to him in the church, and they began there to pray and to sing, so that Rush, as he could not abide the like, was desirous to sneak away. But the Abbot grasped him by the cloak and exorcised him into a red horse, and gave him into the power of Hell. For many years after these events they showed in the Monastery of Esrom Rush's Iron Cauldron and Gridiron."

Friar Rush comes, in fact, from the land of the Pucks. His legend abounds in touches common to the old Northern conceptions of a tricksy and malicious spirit, deepened afterwards in meaning by association with such satire on the earthly life of monks as we have in the old " Land of Cockayne."

So ends the list of the good things in this hamper of romance, which is filled up, by way of packing-straw, with some of the "Hundred Merry Tales." He said "that I had my good wit out of the 'Hundred Merry Tales,'" said Beatrice of Benedict. Only two copies of this once popular book are known, and they were both printed by John Rastell. One of them was partly recovered in 1815 by the Rev. J. J. Conybeare, in leaves, from more than one copy of it that had been used in making the pasteboard found binding another book. It was reprinted at once after its discovery, by Mr. S. W. Singer, in an edition of two hundred and fifty copies, and reprinted again in 1864 by Mr. W. Carew Hazlitt, in the first of the three series of his pleasant collection of "Shakespeare Jest Books." In 1866 Dr. Herman Oesterley published another edition of "A Hundred Merry Tales," from the other known copy, which is dated 1526, and is in the Royal Library of the University of Göttingen, for which it was bought in 1768 at an auction in Lüneburg. The tales here used as packing-straw are taken from Dr. Herman Oesterley's edition of the complete book.

H. M.

Carisbrooke, *July* 1889.

—▸◂—

Of him that fayd that a womàs tong was lightiſt met of degeſtiŏ.

A CERTAYN artificer in londō there was which was fore fyk that coud not well dygeſt hys mete/ to whŏ a phyſycŏ cam to gyue hym councell & feyd yᵗ he muſl vfe to ete metis yᵗ be light of dygeſtyon as fmall byrdys/ as fparous or fwallous & efpecyall yᵗ byrd yᵗ ys callyd a wagtale whofe fleſhe ys merueloufe lyght of dygeſtyŏ becaufe that byrd ys euer mouyng & ſtyryng. The ſik man heryng the pheficion feyd fo anfweryd hym & feyd/ Syr yf that be the caufc yᵗ thofe birdys be lyght of dygeſtyon/ Than I know a mete mych lyghter of dygeſtion thā other fparow fwallow or wagtayle/ & that ys my wyuys tŏg for it is neuer in reſt but euer mouying & ſtyrryng.

¶ By thys tale ye may lerne a good generall rule of pheſyk.

Of the woman that folowyd her fourth huſbandys herce & wept.

A WOMAN ther was whych had had .iiii. huſbādes. It fortunyd alfo that this fourth hufband died & was brought to chirch vppon yᵉ berc/ whŏ this womā folowyd & made gret mone & wext very fory. In fo mych that her neybours thought fhe wold fowne & dy for forow/ wherfor one of her goſſyps cam to her & fpake to her in her ere & bad her for goddes fake to comfort her felf & refrayne that lamentacŏn or ellys it wold hurt her gretly & pauenture put her in ieoperdy of her lyfe. To whŏ this womā āfweryd & fayd/

—

I wys good goſyp I haue gret cauſe to morne if ye knew all/ for I haue byryed .iii. huſbandys befyde thys man/ but I was neuer ĩ the caſe yᵗ I am now/ for there was not one of thē but whē that I folowid the corſe to chyrch yet I was ſure alway of an other huſbãd before that yᵉ corſe cam out of my houſe/ & now I am ſure of no nother huſband & therfore ye may be ſure I haue gret cauſe to be ſad and heuy.

¶ By thys tale ye may ſe that the olde puerbe ys trew that yt is as gret pyte to ſe a woman wepe as a goſe to go barefote.

Of the woman that ſayd her wooer came to late.

A NOTHER woman there was that knelyd at yᵉ mas of requiē whyle the corſe of her huſbande lay on the bere in the chyrch. To whom a yonge man came to ſpeke wyth her in her ere as thoughe hyt had bene for ſom matre concernyng the funerallys/ howe be yt he ſpake of no ſuch matter but only wowyd her that he myghte be her huſbande/ to whome ſhe anſweryde & ſayde thus/ Syr by my trouthe I am ſory that ye come ſo late/ for I am ſped all redy/ For I was made ſure yeſter day to a nother man.

¶ By thys tale ye may perceyue that women ofte tymes be wyſe and lothe to loſe any tyme.

Of the horſman of yrelond that prayd Oconer to hang vp the frere.

ONE callyd Oconer an yriſh lorde toke an horſeman pryſoner that was one of hys gret enmys/ whiche for any requeſt or yntrety yᵗ yᵉ horſman made gaue iugement that he ſhulde incõtynēt be hãgyd/ & made a frere to ſhryue hym and bad hym make hym redy to dye. Thys frere yᵗ ſhroue hym examyned hym of dyuers ſynes & aſkyd hym amõg othere whyche were the grettyſte ſynnys that euer he dyde/ thys horſeman anſweryd & ſayde one of the grettyſt actys that euer I dyde whyche I now moſt repent is that when I toke Oconer the laſte weke in a churche and ther I myght haue brennyd hym church and all & becauſe I had conſcyence

& pyte of brennyng of the church I taryed ye tyme fo long y^e
oconer efcaped/ & that fame deferring of brennyng of the church
& fo long taryeng of that tyme is one of the worft actys y^t euer
I dyd wherof I mofte repente/ Thys frere perceyuyng hym in
that mynd fayd pece man in the name of god & change y^t mynde
& dye in charite or els thou fhalt neuer come in heuen/ nay quod
the hors man I wyll neuer change y^t mynde what fo euer fhall
come to my foule/ thys frere pceyuyng hym thys ftyll to contynew
hys mīde cā to oconer & feyd fyr in ye name of god haue fome
pyte vppō thys mannys fowle & let hym not dye now tyll he be
in a better mynde/ For yf he dye now he ys fo far out of charyte
y^t vtterly hys foule fhalle be dampnyd/ and fhewyd hym what mynde
he was in & all the hole matter as ys before fhewyd. Thys horf-
man heryng ye frere thys intrete for hym fayd to oconer thys/
Oconer thou feeyft well by thys mannys reporte y^t yf I dye now .
I am out of charyte & not redy to go to heuen & fo it ys y^t I am
now out of charyte in dede/ but thou feeft well y^t this frere ys a
good man he is now well dyfpofyd & in charyte/ and he is redy
to go to heuen & fo am not I/ therfore I pray the hang vp thys
frere whyle that he hys redy to go to heuyn and lette me tary
tyl a nother tyme y^t I may be ī charyte and redy & mete to
go to heuyn. This Oconer heryng this mad anfwere of hym
fparyd the man & forgaue hym hys lyfe at that feafon.

¶ By thys ye may fe that he that is in daunger of his enmye
y^t hath no pyte/ he can do no better than fhew to hym the vtter-
mofte of hys malycyous mynde whych that he beryth toward hym.

Of the preft that fayd nother corpus meus nor corpum meum.

THE archdekyn of Effex y^t had bene long in auctoryte in a tyme
of vyfytacion when all the preeftys apperyd before hym callyd
afyde .iii. of ye yōg preftys whych were accufyd y^t they coud not
well fay theyr deuyne feruyce/ & afkyd of thē whē they fayd mas
whether they fayd corpus meus or corpū meū. The furft preeft
fayd y^t he fayd corpus meus. The fecōd fayd y^t he fayd corpū
meū. And thē he afkyd of the thyrd how he fayd/ whych

c

anfweryd & fayd thus/ fyr becaufe it is fo gret a dout & dyuers men be in dyuers opynyons/ therfore becaufe I wold be fure I wold not offend whē I come to yᵉ place I leue it clene out & fay nothyng therfore/ wherfore he then openly rebukyd them all thre.　But dyuers that were prefent thought more defaut in hym becaufe he hym felfe before tyme had admyttyd them to be preeftys.

¶ By thys tale ye may fe that one ought to take hede how he rebukyth an other left it torne moft to hys owne rebuke.

Of the .ii. frerys wherof the one louyd not the ele hed nor the other the tayle.

Two frerys fat at a gentylmans tabyll whych had before hym ŏ a faftyng day an ele & cut the hed of the ele & layd it vppŏ one of yᵉ Freres trĕchars/ but the Frere becaufe he wold haue had of yᵉ myddyll part of the ele fayd to the gentylman he louyd no ele heddes/ this gentylman alfo cut the tayle of yᵉ ele & leyd it on the other Freres trĕchar/ he lykewyfe becaufe he wold haue had of the myddyll pte of yᵉ ele fayd he louyd no ele taylys. Thys gentylmā perceyuyng that: gaue the tayle to the Frere yᵗ fayd he louyd not the hed/ & gaue the hed to hym that fayd he louyd not yᵉ tayle.　And as for the myddell part of the ele he ete part him felf & part he gaue to other folke at yᵉ table/ wherfore thefe freres for anger wold ete neuer a moffell/ & fo they for all theyr craft & fubtylte were not onely deceyued of yᵉ beft moffel of yᵉ ele/ but therof had no part at al.

¶ By this ye fe that they that couet the beft part fomtyme therfore lofe the meane part and all.

Of the welchmā that fhroue hym for brekyng his faft on the fryday.

A WELCHMAN dwellynge in a wylde place of walys came to hys curate in the tyme of lent & was cŏfeffed.　& when his con- feffyon was in maner at the end the curate afked him whether he had any other thyng to say yᵗ greuyd his cŏfcyēce/ whych fore

abafshyd anfweryd no word·a gret whyle/ at laſt by exortacion of
hys gooſtly fader he fayd yᵗ there was one thyng in his mynd that
gretly greuyd his cõfciẽce which he was aſhamed to vtter/ for
it was fo greuous yᵗ he trowid god wold neuer forgyue hym/ to
whom the curate ãfweryd & fayd yᵗ goddys mercy was aboue all/
& bad hym not dyſpayre in the mercy of god/ For what fo
euer it was yf he were repentaũte yᵗ god wold forgyue him/ And
fo by long exortacion at the laſt he ſhewyd it & feyd thus/ Syr
it happenyd onis that as my wyfe was making a chefe vppon a
fryday I wold haue fayed whether it had ben falt or freſh and
toke a lytyll of the whey in my hand & put it in my mouth & or
I was ware part of it went downe my throte agaynſt my wyll &
fo I brake my faſt/ to whom the curate fayd & if ther be no nother
thyng I warant god ſhall forgiue the. So whã he had well com-
fortyd hym wᵗ yᵉ mercy of god the curate prayd hym to anfwer a
queſtion & to tell hym treuth/ & when the welchman had pro·
myſyd to tell the treuth/the curate fayd that there were robberys and
murders done nye the place where he dwelt & dyuers men foũd
ſlayne & aſkyd hym whether he were cõfentyng to any of them/
to whõ he anfwerid & fayd yes & fayd he was ptee to many of
them & dyd helpe to robbe and to ſle dyuers of them. Then
the curate aſkyd hym why he dyd not cõfeſſe him therof/ the
welch man ãſweryd & fayd he toke yᵗ for no fynne for it was a
cuſtome amonge them yᵗ whan any boty came of any rych merchaunt
rydyng yᵗ it was but a good neybours dede one to help a nother
when one callyd a nother/ & fo they toke that but for good fely·
ſhyp & neybourhod.

¶ Here ye may fe yᵗ fome haue remorfe of confcyence of fmall
venyall finys & fere not to do gret offencys w'out ſhame of yᵉ world
or drede of god : & as yᵉ cõen puerb is they ſtũble at a ſtraw &
lepe ouer a blok.

Of the merchaũt of lõdõ that put nobles ĩ his mouth ĩ his deth bed.

A ʀʏᴄʜ couetous marchãte ther was yᵗ dwellyd in Lõdon whych
euer gaderyd money & coud neuer fynd in hys hert to fpend

noght vppon hym felf nor vppon no mã els/ whych fell fore fyk/ & as he lay on hys deth bed had hys purs lyeng at hys beddys hed/ & had fuche a loue to hys money that he put his hand in his purs & toke out thereof .x. or .xii. li ĩ nobles & put them in his mouth/ And becaufe his wyfe and other ꝑceyuyd him very fyk and lyke to dye they exortyd hym to be confeffyd and brought yᵉ curate vnto him/ whych when they had caufyd hym to fey Bene-dicite yᵉ curat bad hym cry god mercy & fhew his fynnys. Than this fyk man began to fey l cry god mercy I haue offendyd in yᵉ .vij. dedly fynnys & brokeɴ the .x. comaundementys/ & be-caufe of the gold in hys mouth he mufflede fo in hys fpeche that the curate cowde not well vnderftande hym/ wherefore the curate afked hym what he hadde in hys mouthe that letted hys fpeche/ I wys maftere perfone quod the fyk man muffelynge I haue nothyng in my mouth but a lyttyll money becaufe I wot not whether I fhall go l thoughte I wolde take fome fpendyng money wyth me for I wot not what nede I fhall haue therof/ And incontynent after that feyynge dyed before he was confeffed or repentant that ony man could perceue/ and fo by lykelyhode went to the deuyll.

¶ By thys tale ye may fe that they that all theyre lyuys wylle neuer do charyte to theyr neyghbours/ that god in tyme of theyr dethe wyll not fuffer them to haue grace of repentaunce.

Of the mylner that ftale the nuttys & of the tayler that ftale a fheep.

THERE was a certayn ryche hufbandman in a vyllage whych loued nottes merueloufly well & fet trees of filberdys & other nut trees in his orchard/ & norifhid them well all hys lyfe/ & when he dyed he made hys executours to make promife to bery wᵗ hym yn hys graue a bage of nottis or els they fholde not be hys executours/ which executours for fere of lofyng theyre romys ful-fyllyd hys wyll & dyd fo. It happenyd yᵗ the fame nyght after that he was beryed there was a mylnere in a whyte cote came to this mãys garden to thētēt tó ftele a bag óf nottis/ & in yᵉ way he met wᵗ a tayler in a blak cote an vnthrift of hys accoyn-taũce & fhewyd hym hys intent/ This tayler lykewyfe fhewyd

hym y^t he intēdyd ye fame tyme to ſtele a ſhepe/ & ſo they
both there agreyd to go forthward euery man ſeuerally w^t hys
purpoſe & after y^t they apoynted to make good chere ech w^t other
& to mete agayne in ye chyrch porch/ & he that came furſt to
tary for the other.

This mylner when he had ſpede of hys nottis came furſt to the
chyrch porche & there taryed for hys felowe and the mene whyle
ſatte ſtyll there & knakked nottys.

It fortuned than the ſexten of the church becauſe yt was abowt
.ix. of the clok cam to ryng curfu. & when he lokyd in ye porch
& ſaw one all in whyte knakkyng nottes/ he had went it had
bene ye dede man ryſen owt of hys graue knakkynge ye nottes
y^t were byryed w^t hym & ran home agayn in all haſt and tolde to
a krepyll y^t was in hys howſe what he had ſene. This crepyll
thus heryng rebukyd y^e ſexten & ſeyd y^t yf he were able to go
he wold go thyder & cōiure y^e ſprite/ by my trouth quod y^e ſexten
& yf thou darſt do y^t I wyl bere the on my nek & ſo they both
agreed. The ſexten toke ye crepul on hys nek & cam in to y^e
chyrchyard agayn/ & ye mylner in ye porch ſaw one comyng
bering a thing on his bak had went it had ben ye taylour cōmyng
w^t the ſhepe & roſe vp to mete thē/ & as he cam towarde thē
he aſkeyd & ſeyd/ Is he fat/ is he fat/ y^e ſexten heryng hym
ſey ſo/ for fere caſt the crepull down & ſeyd fat or lene take hym
ther for me/ and ran away/ & the creple by myracle was made hole
& rā away as faſt as he or faſter/ This mylner perceyuing y^t they
were .ii. & y^t one ran after a nother ſuppoſyng y^t one had ſpyed
ye tayler ſtelyng y^e ſhepe & y^t he had ron after hym to haue taken
hym/ and fered y^t ſom body alſo had ſpyed hym ſtelyng nottes he
for fere left hys nottes behynd hym and as ſecretly as he cowde
ran home to hys myll/ And anon after y^t he was gon ye tayler
cam w^t the ſtolyn ſhepe vppon hys nek to the chyrch porch to
ſeke the mylner & when he fownd ther the not ſhalys he ſuppoſyd
y^t hys felow had be ther and gone home as he was in dede/ wherefore he toke vp y^e ſhepe agayne on hys nek and went to ward
the myl/ But yet duryng this whyle the ſextē which rạn away
went not to hys owne houſe but wēt to the pyſh pryſtis chāber/

& ſhewd hym how the ſpryte of yᵉ man was ryſē out of hys graue knakkīg nottes as ye haue hard before/ wherfor yᵉ preſt ſayd that he wold go cōiure hym yf the ſexten wold go wᵗ hym/ & ſo they both agreed/ yᵉ preſt dyd on hys ſurples & a ſtole about hys nek & toke holy watèr wᵗ hym and cam wᵗ the ſextē toward yᵉ church/ & as ſone as he enteryd in to yᵉ church yarde, The tayler wᵗ the whyte ſhepe on hys nek intendyng as I before haue ſhewid yow to go down to yᵉ myll met wᵗ them & had went yᵗ yᵉ preſt in hys ſurples had ben yᵉ mylner in hys whyte cote/ & ſeyd to hym by god I haue hym I haue hym meanyng by the ſhepe yᵗ he had ſtolyn/ the preſt perceyuynge the tayler all in blak & a whyte thyng on his nek had went it had ben yᵉ deuyll beryng away the ſpryte of yᵉ dede man yᵗ was beryed & ran away as faſte as he coud takyng yᵉ way downe toward the myll/ & yᵉ ſexten ronnyng after hī. This tayler ſeyng one folowyng hī had went yᵗ one had folowed the mylner to haue don hym ſome hurt & thought he wold folow if nede were to help yᵉ mylner. & went forth tyl he cam to the myll & knokked at yᵉ myldore/ yᵉ mylner beyng wᵗyn aſked who was ther yᵉ tayler āſwerd & ſaid by god I haue caught one of them & made hī ſure & tyed hym faſt by yᵉ leggys menynge by the ſhepe yᵗ he had ſtolen & had thē on hys nek tyed faſt by the leggys. But yᵉ mylner heryng hym ſey yᵗ he had hym tyed faſt by the leggys had wente it had bē the conſtable yᵗ had takē the tayler for ſtelyng of the ſhepe & had tyed him by the leggys/ & ſerid yᵗ he had comen to haue taken hym alſo for ſtelyng of the nottys/ wherfore the mylner openyd a bak dore & ran away as faſt as he coud. The taylour heryng the bak dore openyng wēt on yᵉ other ſyde of yᵉ myll/ & there ſaw the mylner ronnyng away/ & ſtode there a littyll whyle muſyng wᵗ yᵉ ſhepe on his nek. Then was the paryſh preeſt & the ſextē ſtandyng there vnder the mylhouſe hydyng them for fere & ſaw the taylour agayn wᵗ yᵉ ſhepe on his nek had wend ſtyll it had bene the dyuyll wᵗ the ſpryt of the dede man on hys nek & for fere ran away/ but becauſe they knew not the ground well/ the preeſt lepte into a dyche almoſt ouer the hed lyke to be drounyd that he cryed wyth a loud voyce help help. Then the taylour lokyd about & ſaw

the mylner rõne away & the fexten a nother way & hard the
preeſt cry help: had wend it had bene the cõſtable wᵗ a gret
cõpany cryeng for help to take hym & to bryng hym to pryſon for
ſtelyng of yᵉ ſhepe wherfore he threw downe the ſhepe & ran
away a nother way as faſte as he coud/ & ſo euery man was afferd
of other wythout cauſe.

¶ By thys ye may ſe well it is foly for any man to fere a thyng
to mych tyll that he ſe ſome proue or cauſe.

Of the woman that powryd the potage in the Tuggys male.

THERE was a iuſtyce but late in yᵉ realme of englond called
maſter Uauyfour a very homly man & rude of condycions &
louyd neuer to ſpẽd mych money/ This maſter Uauyfour rode on
a tyme in hys cyrcute in a place of the north cõtrey where he
had agreed wᵗ the ſhyryf for a certayn ſome of money for hys
chargys thorowe the ſhyre/ ſo that at euery Inne & lodgyng thys
maſter vauefour payd for hys own coſtys. It fortunyd ſo yᵗ when
he cam to a certayn lodgyng he cõmaunded one Torpyn hys
feruãt to ſe yᵗ he vſed good huſbondry & to ſauc ſuche thynges
as were laft & to cary it wᵗ hym to ferue hym at the next baytyng.
Thys Torpyn doyng hys maſters cõmaũdemẽt toke yᵉ brokyn
brede brokyn mete & all ſych thĩg yᵗ was laft & put it in hys male/
The wyfe of yᵉ houſe pceyuyng yᵗ he toke all ſuche fragmentys &
vytayle wᵗ hym yᵗ was laft & put it in hys male/ ſhe brought vp
yᵗ podege yᵗ was laft ĩ the pot & when torpyn had torned hys bak
a lytyll ſyde ſhe pouryd yᵉ podege in to yᵉ male whych ran vpon
hys robe of ſkarlet & other hys garmẽtys & rayed them very
euyll that they were mych hurt therwᵗ. Thys Torpyn fodeynly
tornyd him & faw it/ reuylyd the wyfe therfor & ran to hys
maſter & told hym what ſhe had don/ wherfor maſter Uauefour
incõtinẽt callyd yᵉ wyfe & ſeyd to her thus. Thou drab quod he
what haſt thou dõ why haſt thou pouryd yᵉ podege in my male
& marryd my raymẽt & gere/ O ſyr quod yᵉ wyfe I know well ye
ar a iudge of yᵉ realme/ & I perceyue by you : your mĩd is to do
ryght & to haue that that is your owne/ & your mynd is to haue
all thyng wᵗ you yᵗ ye haue payd for/ both brokyn brede mete

& other thynges y^t is left : & fo it is reafon that ye haue/ & therfore becaufe your feruant hath taken the brede & the mete &
put it ĩ your male I haue therfore put in your male the podege
y^t be laft becaufe ye haue well & truly payd for them for yf I
fhuld kepe ony thyng from you y^t ye haue payd for : peraduenture
ye wold troble me in the law an other tyme.

¶ Here ye may fe y^t he y^t playth the nygarde to mych fome-
tyme yt torneth hym to hys owne loffe.

Of the man that wold haue the pot ftand there as he wold.

A YONGE man late maryed to a wyfe thowght it was good polycy
to get the mayftry of her in the begynnynge.   Cam to her the pot
fethynge ouer ye fyre all though the mete therin were not inough
fodenly cõmaundyd her to take the pot from the fyre. whyche
anfweryd & faydc that ye mete was not redy to ete.   And he
fayd agayne I wyll haue it taken of for my pleafure.   This good
woman loth yet to offend hym fet ye pot befyde the fyre as he
bad.   And anone after he cõmaũded her to fet the pot behynde
the dore/ & fhe fayd therto agayne ye be not wyfe therin.   But
he precifely fayd it fholde be fo as he bad.   And fhe gentylly
agayne did his cõmaũdment.   This man yet not fatysfyed cõmaunded her to fet the pot a hygh vpon the hen roft/ what quod
ye wyf agayne I trow ye be mad.   And he fyerfly than cõmaunded
her to fet it there or els he fayd fhe fholde repẽt   She fome-
what aferde to moue his pacience toke a ladder and fet it to the
rooft/ and wẽt herfelf vp the ladder and toke the pot in her hande
prayeng her hufbande than to holde the ladder faft for flydynge/
whiche fo dyd.

And whenne the hufbande lokyd vp and fawe the Potte ftande
there on hyght he fayde thus.   Lo now ftandyth the pot there as
I wolde haue it This wyfe herynge that fodenly pouryd the hote
potage on his hed & fayd thus.   And now bene the potage there
as I wolde haue them.

¶ By this tale men may fe it is no wyfedome for a man to
attempte a meke womãs pacyẽce to far left it torne to his owne
hurte & damage.

THE HISTORY

OF

REYNARD THE FOX.

EARLY PROSE ROMANCES.

I.

THE HISTORY OF REYNARD
THE FOX.

Here beginneth the History of Reynard the Fox.

𝔍𝔫 𝔱𝔥𝔦𝔰 𝔥𝔦𝔰𝔱𝔬𝔯𝔶 ben written the parables, good lerynge,[1] and diverse points to be marked, by which points men may learn to come to the subtle knowledge of such things as daily ben used and had in the counsels of lords and prelates, ghostly and worldly, and also among merchants and other common people. And this book is made for need and profit of all good folk, as far as they in reading or hearing of it shall mowe[2] understand and feel the foresaid subtle deceits that daily ben used in the world; not to the intent that men should use them, but that every man should eschew and keep him from the subtle false shrews, that they be not deceived. Then who that will have the very understanding of this matter, he must oft and many times read in this book, and earnestly and diligently mark well that he readeth; for it is set subtlely, like as ye shall see in reading of it; and not once to read it, for a man shall not with once over reading find the right understanding ne comprise it well; but ofttimes to read it shall cause it well to be understood. And for them that understandeth it, it shall be right joyous, pleasant, and profitable.

[1] *Lerynge,* doctrine.　　　　[2] *Mowe,* be able to.

CHAPTER I.

How the Lion, King of all Beasts, sent out his commandments that all Beasts should come to his feast and Court.

IT was about the time of Pentecost or Whitsuntide, that the woods commonly be lusty and gladsome, and the trees clad with leaves and blossoms, and the ground with herbs and flowers sweet smelling, and also the fowls and birds singing melodiously in their harmony, that the Lion, the noble King of all Beasts, would in the holy days of this feast hold an open Court at state ; which he did to know [1] over all in his land, and commanded by straight commissions and commandments that every Beast should come thither, in such wise that all the Beasts great and small came to the Court save Reynart the Fox : for he knew himself faulty and guilty in many things against many Beasts that thither should comen, that he durst not adventure to go thither. When the King of all Beasts had assembled all his Court, there was none of them all but that he had complained sore on Reynart the Fox.

CHAPTER II.

The first complaint made Isegrim the Wolf on Reynart.

ISEGRIM the Wolf, with his lineage and friends, came and stood before the King, and said, " High and Mighty Prince, my Lord the King, I beseech you that through your great might, right, and mercy, that ye will have pity on the great trespass and the unreasonable misdeeds that Reynart the Fox hath done to me and to my wife : that is to wit, he is comen in to my house against the will of my wife, and there he hath bepissed my children whereas they lay, in such wise as they thereof ben waxen blind. Whereupon was a day set, and was judged that Reynart should come and have excused him hereof, and have sworn on the holy saints that he was not guilty thereof. And

---

[1] *Did to know*, caused to be made known.

when the book with the saints was brought forth, tho [1] had Reynart bethought him otherwise, and went his way again into his hole, as he had naught set thereby. And, dear King, this knowen well many of the Beasts that now be comen hither to your Court. And yet hath he trespassed to me in many other things. He is not living that could tell all that I now leave untold. But the shame and villainy that he hath done my wife, that shall I never hide ne suffer it unavenged, but that he shall make to me large amends.

CHAPTER III.

The complaint of Courtoys the Hound.

WHEN these words were spoken, so stood there a little Hound and was named Courtoys, and complained to the King, how that in the cold winter in the hard frost he had ben sore forwintered, in such wise as he had kept no more meat than a pudding, which pudding Reynart the Fox had taken away from him.

Tho spake Tybert the Cat.

WITH this so came Tybert the Cat, with an irous [2] mood, and sprang in among them, and said: "My Lord the King, I here hear that Reynart is sore complained on, and here is none but that he hath enough to do to clear himself. That Courtoys here complaineth of, that is passed many years gone, howbeit, that I complain not ; that pudding was mine, for I had won it by night in a mill. The miller lay and slept. If Courtoys had any part hereon, that came by me too."

   Tho spake Panther, "Think ye, Tybert, that it were good that Reynart should not be complained on ? He is a very murderer, a rover, and a thief, he loveth no man so well, not our Lord the King here, but that he well would that he should lose good and worship, so that he might win as much as a leg of a fat hen. I shall tell you what I saw him do yesterday to Cuwart the Hare, that here standeth in the King's peace and safeguard. He promised

---

[1] *Tho*, then.   [2] *Irous*, angry.

to Cuwart and said he would teach him his *Credo*, and make him a good chaplain. He made him go sit between his legs, and sang and cried loud, ' *Credo, Credo !* ' My way lay thereby there that I heard this song. Tho went I near and found Master Reynart that had left that he first read and sang, and began to play his old play. For he had caught Cuwart by the throat, and had I not that time comen he should have taken his life from him, like as ye here may see on Cuwart the Hare the fresh wound yet. Forsooth, my Lord the King, if ye suffer this unpunished, and let him go quit that hath thus broken your peace, and will do no right after the sentence and judgment of your men, your children many years hereafter shall be misprised and blamed therefor."

"Sikerly, Panther," said Isegrim, "ye say truth. It were good that right and justice were done, for them that would fain live in peace."

CHAPTER IV.

How Grymbart the Dasse[1] the Fox's sister's son spake for Reynart and answered tofore the King.

THEN spake Grymbart the Dasse, and was Reynart's sister's son, with an angry mood.

"Sir Isegrim that is evil said. It is a common proverb an enemy's mouth saith seld well. What lie ye and wite[2] ye mine Eme[3] Reynart? I would that ye would adventure that who of you twain had most trespassed to other should hang by the neck as a thief on a tree. But and if he were as well in this court and as well with the King as ye be, it should not be thought in him that it were enow that ye should come and ask him forgiveness; ye have bitten and nipped mine uncle with your fell and sharp teeth many more times than I can tell. Yet will I tell some points that I well know. Know not ye how ye misdealed on the plaice which he threw down from the car, when ye followed after from afar, and ye ate the good plaice alone, and gave him no more than the grate or bones which ye might not eat yourself. In like- ·

---

[1] *Dasse*, Badger (Dutch, dasje). [2] *Wite*, blame. [3] *Eme*, uncle.

wise did ye to him also of the fat flitch of bacon which savoured so well that ye alone ate it in your belly, and when mine Eme asked his part tho answered ye him again in scorn, 'Reynart, fair youngling, I shall gladly give you your part'—but mine Eme gat ne had nought, ne was not the better. Notwithstanding he had won the flitch of bacon with great dread, for the man came and threw him in a sack that he scarcely came out with his life. Such manner things hath Reynart many times suffered through Isegrim. O ye lordes, think ye that this is good? Yet is there more. He complaineth how that Reynart mine Eme hath much trespassed to him by cause of his wife. Mine Eme hath lain by her, but that is well seven years tofore, ere he wedded her; and if Reynart for love and courtesy did with her his will, what was that? She was soon healed thereof. Hereof by right should be no complaint, were Isegrim wise. He should have believéd that he doth to himself no worship thus to slander his wife. She plaineth not. Now maketh Cuwart the Hare a complaint also. That thinketh me a vyseuase.[1] If he read ne learned aright his lesson, should not Reynart his master beat him therefor? If the scholars were not beaten ne smitten and reprised[2] of their truantry, they should never learn. Now complaineth Courtoys that he with pain had gotten a pudding in the winter, at such time as the cost[3] is evil to find. Thereof him had be better to have held his peace, for he had stolen it. *Male quæsisti et male perdidisti.* It is right that it be evil lost that is evil won. Who shall blame Reynart if he have taken from a thief stolen good. It is reason. Who that understandeth the law, and can discern the right, and that he be of high birth as mine Eme Reynart is, knoweth well how he shall resseyue stolen good. Yet all had he Courtoys hanged when he found him with the menour[4] he had not much misdone nor trespassed, save against the Crown, that he had done justice without leave. Wherefore for the honour of the King he did it not, all hath he but little thanks. What scathed it him that he is thus complained

---

[1] *Visevase*, wish-wash.   [2] *Reprised*, reprehended.   [3] *Cost*, food (kost).
[4] *With the menour*, in the very act, *i.e.*, with the thing stolen *in his hands*.

on? Mine Eme is a gentle and true man. He may suffer no falsehood. He doth nothing but by his priest's counsel. And I say you, sith that my lord the King hath do proclaim [1] his peace, he never thought to hurt any man; for he eateth no more than once a day; he liveth as a recluse; he chastiseth his body, and weareth a shirt of hair; it is more than a year that he hath eaten no flesh. As I yesterday heard say of them that came from him he hath left and given over his Castle Maleperduys and hath builded a cluse; therein dwelleth he and hunteth no more ne desireth no winning, but he liveth by alms and taketh nothing but such as men give him for charity, and doth great penance for his sins, and he is waxen much pale and lean of praying and waking, for he would be fain with God."

Thus as Grymbart his Eme stood and preached these words, so saw they coming down the hill to them Chanticleer the Cock and brought on a bier a dead hen of whom Reynart had bitten the head off, and that must be showed to the King for to have knowledge thereof.

CHAPTER V.

How the Cock complained on Reynart.

CHANTICLEER came forth and smote piteously his hands and his feathers; and on each side of the bier wenten tweyne sorrowful hens, that one was called Cantart and that other good hen Crayant, they were two the fairest hens that were between Holland and Arderne. These hens bare each of them a burning taper which was long and straight. These two hens were Coppen's sisters, and they cried so piteously " Alas and weleaway " for the death of their dear sister Coppen. Two young hens bare the bier, which cackled so heavily and wept so loud for the death of Coppen their mother, that it was very hard. Thus came they together tofore the King.

And Chanticleer tho said, "Merciful lord, my lord the King, please it you to hear our complaint and abhor the great scathe

---

[1] *Hath do proclaim,* hath caused to be proclaimed.

that Reynart hath done to me and my children that here stand. It was so that in the beginning of April, when the weather is fair, as that I, as hardy and proud because of the great lineage that I am come of and also had, for I had eight fair sons and seven fair daughters which my wife had hatched, and they were all strong and fat, and went in a yard which was walled round about, in which was a shed wherein were six great dogs which had totore and plucked many a beast's skin in such wise as my children were not afraid. On whom Reynart the thief had great envy because they were so sure that he could none get of them; how well ofttimes hath this fell thief gone round about this wall and hath laid for us in such wise that the dogs have be set on him and have hunted him away; and once they leapt on him upon the bank, and that cost him somewhat for his theft. I saw that his skin smoked. Nevertheless he went his way. God amend it!

"Thus were we quit of Reynart a long while. At last came he in likeness of an hermit, and brought to me a letter for to read, sealed with the King's seal, in which stood written that the King had made peace over all in his realm, and that all manner beasts and fowls should do none harm nor scathe to any other. Yet said he to me more that he was a cloisterer or a closed recluse becomen, and that he would receive great penance for his sins. He showed me his slavyne and pylche [1] and an hairen shirt thereunder, and then said he, 'Sir Chanticleer after this time be no more afraid of me, ne take no heed, for I now will eat no more flesh. I am forthon so old that I would fain remember my soul. I will now go forth, for I have yet to say my sexte, none, and mine evensong. To God I betake [2] you." Tho went Reynart thence, saying his Credo, and laid him under an hawthorn. Then I was glad and merry, and also took none heed, and went to my children and clucked them together, and went without the wall for to walk; whereof is much harm comen to us, for Reynart lay under a bush and came creeping between us and the gate, so that he caught one of my children and laid him in his male. [3] Whereof

---

[1] *Slavyne and pilch*, old shoes (Dutch, *sloffen*) and skincoat.
[2] *Betake*, commend, entrust. [3] *Male*, bag, wallet.

D

we have great harm, for sith he hath tasted of him there might never hunter ne hound save ne keep him from us. He hath waited by night and day in such wise that he hath stolen so many of my children that of fifteen I have but four, in such wise hath this thief forslongen [1] them. And yet yesterday was Coppen my daughter, that here lieth upon the bier, with the hounds rescued. This complain I to you, gracious King, have pity on mine great and unreasonable damage and loss of my fair children !"

CHAPTER VI.

How the King spake touching this complaint.

THEN spake the King:

"Sir Dasse, hear ye this well of the recluse of your Eme? He hath fasted and prayed, that if I live a year he shall abye [2] it. Now hark, Chanticleer, your plaint is enough. Your daughter that lieth here dead, we will give to her the death's rite. We may keep her no longer, we will betake her to God. We will sing her vigil and bring her worshipfully on earth, and then we will speak with these lords and take counsel how we may do right and justice of this great murder, and bring this false thief to the law.

Tho began they *Placebo domino*, with the verses that to longen,[3] which if I should say were me too long. When this vigil was done and the commendation, she was laid in the pit, and there upon her was laid a marble stone polished as clear as any glass, and thereon was hewen in great letters in this wise : COPPE CHAN-TEKLERS DOUGHTER, WHOM REYNART THE FOX HATH BYTEN, LYETH HIER VNDER BURYED, COMPLAYNE YE HER FFOR, SHE IS SHAME-FULLY COMEN TO HER DETH.

After this, the King sent for his lords and the wisest of his council for to take advice how this great murder and trespass should be punished on Reynart the Fox. There was concluded

---

[1] *Forslongen* (verschlungen), swallowed.
[2] *Abye*, pay for.   [3] *To longen*, belong thereto.

and appointed for the best that Reynart should be sent for, and that he left not for any cause, but he came into the King's court for to hear what should be said to him; and that Bruin the Bear should do the message.

The King thought that all this was good and said to Bruin the Bear, "Sir Bruin, I will that ye do this message; but see well to for yourself, for Reynart is a shrew, and fell,[1] and knoweth so many wiles that he shall lie and flatter, and shall think how he may beguile, deceive, and bring you to some mockery."

Then said Bruin, "What, good lord, let it alone! Deceiveth me the Fox, so have I ill learned my *casus*. I trow he shall come too late to mock me." Thus departed Bruin merrily from thence, but it is to dread that he came not so merrily again.

CHAPTER VII.

How Bruin the Bear was sped of Reynart the Fox.

Now is Bruin gone on his way toward the Fox with a stout mood, which supposed well that the Fox should not have beguiled him. As he came in a dark wood in a forest whereas Reynart had a bypath when he was hunted, there beside was an high mountain and land, and there must Bruin in the middle goon over for to go to Maleperduys. For Reynart had many a dwelling-place, but the Castle of Maleperduys was the best and the fastest burgh that he had. There lay he in when he had need, and was in any dread or fear. Now when Bruin was comen to Maleperduys, he found the gate fast shut. Tho went he tofore the gate, and sat upon his tail, and called, "Reynart, be ye at home? I am Browning. The King hath sent me for you that you should come to Court, for to plead your cause. He hath sworn there by his God, come ye not, or bring I you not with me, for to abide such right and sentence as shall be there given, it shall cost you your life. He will hang you or set you on the rack. Reynart, do by my counsel, and come to the Court."

---

[1] *Fell*, cruel.

Reynart lay within the gate, as he oft was wont to do, for the warmth of the sun. When Reynart heard Bruin, tho went he inward into his hole. For Maleperduys was full of holes, here one hole and there another, and yonder another, narrow, crooked and long, with many ways to go out, which he opened and shut after that he had need. When he had any prey brought home, or that he wist that any sought him for his misdeeds and trespasses, then he ran and hid him from his enemies into his secret chambers, that they could not find him; by which he deceived many a beast that sought him. And tho thought Reynard in himself how he might best bring the Bear in charge and need, and that he abode in worship.

In this thought Reynart came out, and said, "Bruin, Eme, ye be welcome! I heard you well tofore, but I was in mine evensong, therefore have I the longer tarried a little. Dear Eme, he hath done to you no good service, and I con him no thank,[1] that hath sent you over this long hill; for I see that ye be also weary, that the sweat runneth down by your cheeks. It was no need: I had nevertheless comen to Court to-morrow: but I sorrow now the less, for your wise counsel shall well help me in the Court. And could the King find none less messenger but you for to send hither? That is great wonder. For next the King ye be the most gentle, and richest of levies and of land. I would well that we were now at the Court, but I fear me that I shall not con well go thither, for I have eaten so much new meat that me thinketh my belly will break or cleave asunder, and because the meat was new I ate the more."

Tho spake the Bear, "Lief Neve,[2] what meat have ye eaten that maked you so full?"

"Dear Eme, that I ate, what might it help you that if I told you? I ate but simple meat. A poor man is no lord, that may ye know, Eme, by me. We poor folk must eat ofttimes such as we gladly would not eat if we had better. They were great honey-

---

[1] *Con him no thank.* To can or con thank was an old phrase for acknowledgment of thanks due.

[2] *Lief neve*, dear nephew.

combs; which I must needs eat for hunger. They have made my belly so great that I can nowhere endure."

Bruin then spake anon, "Alas, Reynart, what say ye! Set ye so little by honey? Me ought to prize and love it above all meat. Lief Reynart, help me that I might get a deal of this honey, and as long as I live I shall be to you a true friend, and abide by you, as far as ye help me that I may have a part of this honey."

CHAPTER VIII.

How Bruin ate the honey.

BRUIN, Eme, I had supposed that ye had japed[1] therewith."

"So help me God, Reynart, nay. I should not gladly jape with you."

Then spake the red Reynart, "Is it then earnest, that ye love so well the honey? I shall do let you have so much that ten of you should not eat it at one meal, might I get therewith your friendship."

"Not we ten, Reynart Neve!" said the Bear. "How should that be? Had I all the honey that is between this and Portugal I should well eat it alone."

Reynart said, "What say ye, Eme? Hereby dwelleth an husbandman named Lantfert, which hath so much honey that ye should not eat in seven years; which ye shall have in your hold if ye will be to me friendly and helping against mine enemies in the King's Court."

Then promised Bruin the Bear to him, that if he might have his belly full he would truly be to him tofore all other a faithful friend.

Hereof laughed Reynart the shrew,[2] and said, "If ye would have seven hamper barrels full I shall well get them and help you to have them." These words pleased the Bear so well, and made him so much to laugh that he could not well stand.

Tho thought Reynart, "This is good luck; I shall lead him thither that he shall laugh by measure."

---

[1] *Japed*, jested.   [2] *Shrew*, malicious deceiver.

Reynart said then, " This matter may not be long tarried.   I must pain myself for you.   Ye shall well understand the very yonste [1] and good will that I bear to you ward.   I know none in all my lineage that I now would labour for thus sore."

That thanked him the Bear and thought he tarried long.

" Now, Eme, let us go a good pace, and follow ye me.   I shall make you to have as much honey as ye may bear."   The Fox meant, of good strokes; but the caitiff marked not what the Fox meant; and they went so long together, that they came unto Lantfert's yard.   Tho was sir Bruin merry.

Now hark of Lantfert.   Is it true that men say, so was Lantfert a strong carpenter of great timber, and had brought that other day tofore into his yard a great oak, which he had begun to cleave.   And as men be woned [2] he had smitten two betels [3] therein one after that other, in such wise the oak was wide open. Whereof Reynart was glad, for he had found it right as he wished, and said to the Bear all laughing, " See now well sharply to !   In this tree is so much honey that it is without measure.   Assay if ye can come therein, and eat but little, for though the honey-combs be sweet and good, yet beware that ye eat not too many, but take of them by measure, that ye catch no harm in your body ; for, sweet Eme, I should be blamed if they did you any harm."

" What, Reynart, cousin, sorrow ye not for me !   Ween ye that I were a fool ? "

" Measure is good in all meat," Reynart said.   " Ye say truth.   Wherefore should I sorrow?   Go to the end and creep therein."

Bruin the Bear hasted sore toward the honey, and trode in with his two foremost feet, and put his head over his ears into the clift of the tree.   And Reynart sprang lightly and brake out the betle of the tree.   Tho helped the Bear neither flattering ne chiding ; he was fast shut in the tree.   Thus hath the Neve, with deceit, brought his Eme in prison in the tree, in such wise as he could not get out with might ne with craft, head ne foot.

---

[1] *Yonste* (gunst), favour.   [2] *Woned*, accustomed.
[3] *Betels*, heavy mallets used for beating in wedges, &c.

What profiteth Bruin the Bear that he strong and hardy is? That may not help him. He saw well that he was beguiled. He began to howl, and to bray, and crutched with the hinder feet, and made such a noise and rumour, that Lantfert came out hastily, and knew nothing what this might be, and brought in his hand a sharp hook. Bruin the Bear lay in the clift of the tree, in great fear and dread, and held fast his head, and nipped both his fore feet. He wrang, he wrestled, and cried, and all was for naught. He wist not how he might get out.

Reynart the Fox saw from far how that Lantfert the carpenter came, and tho spake Reynart to the Bear, " Is that honey good? How is it now? Eat not too much, it should do you harm ; ye should not then well con go to the Court. When Lantfert cometh, if ye have well eaten he shall give you better to drink, and then it shall not stick in your throat."

After these words tho turned him Reynart toward his castle, and Lantfert came and found the Bear fast taken in the tree. Then ran he fast to his neighbours and said " Come all in to my yard, there is a bear taken ! " The word anon sprang over all in the thorp. There ne bleef[1] neither man ne wife, but all ran thither as fast as they could, every one with his weapon, some with a staff, some with a rake, some with a broom, some with a stake of the hedge, and some with a flail ; and the priest of the church had the staff of the cross, and the clerk brought a vane. The priest's wife Julocke came with her distaff,—she sat tho and span, —there came old women that for age had not one tooth in their head.

Now was Bruin the Bear nigh much sorrow that he alone must stand against them all. When he heard all this great noise and cry he wrestled and plucked so hard and so sore that he gat out his head. But he left behind all the skin and both his ears, in such wise that never man saw fouler ne loather beast, for the blood ran over his eyes. And or he could get out his feet he must lete[2] there his claws or nails and this rough hand. This market came to him evil, for he supposed never to have gone, his

---

[1] *Bleef* (blieb), remained.   [2] *Lete*, leave.

feet were so sore, and he might not see for the blood which ran
so over his eyes.

Lantfert came to him with the priest, and forthwith all the
parish, and began to smite and strike sore upon his head and
visage.   He received there many a sore stroke.   Every man
beware hereby : who hath harm and scathe, every man will be
thereat and put more to.   That was well seen on the Bear, for
they were all fierce and wroth on the Bear, great and small, yea
Hughelyn with the crooked leg, and Ludolf with the broad long
nose, they were both wroth.   That one had a leaden malle, and
that other a great leaden wapper, therewith they wappred and all
forslingred[1] him, Sir Bertolt with the long fingers, Lantfert, and
Ottram the long.   This did to the Bear more harm than all the
other, that one had a sharp hook and the other a crooked staff
well leaded on the end for to play at the ball.   Baetkyn and
Aue, Abelquak, my dame Baue, and the priest with his staff, and
dame Julocke his wife, these wroughten to the Bear so much harm
that they would fain have brought him from his life to death,
they smote and stack him all that they could.

Bruin the Bear sat and sighed and groaned, and must take
such as was given to him.   But Lantfert was the worthiest of
birth of them all, and made most noise; for dame Pogge of
Chafporte was his mother, and his father was Macob the stoppel-
maker, a much stout man.   There as he was alone Bruin received
of them many a cast of stones.   Tofore them all sprang first
Lantfert's brother with a staff, and smote the Bear on the head
that he ne heard ne saw; and therewith the Bear sprang up
between the bush and the river among a heap of wives, that he
threw a deal of them in the river, which was wide and deep.

There was the parson's wife one of them, wherefore he was
full of sorrow when he saw his wife lie in the water.   He lusted
no longer to smite the Bear, but called, " Dame Julocke in the
water !   Now every man see to, All they that may help her !

---

[1] *Wappered and forslingered*, beat at and overwhelmed with blows.   The Low
German *slingen*, to swallow, is to be distinguished from Low German, *slingern*,
the word here.

Be they men or women, I give to them all pardon of their penance, and release all their sins!" All they then left Bruin the
Bear lie, and did that the priest bade.

When Bruin the Bear saw that they ran all from him, and ran
to save the women, tho sprang he into the water and swam all
that he could. Then made the priest a great shout and noise,
and ran after the Bear with great anger, and said, "Come and
turn again, thou false thief!" The Bear swam after the best of
the stream and let them call and cry, for he was glad that he was
so escaped from them. He cursed and banned the honey tree,
and the Fox also that had so betrayed him that he had crept
therein so deep that he lost both his hood and his ears. And so
forth he drove in the stream well a two or three mile. Tho wax
he so weary that he went to land for to sit and rest him, for he
was heavy; he groaned and sighed, and the blood leapt over his
eyes, he drew his breath like as one should have died.

Now hark how the Fox did. Ere he came from Lantfert's
house he had stolen a fat hen and had laid her in his male, and
ran hastily away by a bye path where he weened that no man
should have comen. He ran toward the river, that he sweat, he
was so glad that he wist not what to do for joy, for he hoped
that the Bear had been dead. He said, "I have now well
sped, for he that should most have hindered me in the Court
is now dead, and none shall wite[1] me thereof, may I not, then,
by right be well glad?" With these words the Fox looked to the
riverward, and espied where Bruin the Bear lay and rested him.
Tho was the Fox sorrier and heavier than tofore was merry, and
·was as angry, and said in chiding to Lantfert, "Alas, Lantfert,
lewd fool! God give him a shames death that hath lost such
good venison, which is good and fat, and hath let him go which
was taken to his hand! Many a man would gladly have eaten of
him. He hath lost a rich and fat Bear." Thus all chiding he
came to the river, where he found the Bear sore wounded, bebled,
and right sick, which he might thank none better thereof than
Reynart, which he spake to the Bear in scorn:

[1] *Wite,* blame.

"*Chiere priestre, Dieu vous garde!* Will ye see the red thief?"

Said the Bear to himself, "The ribaud and the fell deer,[1] here I see him coming."

Then said the Fox, "Have ye aught forgotten at Lantfert's? Have ye also paid him for the honeycombs that ye stole from him? If ye have not, it were a great shame, and not honest; I will rather be the messenger myself for to go and pay him. Was the honey not good? I know yet more of the same prize. Dear Eme, tell me ere I go hence into what order will ye go that wear this new hood? Were ye a monk or an abbot? He that shaved your crown hath nipped off your ears, ye have lost your top and don off your gloves, I trow verily that ye will go sing compline."

All this heard Bruin the Bear, and waxed all angry, and sorry for he might not avenge him. He let the Fox say his will, and with great pain suffered it, and start again in the river, and swam down with the stream to that other side.

Now must he sorrow how that he should come to the Court, for he had lost his ears and the skin with the claws of his forefeet; for though a man should have slain him he could not go; and yet he must needs forth, but he wist not how.

Now hear how he did. He sat upon his hams and began to rustle over his tail; and when he was so weary, he wentled [2] and tumbled nigh half a mile; this did he with great pain so long till at last he came to the Court. And when he was seen so coming from far, some doubted what it might be that came so wenteling.

The King at last knew him, and was not well paid,[3] and said, "This is Bruin the Bear, my friend! Lord God, who hath wounded him thus? He is passing red on his head: me thinketh he is hurt unto the death. Where may he have been?"

Therewith is the Bear came tofore the king, and said:

[1] *Deer*, wild beast.

[2] *Wentled*, twisted, wriggled round and round. There is a mollusc called for its spiral "wentle-trap" from G. wendel-treppe, a winding staircase.

[3] *Paid*, satisfied.

CHAPTER IX.

The complaint of the Bear upon the Fox.

"I COMPLAIN to you, merciful lord, sir King, so as ye may see how that I am handled, praying you to avenge it upon Reynart the fell beast; for I have gotten this in your service. I have lost both my foremost feet, my cheeks, and mine ears, by his false deceit and treason."

The King said, "How durst this false thief Reynart do this? I say to you, Bruin, and swear by my crown, I shall so avenge you on him that ye shall con me thank!"

He sent for all the wise beasts and desired counsel how that he might avenge this over-great wrong that the Fox had done. Then the council concluded, old and young, that he should be sent for, and dayed [1] earnestly again, for to abide such judgment as should there be given on him of all his trespasses. And they thought that the cat Tybert might best do this message if he would, for he is right wise. The King thought this counsel good.

CHAPTER X.

How the King sent another time Tybert the Cat for the Fox, and how Tybert sped with Reynart the Fox.

THEN the King said, "Sir Tybert, ye shall now go to Reynart and say to him this second time, that he come to Court unto the plea for to answer; for though he be fell to other beasts, he trusteth you well and shall do by your counsel. And tell him if he come not he shall have the third warning and be dayed, and if he then come not, we shall proceed by right against him and all his lineage without mercy.

Tybert spake, "My lord the King, they that this counselled you were not my friends. What shall I do there? He will not, for me neither, come ne abide. I beseech you, dear King, send

---

[1] *Dayed*, cited for an appointed *day*.

some other to him. I am little and feeble. Bruin the Bear, which
was so great and strong, could not bring him. How should I
then take it on hand?"

"Nay," said the King, "Sir Tybert, ye ben wise and well
learned. Though ye be not great, there lieth not on. Many do
more with craft and cunning than with might and strength."

Then said the Cat, "Sith it must needs be done, I must then
take it upon me. God give grace that I may well achieve it, for
my heart is heavy, and evil willed thereto."

Tybert made him soon ready toward Maleperduys. And he
saw from far come flying one of Saint Martin's birds, tho
cried he loud and said, "All hail, gentle bird, turn thy wings
hitherward, and fly on my right side." The bird flew forth upon
a tree which stood on the left side of the Cat. Tho was Tybert
woe; for he thought it was a shrewd token and a sign of harm.
For if the bird had flown on his right side he had been merry
and glad, but now he sorrowed that his journey should turn to
unhappe. Nevertheless he did as many do, and gave to himself
better hope than his heart said. He went and ran to Maleperduys ward, and there he found the Fox alone standing tofore his
house.

Tybert said, "The rich God give you good even, Reynart.
The King hath menaced you for to take your life from you if ye
come not now with me to the court."

The Fox tho spake and said, "Tybert, my dear cousin, ye be
right welcome. I would well truly that ye had much good luck."
What hurted the Fox to speak fair. Though he said well, his heart
thought it not, and that shall be seen ere they depart.

Reynart said, "Will we this night be together. I will make
you good cheer, and to-morrow early in the dawning we will
together go to the Court. Good Nephew, let us so do, I have
none of my kin that I trust so much to as to you. Here was
Bruin the Bear,—the traitor! He looked so shrewdly on me,
and methought he was so strong, that I would not for a
thousand mark have gone with him; but, cousin, I will to-
morrow early go with you."

Tybert said, "It is best that we now go, for the moon shineth all so light as it were day; I never saw fairer weather."

"Nay, dear cousin, such might meet us by day-time that would make us good cheer and by night peradventure might do us harm. It is suspicious to walk by night. Therefore abide this night here by me."

Tybert said, "What should we eat if we abode here?"

Reynart said, "Here is but little to eat. Ye may well have an honeycomb, good and sweet. What say ye, Tybert, will ye any thereof?"

Tybert answered, "I set nought thereby. Have ye nothing else? If ye gave me a good fat mouse I should be better pleased."

"A fat mouse!" said Reynart. "Dear cousin, what say ye? Hereby dwelleth a priest and hath a barn by his house; therein ben so many mice that a man should not lead them away upon a wain. I have heard the priest many times complain that they did him much harm."

"Oh, dear Reynart, lead me thither for all that I may do for you!"

"Yea, Tybert, say ye me truth? Love ye well mice?"

"If I love them well?" said the Cat. "I love mice better than anything that men give me. Know ye not that mice savour better than venison, yea, than flawnes[1] or pasties? Will ye well do, so lead me thither where the mice ben, and then shall ye win my love, yea all had ye slain my father, mother, and all my kin."

Reynart said, "Ye mock and jape therewith."

The Cat said, "So help me God, I do not!"

"Tybert," said the Fox, "wist I that verily, I would yet this night make that ye should be full of mice."

"Reynart!" quoth he, "Full? That were many."

"Tybert, ye jape!"

"Reynart," quoth he, "in truth I do not. If I had a fat mouse I would not give it for a golden noble."

---

[1] *Flawns*, custard tarts.

"Let us go, then, Tybert," quoth the Fox, "I will bring you to the place ere I go from you."

"Reynart," quoth the Cat, "upon your safe-conduct, I would well go with you to Monpelier."

"Let us then go," said the Fox, "we tarry all too long."

Thus went they forth, without letting [1] to the place whereas they would be, to the Priest's barn, which was fast walled about with a mud wall. And the night tofore the Fox had broken in, and had stolen from the Priest a good fat hen; and the Priest, all angry, had set a gryn [2] tofore the hole to avenge him; for he would fain have taken the Fox. This knew well the fell thief, the Fox, and said, "Sir Tybert, cousin, creep into this hole, and ye shall not long tarry but that ye shall catch mice by great heaps. Hark how they pipe! When ye be full, come again; I will tarry here after you before this hole. We will to-morrow go together to the Court. Tybert, why tarry ye thus long? Come off, and so may we return soon to my wife which waiteth after us, and shall make us good cheer."

Tybert said, "Reynart, cousin, is it then your counsel that I go into this hole? These Priests ben so wily and shrewish I dread to take harm."

"Oh ho, Tybert!" said the Fox, "I saw you never so sore afraid. What aileth you?"

The Cat was ashamed, and sprang into the hole. And anon he was caught in the gryn by the neck, ere he wist. Thus deceived Reynart his guest and cousin.

As Tybert was ware of the gryn, he was afraid and sprang forth; the gryn went to. Then he began to wrawen, for he was almost y-strangled. He called, he cried, and made a shrewd noise.

Reynart stood before the hole and heard all, and was well paid, and said, "Tybert, love ye well mice? Be they fat and good? Knew the Priest hereof, or Mertynet, they be so gentle that they would bring you sauce. Tybert, ye sing and eat, is

---

[1] *Letting*, hindrance.
[2] *Gryn*, snare or trap. A word used by Chaucer.

that the guise of the Court? Lord God, if Isegrim were there by you, in such rest as ye now be, then should I be glad; for oft he hath done me scathe and harm."

Tybert could not go away, but he mawed and galped so loud, that Mertynet sprang up, and cried loud, "God be thanked, my gryn hath taken the thief that hath stolen our hens. Arise up, we will reward him!"

With these words arose the Priest in an evil time, and waked all them that were in the house, and cried with a loud voice, "The Fox is taken!"

There leapt and ran all that there was. The Priest himself ran, all mother naked. Mertynet was the first that came to Tybert. The Priest took to Locken his wife an offering candle, and bade her light it at the fire, and he smote Tybert with a great staff. There received Tybert many a great stroke over all his body. Mertynet was so angry that he smote the Cat an eye out. The naked Priest lift up and should have given a great stroke to Tybert, but Tybert that saw that he must die sprang between the Priest's legs with his claws and with his teeth. That leap became ill to the Priest and to his great shame.

When Dame Julocke knew that, she sware by her father's soul, that she would it had cost her all the offering of a whole year, that the Priest had not had that harm, hurt, and shame, and that it had not happened; and said, "In the Devil's name was the gryn there set! See Mertynet, lief son, this is a great shame and to me a great hurt!" The Fox stood without, tofore the hole, and heard all these words, and laughed so sore that he vnnethe[1] could stand. Thus scorned and mocked the Fox the Priest's wife, Dame Julocke, that was full of sorrow. The Priest fell down aswoon. They took him up, and brought him again to bed. Tho went the Fox again in to his burgh ward and left Tibert the Cat in great dread and jeopardy, for the Fox wist none other but that the Cat was nigh dead. But when Tibert the Cat saw them all busy about the Priest, tho began he to bite and gnaw the gryn in the middle asunder, and sprang out of

---

[1] *Unnethe*, not easily.

the hole, and went rolling and wentling towards the King's Court. Ere he came thither it was fair day, and the sun began to rise. And he came to the Court as a poor wight. He had caught harm at the Priest's house by the help and counsel of the Fox. His body was all tobeaten, and blind on the one eye. When the King wist this, that Tibert was thus arrayed, he was sore angry, and menaced Reynart the thief sore, and anon gathered his council to wit what they would advise him, how he might bring the Fox to the law, and how he should be fetched.

Tho spake Sir Grymbart, which was the Fox's sister son, and said, "Ye lords, though my Eme were twice so bad and shrewish, yet is there remedy enough. Let him be done to as to a free man. When he shall be judged he must be warned the third time for all; and if he come not then, he is then guilty in all the trespasses that ben laid against him and his, or complained on."

"Grymbart, who would ye that should go and daye him to come? Who will adventure for him his ears, his eye, or his life; which is so fell a beast? I trow there is none here so much a fool."

Grymbart spake, "So help me God, I am so much a fool that I will do this message myself to Reynart, if ye will command me."

CHAPTER XI.

How Grymbart the Dasse brought the Fox to the law tofore the King.

"Now go forth, Grymbart, and see well tofore you. Reynart is so fell and false, and so subtle, that ye need well to look about you and to beware of him."

Grymbart said he should see well to.

Thus went Grymbart to Maleperduys ward, and when he came thither he found Reynart the Fox at home, and Dame Ermelyn his wife lay with her whelps in a dark corner.

Tho spake Grymbart and saluted his Eme and his Aunt, and said to Reynart, "Eme, beware that your absence hurt you not in such matters as be laid and complained on you; but if ye think it good, it is high time that ye come with me to the Court. The withholding you from it can do you no good. There is much thing complained over you, and this is the third warning; and I tell you for truth, if ye abide to-morrow all day, there may no mercy help you. Ye shall see that within three days that your house shall be besieged all about, and there shall be made tofore it gallows and rack. I say you truly ye shall not then escape, neither with wife ne with child, the King shall take all your lives from you. Therefore it is best that ye go with me to the Court. Your subtle wise counsel shall peradventure avail you. There ben greater adventures falle, ere this; for it may hap ye shall go quit of all the complaints that ben complained on you, and all your enemies shall abide in the shame. Ye have ofttimes done more and greater things than this."

Reynart the Fox answered, "Ye say sooth. I trow it is best that I go with you, for there lacketh my counsel. Peradventure the King shall be merciful to me if I may come to speak with him, and see him under his eyen. Though I had done much more harm, the Court may not stand without me; that shall the King well understand. Though some be so fell to me ward, yet it goeth not to the heart. All the council shall conclude much by me. Where great Courts ben gathered, of kings or of great lords, whereas needeth subtle counsel, there must Reynart find the subtle means. They may well speak and say their advice, but tho mine is best, and that goeth tofore all other. In the Court ben many that have sworn to do me the worst they can, and that causeth me a part to be heavy in my heart, for many may do more than one alone that shall hurt me. Nevertheless, nephew, it is better I go with you to the Court and answer for myself, than to set me my wife and my children in adventure for to be lost. Arise up, let us go hence. He is over mighty for me. I must do as he will. I cannot better it; I shall take it patiently and suffer it."

Reynart said to his wife Dame Ermelyn, "I betake you my children, that ye see well to them and specially to Reynkin, my youngest son. He beliketh me so well I hope he shall follow my steps. And there is Rossel a passing fair thief, I love them as well

E

as any may love his children.   If God give me grace that I may
escape, I shall, when I come again, thank you with fair words."
Thus took Reynart leave of his wife.

Ah, gods ! how sorrowful abode Ermelyn with her small whelps,
for the victualler and he that sorrowed [1] for Maleperduys was gone
his way, and the house not purveyed nor victualled.

CHAPTER XII.

How Reynart shrove him.

WHEN Reynart and Grymbart had gone a while together, tho said
Reynart, " Dear Cousin, now am I in great fear, for I go in dread
and jeopardy of my life.   I have so much repentance for my sins
that I will shrive me, dear Cousin, to you ; here is none other
priest to get.   If I were shriven of my sins my soul should be the
clearer."

Grymbart answered, " Eme, will ye shrive you, then must ye
promise first to leave your stealing and roving."

Reynart said, that wist he well.   " Now hark, dear Cousin,
what I shall say.   *Confiteor tibi, pater,* of all the misdeeds that I
have done, and gladly will receive penance for them."

Grymbart said, " What say ye, will ye shrive you ?   Then say
it in English, that I may understand you."

Reynart said, " I have trespassed against all the beasts that
live ; in especial against Bruin the Bear, mine Eme, whom I made
his crown all bloody ; and taught Tybert the Cat to catch mice,
for I made her leap in a grynne where she was all to-beaten ; also
I have trespassed greatly against Chanticleer with his children, for
I have made him quit of a great deal of them.   The King is not
gone all quit, I have slandered him and the Queen many times,
that they shall never be clear thereof.   Yet have I beguiled
Isegrim the Wolf, oftener than I can tell well.   I called him
Eme, but that was to deceive him ; he is nothing of my kin.   I
made him a monk at Eelmare, where I myself also became one ;

1 *Sorrowed*, took care (sorge).

and that was to his hurt and no profit. I made bind his feet to
the bell rope, the ringing of the bell thought him so good that he
would learn to ring; whereof he had shame, for he rang so sore
that all the folk in the street were afraid thereof and marvelled
what might be on the bell, and ran thither tofore he had comen
to axe the religion, wherefore he was beaten almost to the death.
After this I taught him to catch fish, where he received many a
stroke; also I led him to the richest priest's house that was in
Vermedos, this priest had a spynde wherein hung many a good
flitch of bacon wherein many a time I was wont to fill my belly;
in this spynde I had made an hole in which I made Isegrim to
creep. There found he tubs with beef and many good flitches of
bacon, whereof he ate so much without measure that he might
not come out at the hole where he went in; his belly was so great
and full of the meat, and when he entered his belly was small; I
went in to the village and made there a great shout and noise; yet
hark what I did then, I ran to the priest where he sat at the table
and ate, and had tofore him as fat capon as a man might find:
that capon caught I, and ran my way therewith all that I might.
The priest cried out, and said, 'Take and slay the Fox! I trow
that man never saw more wonder. The Fox cometh in my house
and taketh my capon from my table: where saw ever man an
hardier thief!' and as me thought he took his table knife and
cast it at me, but he touched me not. I ran away, he shoved the
table from him and followed me crying 'Kill and slay him!' I
too go, and they after, and many moo came after, which all
thought to hurt me.

"I ran so long that I came whereas Isegrim was, and there I
let fall the capon, for it was too heavy for me, and against my will
I left it there, and then I sprang through a hole whereas I would
be. And as the priest took up the capon, he espied Isegrim
and cried, 'Smite down here, friends, here is the thief, the Wolf!
See well to, that he escape us not!' They ran all together with
stocks and staves, and made a great noise, that all the neighbours
camen out, and gave him many a shrewd stroke, and threw at
him great stones, in such wise that he fell down as he had been

dead. They slipped him and drew him over stones and over blocks without the village and threw him into a ditch, and there he lay all the night. I wot never how he came thence, sith I have goten of him, for as much as I made him to fill his belly, that he sware he would be mine help a whole year.

"Tho led I him to a place where I told him there were seven hens and a cock which sat on a perch and were much fat And there stood a fall-door by, and we climbed thereup. I said to him if he would believe me, and that he would creep into the door, he should find many fat hens. Isegrim went all laughing to the doorward, and crept a little in, and tasted here and there, and at last he said to me, 'Reynart, ye bord and jape with me, for what I seek I find not.' Then said I, 'Eme, if ye will find, creep further in. He that will win, he must labour and adventure. They that were wont to sit there, I have them away.' Thus I made him to seek further in, and shoved him forth so far, that he fell down upon the floor, for the perch was narrow. And he fell so great a fall, that they sprang up all that slept, and they that next the fire cryden that the fall-door was open and something was falle, and they wist not what it might be. They rose up and light a candle, and when they saw him, they smiten, beaten, and wounded him to the death. I have brought him thus in many a jeopardy, more than I can now reckon. I should find many more, if I me well bethought, which I shall tell you here-after. Also I have bedriuen[1] with dame Ersewynde his wife. I would I had not done it. I am sorry for it. It is to her great shame, and that me repenteth."

Grymbart said, "Eme, I understand you not."

He said, "I have trespassed with his wife."

"Ye shrive you, as though ye held somewhat behind. I wot not what ye mean, ne where ye have learned this lan-guage."

"Ach, Dear Neve, it were great shame if I should say it openly as it happened. I have lain by mine aunt, I am your Eme, I should anger you if I spake villainy of women. Nephew, now

---

[1] *Bedriuen*, had experience (Dutch, *bedreven ;* German, *betrieben*).

have I told you all that I can think on. Set me penance, and assoil me, for I have great repentance."

Grymbart was subtle and wise. He broke a rod off a tree and said, "Eme, now shall ye smite yourself thrice with this rod on your body, and then lay it down upon the ground, and spring three times thereover, without bowing of your legs and without stumbling, and then shall ye take it up and kiss it friendly in token of meekness and obedience of your penance that I gave you. Herewith be ye quit of all sins that ye have done to this day, for I forgive it you all."

The Fox was glad.

Tho said Grymbart to his Eme, "Eme, see now forthon that ye do good works: read your psalms, go to church, fast, and keep your holydays, and give your alms; and leave your sinful and ill life, your theft, and your treason, and so may ye come to mercy."

The Fox promised that he would so do, and then went they both together to the Court ward.

A little beside the way as they went stood a cloister of black nuns, where many geese, hens and capons went without the walls; and as they went talking the Fox brought Grymbart out of the right way thither, and without the walls by the barn went the polaylle. The Fox espied them, and saw a fat young capon which went alone from his fellows, and leapt, and caught him that the feathers flew about his ears, but the capon escaped.

Grymbart said, "What, Eme, cursed man, what will ye do! Will ye for one of these pullets fall again in all your sins of which ye have shriven you? Ye ought sore repent you."

Reynart answered, "Truly, cousin, I had all forgotten. Pray God that he forgive it me, for I will never do so more."

Then turned they again over a little bridge, yet the Fox alway looked after the polaylle; he could not refrain himself; that which clevid by the bone might not out of the flesh: though he should be hanged he could not let the looking after the polaylle as far as he might see them.

Grymbart saw his manner, and said, " Foul false deceiver, how go your eyen so after the polaylle ! "

The Fox said, "Cousin, ye misdo to say to me any such words.   Ye bring me out of my devotion and prayers.   Let me say a *pater noster* for all the souls of polaylle and geese that I have betrayed, and oft with falsehood stolen from these holy nuns."

Grymbart was not well apaid, but the Fox had ever his eyen toward the polaylle [1] till at last they came in the way again, and then turned they to the Courtward.   How sore quaked tho Reynart when they approached the Court !   For he wist well that he had for to answer to many a foul feat and theft that he had done.

CHAPTER XIII.

How the Fox came to the Court, and how he excused him tofore the King.

AT the first when it was known in the Court that Reynart the Fox and Grymbart his cousin were comen to the Court, there was none so poor nor so feeble of kin and friends but that he made him ready for to complain on Reynart the Fox.

Reynart looked as he had not been afraid, and held him better than he was, for he went forth proudly with his nephew through the highest street of the Court, right as he had been the King's son, and as he had not trespassed to any man the value of an hair : and went in the middle of the place standing tofore Noble the King and said—

" God give you great honour and worship.   There was never King that ever had a truer servant than I have been to your good grace, and yet am.   Nevertheless, dear lord, I know well that there ben many in this Court that would destroy me if ye would believe them ; but nay, God thank you, it is not fitting to your crown to believe these false deceivers and liars lightly.   To God mote it be complained how that these false liars and flatterers now-adays in the lord's Courts ben most heard and believed, the

---

[1] *Polaille*, poultry.

shrews and false deceivers ben borne up for to do to good men
all the harm and scathe they may. Our Lord God shall once
reward them their hire."

The King said, "Peace, Reynart, false thief and traitor ! How
well can ye bring forth fair tales ! And all shall not help you a
straw. Ween ye with such flattering words to be my friend, ye
have so oft served me so as ye now shall well know. The peace
that I have commanded and sworn, that have ye well holden,
have ye ?"

Chanticleer could no longer be still, but cried, "Alas, what
have I by this peace lost !"

"Be still, Chanticleer, hold your mouth. Let me answer
this foul thief. Thou shrewd fell thief," said the King, "thou
sayest that thou lovest me well : that hast thou showed well on
my messengers, these poor fellows, Tibert the Cat and Bruin the
Bear, which yet ben all bloody; which chide not ne say not
much, but that shall this day cost thee thy life. *In nomine Patris
et Christi filii.*"

Said the Fox, "Dear lord and mighty King, if Bruin's crown
be bloody what is that to me ? When he ate honey at Lantfert's
house in the village and did him hurt and scathe, there was he
beaten therefor; if he had willed, he is so strong of limbs, he
might well have be avenged ere he sprang into the water. Tho
came Tybert the Cat, whom I received friendly. If he went out
without my counsel for to steal mice to a priest's house, and the
priest did him harm, should I abye that, then might I say I were
not happy. Not so, my liege lord. Ye may do what ye will,
though my matter be clear and good ; ye may siede[1] me, or roast,
hang, or make me blind. I may not escape you. We stand all
under your correction. Ye be mighty and strong. I am feeble,
and my help is but small. If ye put me to the death it were a
small vengeance."

Whiles they thus spake, up sprang Bellyn the Ram and his ewe
Dame Olewey, and said, "My lord the King, hear our complaint." Bruin the Bear stood up with all his lineage and his

---

[1] *Siede,* seethe, boil.

fellows. Tybert the Cat, Isegrim the Wolf, Cuwart the Hare, and Panther; the Boar, the Camel, and Brunel the Goose; the Kid and Goat; Boudewyn the Ass, Borre the Bull, Hamel the Ox, and the Weasel; Chanticleer the Cock, Pertelot with all their children, all these made great rumour and noise, and came forth openly tofore their lord the King, and made that the Fox was taken and arrested.

CHAPTER XIV.

How the Fox was arrested and judged to death.

HEREUPON was a Parliament; and they desired that Reynart should ben dead. And whatsomever they said against the Fox he answered to each to them. Never heard man of such beasts such plaints of wise counsel and subtle inventions. And on that other side, the Fox made his excuse so well and formably thereon, that they that heard it wondered thereof. They that heard and saw it may tell it forth for truth; I shall short the matter and tell you forth of the Fox. The King and the Council heard the witnesses of the complaints of Reynart's misdeeds. It went with them as it oft does, the feeblest hath the worst. They gave sentence, and judged that the Fox should be dead and hanged by the neck. Tho list not he to play. All his flattering words and deceits could not help him. The judgment was given, and that must be done. Grymbart, his nephew, and many of his lineage might not find in their hearts to see him die, but took leave sorrowfully, and roomed the court.[1]

The King bethought him, and marked how many a youngling departed from thence all weeping, which were nigh of his kin, and said to himself, "Here behoveth other counsel hereto; though Reynart be a shrew, there be many good of his lineage."

Tybert the Cat said, "Sir Bruin and Sir Isegrim, how be ye thus slow? It is almost even. Here ben many bushes and hedges. If he escaped from us and were delivered out of this peril, he is so subtle, and so wily, and can so many deceits, that

---

[1] *Roomed*, vacated (räumen).

he should never be taken again. Shall we hang him? How
stand ye all thus? Ere the gallows can be made ready it shall
be night."

Isegrim bethought him tho, and said, "Hereby is a gibbet or
gallows." And with that word he sighed.

And the Cat espied that, and said, "Isegrim, ye be afraid.
Is it against your will? Think ye not that he himself went and
laboured that both your brethren were hanged? Were ye good
and wise, ye should thank him, and ye should not therewith so
long tarry."

CHAPTER XV.

How the Fox was led to the gallows.

ISEGRIM balked [1] and said, "Ye make much ado, Sir Tybert; had
we an halter which were meet for his neck and strong enough,
we should soon make an end."

Reynart the Fox, which long had not spoken, said to Isegrim,
"Short my pain. Tybert hath a strong cord which caught him
in the Priest's house. He can climb well, and is swift; let him
bear up the line. Isegrim and Bruin, this becometh you well,
that ye thus do to your Nephew! I am sorry that I live thus
long; haste you, ye be set thereto ; it is evil doo that ye tarry thus
long. Go tofore, Bruin, and lead me; Isegrim, follow fast, and
see well to, and be ware that Reynart go not away."

Tho said Bruin, "It is the best counsel that I ever yet heard,
that Reynart here saith."

Isegrim commanded anon and bad his kin and friends that
they should see to Reynart that he escaped not, for he is so wily
and false. They helden him by the feet, by the beard; and so
kept him that he escaped not from them.

The Fox heard all these words, which touched him nigh, yet
spake he and said, "Oh, dear Eme, methinketh ye pain yourself
sore for to do me hurt and scathe. If I durst, I would pay you
of mercy, though my hurt and sorrow is pleasant to you. I wot

---

[1] *Balked*, brayed (Dutch, *balken ;* vulg., bölken).

well, if mine Aunt, your wife, bethought her well of old ferners,[1] she would not suffer that I should have any harm; but now I am he that now ye will do on me what it shall please you. Ye Bruin and Tybert, God give you shames death but ye do to me your worst. I wot whereto I shall. I may die but once, I would that I were dead already. I saw my father die, he had soon done."

Isegrim said, "Let us go, for ye curse us because we lengthen the time. Evil might we fare if we abide any longer."

He went forth with great envy on that one side, and Bruin stood on the other side, and so led they him forth to the gallows ward. Tybert ran with a good will tofore, and bare the cord; and his throat was yet sore of the grynne, and his croppe did him woe of the stroke that he was take in; that happened by the counsel of the Fox, and that thought he now to quit.

Tybert Isegrim and Bruin went hastily with Reynart to the place there as the felons ben wont to be put to death. Noble the King and the Queen and all that were in the Court followed after, for to see the end of Reynart. The Fox was in great dread if him myshapped, and bethought him oft how he might save him from the death; and tho three that so sore desired his death, how he might deceive them and bring them to shame; and how he might bring the King with leasings for to hold with him against them. This was all that he studied, how he might put away his sorrow with wiles, and thought thus: "Though the King and many one be upon me angry, it is no wonder, for I have well deserved it; nevertheless, I hope for to be yet their best friend. And yet shall I never do them good. How strong that the King be, and how wise that his council be, if I may brook[2] my words I know so many an invention, I shall come to mine above[3] as far as they would comen to the gallows."

Tho said Isegrim, "Sir Bruin, think now on your red crown which by Reynart's mean ye caught; we have now the time that we may well reward him. Tybert, clime up hastily and bind the

---

[1] *Old ferners*, auld lang syne.   [2] *Brook*, have use of (brauchen).
[3] *Come to mine above*, rise in the world.

cord fast to the lynde, and make a riding knot or a strope, ye be the lightest ; ye shall this day see your will of him. Bruin, see well to, that he escape not, and hold fast. I will help that the ladder be set up, that he may go upward thereon."

Bruin said, " Do. I shall help him well."

The Fox said, "Now may my heart be well heavy for great dread ; for I see the death tofore mine eyen, and I may not escape. My lord the King, and dear Queen, and forth all ye that here stand, ere I depart from this world I pray you of a boone : that I may tofore you all make my confession openly, and tell my defaults all so clearly that my soul may not be acum-bred, and also that no man hereafter bear no blame for my theft ne for my treason. My death shall be to me the easier, and pray ye all to God that he have mercy on my soul."

CHAPTER XVI.

How the Fox made openly his confession tofore the King and tofore all them that would hear it.

ALL they that stood there had pity when Reynart said tho words, and said it was but a little request if the King would grant it him, and they prayed the King to grant it him.

The King gave him leave.

Reynart was well glad, and hoped that it might fall better, and said thus :

"Now help, *Spiritus Domini*, for I see here no man but I have trespassed unto. Nevertheless yet was I, unto the time that I was weaned from the teat, one of the best children that could anywhere be found. I went tho and played with the lambs, because I heard them gladly bleat. I was so long with them that at the last I bit one; there learned I first to lappen of the blood. It savoured well ; me thought it right good. And after I began to taste of the flesh thereof, I was licorous ; so that after that I went to the gate into the wood, there heard I the kids bleat and I slew of them twain. I began to wax hardy

after. I slew hens, polaylle and geese wherever I found them.
Thus worden[1] my teeth all bloody. After this, I wex so fell and
so wroth that whatsomever I found that I might over, I slew all.
Thereafter came I by Isegrim, now in the winter, where he hid
him under a tree, and reckoned to me that he was mine eme.
When I heard him then reckon alliance, we became fellows,
which I may well repent. We promised each to other to be
true, and to use good fellowship, and began to wander together.
He stole the great things and I the small, and all was common
between us. Yet he made it so that he had the best deal[2]; I got
not half my part. When that Isegrim gat a calf a ram or a
wether, then grimmed he, and was angry on me, and drove me
from him, and held my part and his too, so good is he. Yet
this was of the least. But when it so lucked that we took an
ox or a cow, then came thereto his wife with seven children;
so that unto me might vnnethe come one of the smallest ribs,
and yet, had they eaten all the flesh thereof, therewithall must
I be content; not for that I had so great need, for I have so
great scatte[3] and good of silver and of gold, that seven wains
should not can carry it away."

When the King heard him speak of this great good and riches,
he burned in the desire and covetyse thereof, and said, " Reynart,
where is the riches becomen? tell me that."

The Fox said, "My lord, I shall tell you. The riches was
stolen. And had it not be stolen, it should have cost you your life
and you should have been murdered,—which God forbid!—and
should have been the greatest hurt in the world."

When the Queen heard that, she was sore afraid and cried
aloud, "Alas and weleaway! Reynart, what say ye? I conjure
you by the long way that your soul shall go, that ye tell us openly
the truth hereof, as much as ye know of this great murder that
should have be done on my lord, that we all may hear it!"—

Now hearken how the Fox shall flatter the King and Queen,
and shall win both their good will and loves, and shall hinder

---

[1] *Worden*, became.   [2] *Deal*, share, division.
[3] *Scatte*, treasure, money; "shot" in the locker.

them that labour for his death. He shall unbind his pack and lie, and by flattery and fair words shall bring forth so his matters that it shall be supposed for truth.

In a sorrowful countenance spake the Fox to the Queen, " I am in such case now that I must needs die, and had ye me not so sore conjured I will not jeopardise my soul, and if I so died I should go therefor in to the pain of hell. I will say nothing but that I will make it good, for piteously he should have been murdered of his own folk. Nevertheless they that were most principal in this feat were of my next kin, whom gladly I would not betray, if the sorrow were not of the hell."

The King was heavy of heart, and said, "Reynart, sayest thou to me the truth?"

"Yes," said the Fox. "See ye not how it standeth with me? Ween ye that I shall damn my soul? What should it avail me if I now said otherwise than truth? My death is so nigh. There may neither prayer ne good help me." Tho trembled the Fox, by dissembling, as he had been afraid.

The Queen had pity on him, and prayed the King to have mercy on him, in eschewing of more harm, and that he should doo the people hold their peace, and give the Fox audience, and hear what he should say.

Tho commanded the King openly that each of them should be still, and suffer the Fox to say unberisped[1] what that he would.

Then said the Fox, "Be ye now all still, sith it is the King's will, and I shall tell you openly this treason. And therein will I spare no man that I know guilty."

CHAPTER XVII.

How the Fox brought them in danger that would have brought him to death, and how he got the grace of the King.

Now hearken how the Fox began. In the beginning he appealed Grymbart his dear Cousin, which ever had helped him in his need.

---

[1] *Unberisped*, untroubled, unexcited (Dutch, *rispen*).

He did so because his words should be the better believed; and
that he forthon might the better lie on his enemies. Thus began
he first and said:

"My lord, my father had found King Ermeryk's treasure dolven
in a pit; and when he had this great good, he was so proud and
orguillous that he had all other beasts in despite which tofore had
been his fellows. He made Tybert the Cat to go into that wild
land of Ardenne to Bruin the Bear for to do him homage, and
bad him say, if he would be King that he should come in to
Flanders. Bruin the Bear was glad hereof, for he had long desired it, and went forth in to Flanders; where my father received
him right friendly. Anon he sent for the wise Grymbart, mine
nephew, and for Isegrim the Wolf, and for Tybert the Cat. Tho
these five came between Gaunt and the thorp called Yfte, there
they held their council an whole dark night long. What with
the devil's help and craft, and for my father's riches, they concluded and swore there the King's death. Now hearken, and
hear this wonder. The four swore upon Isegrim's crown that
they should make Bruin a king and a lord, and bring him in the
stool at Akon,[1] and set the crown on his head; and if there were
any of the King's friends or lineage that would be contrary or
against this, him should my father with his good and treasure
fordrive, and take from him his might and power.

"It happed so that on a morrowtide early when Grymbart, my
nephew, was of wine almost drunk, that he told it to Dame Sloep-
cade, his wife, in counsel, and bade her keep it secret. But she
anon forgat it, and said it forth in confession to my wife upon
an heath where they both wenten a pilgrimage, but she must first
swear, by her truth and by the holy Three Kings of Cologne, that
for love ne for hate she should never tell it forth, but keep it
secret. But she held it not, and kept it no longer secret but till
she came to me; and she then told to me all that she heard, but
I must keep it in secret. And she told me so many tokens that
I felt well it was truth; and for dread and fear mine hair stood
right up, and my heart became as heavy as lead and as cold as

1 *Akon*, Aachen, Aix-la-Chapelle.

ice. I thought by this a likeness which here aforetime befell to the frosshis[1] which were free and complained that they had none lord ne were not bydwongen,[2] for a comynte[3] without a governor was not good, and they cried to God with a loud voice that he would ordain one that might rule them, this was all that they desired. God heard their request, for it was reasonable, and sent to them a Stork which ate and swallowed them in, as many as he could find; he was alway to them unmerciful. Tho complained they their hurt, but then it was too late; they that were tofore free and were afraid of nobody ben now bound and must obey to strength their king : herefor, ye rich and poor, I sorrowed, that it might happen us in likewise.

"Thus, my lord the King, I have had sorrow for you whereof ye can me but little thank. I know Bruin the Bear for such a shrew and ravener, wherefore I thought if he were king we should be all destroyed and lost. I know our sovereign lord the King of so high birth, so mighty, so benign and merciful, that I thought truly it had been an evil change for to have a foul stinking thief and to refuse a noble mighty stately Lion; for the Bear hath more mad folly in his unthrifty head, and all his ancestors, than any other hath. Thus had I in mine heart many a sorrow, and thought alway how I might break and foredo my father's false counsel, which of a churl and a traitor and worse than a thief would make a lord and a king. Alway I prayed God that he would keep our King in worship and good health, and grant him long life, but I thought well if my father held his treasure he should with his false fellows well find the way that the King should be deposed and set aside. I was sore bethought how I might best wit[4] where my father's good lay. I awaited at all times as nigh as I could, in woods, in bushes, in fields; where my father laid his eyen; were it by night or by day, cold or wet, I was alway by him to espy and know where his treasure was laid.

"On a time I lay down all plat on the ground and saw my

---

[1] *Frosshis*, frogs.
[2] *Bydwongen*, held in restraint (Dutch, *bedwingen ;* German, *beswingen*).
[3] *Comynte*, community.   [4] *Wit*, know.

father come running out of an hole. Now hark what I saw him
do. When he came out of the hole, he looked fast about if any-
body had seen him. And when he could nowhere none see, he
stopped the hole with sand and made it even and plain like to
the other ground by. He knew not that I saw it. And where
his footspore stood, there stryked he with his tail, and made it
smooth with his mouth, that no man should espy it. That learned
I there of my false father, and many subtleties that I tofore knew
nothing of. Then departed he thence and ran to the village
ward for to do his things; and I forgot not, but sprang and leapt
to the hole ward, and how well that he had supposed that he
had made all fast I was not so much a fool but that I found the
hole well, and scratched and scraped with my feet the sand out
of the hole, and crept therein. There found I the most plenty
of silver and of gold that ever I saw. Here is none so old that
ever so much saw on one heap in all his life. Tho took I Ermelyne my wife to help, and we ne rested night ne day to bear and
carry away, with great labour and pain, this rich treasure in to
another place that lay for us better, under an hawe in a deep hole.
In the mean while that mine housewife and I thus laboured, my
father was with them that would betray the King. Now may ye
hear what they did. Bruin the Bear and Isegrim the Wolf sent
all the land about if any man would take wages that they should
come to Bruin and he would pay them their souldye or wages
tofore. My father ran all over the land and bare the letters. He
wist little that he was robbed of his treasure; yea though he might
have wonnen all the world, he had not conne find a penny
thereof.

"When my father had been over all in the land between the
Elbe and the Somme, and had gotten many a soldier that
should the next summer have comen to help Bruin, tho came he
again to the Bear and his fellows, and told them in how great a
venture he had be tofore the boroughs in the land of Saxon, and
how the hunters daily ridden and hunted with hounds after him
in such wise that he unnethes escaped with his life. When he had
told this to these four false traitors, then showed he them letters

that pleased much. To Bruin therein were written twelve hundred of Isegrim's lineage by name, without the bears, the foxes, the cats, and the dassen, all these had sworn that with the first messenger that should come for them they should be ready, and come for to help the Bear if they had their wages a month tofore. This aspied I, I thank God. After these words my father went to the hole where his treasure had lain, and would look upon it. Tho began he a great sorrow; that he sought he found nothing. He found his hole broken, and his treasure borne away. There did he that I may well sorrow and bewail, for great anger and sorrow he went and hung himself. Thus abode the treason of Bruin by my subtilty after. Now see mine infortune. These traitors Isegrim and Bruin ben now most privy of counsel about the King, and sit by him on the high bench. And I, poor Reynart, have ne thanks ne reward. I have buried mine own father, because the King should have his life. My lord," said the Fox, "where ben they that would so do, that is, to destroy them self for to keep you."

The King and the Queen hoped to win the treasure and without council took to them Reynart and prayed him that he would do so well as to tell them where this treasure was.

Reynart said, "How should I tell the King, or them that would hang me for love of the traitors and murderers which by their flattery would fain bring me to death? Should I tell to them where my good is, then were I out of my wit."

The Queen then spake, "Nay, Reynart, the King shall let you have your life, and shall altogether forgive you, and ye shall be from henceforth wise and true to my lord."

The Fox answered to the Queen, "Dear lady, if the King will believe me, and that he will pardon and forgive me all my old trespasses, there was never King so rich as I shall make him. For the treasure that I shall do him have is right costly and may not be numbered."

The King said, "Ach Dame, will ye believe the Fox? Save your reverence, he is born to rob, steal, and to lie. This cleaves to his bones, and can not be had out of the flesh."

The Queen said, " Nay, my lord, ye may now well believe him. Though he were tofore fell, he is now changed otherwise than he was.   Ye have well heard that he hath impeached his father and the Dasse his nephew, which he might well have laid on other beasts if he would have been false, fell, and a liar."

The King said, "Dame, will ye then have it so, and think ye it best to be don, though I supposed it should hurt me I will take all these trespasses of Reynart upon me and believe his words. But I swear by my crown, if he ever hereafter misdo and trespass, that shall he dear abye and all his lineage unto the ninth degree."

The Fox looked on the King stoundmele,[1] and was glad in his heart, and said, " My lord, I were not wise if I should say things that were not true."

The King took up a straw from the ground, and pardoned and forgave the Fox all the misdeeds and trespasses of his father and of him also.

If the Fox was tho merry and glad, it was no wonder; for he was quit of his death and was all free and frank of all his enemies.

The Fox said, " My Lord the King and noble Lady the Queen, God reward you this great worship that ye do to me.   I shall think and also thank you for it in such wise that ye shall be the richest king of the world ; for there is none living under the sun that I vouchsafe better my treasure on, than on you both."

Then took the Fox up a straw and proffered it to the King, and said, " My most dear Lord, please it you to receive here the rich treasure which King Ermeryk had.   For I give it unto you with a free will, and knowledge it openly."

The King received the straw, and threw it merely from him with a joyous visage, and thanked much the Fox.

The Fox laughed in himself.

The King then hearkened after the counsel of the Fox.   And all that there were were at his will.

" My Lord," said he, " hearken and mark well my words.   In

<hr />

[1] *Stoundmele,* for a space of time.

the west side of Flanders there standeth a wood and is named Hulsterlo, and a water that is called Krekenpyt lieth thereby. This is so great a wilderness, that oft in a whole year man nor wife cometh therein, save they that will, and they that will not eschew it. There lieth this treasure hidden. Understand well that the place is called Krekenpyt, for I advise you, for the least hurt, that ye and my Lady go both thither; for I know none so true that I durst on your behalf trust; wherefore go yourself. And when ye come to Krekenpyt ye shall find there two birch trees standing althernext[1] the pit. My Lord, to tho birch trees shall ye go: there lieth the treasure untherdolven.[2] There must ye scrape and dig away a little the moss on the one side. There shall ye find many a jewel of gold and silver, and there shall ye find the crown which King Ermeryk wore in his days. That should Bruin the Bear have worn, if his will had gone forth. Ye shall see many a costly jewel, with rich stones set in gold work, which cost many a thousand mark. My Lord the King, when ye now have all this good, how oft shall ye say in your heart and think, 'Oh how true art thou, Reynart the Fox, that with thy subtle wit delvest and hidest this great treasure! God give thee good hap and welfare wherever thou be!'"

The King said, "Sir Reynart, ye must come and help us to dig up this treasure. I know not the way. I should never conne find it. I have heard often named Paris, London, Aachen, and Cologne; as me thinketh this treasure lieth right as ye mocked and japed, for ye name Krekenpyt. That is a feigned name."

These words were not good to the Fox, and he said with an angry mood, and dissembled and said, "Yea, my Lord the King, ye be also nigh that as from Rome to Maye. Ween ye that I will lead you to flume[3] Jordan. Nay, I shall bring you out of weening and show it you by good witness."

He called loud, "Cuwart the Hare, come here tofore the King." The beasts saw all thitherward and wondered what the King would.

---

[1] *Althernext*, next of all.   [2] *Untherdolven*, dug under.
[3] *Flume*, river.

The Fox said to the Hare, " Cuwart, are ye acold ; how tremble ye and quake so ? Be not afraid ; and tell my Lord the King here the truth, and that I charge you, by the faith and truth that ye owe him and to my Lady the Queen, of such thing as I shall demand of you."

Cuwart said, " I shall say the truth, though I should lose my neck therefor.   I shall not lie, ye have charged me so sore, if I know it."

" Then say, know ye not where Krekenpyt standeth ?   Is that in your mind ? "

The Hare said, " I knew that well twelve year agone, where that standeth.   Why ask ye that ?   It standeth in a wood named Hulsterlo, upon a warande [1] in the wilderness.   I have suffered there much sorrow for hunger and for cold, yea, more than I can tell.   Pater Symonet the Friese was woned [2] to make there false money, wherewith he bare himself out and all his fellowship ; but that was tofore ere I had fellowship with Ryn the Hound, which made me escape many a danger ; as he could well tell if he were here, and that I never in my days trespassed against the King otherwise than I ought to do with right."

Reynart said to him, " Go again to yonder fellowship.   Hear ye, Cuwart?   My Lord the King desireth no more to know of you."

The Hare returned and went again to the place he came from.

The Fox said, " My Lord the King, is it true that I said ? "

" Yea, Reynart," said the King, " forgive it me ; I did evil that I believed you not.   Now, Reynart, friend, find the way that ye go with us to the place and pit where the treasure lieth."

The Fox said, " It is a wonder thing.   Ween ye that I would not fain go with you ; if it were so with me that I might go with you in such wise that it no shame were unto your lordship, I would go.   But nay, it may not be.   Hearken what I shall say, and must needs, though it be to me villainy and shame.   When

---

[1] *Warande,* warren, a place privileged by a franchise from the King for keeping or hunting certain animals, to the exclusion of all persons entering without permission.   [2] *Woned,* accustomed.

Isegrim the Wolf, in the devil's name, went into religion and became a monk shorn in the order, tho the provender of six monks was not sufficient to him, and had not enough to eat, he then plained and wailed so sore that I had pity on him, for he became slow and sick. And because he was of my kin, I gave him counsel to run away, and so he did. Wherefore I stand accursed, and am in the Pope's ban and sentence. I will to-morrow betimes, as the sun riseth, take my way to Rome for to be assoiled [1] and take pardon. And from Rome I will over the sea into the Holy Land, and will never return again till I have done so much good that I may with worship go with you. It were great reproof to you, my Lord the King, in what land that I accompanied you that men should say ye reysed [2] and accompanied yourself with a cursed and person agravate."

The King said, "Sith that ye stand accursed in the censures of the Church, if I went with you men should arette villainy unto my crown. I shall then take Cuwart or some other to go with me to Krekenpyt; and I counsel you, Reynart, that ye put you yourself out of this curse."

"My Lord," quoth the Fox, "therefore will I go to Rome as hastily as I may. I shall not rest by night nor day till I be assoiled."

"Reynart," said the King, "me thinketh ye ben turned into a good way. God give you grace to accomplish well your desire."

As soon as this speaking was done, Noble the King went and stood upon an high stage of stone and commanded silence to all the beasts, and that they should sit down in a ring round upon the grass, everiche in his place after his estate and birth. Reynart the Fox stood by the Queen, whom he ought well to love.

Then said the King, "Hear ye all that be poor and rich, young and old, that standeth here. Reynart, one of the head officers of my house, had done so evil, which this day should have been hanged, hath now in this Court done so much, that I and my wife the Queen have promised to him our grace and

---

[1] *Assoiled*, absolved.   [2] *Reysed*, travelled (*reisen*).

friendship. The Queen hath prayed much for him, insomuch that I have made peace with him. And I give to him his life and member freely again, and I command you upon your life that ye do worship to Reynart and his wife, and to his children, wheresomever ye meet them by day or night. And I will also hear no more complaints of Reynart. If he hath heretofore misdone and trespassed, he will no more misdo ne trespass, but now better him. He will to-morrow early go to the Pope for pardon and forgiveness of all his sins, and forth over the sea to the Holy Land, and he will not come again till he bring pardon of all his sins."

This tale heard Tyselyn the Raven and leapt to Isegrim to Bruin and to Tybert, there as they were, and said, "Ye caitifs, how goeth it now? Ye unhappy folk, what do ye here? Reynart the Fox is now a squire and a courtier, and right great and mighty in the Court. The King hath skylled him quite of all his brokes,[1] and forgiven him all his trespasses and misdeeds. And ye be all betrayed and appeached."

Isegrim said, "How may this be? I trow Tyselyn that ye lie."

" I do not, certainly," said the Raven.

Tho went the Wolf and the Bear to the King. Tybert the Cat was in great sorrow, and he was so sore afraid that for to have the Fox's friendship he would well forgive Reynart the loss of his one eye that he lost in the priest's house ; he was so woe he wist not what to do, he would well that he never had seen the Fox.

CHAPTER XVIII.

How the Wolf and the Bear were arrested by the labour of Reynart the Fox.

ISEGRIM came proudly over the field tofore the King, and he thanked the Queen, and spake with a fell mood ill words on the Fox, in suchwise that the King heard it and was wroth, and

---

[1] *Skylled him quite of all his brokes*, judged him acquitted of all his dealings.

made the Wolf and the Bear anon to be arrested. Ye saw never wood [1] dogs do more harm than was done to them. They were both fast bounden, so sore that all that night they might not stir hand ne foot. They might scarcely roar ne move any joint. Now hear how the Fox forth did. He hated them. He laboured so to the Queen that he got leave for to have as much of the Bear's skin upon his rigge [2] as a foot long and a foot broad, for to make him thereof a scrip; then was the Fox ready if he had four strong shoon. Now hear how he did for to get these shoon.

He said to the Queen, "Madam, I am your pilgrim. Here is mine Eme, Sir Isegrim, that hath four strong shoon which were good for me. If he would let me have two of them I would on the way busily think on your soul, for it is right that a pilgrim should always think and pray for them that do him good. Thus may ye do your soul good if ye will. And also if ye might get of mine aunt Dame Ersewynde also two of her shoon to give me, she may well do it, for she goeth but little out, but abideth alway at home."

Then said the Queen, "Reynart, you behoveth well such shoes; ye may not be without them. They shall be good for you to keep your feet whole for to pass with them many a sharp mountain and stony rocks. Ye can find no better shoes for you than such as Isegrim and his wife have and wear. They be good and strong. Though it should touch their life, each of them shall give you two shoes for to accomplish with your high pilgrimage."

CHAPTER XIX.

How Isegrim and his wife Ersewynde must suffer their shoes to be plucked off, and how Reynart did on the shoes for to go to Rome with.

THUS hath this false pilgrim gotten from Isegrim two shoes from his feet, which were hauled off the claws to the sinews. Ye saw never fowl that men roasted lay so still as Isegrim did when his

---

[1] *Wood*, mad.   [2] *Rigge*, back.

shoes were hauled off. He stirred not, and yet his feet bled.
Then when Isegrim was unshod tho must Dame Ersewynde his
wife lie down in the grass with an heavy cheer. And she lost
there her hinder shoes.

Tho was the Fox glad, and said to his Aunt in scorn, " My dear
Aunt, how much sorrow have ye suffered for my sake, which me
sore repenteth, save this, hereof I am glad for ye be the liefest [1] of
all my kin. Therefore I will gladly wear your shoes. Ye shall
be partner of my pilgrimage and deal of the pardon that I shall
with your shoes fetch over the sea."

Dame Ersewynde was so woe that she unnethe might speak.
Nevertheless this she said, " Ah, Reynart, that ye now all thus
have your will, I pray God to wreak [2] it ! "

Isegrim and his fellow the Bear held their peace and were all
still.   They were evil at ease for they were bound and sore
wounded.   Had Tybert the Cat have been there, he should also
somewhat have suffered, in such wise as he should not have
escaped thence without hurt or shame.

The next day, when the sun arose, Reynart then did grease
his shoes which he had of Isegrim and Ersewynde his wife, and did
them on, and bound them to his feet, and went to the King and
to the Queen and said to them with a glad cheer, " Noble Lord
and Lady, God give you good morrow, and I desire of your grace
that I may have male [3] and staff blessed as belongeth to a
pilgrim."

Then the King anon sent for Bellyn the Ram, and when he
came he said, " Sir Bellyn, ye shall do mass tofore Reynart, for
he shall go on pilgrimage ; and give to him male and staff."

The Ram answered again and said, " My Lord, I dare not do
that, for he hath said that he is in the Pope's curse."

The King said what thereof master Gelys hath said to us, if a
man had don as many sins as all the world and he would tho
sins forsake, shrive him and receive penance, and do by the
priest's counsel, God will forgive them and be merciful unto him.

---

[1] *Liefest*, best loved.   [2] *Wreak*, avenge.
[3] *Male*, bag, scrip.

Now will Reynart go over the sea into the Holy Land, and make him clear of all his sins.

Then answered Bellyn to the King, "I will not do little ne much herein but if ye save me harmless in the spiritual court, before the bishop Prendelor and tofore his archdeacon Looswinde and tofore Sir Rapiamus his official."

The King began to wax wroth, and said, "I shall not bid you so much in half a year! I had liever hang you than I should so much pray you for it!"

When the Ram saw that the King was angry, he was so sore afraid that he quoke for fear, and went to the altar and sang in his books and read such as him thought good over Reynart, which little set thereby save that he would have the worship thereof.

When Bellyn the Ram had all said his service devoutly, then he hung on the fox's neck a male covered with the skin of Bruin the Bear and a little psalter thereby. Tho was Reynart ready toward his journey. Tho looked he toward the King, as he had been sorrowful to depart; and feigned as he had wept, right as he had yamerde[1] in his heart; but if he had any sorrow it was because all the other that were there were not in the same plight as the Wolf and Bear were brought in by him. Nevertheless he stood and prayed them all to pray for him, like as he would pray for them. The Fox thought that he tarried long and would fain have departed, for he knew himself guilty.

The King said, "Reynart, I am sorry ye be so hasty, and will no longer tarry."

"Nay, my Lord, it is time, for we ought not spare to do well, I pray you to give me leave to depart: I must do my pilgrimage."

The King said, "God be with you," and commanded all them of the court to go and convey Reynart on his way, save the Wolf and the Bear which fast lay bounden. There was none that durst be sorry therefor, and if ye had seen Reynart how personably he went with his male and psalter on his shoulder, and the shoes on his feet, ye should have laughed. He went and showed him

---

[1] *Yamerde*, grief (jammer).

outward wisely, but he laughed in his heart that all they brought
him forth which had a little tofore been with him so wroth.
And also the King which so much hated him, he had made him
such a fool that he brought him to his owne intent.   He was a
pilgrim of deuce ace."

"My Lord the King," said the Fox, "I pray you to return
again.   I will not that ye go any further with me.   Ye might
have harm thereby.   Ye have there two murderers arrested.   If
they escape you, ye might be hurt by them.   I pray God keep
you from misadventure!"   With these words he stood up on his
afterfeet, and prayed all the beasts, great and small, that would
be partners of his pardon, that they should pray for him.

They said that they all would remember him.

Then departed he from the King so heavily that many of them
ermed.[1]

Then said he to Cuwart the Hare and to Bellyn the Ram
merrily, "Here, friends, shall we now depart?   Yea, with a good
will accompany me further.   Ye two made me never angry.   Ye
be good for to walk with, courteous, friendly, and not complained
on of any beast.   Ye be of good conditions and ghostly of your
living; ye live both as I did when I was a recluse.   If ye have
leaves and grass ye be pleased, ye reck not of bread of flesh ne
such manner meat."

With such flattering words hath Reynart these two flattered
that they went with him till they came tofore his house Maleperduys.   .

CHAPTER XX.

How Cuwart the Hare was slain by the Fox.

WHEN the Fox was come tofore the gate of his house, he said
to Bellyn the Ram, "Cousin, ye shall abide here without, I and
Cuwart will go in, for I will pray Cuwart to help me to take my
leave of Ermelyne my wife, and to comfort her and my children."

Bellyn said, "I pray him to comfort them well."

---

[1] *Ermed*, grieved.

With such flattering words brought he the Hare into his hole in an evil hour. There found they Dame Ermelyne lying on the ground with her younglings, which had sorrowed much for dread of Reynart's death. But when she saw him come, she was glad. But when she saw his male and psalter, and espied his shoes, she marvelled and said, " Dear Reynart, how have ye sped ? "

He said I was arrested in the court, but the King let me gon. I must go a pilgrimage. Bruin the Bear and Isegrim the Wolf they be pledge for me. I thank the King he hath given to us Cuwart here, for to do with him what we will. The King said himself that Cuwart was the first that on us complained, and by the faith that I owe you I am right wroth on Cuwart."

When Cuwart heard these words he was sore afraid. He would have fled but he might not, for the Fox stood between him and the gate, and he caught him by the neck. Tho cried the Hare, " Help, Bellyn, help ! Where be ye ? This pilgrim slayeth me ? " But that cry was soon done, for the Fox had anon bitten his throat a two.

Tho said he, " Let us go eat this good fat hare." The young whelps came also. Thus held they a great feast, for Cuwart had a good fat body. Ermelyne ate the flesh and drank the blood ; she thanked oft the King that he had made them so merry. The Fox said, " Eat as much as ye may, he will pay for it if we will fetch it."

She said, " Reynart, I trow ye mock. Tell me the truth how ye be departed thence."

" Dame, I have so flattered the king and the queen that I suppose the friendship between us shall be right thin. When he shall know of this he shall be angry, and hastily seek me for to hang me by mine neck. Therefore let us depart, and steal secretly away in some other forest where we may live without fear and dread, and there that we may live seven year and more an they find us not. There is plenty of good meat of partridges, woodcocks, and much other wild fowl, Dame, and if ye will come with me thither there ben sweet wells and fair and clear running brooks ; Lord God, how sweet air is there. There may we be in peace and ease, and live in great wealth. For the King hath let me gon because I told him that there was great treasure in Krekenpyt, but there shall he find nothing though he sought ever. This shall sore anger him when he knoweth that he is thus deceived. What ! trow ye how many a great leasing must I lie ere I could escape from him. It was hard that I escaped out of prison ; I was never in greater peril ne nearer my death. But how it ever go I shall by my will never more come in the King's danger. I have now gotten my thumb out of his mouth, that thank I my subtilty."

Dame Ermelyne said, "Reynart, I counsel that we go not into another forest where we should be strange and elenge. We have here all that we desire. And ye be here lord of our neigh-bours ; wherefore shall we leave this place and adventure us in a worse ? We may abide here sure enough. If the King would do us any harm or besiege us, here ben so many by or side holes, in such wise as we shall escape from him ; in abiding here we may not do amiss. We know all bypaths over all, and ere he take us with might he must have much help thereto. But that ye have sworn that ye shall go oversea and abide there, that is the thing that toucheth me most."

"Nay, Dame, care not therefor. How more forsworn, how more forlorn. I went once with a good man that said to me that a bedwongen [1] oath, or oath sworn by force, was none oath. Though I went on this pilgrimage it should not avail me a cat's tail. I will abide here and follow your counsel. If the King hunt after me, I shall keep me as well as I may. If he be me too mighty, yet I hope with subtlety to beguile him. I shall unbind my sack. If he will seek harm he shall find harm."

Now was Bellyn the Ram angry that Cuwart his fellow was so long in the hole, and called loud, "Come out, Cuwart, in the devil's name ; how long shall Reynart keep you there ? Haste you, and come ! Let us go."

When Reynart heard this, he went out and said softly to Bellyn the Ram, " Lief Bellyn, wherefore be ye angry ? Cuwart speaketh with his dear Aunt. Methinketh ye ought not to be displeased

---

[1] *Bedwongen*, enforced.

therefor. He bade me say to you ye might well go tofore, and he shall come after; he is lighter of foot than ye. He must tarry awhile with his Aunt and her children, they weep and cry because I shall go from them."

Bellyn said, "What did Cuwart? Methought he cried after help."

The Fox answered, "What say ye, Bellyn? Ween ye that he should have any harm? Now hark what he then did. When we were comen into mine house, and Ermelyne my wife understood that I should go over sea, she fell down in a swoon; and when Cuwart saw that, he cried loud, 'Bellyn, come help mine Aunt to bring her out of her swoon.'"

Then said the Ram, "In faith I understood that Cuwart had been in great danger."

The Fox said, "Nay truly, or Cuwart should have any harm in my house I had liever that my wife and children should suffer much hurt."

CHAPTER XXI.

How the Fox sent the head of Cuwart the Hare to the King by Bellyn the Ram.

THE Fox said, "Bellyn, remember ye not that yesterday the King and his council commanded me that ere I should depart out of this land I should send to him two letters? Dear cousin, I pray you to bear them, they be ready written."

The Ram said, "I wot never. If I wist that your inditing and writing were good, ye might peradventure so much pray me that I would bear them, if I had anything to bear them in."

Reynart said, "Ye shall not fail to have somewhat to bear them in. Rather than they should be unborne I shall rather give you my male that I bear; and put the King's letters therein, and hang them about your neck. Ye shall have of the King great thanks therefor, and be right welcomen to him."

Hereupon Bellyn promised him to bear these letters.

Tho returned Reynart into his house and took the male and

put therein Cuwart's head, and brought it to Bellyn for to bring him in danger, and hang it on his neck, and charged him not to look in the male if he would have the King's friendship. "And if ye will that the King take you into his grace and love you, say that ye yourself have made the letter and indited it, and have given the counsel that it is so well made and written. Ye shall have great thanks therefor."

Bellyn the Ram was glad hereof, and thought he should have great thanks, and said, "Reynart, I wot well that ye now do for me. I shall be in the Court greatly praised when it is known that I can indite and make a letter, though I cannot make it. Ofttimes it happeneth that God suffereth some to have worship and thank of the labours and cunning of other men, and so it shall befall me now. Now, what counsel ye, Reynart? Shall Cuwart the Hare come with me to the Court?"

"Nay," said the Fox, "he shall anon follow you. He may not yet come, for he must speak with his Aunt. Now go ye forth tofore. I shall show to Cuwart secret things which ben not yet known."

Bellyn said, "Farewell, Reynart," and went him forth to the Court. And he ran and hasted so fast, that he came tofore midday to the Court, and found the King in his palace with his Barons. The King marvelled when he saw him bring the male again which was made of the Bear's skin. The King said, "Say on, Bellyn, from whence come ye? Where is the Fox? How is it that he hath not the male with him?"

Bellyn said, "My Lord, I shall say you all that I know. I accompanied Reynart unto his house. And when he was ready, he asked me if I that would for your sake bear two letters to you. I said, for to do you pleasure and worship, I would gladly bear to you seven. Tho brought he to me this male wherein the letters be, which ben indited by my cunning, and I gave counsel of the making of them. I trow ye saw never letters better ne craftlier made ne indited."

The King commanded anon Bokart, his secretary, to read the letters, for he understood all manner languages. Tybert the Cat and he took the male off Bellyn's neck, and Bellyn hath so far said and confessed that he therefore was dampned.[1]

The clerk Bokwart undid the male, and drew out Cuwart's head, and said, "Alas, what letters ben these! Certainly, my Lord, this is Cuwart's head."

"Alas," said the King, "that ever I believed so the Fox!" There might men see great heaviness of the King and of the Queen. The King was so angry that he held long down his head, and at last, after many thoughts, he made a great cry, that all the beasts were afraid of the noise.

Tho spake Sir Firapeel the Leopard, which was sybbe[2] somewhat to the King, and said, "Sire King, how make ye such a noise! Ye make sorrow enough though the Queen were dead. Let this sorrow go, and make good cheer. It is great shame. Be ye not a Lord and King of this land? Is it not all under you, that here is?"

The King said, "Sir Firapeel, how should I suffer this? One false shrew and deceiver has betrayed me and brought me so far, that I have forwrought[3] and angered my friends the stout Bruin the Bear and Isegrim the Wolf, which sore me repenteth. And this goeth against my worship, that I have done amiss against my best Barons, and that I trusted and believed so much the false Fox. And my wife is cause thereof. She prayed me so much that I heard her prayer, and that me repenteth, though it be too late."

"What though, Sir King," said the Leopard. "If there be any thing misdone it shall be amended. We shall give to Bruin the Bear to Isegrim the Wolf and to Ersewynde his wife for the piece of his skin and for their shoes, for to have good peace, Bellyn the Ram. For he hath confessed himself that he gave counsel and consented to Cuward's death. It is reason that he abye it. And we all shall go fetch Reynart, and we shall arrest him and hang him by the neck, without law or judgment. And there with all shall be content."

---

[1] *Dampned*, condemned.   [2] *Sybbe*, related by blood.
[3] *Forwrought*, overwrought.

CHAPTER XXII.

How Bellyn the Ram and all his lineage were given in the hands of Isegrim and Bruin, and how he was slain.

THE King said, " I will do it gladly."

Firapeel the Leopard went tho to the prison and unbound them first, and then he said, "Ye, sirs, I bring to you a fast pardon and my lord's love and friendship. It repenteth him, and is sorry, that he ever hath done spoken or trespassed against you, and therefore ye shall have a good appointment. And also amends he shall give to you, Bellyn the Ram and all his lineage fro now forthon to doomsday, in such wise that wheresomever ye find them, in field or in wood, that ye may freely bite and eat them without any forfeit. And also the King granteth to you that ye may hunt and do the worst ye can to Reynart and all his lineage without misdoing. This fair great privilege will the King grant to you ever to hold of him. And the King will that ye swear to him never to misdo, but do him homage and fealty. I counsel you to do this, for ye may do it honourably."

Thus was the peace made by Firapeel the Leopard, friendly and well. And that cost Bellyn the Ram his tabart[1] and also his life, and the Wolf's lineage hold these privileges of the King. And in to this day they devour and eat Bellyn's lineage where that they may find them. This debate was begun in an evil time, for the peace could never sith[2] be made between them.

The King did forth with his Court and feast length twelve days longer for love of the Bear and the Wolf, so glad was he of the making of this peace.

CHAPTER XXIII.

How the King held his feast, and how Lapreel the Cony complained unto the King upon Reynart the Fox.

To this great feast came all manner of beasts, for the King did do cry this feast over all in that land. There was the most joy and

---

[1] *Tabart,* cont. The sleeveless coat of a labourer.   [2] *Sith,* after.

mirth that ever was seen among beasts. There was danced mannerly the hovedance,[1] with shalms, trumpets, and all manner of minstrelsy. The King did do ordain so much meat that everych found enough. And there was no beast in all his land so great ne so little but he was there, and there were many fowls and birds also, and all they that desired the King's friendship were there, saving Reynart the Fox, the red false pilgrim which lay in await to do harm and thought it was not good for him to be there. Meat and drink flowed there. There were plays and esbatemens. The feast was full of melody. One might have lust to see such a feast.

And right as the feast had dured eight days, about mid-day came in the Cony Lapreel tofore the King, where he sat on the table with the Queen, and said all heavily that all they heard him that were there, " My lord, have pity on my complaint, which is of great force and murder that Reynart the Fox would have done to me yester morrow as I came running by his borough at Maleperduys. He stood before his door without, like a pilgrim. I supposed to have passed by him peaceably toward this feast, and when he saw me come he came against me saying his beads. I saluted him, but he spake not one word, but he raught out his right foot and dubbed me in the neck between mine ears that I had weened I should have lost my head, but God be thanked I was so light that I sprang from him. With much pain came I off his claws. He grimmed as he had been angry by cause he held me no faster. Tho I escaped from him I lost mine one ear, and I had four great holes in my head of his sharp nails that the blood sprang out and that I was nigh all aswoon, but for the great fear of my life I sprang and ran so fast from him that he could not overtake me. See, my Lord these great wounds that he hath made to me with his sharp long nails. I pray you to have pity of me, and that ye will punish this false traitor and murderer, or else shall there no man go and come over the heath in safety whiles he haunteth his false and shrewd rule."

---

[1] *Hovedance,* court (hof) dance.

CHAPTER XXIV.

How Corbant the Rook complained on the Fox for the death of his wife.

RIGHT as the Cony had made an end of his complaint, came in Corbant the Rook flowen in the place tofore the King and said, "Dear Lord, hear me. I bring you here a piteous complaint. I went to-day by the morrow[1] with Sharpebek my wife for to play upon the heath. And there lay Reynart the Fox down on the ground, like a dead caitiff. His eyes stared and his tongue hung long out of his mouth, like an hound had been dead. We tasted[2] and felt his belly but we found thereon no life. Tho went my wife and hearkened, and laid her ear tofore his mouth for to wit if he drew his breath, which misfell her evil: For the false fell Fox awaited well his time, and when he saw her so nigh him he caught her by the head and bit it off. Tho was I in great sorrow and cried loud, 'Alas! alas! what is there happened?' Then stood he hastily up and raught so covetously after me that for fear of death I trembled, and flew upon a tree thereby, and saw from far how the false caitiff ate and slonked[3] her in, so hungrily that he left neither flesh ne bone, no more but a few feathers. The small feathers he slang them in with the flesh; he was so hungry, he would well have eaten twain. Tho went he his strete. Tho flew I down with great sorrow, and gathered up the feathers for to show them to you here. I would not be again in such peril and fear as I was there for a thousand mark of the finest gold that ever came of Araby. My Lord the King, see here this piteous work. This ben the feathers of Sharpebek my wife! My Lord, if ye will have worship ye must do herefor justice, and avenge you in such wise as men may fear and hold of you, for if ye suffer thus your safe conduct to be broken, ye yourself shall not go peaceably in the highway. For the lords that do not justice, and suffer that the law be not executed upon the

---

[1] *Morrow*, morning.   [2] *Tasted*, touched.
[3] *Slonked*, swallowed (schlingen).

thieves, murderers, and them that misdo, they be partners tofore
God of all their misdeeds and trespasses, and eueryche then will
be a lord himself. Dear Lord see well to, for to keep yourself."

CHAPTER XXV.

How the King was sore angry of these complaints.

NOBLE the King was sore moved and angry when he had heard
these complaints of the Cony and of the Rook. He was so
frightful to look on that his eyen glimmered as fire ; he brayed as
loud as a bull, in such wise that all the Court quoke for fear; at
the last he said, crying, " By my crown, and by the truth that I
owe to my wife, I shall so awreak and avenge these trespasses that
it shall be long spoken of after. That my safe conduct and my
commandment is thus broken, I was over nice that I believed so
lightly the false shrew. His false flattering speech deceived me.
He told me he would go to Rome, and from thence over the sea to
the Holy Land. I gave him male and psalter, and made of him
a pilgrim, and meant all truth. Oh, what false touches can he !
How can he stuff the sleeve with flocks ! But this caused my
wife. It was all by her counsel. I am not the first that have
been deceived by women's counsel, by which many a great hurt
hath befallen. I pray and command all them that hold of me,
and desire my friendship, be they here or wheresomever they be,
that they with their counsel and deeds help me to avenge this over
great trespass, that we and ours may abide in honour and worship
and this false thief in shame. That he no more trespass against
our safeguard, I will myself in my person help thereto all that I
may."

Isegrim the Wolf and Bruin the Bear heard well the King's
words, and hoped well to be avenged on Reynart the Fox, but
they durst not speak one word. The King was so sore moved
that none durst well speak.

At last the Queen spake, " *Sire, pour dieu ne croyes mye toutes
choses que on vous dye, et ne Iures pas legierment.* A man of

worship should not lightly believe, ne swear greatly, unto the
time he knew the matter clearly; and also he ought by right
hear that other party speak.   There ben many that complain on
other and ben in the default themself.   *Audi alteram partem:*
hear that other party.   I have truly holden the Fox for good, and
upon that that he meant no falsehood I helped him that I might.
But howsomever it cometh or goeth, is he evil or good, me
thinketh for your worship that ye should not proceed against
him over hastily.   That were not good ne honest, for he may
not escape from you.   Ye may prison him or flay him, he must
obey your judgment."

Then said Firapeel the Leopard, "My Lord, me thinketh my
Lady here hath said to you truth and given you good counsel; do
ye well and follow her, and take advice of your wise council.
And if he be founden guilty in the trespasses that now to you
be showed, let him be sore punished according to his trespasses.
And if he come not hither ere this feast be ended, and excuse
him as he ought of right to do, then do as the council shall
advise you.   But and if he were twice as much false and ill as
he is, I would not counsel that he should be done to more than
right."

Isegrim the Wolf said, "Sir Firapeel, all we agree to the same;
as far as it pleaseth my lord the King, it cannot be better.   But
though Reynart were now here, and he cleared him of double so
many plaints, yet should I bring forth against him that he had
forfeited his life.   But I will now be still and say not, because
he is not present.   And yet, above all this, he hath told the
King of certain treasure lying in Krekenpyt in Hulsterlo.   There
was never lied a greater leasing; therewith he hath us all beguiled,
and hath sore hindered me and the Bear.   I dare lay my life
thereon that he said not thereof a true word.   Now robbeth he
and stealeth upon the heath all that goeth forth by his house.
Nevertheless, Sir Firapeel, what that pleaseth the King and you
that must well be done.   But and if he would have comen hither
he might have been here, for he had knowledge by the King's
messenger."

The King said, "We will none otherwise send for him, but I command all them that owe me service and will my honour and worship that they make them ready to the war at the end of six days, all them that ben archers and have bows, guns, bombards, horsemen and footmen, that all these be ready to besiege Maleperduys. I shall destroy Reynart the Fox if I be a king. Ye lords and sirs, what say ye hereto? Will ye do this with a good will?"

And they said and cried all, "Yea we, Lord, when that ye will, we shall all go with you!"

CHAPTER XXVI.

How Grymbart the Dasse warned the Fox that the King was wroth with him and would slay him.

ALL these words heard Grymbart the Dasse, which was his brother son. He was sorry and angry. If it might have profited he ran then the highway to Maleperduys ward. He spared neither bush ne hawe, but he hasted so sore that he sweat. He sorrowed in himself for Reynart his rede Eme, and as he went he said to himself, "Alas, in what danger be ye comen in! Where shall ye become! Shall I see you brought from life to death, or else exiled out of the land! Truly I may be well sorrowful, for ye be head of all our lineage; ye be wise of council, ye be ready to help your friends when they have need, ye can so well show your reasons that where ye speak ye win all."

With such manner wailing and piteous words came Grymbart to Maleperduys, and found Reynart his Eme there standing, which had gotten two pigeons as they came first out of their nest to assay if they could fly, and because the feathers on their wings were too short they fell down to the ground; and as Reynart was gone out to seek his meat he espied them and caught them, and was comen home with them.

And when he saw Grymbart coming, he tarried and said, "Welcome, my best beloved Nephew that I know in all my kindred.   Ye have run fast, ye ben all besweat ; have ye any new tidings ? "

"Alas," said he, "lief Eme, it standeth evil with you. Ye have lost both life and good.   The King hath sworn that he shall give you a shameful death.   He hath commanded all his folk within six days for to be here.   Archers, footmen, horsemen, and people in wains !   And he hath guns, bombards, tents, and pavilions. And also he hath do laden torches.   See tofore you, for ye have need.   Isegrim and Bruin ben better now with the King than I am with you.   All that they will is done.   Isegrim hath don him to understand that ye be a thief and a murderer ; he hath great envy to you.   Lapreel the Cony, and Corbant the Rook have made a great complaint also.   I sorrow much for your life, that for dread I am all sick."

"Puf !" said the Fox.   "Dear Nephew, is there nothing else ? Be ye so sore afraid hereof ? Make good cheer hardily.   Though the King himself and all that ben in the Court hath sworn my death, yet shall I be exalted above them all.   They may all fast jangle, clatter, and give counsel, but the Court may not prosper without me and my wiles and subtlety.

CHAPTER XXVII.

How Reynart the Fox came another time to the Court.

"DEAR Nephew, let all these things pass, and come here in and see what I shall give you ; a good pair of fat pigeons.   I love no meat better.   They ben good to digest.   They may almost be swolowen in all whole ; the bones ben half blood ; I eat them with that other.   I feel myself other while encumbered in my stomach, therefore eat I gladly light meat.   My wife Ermelyne shall receive us friendly, but tell her nothing of this thing for she should take it over heavily.   She is tender of heart ; she might for fear fall in some sickness ; a little thing goeth sore to her heart.   And to-morrow early I will go with you to the Court, and if I may come to speech and may be heard, I shall so answer that I shall touch some nigh ynowh. Nephew, will not ye stand by me as a friend ought to do to another?"

"Yes truly, dear Eme," said Grymbart, "and all my good is at your commandment."

"God thank you, Nephew," said the Fox. "That is well said. If I may live, I shall quite it you."

"Eme," said Grymbart, "ye may well come tofore all the lords and excuse you. There shall none arrest you ne hold as long as ye be in your words. The Queen and the Leopard have gotten that."

Then said the Fox, "Therefor I am glad; then I care not for the best of them an hair; I shall well save myself."

They spoke no more hereof, but went forth into the burrow, and found Ermelyne there sitting by her younglings, which arose up anon and received them friendly. Grymbart saluted his aunt and the children with friendly words. The two pigeons were made ready for their supper, which Reynart had taken. Each of them took his part, as far as it would stretch; if each of them had had one more there should but little have left over. The Fox said, "Lief Nephew, how like ye my children Rossel and Reynerdine? They shall do worship to all our lineage. They begin already to do well. That one catcheth well a chicken, and that other a pullet. They conne well also duck in the water after lapwings and ducks. I would oft send them for provender, but I will first teach them how they shall keep them from the grynnes, from the hunters, and from the hounds. If they were so far comen that they were wise, I durst well trust to them that they should well victual us in many good divers meats that we now lack. And they like and follow me well, for they play all grimming, and where they hate they look friendly and merrily; for thereby they bring them under their feet, and bite the throat asunder. This is the nature of the Fox. They be swift in their taking, which pleaseth me well."

"Eme," said Grymbart, "ye may be glad that ye have such wise children. And I am glad of them also because they be of my kin."

"Grymbart," said the Fox, "ye have sweat and be weary. It were high tide that ye were at your rest."

"Eme, if it pleaseth you, it thinketh me good." Tho lay they down on a litter made of straw. The Fox his wife and his children went all to sleep, but the Fox was all heavy and lay, sighed, and sorrowed[1] how he might best excuse himself.

On the morrow early he roomed[2] his castle and went with Grymbart. But he took leave first of Dame Ermelyne his wife and of his children, and said, "Think not long. I must go to the Court with Grymbart, my cousin. If I tarry somewhat, be not afraid; and if ye hear any ill tidings, take it alway for the best. And see well to yourself and keep our castle well. I shall do yonder the best I can, after that I see how it goeth."

"Alas, Reynart," said she, "how have ye now thus taken upon you for to go to the Court again? The last time that ye were there, ye were in great jeopardy of your life. And ye said ye would never come there more."

"Dame," said the Fox, "the adventure of the world is wonderly; it goeth otherwhile by weening. Many one weeneth to have a thing which he must forego. I must needs now go thither. Be content. It is all without dread. I hope to come at altherlengest within five days again."

Herewith he departed, and went with Grymbart to the Court ward. And when they were upon the heath then said Reynart, "Nephew, sith I was last shriven I have done many shrewd turns. I would ye would hear me now of all that I have trespassed in: I made the Bear to have a great wound for the male which was cut out of his skin; and also I made the Wolf and his wife to lose their shoon; I peased[3] the King with great leasings, and bare him on hand that the Wolf and the Bear would have betrayed him and would have slain him, so I made the King right wroth with them where they deserved it not; also I told to the King that there was great treasure in Hulsterlo of which he was never the better ne richer, for I lied all that I said; I led Bellyn

---

[1] *Sorrowed*, took careful thought.   [2] *Roomed*, vacated.
[3] *Peased*, pacified, appeased.

the Ram and Cuwart the Hare with me, and slew Cuwart and
sent to the King by Bellyn Cuwart's head in scorn; and I dowed[1]
the Cony between the ears that almost I benamme[2] his life from
him, for he escaped against my will, he was to me overswift; the
Rook may well complain for I swallowed in Dame Sharpebek his
wife. And also I have forgotten one thing, the last time that I
was shriven to you, which I have sith bethought me; and it was
of great deceit that I did; which I now will tell you.

"I came with the Wolf walking between Houthulst and Elver-
dynge. There saw we go a red mare, and she had a black colt
or a foal of four months old which was good and fat. Isegrim
was almost storven for hunger, and prayed me go to the Mare
and wit of her if she would sell her foal.

"I ran fast to the Mare and asked that of her. She said she
would sell it for money.

"I demanded of her, how she would sell it.

"She said, 'It is written on my hinder foot. If ye can read
and be a clerk ye may come see and read it.'

"Tho wist I well where she would be, and I said, 'Nay, for
sooth, I cannot read. And also I desire not to buy your child.
Isegrim hath sent me hither, and would fain know the price
thereof.'

"The Mare said, 'Let him come then himself, and I shall let
him have knowledge.'

"I said, 'I shall;' and hastily went to Isegrim, and said, 'Eme
will you eat your bellyful of this colt, so go fast to the Mare for
she tarrieth after you. She hath do write the price of her colt
under her foot. She would that I should have read it, but I can
not one letter, which me sore repenteth for I went never to school.
Eme will ye buy that colt? Can ye read, so may ye buy it.'

"'Oh, Nephew, that can I well. What should me let? I can
well French, Latin, English, and Dutch. I have gone to school
at Oxenford, I have also with old and ancient doctors been in
the audience and heard pleas, and also have given sentence, I
am licensed in both laws; what manner writing that any man

---

[1] *Dowed*, struck.   [2] *Benamme*, took away.

can devise I can read it as perfectly as my name : I will go to her, and shall anon understand the price,' and he bade me to tarry for him, and he ran to the Mare, and asked her how she would sell her foal or keep it. She said, 'The sum of the money standeth written after on my foot.' He said, 'Let me read it.' She said, 'Do,' and lifte up her foot, which was new shod with iron and six strong nails ; and she smote him, without missing, on his head, that he fell down as he had been dead. A man should well have ridden a mile ere he arose. The Mare trotted away with her colt, and she left Isegrim lying shrewdly hurt and wounded. He lay and bled, and howled as an hound. I went tho to him and said, 'Sir Isegrim, dear Eme, how is it now with you ? Have you eaten yenowh of the colt ? Is your belly full ? Why give ye me no part ? I did your errand. Have slept ye your dinner ? I pray you tell me, what was written under the mare's foot ? What was it, prose or rhyme, metre or verse ? I would fain know it. I trow it was *cantum,* for I heard you sing, me thought, from fear ; for ye were so wise that no man could read it better than ye.'

"'Alas, Reynart, alas !' said the Wolf, 'I pray you to leave your mocking. I am so foul arrayed and sore hurt than an heart of stone might have pity on me. The Mare with her long leg had an iron foot, I weened the nails thereof had been letters, and she hit me at the first stroke six great wounds in my head that almost it is cloven. Such manner letters shall I never more desire to read.' 'Dear Eme, is that truth that ye tell me ? I have great mervaylle. I held you for one of the wisest clerks that now live. Now I hear well it is true that I long since have read and heard, that the best clerks ben not the wisest men. The lay people otherwhile wax wise. The cause that these clerks ben not the wisest is that they study so much in the cunning and science that they therein doole.' Thus brought I Isegrim in this great laste and harm, that he vnneth byhelde his life.

"Lief Nephew now have I told you all my sins that I remember. Whatsoever falle at the Court—I wote never how it shall stand with me there—I am not now so sore afraid, for I am clear from sin. I will gladly come to mercy and receive penance by your counsel."

Grymbart said, "The trespasses ben great. Nevertheless who that is dead must abide dead, and therefore I will forgive it you altogether, with the fear that ye shall suffer therefor ere ye shall conne excuse you of the death, and hereupon I will assoil you. But the most hinder that ye shall have shall be, that ye sent Cuwart's head to the Court, and that ye blinded the King with sutthe[1] lies. Eme, that was right evil done."

The Fox said, "What, lief nephew! Who that will go through the world this to hear and that to see and that other to tell, truly it may not clearly be done. How should any man handle honey but if he licked his fingers? I am ofttimes rored and pricked in my conscience as to love God above all thing and mine even Crysten as myself, as is to God well acceptable and according to his law. But how ween ye that reason within forth fighteth against the outward will, then stand I all still in myself, that me thinketh I have lost all my wits, and wote not what me aileth, I am then in such a thought I have now all left my sins, and hate all thing that is not good, and climb in high contemplation abone his commandments. But this special grace have I when I am alone; but in a short while after, when the world cometh in me, then find I in my way so many stones, and the foot spores[2] that these loose prelates and rich priests go in, that I am anon taken again. Then cometh the world and will have this; and the flesh will live pleasantly; which lay tofore me so many things that I then lose all my good thoughts and purpose. I hear there sing, pipe, laugh, play, and all mirth, and I hear that these prelates and rich curates preach and say all otherwise than they think and do. There learn I to lie, the leasings ben most used in the lord's courts; certainly lords, ladies, priests, and clerks, maken most leasings. Men dare not tell to the lords now the truth. There is default. I must flatter and lie also or else I should be shut without the door. I have often heard men say truth and rightfully, and have their reason made with a leasing like to their

[1] *Sutthe*, flattering.   [2] *Spores*, tracks.

purpose, who brought it in and went through because their matter should seem the fairer. The leasing ofttimes cometh unavised, and falleth in the matter unwittingly, and so, when she is well clad, it goeth forth through with that other.

"Dear Nephew thus must men now lie nere and there, say sooth, flatter and menace, pray and curse, and seek every man upon his feeblest and weakest. ·Who otherwise will now haunt and use the world than devise a leasing in the fairest wise, and that bewimple with kerchiefs about in such wise that men take it for a truth, he is not run away from his master. Can he that subtilty in such wise that he stammer not in his words, and may then be heard, Nephew, this man may do wonder. He may wear scarlet and grise.[1] He winneth in the spiritual law and temporal also, and wheresomever he hath to do. Now ben there many false shrews that have great envy that they have so great fardel,[2] and ween that they can also well lie ; and take on them to lie and to tell it forth. He would fain eat of the fat morsels. But he is not believed ne heard. And many ben there that be so plump and foolish that when they ween best to pronounce and show their matter and conclude, they fall beside and out thereof, and cannot then help themself, and leave their matter without tail or head ; and he is acompted for a fool; and many mock them therewith. But who can give to his leasing a conclusion, and pronounce it without tatelying, like as it were written tofore him, and that he can so blind the people that his leasing shall better be believed than the truth : that is the man. What cunning is it to say the truth that is good to do? How laugh these false subtle shrews that give counsel, to make these leasings and set them forth, and maken unright go above right, and maken bills and set in things that never were thought ne said, and teach men see through their fingers ; and all for to win money and let their tongues to hire for to maintain and strengthen their leasings. Alas, Nephew, this is an evil cunning, of which life-scathe and hurt may come thereof.

"I say not but that otherwhile men must jape, bourd,[3] and lie

---

[1] *Grise*, fur.   [2] *Fardel*, burden.   [3] *Bourd*, jest.

in small things ; for whoso saith alway truth, he may not now go nowhere through the world. There ben many that play *Placebo.* Whoso alway saith truth, shall find many lettings in his way. Men may well lie when it is need, and after amend it by counsel. For all trespasses there is mercy. There is no man so wise, but he dooleth[1] other while."

Grymbart said, "Well, dear Eme, what thing shall you let ? Ye know all thing at the narrowest. Ye should bring me hastily in doting ; your reasons passen my understanding. What need have ye to shrive you ? Ye should yourself by right be the priest, and let me and other sheep come to you for to be shriven. Ye know the state of the world in such wise as no man may halt tofore you."

With such manner talking they came walking in to the Court. The Fox sorrowed somewhat in his heart, nevertheless he bare it out and striked forth through all the folk till he came into the place where the King himself was.

And Grymbart was alway by the Fox and said, " Eme, be not afraid, and make good cheer ! Who that is hardy, the adventure helpeth him.[2] Ofttimes one day is better than sometime a whole year."

The Fox said, "Nephew, ye say truth. God thank you, ye comfort me well."

And forth he went, and looked grimly here and there, as who saith, "What will ye ? here come I." He saw there many of his kin standing which yonned[3] him but little good, as the Otter, Beaver, and other to the number of ten whom I shall name afterward. And some were there that loved him.

The Fox came in and fell down on his knees tofore the King, and began his words and said :—

---

[1] *Dooleth*, errs (Dutch, *doolen*).
[2] Fortune favours the bold.
[3] *Yonned*, conceded. First English *unnan*, to grant.

CHAPTER XXVIII.

How Reynart the Fox excused him before the King.

" GOD from whom nothing may be hid, and above all thing is mighty, save my Lord the King and my Lady the Queen and give him grace to know who hath right and who hath wrong. For there live many in the world that seem otherwise outward than they be within. I would that God showed openly every man's misdeeds, and all their trespasses stooden written in their foreheads, and it cost me more than I now say ; and that ye, my Lord the King, knew as much as I do how I dispose me both early and late in your service. And therefore am I complained on of the evil shrews, and with leasings am put out of your grace and conceit, and would charge me with great offences, without deserving, against all right. Wherefore I cry out harowe on them that so falsely have belied me, and brought me in such trouble. Howbeit, I hope and know you both my Lord and my Lady for so wise and discreet, that ye be not led nor believe such leasings ne false tales out of the right way, for ye have not be woned so to do. Therefore, dear Lord, I beseech you to consider by your wisdom all things by right and law. Is it in deed or in speech, do every man right. I desire no better. He that is guilty and found faulty, let him be punished. Men shall well know ere I depart out of this Court who that I am. I cannot flatter, I will always show openly my head."

How the King answered upon Reynart's excuse.

ALL they that were in the palace weren all still and wondered that the Fox spake so stoutly.

The King said, " Ha, Reynart, how well can ye your fallacy and salutation doon ! But your fair words may not help you. I think well that ye shall, this day, for your works be hanged by your neck. I will not much chide with you, but I shall short your pain. That ye love us well, that have ye well showed on the Cony and on Corbant the Rook. Your falseness and your false inventions shall without long tarrying make you to die. A pot may go so long to water, that at the last it cometh tobroken home. I think your pot, that so oft hath deceived us, shall now hastily be broken."

Reynart was in great fear of these words. He would well he had ben at Cologne when he came thither. Then thought he I must here through, how that I do.

" My Lord the King," said he, " it were well reason that ye heard my words all out. Though I were dampned to the death, yet ought ye to hear my words out. I have yet heretofore time given to you many a good counsel and profitable, and in need alway have biden by you where other beasts have wyked[1] and gone their way. If now the evil beasts with false matters have tofore you with wrong belied me, and I might not come to mine excuse, ought I not then to plain? I have tofore this seen that I should be heard before another; yet might these things well change and come in their old state. Old good deeds ought to be remembered. I see here many of my lineage and friends stand-ing, that seem they set now little by me, which nevertheless should sore dere[2] in their hearts, that ye, my Lord the King, should destroy me wrongfully. If ye so did, ye should destroy the truest servant that ye have in all your lands. What ween ye, Sir King, had I knowen myself guilty in any feat or broke,[3] that I would have comen hither to the law among all mine enemies? Nay, sire, nay. Not for all the world of red gold. For I was free and at large. What need had I to do that? But, God be thanked, I know myself clear of all misdeeds, that I dare welcome openly in the light and to answer to all the complaints that any man can say on me. But when Grymbart brought me first these tidings, tho was I not well pleased but half from myself, that I leapt here and there as an unwise man, and had I not been in the censures of the Church I had without tarrying have comen, but I went dolynge[4] on the heath, and wist not what to do for sorrow.

---

[1] *Wyked,* flinched (Dutch, *wyken ;* German, *weichen*).
[2] *Dere,* take hurt.   [3] *Broke,* usage.   [4] *Dolynge,* grieving.

And then it happened that Mertyne, mine Eme, the Ape, met with me, which is wiser in clergy than some priest. He hath ben advocate for the Bishop of Cameryk nine year during. He saw me in this great sorrow and heaviness, and said to me, 'Dear Cousin, me thinketh ye are not well with yourself, what aileth you? Who hath displeased you? Thing that toucheth charge ought to be given in knowledge to friends. A true friend is a great help; he findeth oft better counsel than he that the charge resteth on, for whosomever is charged with matters is so heavy and acombred with them that oft he can not begin to find the remedy, for such be so woe like as they had lost their inwytte.'[1] I said 'Dear Eme, ye say truth, for in likewise is fallen to me. I am brought into a great heaviness, undeserved and not guilty, by one to whom I have alway been an hearty and great friend; that is the Cony which came to me yesterday in the morning whereas I sat tofore my house and said matins.'

" He told me he would go to the Court, and saluted me friendly, and I him again.

"Tho said he to me, 'Good Reynart, I am an hungred and weary. Have ye any meat?'

"I said, 'Yea, ynowh; come near.'

" Tho gave I him a couple of manchets[2] with sweet butter. It was upon a Wednesday, on which day I am not wont to eat any flesh, and also I fasted because of this feast of Whitsuntide which approached. For who that will taste of the overest wisehede, and live ghostly in keeping the commandments of our Lord, he must fast and make him ready against the high feasts. *Et vos estote parati.* Dear Eme, I gave him fair white bread with sweet butter, wherewith a man might well be eased that were much hungry.

"And when he had eaten his bellyful, tho came Rossel, my youngest son, and would have taken away that was left. For young children would alway fain eten. And with that he tasted for to have taken somewhat, the Cony smote Rossel tofore his mouth that his teeth bled, and he fell down half aswoon. When

---

[1] *Inwytte,* inner consciousness.
[2] *Manchets,* small loaves of white bread.

Reynardyn, mine eldest son, saw that, he sprang to the Cony and caught him by the head, and should have slain him had I not rescued him. I helped him, that he went from him, and beat my child sore therefor.

"Lapreel the Cony ran to my Lord the King and said I would have murdered him. See, Eme, thus come I in the words and I am laid in the blame. And yet he complaineth, and I plain not.

"After this came Corban the Rook fleeing with a sorrowful noise. I asked what him ailed.

"And he said, 'Alas my wife is dead. Yonder lieth a dead hare full of moths and worms, and there she ate so much thereof that the worms have bitten atwo her throat.'

"I asked him how cometh that by. He would not speak a word more, but flew his way, and let me stand.

"Now saith he that I have bitten and slain her. How should I come so nigh her? For she fleeth and I go afoot. Behold, dear Eme, thus I am born on hand. I may say well that I am unhappy. But peradventure it is for mine old sins. It were good for me if I could patiently suffer it.

"The Ape said to me, 'Nephew, ye shall go to the Court tofore the lords, and excuse you.'

"'Alas, Eme, that may not be, for the Archdeacon hath put me in the Pope's curse because I counselled Isegrim the Wolf for to leave his religion at Elmare and forsake his habit. He complained to me that he lived so straitly, as in long fasting, and many things reading and singing, that he could not endure it; if he should long abide there, he should die. I had pity of his complaining, and I holpe him as a true friend, that he came out. Which now me sore repenteth, for he laboureth all that he can against me to the King for to do me be hanged. Thus doth he evil for good. See, Eme, thus am I at the end of all my wits and of counsel. For I must go to Rome for an absolution, and then shall my wife and children suffer much harm and blame. For these evil beasts that hate me shall do to them all the hurt they may, and fordrive them where they can. And I would well defend them if I were free of the curse, for then I would go to

H

the Court and excuse me, where now I dare not. I should do
great sin if I came among the good people, I am afraid God should
plague me.'

" 'Nay, cousin, be not afraid. Ere I should suffer you in this
sorrow, I know the way to Rome well. I understand me on this
work. I am called there Mertyne the bishop's clerk, and am well
beknowen there. I shall do cite the Archdeacon and take a plea
against him, and shall bring with me for you an absolution against
his will, for I know there all that is for to be done or left. There
dwelleth Simon, mine Eme, which is great and mighty there.
Who that may give aught, he helpeth him anon. There is Pren-
tout, Wayte, Scathe, and other of my friends and allies. Also I
shall take some money with me if I need any. The prayer is
with gifts hardy[1]; with money alway the right goeth forth. A true
friend shall for his friend adventure both life and good, and so
shall I for you in your right. Cousin, make good cheer! I shall
not rest after to-morrow till I come to Rome, and I shall solicit
your matters. And go ye to the Court as soon as ye may. All
your misdeeds and the sins that have brought you in the great
sentence and curse, I make you quit of them and take them in
myself. When ye come to the Court ye shall find there Rukenawe
my wife, her two sisters, and my three children, and many more
of our lineage. Dear cousin, speak to them hardily. My wife is
sondrely[2] wise, and will gladly do somewhat for her friends. Who
that hath need of help shall find in her great friendship. One
shall alway seek on his friends, though he hath angered them, for
blood must creep where it cannot go. And if so be that ye be
so overcharged that ye may have no right, then send to me by
night and day to the Court of Rome, and let me have knowledge
thereof, and all tho that ben in the land, is it King or Queen,
wife or man, I shall bring them all in the Pope's Curse and send
there an interdict that no man shall read ne singen ne christen
children, ne bury the dead, ne receive sacrament, till that ye
shall have good right. Cousin, this shall I well get, for the
Pope is so sore old that he is but little set by, and the cardinal

---

[1] *Hardy*, bold.   [2] *Sondrely*, peculiarly.

of Pure Gold hath all the might of the Court. He is young and great of friends, he hath a concubine whom he much loveth, and what she desireth that getteth she anon. See, Cousin, she is mine niece, and I am great and may do much with her, in such wise what I desire I fail not of it but am alway furthered therein. Wherefore, Cousin, bid my Lord the King that he do you right I wote well he will not warn [1] you, for the right is heavy enough to every man.'

"My Lord the King, when I heard this I laughed, and with great gladness came hither, and have told you all truth. If there be any in this Court that can lay on me any other matter with good witness, and prove it, as ought to be to a noble man, let me then make amends according to the law; and if ye will not leave off hereby, then set me day and field, and I shall make good on him all so ferre as he be of as good birth as I am and to me like, and who that can with fighting get the worship of the field, let him have it. This right hath standen yet hitherto, and I will not it should be broken by me. The law and right doth no man wrong."

All the beasts both poor and rich were all still when the Fox spake so stoutly. The Cony Lapreel and the Rook were so sore afraid that they durst not speak, but piked and striked them out of the Court both two, and when they were a room far in the plain they said, "God grant that this fell murderer may fare evil. He can bewrap and cover his falsehood, that his words seem as true as the gospel. Hereof knoweth no man than we: how should we bring witness. It is better that we wyke [2] and depart, than we should hold a field and fight with him; he is so shrewd, yea though there of us were five we could not defend us, but that he should slay us all."

Isegrim the Wolf and Bruin the Bear were woe in themself when they saw these twain room the court.

The King said, "If any man will complain, let him come forth, and we shall hear him: yesterday camen here so many, where ben they now Reynart is here?"

The Fox said, "My Lord, there ben many that complain that

---

[1] *Warn*, refuse. [2] *Wyke*, flinch, yield.

and if they saw their adversary they would be still and make no plaint; witness now of Lapreel the Cony and Corbant the Rook, which have complained on me to you in my absence, but now that I am comen in your presence they flee away, and dare not abide by their words. If men should believe false shrews it should do much harm and hurt to the good men, as for me it skilleth not. Nevertheless, my lord, if they had by your commandment asked of me forgiveness, how be it they have greatly trespassed, yet I had for your sake pardoned and forgive them; for I will not be out of charity, ne hate ne complain on mine enemies. But I set all thing in God's hand, he shall work and avenge it as it pleaseth him."

The King said, "Reynart, me thinketh ye be grieved as ye say. Are ye withinforth as ye seem outward? Nay, it is not so clear ne so open, nowhere nigh, as ye here have showed. I must say what my grief is, which toucheth your worship and life, that is to wit that you have done a foul and shameful trespass when I had pardoned you all your offences and trespasses, and ye promised to go over the sea on pilgrimage, and gave to you male and staff. And after this ye sent me by Bellyn the Ram the male again and therein Cuwart's Head. How might ye do a more reprovable trespass? How were ye so hardy to dare to me do such a shame? Is it not evil done to send to a lord his servant's head? Ye cannot say nay hereagainst, for Bellyn the Ram, which was our chaplain, told us all the matter how it happed? Such reward as he had when he brought us the message, the same shall ye have, or right shall fail."

Tho was Reynart so sore afraid that he wist not what to say. He was at his wit's end, and looked about him piteously, and saw many of his kin and allies that heard all this, but nought they said. He was all pale in his visage, but no man proffered him hand ne foot to help him.

The King said, "Thou subtle fellow and false shrew, why speakest thou not? Now dumb?"

The Fox stood in great dread, and sighed sore that all heard him. But the Wolf and the Bear were glad thereof.

CHAPTER XXIX.

How Dame Rukenawe answered for the Fox to the King.

DAME Rukenawe the She Ape, Reynart's Aunt, was not well pleased. She was great with the Queen and well beloved. It happened well for the Fox that she was there, for she understood all wisdom, and she durst well speak, where as it to do was. Wherever she came everich was glad of her.

She said, " My Lord the King, ye ought not to be angry when ye sit in judgment, for that becometh not your nobleness. A man that sitteth in judgment ought to put from him all wrath and anger. A lord ought to have discretion that should sit in justice. I know better the points of the law than some that wear furred gowns, for I have learned many of them and was made cunning in the law. I had in the Pope's palace of Woerden a good bed of hay, where other beasts lay on the hard ground, and also when I had there to do I was suffered to speak, and was heard tofore another because I knew so well the law. Seneca writeth that a lord shall overall do right and law, he shall charge none to whom he hath given his safeguard to above the right and law; the law ought not to halt for no man. And every man that standeth here would well bethink him what he hath done and bedriven[1] in his days, he should the better have patience and pity on Reynart. Let every man know him self, that is my counsel. There is none that standeth so surely but otherwhile he falleth or slideth. Who that never misdid ne sinned is holy and good, and hath no need to amend him. When a man doth amiss and then by counsel amendeth it, that is humanly and so ought he to do ; but alway to misdo and trespass and not to amend him, that is evil and a devily life. Mark then what is written in the gospel, *Estote misericordes*, be ye merciful ; yet standeth there more, *Nolite judicare et non judicabimini*, deem ye no man and ye shall not be deemed. There standeth also how the pharisees brought a woman taken in adultery and would have stoned her to death. They

---

[1] *Bedriven*, experienced (Dutch, *bedreven*).

asked Our Lord what he said thereto; he said, 'Who of you all is without sin let him cast the first stone.' Tho abode no man but left her there standing. Me thinketh it is so here. There be many that see a straw in another's eye that can not see a balke in his own. There be many that deem other, and himself is worst of all. Though one fall oft, and at last ariseth up and cometh to mercy, he is not thereof damned. God receiveth all them that desire his mercy. Let no man condemn another though they wist that he had done amiss; yet let them see their own defaults, and then may they themself correct first, and then Reynart my Cousin should not fare the worse. For his father and his grandfather have alway been in more love and reputation in this Court than Isegrim the Wolf or Bruin the Bear with all their friends and lineage. It hath been heretofore an unlike comparison, the wisdom of Reynart my Cousin, and the honour and worship of him, that he hath done, and the counsel of them; for they know not how the world goeth. Me thinketh this Court is all turned upside down. These false shrews, flatterers, and deceivers, arise and wax great by the lordes, and ben enhanced up; and the good, true, and wise ben put down, for they have been wont to counsel truly and for the honour of the King. I cannot see how this may stand long."

Then said the King, "Dame, if he had done to you such trespass as he hath done to other it should repent you. Is it wonder that I hate him? He breaketh away my safeguard. Have ye not heard the complaints that here have been showed of him, of murder, of theft, and of treason? Have ye such trust in him? Think ye that he is thus good and clear? then set him up on the altar, and worship and pray to him as to a saint. But there is none in all the world that can say any good of him; ye may say much for him, but in the end ye shall find him all nought. He hath neither kin ne one friend that will enterprise to help him. He hath so deserved. I have great marvel of you. I heard never of none that hath fellowshipped with him that ever thanked him or said any good of him, save you now, but alway he hath striked them with his tail."

Then the She Ape answered and said, "My lord, I love him and have him in great charity. And also I know a good deed that he once in your presence did, whereof ye could him great thank. Though now it be thus turned, yet shall the heaviest weigh most. A man shall love his friend by measure, and not his enemy hate overmuch. Steadfastness and constancy is fitting and behoveth to the lords, how soever the world turneth. Me ought not to praise too much the day, till even be come. Good counsel is good for him that will do thereafter.

CHAPTER XXX.

A parable of a Man that delivered a Serpent from peril of death.

"Now two year past came a Man and a Serpent here into this Court for to have judgment, which was to you and yours right doubtful. The Serpent stood in an hedge whereas he supposed to have gone through, but he was caught in a snare by the neck that he might not escape without help, but should have lost his life there. The Man came forth by, and the Serpent called to him and cried, and prayed the Man that he would help him out of the snare, or else he must there die.

"The Man had pity of him, and said, 'If thou promise to me that thou wilt not envenom me, ne do me none harm ne hurt, I shall help thee out of this peril.'

"The Serpent was ready, and swore a great oath that he now ne never should do him harm ne hurt.

"Then he unloosed him and delivered him out of the snare. And they went forth together a good while that the Serpent had great hunger, for he had not eaten a great while tofore, and sterte to the Man and would have slain him. The Man sterte away and was afraid, and said, 'Wilt thou now slay me? hast thou forgotten the oath that thou madest to me that thou shouldest not misdo ne hurt me?'

"The Serpent answered, 'I may do it good tofore all the world that I do. The need of hunger may cause a man to break his oath.'

"The Man said, 'If it may be not better, give me so long respite till we meet and find that may judge the matter by right.'

"The Serpent granted thereto. Thus they went together so long that they found Tyseln the Raven and Slyndpere his son; there rehearsed they their reasons.

"Tyseln the Raven judged anon that he should eat the Man. He would fain have eaten his part, and his son also.

"The Serpent said to the Man, 'How is it now? What think ye? Have I not won?'

"The Man said, 'How should a robber judge this? He should have avail thereby. And also he is alone: there must be two or three at least together, and that they understand the right and law, and that done let the sentence gon; I am nevertheless ill on enough.'

"They agreed and went forth both together so long that they found the Bear and the Wolf, to whom they told their matter.

"And they anon judged that the Serpent should slay the Man. For the need of hunger breaketh oath alway. The Man then was in great doubt and fear, and the Serpent came and cast his venom at him; but the Man leapt away from him with great pain, and said, 'Ye do great wrong that ye thus lie in await to slay me. Ye have no right thereto.'

"The Serpent said, 'Is it not enough yet? It hath been twice judged.'

"'Yea,' said the Man, 'that is of them that ben wont to murder and rob. All that ever they swear and promise they hold not. But I appeal this matter into the Court tofore our Lord the King, and that thou mayst not forsake.[1] And what judgment that shall be given there, shall I obey and suffer, and never do the contrary.'

"The Bear and the Wolf said that it should be so, and that the Serpent desired no better. They supposed if it should come tofore you it should go there as they would. I trow ye be well remembered hereof. Tho came they all to the Court tofore you; and the Wolf's two children came with their father, which were called Empty Belly and Never Full, because they would eat of

---

[1] *Forsake*, deny.

the Man ; for they howled for great hunger. Wherefore ye commanded them to avoid your Court.

"The Man stood in great dread, and called upon your good grace, and told how the Serpent would have taken his life from him, to whom he had saved his life, and that, above his oath and promise, he would have devoured him.

"The Serpent answered, 'I have not trespassed, and that I report me wholly unto the King. For I did it to save my life, for need of life one may break his oath and promise.'

"My Lord that time were ye and all your Council herewith accombred. For your noble grace saw the great sorrow of the Man, and ye would not that a man should for his gentleness and kindness be judged to death. And on that other, sith hunger, and need to save the life, seeketh narrowly to be holpen, here was none in all the Court that could ne knew the right hereof. There were some that would fain the Man had be holpen. I see them here standing. I wot well they said that they could not end this matter.

"Then commanded ye that Reynart, my nephew, should come and say his advice in this matter. That time was he above all other believed and heard in this Court, and ye bade him give sentence according to the best right and we all shall follow him, for he knew the ground of the law.

"Reynart said, 'My Lord, it is not possible to give a true sentence after their words, for in hearsaying ben oft leasings. But and if I might see the Serpent in the same peril and need that he was in when the Man loosed him and unbound, then wist I well what I should say. And who that would do otherwise he should misdo against right.'

"Then said ye, my Lord, 'Reynart, that is well said. We all accord hereto ; for no man can say better.'

"Then went the Man and the Serpent into the place whereas he found the Serpent. Reynart bade that the Serpent should be set in the snare in likewise as he was. And it was done.

"Then said ye, my Lord, 'Reynart, how thinketh you now? What judgment shall we give?'

"Then said Reynart the Fox, 'My Lord, now ben they both like as they were tofore. They have neither won ne lost. See, my Lord, how I judge for a right, also ferre as it shall please your noble grace. If the Man will now loose and unbind the Serpent, upon the promise and oath that he tofore made to him, he may well do it. But if he think that he for anything should be encumbered or hindered by the Serpent, or for need of hunger would break his oath and promise, then judge I that the Man may go freely where he will, and let the Serpent abide still bounden, like as he might have done at the beginning: for he would have broken his oath and promise, whereas he holp him out of such fearful peril. Thus thinketh me a rightful judgment that the Man shall have his free choice like as he tofore had.'

"Lo my Lord this judgment thought you good, and all your council which at that time were by you; and followed the same, and praised Reynart's wisdom, that he had made the Man quit and free. Thus the Fox wisely kept your noble honour and worship, as a true servant is bound to do to his Lord. Where hath the Bear or the Wolf done ever to you so much worship? They conne well huylen and blasen, steal and rob, and eat fat morsels and fill their bellies, and then judge they for right and law that small thieves that steal hens and chickens should be hanged; but they themself that steal kine, oxen, and horses, they shall go quit and be lords. And same as though they were wiser than Solomon, Avicene, or Aristoteles; and each will be holden high proud, and praised of great deeds and hardy; but and they come where as it is to do, they ben the first that flee. Then must the simple go forth tofore, and they keep the reward behind. Och, my Lord, these and other like to them be not wise, but they destroy town, castle, land, and people. They reck not whose house burneth, so that they may warm them by the coals. They seek all their own avail and singular profit. But Reynart the Fox and all his friends and lineage sorowen[1] and think to prefer the honour, worship, fordeel,[2] and profit of their lord, and for wise counsel

---

[1] *Sorowen*, take care.

[2] *Fordeel*, advantage (Dutch, *Voordeel;* German, *Vortheil*).

which oft more profiteth here than pride and boast. This doth Reynart, though he have no thank. At long it shall be well known who is best and doth most profit. My Lord, ye say that his kin and lineage draw all afterward from him, and stand not by him for his falsehood and deceivable and subtle touches. I would another had said that; there should then such wrake be taken thereof that him might growl that ever he saw him. But, my Lord, we will forbear you; ye may save your pleasure; and also I say it not by you. Were there any that would bedrive anything against you, with words or with werkes, him that would we so do to, that men should say we had been there. There as fighting is, we ben not wont to be afraid. My Lord, by your leave, I may well give you knowledge of Reynart's friends and kin. There ben many of them that for his sake and love will adventure life and good. I know myself for one. I am a wife. I should, if he had need, set my life and good for him. Also I have three full waxen children which ben hardy and strong, whom I would all together adventure for his love, rather than I should see him destroyed; yet had I liever die than I saw them mis-carry tofore mine eyes, so well love I them.

CHAPTER XXXI.

Which ben friends and kin unto Reynart the Fox.

"The first child is named Bytelouse, which is much cherished and can make much sport and game, wherefore is given to him the fat trenchours and much other good meat, which cometh well to profit of Fulrompe his brother. And also my third child is a daughter, and is named Hatenit, she can well pick out lice and nits out of men's heads. These three ben to each other true, wherefore I love them well."

Dame Rukenawe called them forth and said, " Welcome, my dear children : to me forth, and stand by Reynart, your dear nephew."

Then said she, "Come forth all ye that be of my kin and Reynart's, and let us pray the King that he will do to Reynart right of the land."

Tho came forth many a beast anon, as the Squirrel, the Musk-rat, the Fitchews, the Marten, the Beaver with his wife Ordegale, the Genete,[1] the Otter, the Boussyng, and the Ferret, these twain eat as fain polaylle as doth Reynart. The Otter and Pante-croet his wife, whom I had almost forgotten, yet were they tofore, with the Beaver, enemies to the Fox, but they durst not gainsay Dame Rukenawe, for they were afraid of her. She was also the wisest of all his kin of counsel and was most doubted.[2] There came also more than twenty other, because of her, for to stand by Reynart. There came also Dame Atrote with her two sisters, Weasel and Hermelin, the Ass, the Badger, the Water-rat, and many more to the number of forty, which all camen and stoden by Reynart the Fox.

"My Lord the King," said Rukenawe, "come and see here if Reynart have any friends. Here may ye see we ben your true subjects, which for you would adventure both life and good if ye had need. Though ye be hardy, mighty, and strong, our well-willed friendship cannot hurt you. Let Reynart the Fox well bethink him upon these matters that ye have laid against him, and if he cannot excuse them, then do him right. We desire no better. And this by right ought to no man be warned."[3]

The Queen then spake, "This said I to him yesterday. But he was so fierce and angry that he would not hear it."

The Leopard said also, "Sire, ye may judge no further than your men give their verdict; for if ye would go forth by will and might, that were not worshipful for your estate. Hear always both parties, and then by the best and wisest counsel give judgment discreetly according to the best right."

The King said, "This is all true, but I was so sore moved when I was informed of Cuwart's death and saw his head, that I was hot and hasty. I shall hear the Fox. Can he answer and

---

[1] *The genete* is related to the civet cat.
[2] *Doubted*, feared.   [3] *Warned*, refused.

excuse him of that is laid against him, I shall gladly let him go quit ; and also at request of his good friends and kin."

Reynart was glad of these words, and thought, God thank mine Aunt, she hath the rys do blosme again.[1] She hath well holpen me forth now. I have now a good foot to dance on. I shall now look out of mine eyen, and bring forth the fairest leasing that ever man heard, and bring myself out of this danger.

CHAPTER XXXII.

How the Fox with subtlety excused him for the death of Cuwart the Hare and of all other matters that were laid against him, and how with flattering he gat again his peace of the King.

THEN spake Reynart the Fox and said, " Alas, what say ye ! is Cuwart dead ? And where is Bellyn the Ram ? What brought he to you when he came again ? For I delivered to him three jewels ; I would fain know where they ben becomen. That one of them should he have given to you, my Lord the King, and the other two to my Lady the Queen."

The King said, "Bellyn brought us nought else but Cuwart's head, like as I said you tofore ; whereof I took on him wrake. I made him to lose his life, for the foul caitiff said to me that he himself was of the counsel of the letters making that were in the male."

" Alas, my lord, is this very truth ? Woe to me caitiff that ever I was born ! Sith that these good jewels be thus lost, mine heart will break for sorrow. I am sorry that I now live ! What shall my wife say when she heareth hereof ? She shall go out of her wit for sorrow . I shall never, all so long as I live, have her friendship. She shall make much sorrow when she heareth thereof." .

The She Ape said, " Reynart, dear Nephew, what profiteth that ye make all this sorrow ? Let it pass, and tell us what these jewels were. Peradventure we shall find counsel to have them again. If they be above earth Master Akeryn shall labour for them in

---

[1] She has made the twig blossom again.

his books, and also we shall curse for them in all the churches, unto the time that we have knowledge where they been. They may not be lost."

"Nay, Aunt, think not that, for they that have them will not lightly depart from them. There was never King that ever gave so rich jewels as these be. Nevertheless ye have somewhat with your words eased mine heart and made it lighter than it was. Alas, lo, here ye may see how he or they to whom a man trusteth most is often by him or them deceived. Though I should go all the world through, and my life in adventure set therefor, I shall wit where these jewels ben becomen."

With a dismalled and sorrowful speech, said the Fox : " Hearken ye all my kin and friends, I shall name to you these jewels what they were, and then may ye say that I have a great loss. That one of them was a ring of fine gold, and within the ring next the finger were written letters enamelled with sable and azure, and there were three Hebrew names therein. I could not myself read ne spell them, for I understand not that language ; but Master Abrion of Trier he is a wise man, he understandeth well all manner of languages and the virtue of all manner herbs, and there is no beast so fierce ne strong but he can dompte him, for if he see him once he shall do as he will, and yet he believeth not on God. He is a Jew, the wisest in conning, and specially he knoweth the virtue of stones. I showed him once this ring. He said that they were tho three names that Seth brought out of Paradise when he brought to his father Adam the Oyle of Mercy, and whosomever beareth on him these three names he shall never be hurt by thunder ne lightning, ne no witchcraft shall have power over him, ne be tempted to do sin. And also he shall never take harm by cold though he lay three winters long nights in the field, though it snowed, stormed, or frore, never so sore, so great might have these words, witness of Master Abrion. Without forth on the ring stood a stone of three manner colours ; the one part was like red crystal, and shone like as fire had been therein, in such wise that if one would go by night him behoved none other light, for the shining of the stone made and gave as great a light as it had been midday; that other part of the stone was white and clear as it had been burnished, who so had in his eyen any smart or soreness, or in his body any swelling, or headache, or any sickness, withoutforth if he striked this stone on the place where the grief is he shall anon be whole; or if any man be sick in his body of venom, or ill meat in his stomach, of colic, strangulation, stone, fistel, or cancer, or any other sickness, save only the very death, let him lay this stone in a little water and let him drink it, and he shall forthwith be whole and all quit of his sickness. Alas," said the Fox, "we have good cause to be sorry to lose such a jewel! Furthermore the third colour was green like glass, but there were some sprinkles therein like purple; the master told for truth, that who that bare this stone upon him should never be hurt of his enemy, and was no man, were he never so strong and hardy, that might misdo him; and wherever that he fought he should have victory, were it by night or by day, also ferre as he beheld it fasting; and also thereto, wheresomever he went and in what fellowship, he should be beloved, though he had hated him tofore, if he had the ring upon him they should forget their anger as soon as they saw him. Also though he were all naked in a field again an hundred armed men, he should be well hearted and escape from them with worship; but he must be a noble gentleman and have no churl's conditions, for then the stone had no might. And because this stone was so precious and good, I thought in myself that I was not able ne worthy to bear it, and therefore I sent it to my dear Lord the King, for I know him for the most noble that now liveth, and also all our welfare and worship lieth on him, and for he should be kept from all dread, need, and ungheluck.[1]

"I found this ring in my father's treasure, and in the same place I took a glass or a mirror and a comb which my wife would algates have. A man might wonder that saw these jewels. I sent these to my Lady the Queen, for I have founden her good and gracious to me. This Comb might not be too much praised. It was made of the bone of a clean noble beast named Panthera,

[1] *Ungheluck*, misfortune (unglück).

which feedeth him between the great Inde and Earthly Paradise.
He is so lusty fair and of colour, that there is no colour under the
heaven but some likeness is in him; thereto he smelléth so sweet,
that the savour of him boteth [1] all sickness; and for his beauty and
sweet smelling all other beasts follow him, for by his sweet savour
they ben healed of all sickness. This Panthera hath a fair bone,
broad and thin; when so is that this beast is slain all the sweet
odour rested in the bone, which cannot be broken, ne shall never
rot, ne be destroyed by fire, by water, ne by smiting, it is so
hardy, tight and fast, and yet it is light of weight. The sweet odour
of it hath great might; that who that smelleth it sette nought by
none other lust in the world, and is eased and quit of all manner
diseases and infirmities, and also he is jocund and glad in his
heart. This Comb is polished as it were fine silver, and the teeth
of it be small and strait, and between the greater teeth and the
smaller is a large field and space where is carven many an image
subtilly made and enamelled about with fine gold; the field is
checked with sable and silver, enamelled with cybore [2] and azure,
and therein is the history how Venus, Juno, and Pallas strove for
the apple of gold which each of them would have had, which con-
troversy was set upon Paris that he should give it to the fairest
of them three.

"Paris was that time an herdman, and kept his father's beasts
and sheep without Troy. When he had received the apple, Juno
promised to him if he would judge that she might have the apple,
he should have the most riches of the world. Pallas said if she
might have the apple she would give him wisdom and strength,
and make him so great a lord that he should overcome all his
enemies and whom he would. Venus said, 'What needest thou
riches or strength, art not thou Priamus' son, and Hector is thy
brother, which have all Asia under their power? Art not thou
one of the possessors of great Troy? If thou wilt give to me the
apple, I shall give thee the richest treasure of the world, and that

---

[1] *Boteth*, is boot for, remedies.
[2] *Cybore*, "cyboire" was the decorated case that contained the consecrated
elements of the host. From Greek κιβώριον.

shall be the fairest woman that ever had life on earth, ne never
shall none be born fairer than she. Then shalt thou be richer
than rich, and shalt climb above all other, for that is the treasure
that no man can prize enough; for honest fair and good women
can put away many a sorrow from the heart, they be shamefast
and wise, and bring a man in very joy and bliss.' Paris heard
this Venus, which presented him this great joy and fair lady, and
prayed her to name this fair lady that was so fair, and where she
was. Venus said, 'It is Helen, King Menelaus' wife of Greece,
there liveth not a nobler, richer, gentler, ne wiser wife in all the
world. Then Paris gave to her the apple, and said that she was
fairest. How that he gat afterward Helen by the help of Venus,
and how he brought her in to Troy and wedded her, the great love
and jolly life that they had together, was all carven in the field,
everything by himself, and the story written.

"Now ye shall hear of the Mirror. The glass that stood thereon
was of such virtue that men might see therein all that was done
within a mile, of men of beasts and of all thing that me would [1]
desire to wit and know. And what man looked in the glass, had
he only disease of pricking or motes, smart, or pearls in his eyen,
he should be anon healed of it, such great virtue had the glass.
Is it then wonder if I be moved and angry for to lose such
manner jewels? The tree in which this glass stood was light and
fast and was named Cetyne.[2] It should endure ever ere it would
rot, or worms should hurt it, and therefore King Solomon ceiled
his temple with the same wood withinforth. Men praised it dearer
than fine gold; it is like to tree of hebenus, of which wood King
Crompart made his horse of tree for love of King Morcadigas'
daughter that was so fair, whom he had weened for to have won.
That horse was so made within, that whosoever rode on it, if
he would, he should be within less than one hour an hundred
miles thence; and that was well proved, for Cleomedes the king's
son would not believe that that horse of tree had such might and
virtue. He was young, lusty, and hardy, and desired to do great

---

[1] *Me would*, one would. "Man" and "me" were our Teutonic forms for the
French "*on*."   [2] Shittim wood.

I

· deeds of praise for to be renowned in this world, and leapt on this horse of tree.   Crompart turned a pin that stood on his breast, and anon the horse lift him up and went out of the hall by the window, and ere one might say his *pater noster* he was gone more than ten mile away.   Cleomedes was sore afraid, and supposed never to have turned again, as the history[1] thereof telleth more plainly.   But how great dread he had, and how far that he rode upon that horse made of the tree of hebenus ere he could know the art and craft how he should turn him; and how joyful he was when he knew it; and how men sorrowed for him ; and how he knew all this, and the joy thereof when he came again, all this I pass over for losing of time ; but the most part of all came to by the virtue of the wood, of which wood the tree that the glass stood in was made.   And that was, without forth of the glass, half a foot broad, wherein stood some strange histories, which were of gold, of sable, of silver, of yellow, azure, and cynope, these six colours were therein wrought in such wise as it behoved ; and under every history the words were graven and enamelled, that every man might understand what each history was.   After my judgment there was never mirror so costly, so lustly, ne so pleasant.   In the beginning stood there an Horse, made fat, strong, and sore envious upon an Hart which ran in the field so far and swiftly that the Horse was angry that he ran so far tofore him and could not overtake him.   He thought he should catch him and subdue him, though he should suffer much pain therefor.   The Horse spake tho to a Herdman in this wise, ' If thou couldst taken an Hart that I well can show thee, thou shouldst have great profit thereof; thou shouldst sell dear his horns, his skin, and his flesh.'   The Herdman said, ' How may I come by him ? '   The Horse said, ' Sit upon me, and I shall bear thee, and we shall hunt him till he be take.'   The Herdman sprang and sat upon the Horse, and saw the Hart ; and he rode after ; but the Hart was light of foot and swift, and outran the Horse far.   They hunted so far after him that the Horse was weary, and said to the Herdman that sat on him, ' Now sit off,

[1] The romance of Clyomon and Clamydes.

I will rest me, I am all weary, and give me leave to go from thee.'
The Herdman said, 'I have arrested thee; thou mayst not
escape from me; I have a bridle on thy head and spurs on my
heels; thou shalt never have thank hereof; I shall bedwynge and
subdue thee, hadst thou sworn the contrary.'

"See how the Horse brought himself in thraldom and was
taken in his own net. How may one better be taken than by his
own proper envy suffer himself to be taken and ridden. There
ben many that labour to hurt other, and they themselven ben hurt
and rewarded with the same.

"There was also made an Ass and an Hound which dwelled
both with a rich man. The man loved his Hound well, for he
played oft with him as folk do with Hounds. The Hound leapt
up and played with his tail, and licked his master about the
mouth. This saw Howdwin the Ass, and had great spite thereof
in his heart, and said to himself, 'How may this be? and what
may my lord see on his foul Hound, whom I never see doth
good ne profit save springeth on him and kisseth him? But me,
whom men putten to labour, to bear and draw and do more in a
week than he with his fifteen should do in a whole year,—and
yet sitteth he nevertheless by him at the table and there eateth
bones, flesh, and fat trenchours,—and I have nothing but thistles
and nettles, and lie on nights on the hard earth, and suffer many
a scorn. I will no longer suffer this. I will think how I may
get my lord's love and friendship, like as the Hound doth. Therewith came the lord, and the Ass lift up his tail and sprang with
his fore feet on the lord's shoulders and blared, grinned, and sang,
and with his feet made two great boles about his ears, and put
forth his mouth and would have kissed the lord's mouth as he
had seen the Hound done. Tho cried the lord, sore afraid,
'Help! help! this Ass will slay me!' Then came his servants
with staves and smiten and beat the Ass so sore that he had
weened he should have lost his life. Tho returned he to his stable
and ate thistle and nettles and was an Ass as he tofore was. In
likewise whoso have enough and spite of another's welfare, and were
served in likewise, it should be well behoveful. Therefore it is

concluded that the Ass shall eat thistles and nettles and bear the sack. Though men would do him worship he cannot understand it, but must use old lewd manners. Whereas asses getten lordships, there men see seldom good rule. For they take heed of nothing but on their singular profit; yet ben they take up and risen great, the more pity is.

"Hearken further how my father and Tybert the Cat went together, and had sworn by their truth that for love ne hate they should not depart. And what they gat they should depart to each the half. Then on a time they saw hunters coming over the field with many hounds. They leapt and ran fast from themward all that they might, as they that were afraid of their life.

"'Tybert,' said the Fox, 'whither shall we now best flee? the hunters have espied us. Know ye any help?' My father trusted on the promise that each made to other, and that he would for no need depart from him. 'Tybert,' said he, 'I have a sackful of wiles if we have need; as far as we abide together we need not to doubt hunters ne hounds.'

"Tybert began to sigh and was sore afraid, and said, 'Reynart, what availlen many words? I know but one wile, and thither must I too.'

"And tho clamb he up on a high tree into the top under the leaves, whereas hunter ne hound might do him none harm, and left my father alone in jeopardy of his life, for the hunters set on him the hounds all that they could. Men blew the horns, and cried, and hallooed, 'The Fox! Slee and take!' When Tybert the Cat saw that, he mocked and scorned my father and said, 'What, Reynart, cousin, unbind now your sack where all the wiles ben in! It is now time. Ye be so wise called; help yourself, for ye have need.'

"This much must my father hear of him to whom he had most his trust on, and was almost taken, and nigh his death. And he ran and fled with great fear of his life, and let his male slide off because he would be the lighter. Yet all that could not help him, for the hounds were too swift and should have bitten him; but he had one adventure that thereby he found an old hole, wherein he crept, and escaped thus the hunters and hounds.

"Thus held this false deceiver Tybert his sykernes that he had promised. Alas, how many ben there now a days that keep not their promise, and set not thereby though they break it! And though I hate Tybert herefor, is it wonder? But I do not. Sikerly, I love my soul too well thereto. Nevertheless, if I saw him in adventure and misfall in his body or in his goods, I trow it should not much go to my heart, so that another did it. Nevertheless, I shall neither hate him ne have envy at him. I shall, for God's love, forgive him. Yet is it not so clear out of mine heart but a little ill-will to himward abideth therein as this cometh to my remembrance; and the cause is that the sensuality of my flesh fighteth against reason.

"Ther stood also in that Mirror, of the Wolf, how he found once upon a heath a dead horse flayen, but all the flesh was eaten. Then went he and bote great morsels of the bones, that for hunger he took three or four at once and swallowed them in, for he was so greedy that one of the bones stack thwart in his mouth. Whereof he had great pain, and was of great fear of his life. He sought all about for wise masters and surgeons, and promised great gifts for to be healed of his disease. At last, when he could nowhere find remedy, he came to the Crane with his long neck and bill, and prayed him to help him, and he would love and reward him so well that he should ever be the better. The Crane hearked after this great reward, and put his head into his throat, and brought out the bone with his bill.

"The Wolf start aside with the plucking, and cried out, 'Alas, thou doest me harm! but I forgive it thee. Do no more so, I would not suffer it of another.'

The Crane said, 'Sir Isegrim, go and be merry, for ye be all whole. Now give to me that ye promised.'

"The Wolf said, 'Will ye hear what he saith? I am he that hath suffered and have cause to plain, and he will have good of me! He thanketh not me of the kindness that I did to him. He put his head in my mouth, and I suffered him to draw it out whole without hurting; and he did to me also harm. And if any here should have a reward, it should be I, by right.'

"Thus the unkind men nowadays reward them that do them good. When the false and subtle arise and become great, then goeth worship and profit all to nought. There ben many, of right that ought reward and do good to such as have helpen them in their need, that now find causes and say they be hurt, and would have amends where they ought to reward and make amends themself. Therefore it is said, and truth it is, who that will chide or chastise see that he be clear himself.

" All this and much more than I now can well remember was made and wrought in this glass. The master that ordained it was a cunning man and a profound clerk in many sciences. And because these jewels were over good and precious for me to keep and have, therefore I sent them to my dear Lord the King and to the Queen in present. Where ben they now that give to their lords such presents. The sorrow that my two children made when I sent away the glass was great ; for they were wont to look therein and see themself how their clothing and array became them on their bodies. Oh, alas ! I knew not that Cuwart the Hare was so nigh his death when I delivered him the male with these jewels. I wist not to whom I might better have taken them, though it should have cost me my life, than him and Bellyn the Ram. They were two of my best friends. Out, alas ! I cry upon the murderer. I shall know who it was, though I should run through all the world to seek him, for murder abideth not hid, it shall come out. Peradventure he is in this. company that knoweth where Cuwart is becomen, though he telleth it not; for many false shrews walk with good men, from whom no man can keep him, they known their craft so well and can well cover their falseness. But the most wonder that I have is that my Lord the King here sayeth so felly, that my father nor I did him never good. That thinketh me marvel, of a king. But there come so many things tofore him that he forgetteth that one with that other, and so fareth by me. Dear Lord, remember not ye when my Lord your father lived, and ye an youngling of two year were, that

my father came from school from Monpellier whereas he had five
year studied in recipes of medicines. He knew all the tokens of
the urine as well as his hand, and also all the herbs, and nature
of them which were viscous or laxative. He was a singular master
in that science. He might well wear cloth of silk and a gilt
girdle. When he came to Court he found the King in a great
sickness, whereof he was sorry in his heart, for he loved him
above all other lords. The King would not forego him, for when
he came all other had leave to walk where they would; he trusted
none so much as him. He said, 'Reynart, I am sick, and feel
me the longer the worse.' My father said, 'My dear Lord, here
is an urinal: make your water therein, and as soon as I may see
it I shall tell what sickness it is and also how ye shall be holpen.'
The King did as he counselled him, for he trusted no man better
that lived. Though so were that my father did not as he should
have done to you, but that was by counsel of evil and foul beasts
—I had wonder thereof—but it was a raising against his death.
He said, 'My Lord, if ye will be whole ye must eat the liver of a
wolf of seven year old, that may ye not leave or else ye shall die;
for your urine showeth it plainly.'

"The Wolf stood thereby and said nought.

"But the King said to him, 'Sir Isegrim, now, ye hear well that
I must have your liver if I will be whole.'

"Tho answered the Wolf and said, 'Nay my lord not so, I
wot well I am not yet five year old. I have heard my mother
say so.'

"My father said, 'What skilleth these words? Let him be
opened, and I shall know by the liver if it be good for you or
not.'

"And therewith the Wolf was taken to kitchen, and his liver
taken out, which the King ate and was anon all whole of all his
sickness. Then thanketh he my father much, and commanded
all his household upon their lives that after that time they should
call him Master Reynart.

"He abode still by the King, and was believed of all things,
and must always go by his side; and the King gave to him a gar-

land of roses which he must always wear on his head. But now
this is all turned. All the old good things that he did be forgotten, and these covetous and ravenous shrews ben taken up and
set on the high bench, and ben heard and made great, and the
wise folk ben put aback, by which these lords oft lack, and
cause them to be in much trouble and sorrow. For when a
covetous man of low birth is made a lord, and is much great, and
above his neighbours hath power and might, then he knoweth not
himself, ne whence he is comen, and hath no pity on no man's
hurt, ne heareth no man's request, but if he may have great gifts.
All his intent and desire is to gather good, and to be greater.
Oh, how many covetous men ben now in lords' courts! They
flatter and smeke,[1] and please the prince, for their singular avail,
but and the prince had need of them or their good, they should
rather suffer him to die, or fare right hard, ere they would give
or lend him. They be like the Wolf that had liefer the King had
died than he would give him his liver. Yet had I liefer ere that
the King or the Queen should fare amiss, that twenty such wolves
should lose their lives; it were also the least loss. My lord, all
this befell in your youth, that my father did thus. I trow ye
have forgotten it.

"And also I have my self done you reverence, worship, and
courtesy. Unroused be it, though ye now thank me but little,
but peradventure ye remembered not that I shall now say,—not
to any forwitting of you, for ye be worthy all worship and reverence
that any man can do; that have ye of Almighty God by inheritance of your noble progenitors, wherefore I your humble subject
and servant am bounden to do to you all the service that I can or
may. I came on a time walking with the Wolf Isegrim, and we
had gotten under us both a Swine. And for his loud crying we bit
him to death; and, sire, ye came from far out of a grove against us.
Ye saluted us friendly, and said we were welcome, and that ye
and my Lady the Queen, which came after you, had great hunger
and had nothing for to eat, and prayed us for to give you part of
our winning. Isegrim spake so soft that a man unnethe might

[1] *Smeke*, flatter (schmeicheln).

hear him, but I spake out and said, 'yea, my lord, with a good will. Though it were more, we will well that ye have part.' And then the Wolf departed as he was wont to do; departed, and took that one half for himself, and he gave you a quarter for you and for the Queen. That other quarter he ate and bit as hastily as he might, because he would eat it alone. And he gave to me but half the lungs, that I pray God that evil might he fare.

"Thus showed he his conditions and nature. Ere men should have sungen a *Credo*, ye, my lord, had eaten your part, and yet would ye fain have had more, for ye were not full. And because he gave you no more, ne proffered you, ye lift up your right foot and smote him between the ears that ye tore his skin over his eyen, and tho he might no longer abide, but he bled, howled, and ran away, and left his part there lying. Tho said ye to him, 'Haste ye again hither, and bring to us more. And here after see better to how ye deal and part.' Then said I, 'My lord, if it please you I will go with him, I wot well what ye said.' I went with him. He bled and groaned, as sore as he was, all softly; he durst not cry loud. We went so far that we brought a calf. And when ye saw us come therewith ye laughed, for ye were well pleased, ye said to me that I was swift in hunting: 'I see well that ye can find well when ye take it upon you. Ye be good to send forth in a need. The calf is good and fat, hereof shall ye be the dealer.' I said, 'My lord, with a good will. The one half, my lord, shall be for you. And that other half for my lady the Queen. The moghettis, liver, lungs, and the inward, shall be for your children. The head shall Isegrim the Wolf have, and I will have the feet.' Tho said ye, 'Reynart, who hath taught you to depart so courteously?' 'My lord,' said I, 'that hath done this priest that sitteth here with the bloody crown. He lost his skin with the uncourteous departing of the swine, and for his courtesy and ravin he hath hurt and shame.'

"Alas there be many wolves now a days that, without right and reason, destroy and eat them that they may have the overhand of. They spare neither flesh ne blood, friend ne enemy. What they can get that take they. O, woe be to that land and to towns where as the wolves have the overhand !

"My lord, this and many other good thing have I done for you, that I could well tell if it were not too long, of which now ye remember little by the words I hear of you. If ye would all thing oversee well, ye would not say as ye do. I have seen the day that there should no great matter be concluded in this Court without mine advice. Albeit that this adventure is now fallen, it might happen yet that my words shall be heard and also believed as well as another's, as far as right will, for I desire none other. For if there be any can say and make good by sufficient witnesses that I have trespassed, I will abide all the right and law that may come thereof; and if any say on me anything of which he can bring no witnesses, let me then be ruled after the law and custom of this court."

The King said, "Reynart, ye say reasonably. I know not of Cuwart's death more than that Bellyn the Ram brought his head hither in the male. Thereof I let you go quit, for I have no witness thereof."

"My dear lord," said Reynart, "God thank you. Sykerly ye do well. For his death maketh me so sorrowful that methinketh my heart will break in two. Oh, when they departed from me, mine heart was so heavy that I should have swooned. I wot well it was a token of the loss that tho was so nigh coming to me."

All the most part of them that were there and heard the Fox's words of the jewels, and how he made his countenance and stretched him, had verily supposed that it had not be feigned but that it had be true. They were sorry of his loss and misadventure, and also of his sorrow. The King and the Queen had both pity of him, and bade him to make not too much sorrow, but that he should endeavour him to seek them. For he had so much praised them that they had great will and desire to have them. And because he had made them to understand that he had sent these jewels to them, though they never had them yet they thanked him, and prayed him to help that they might have them.

The Fox understood their meaning well, he thought toward

them but little good for all that. He said, "God thank you, my
lord and my lady, that ye so friendly comfort me in my sorrow.
I shall not rest night ne day, ne all they that will do anything
for me, but run, and pray, threaten, and ask all the four corners
of the world, though I should ever seek, till that I know where
they ben bicomen. And I pray you, my Lord the King, that
if they were in such place as I could not get them by prayer, by
might, ne by request, that ye would assist me and abide by me;
for it toucheth yourself, and the good is yours; and also it is
your part to do justice on theft and murder, which both ben in
this case."

"Reynart," said the King, "that shall I not leave, when ye
know where they ben. Mine help shall be alway ready for you."

"Oh, dear lord, this is too much presented to me. If I had
power and might I should deserve against you."

Now hath the Fox his matter fast and fair, for he hath the
King in his hand as he would. Him thought that he was in
better case than it was like to have be; he hath made so many
leasings that he may go freely where he will, without complaining
of any of them all, save of Isegrim, which was to himward angry
and displeased, and said, "O noble King, are ye so much childish
that ye believe this false and subtle shrew, and suffer yourself
with false lies thus to be deceived? Of faith it should be long or
I should believe him, he is in murder and treason all bewrapped,
and he mocketh you tofore your visage. I shall tell him another
tale. I am glad that I see now him here. All his leasings shall
not avail him ere he depart from me."

CHAPTER XXXIII.

How Isegrim the Wolf complained again on the Fox.

"My lord, I pray you to take heed. This false thief betrayed my
wife once foul and dishonestly. It was so that in a winter's day
they went together through a great water, and he bare my wife
an honde that he would teach her take fish with her tail, and that

she should let it hang in the water a good while and there should
so much fish cleave on it that four of them should not conne eat
it. The fool, my wife, supposed he had said truth. And she
went in the mire ere she came into the water, and when she was
in the deepest of the water he bad her hold her tail till that the fish
were comen. She held her tail so long that it was frozen hard
in the ice and could not pluck it out. And when he saw that,
he sprang up after on her body. She could not defend herself,
the silly beast, she stood so deep in the mire. Hereof he cannot
say nay, for I found him with the deed. Alas, what pain suffered
I tho at my heart! I had almost for sorrow lost my five wits, and
cried as loud as I might, and when he saw me so nigh he went
his way. I went to her in a great heaviness, and went deep in
that mire and that water ere I could break the ice, and much
pain suffered she ere she could have out her tail, and yet left
a gobbet of her tail behind her. And we were like both thereby
to have lost our lives, for she yelped and cried so loud for the
smart that she had ere she came out, that the men of the village
came out, with staves and bills, with flail and pickforks, and
the wives with their distaffs, and cried despitously, "Slay! slay!
and smite down right!" I was never in my life so afraid, for
unnethe we escape. We ran so fast that we sweat. There was
a villain that stake on us with a pike which hurted us sore; he
was strong and swift a foot. Had it not be night, certainly we
had been slain. The foul old queans would fain have beaten
us. They said that we had bitten their sheep. They cursed us
with many a curse. Tho came we in a field full of broom and
brambles, there hid we us from the villains, and they durst not
follow us further by night, but returned home again. See my
lord this foul matter. Ye ought to do justice thereon sharply."

Reynart answered and said, "If this were true, it should go too
nigh mine honour and worship. God forbid that it should be
found true! It is well true that I taught her how she should in
a place catch fish, and showed her a good way for to go over into
the water without going into the mire. But she ran so desirously
when she heard me name the fish, that she neither way ne path

held, but went into the ice wherein she was forfrorn. And that
was because she abode too long. She had fish enough, if she
could have be pleased with measure. It falleth oft, who that
would have all loseth all. Over covetous was never good. For
the beast cannot be satisfied, and when I saw her in the ice so
fast I went to have holpen her, and to have brought her out, but
it was all pain lost, for she was too heavy for me. Tho came
Isegrim, and saw how I did all my best, and he, as a foul churl,
foul and rybadously slandereth me with her, as these foul
unthrifts ben wont to do. But, my dear Lord, it was none
otherwise. He belieth me falsely. Peradventure his eyen
dazzled as he looked from above down. He cried and cursed
me, and swore many an oath I should dear abye it. When
I heard him so curse and threaten I went my way, and let
him curse and threaten till he was weary. And tho went he
and help his wife out, and then he leapt and ran, and she also,
for to get them an heat and to warm them, or else they should
have died for cold. And whatsomever I have said, afore or
after, that is clearly all truth. I would not for a thousand mark
of fine gold lie to you one leasing. It were not fitting for me.
Whatsomever fall of me, I shall say the truth, like as mine elders
have always done sith the time that we first understood reason.
And if ye be in doubt of anything that I have said otherwise than
truth, give me respite of eight days, that I may have counsel, and
I shall bring such information with good true and sufficient
record that ye shall all your life during trust and believe me, and
so shall all your council also. What have I to do with the Wolf?
It is tofore clearly enough showed that he is a foul villainous caitiff,
and an unclean beast, when he dealed and departed the swine. So
it is now knowen to you all by his own words, that he is a defamer
of women as much as in him is, ye may well mark euerychone.
Now ask ye his wife if it be so as he saith. If she will say the
truth I wot well she shall say as I do."

Tho spake Ersewynde the Wolf's wife, "Ach, fell Reynart, no
man can keep himself from thee,—thou canst so well utter thy
words and thy falseness and·reason set forth. But it shall be

evil rewarded in the end. How broughtest thou me once into
the well, where the two buckets hung by one cord running through
one pulley, which went one up and another down, thou sattest
in that one bucket beneath in the pit in great dread. I came
thither and heard thee sigh and make sorrow, and asked thee
how thou camest there. Thou saidst that thou hadst there so
many good fishes eaten out of the water that thy belly would
burst. I said, 'Tell me how I shall come to thee.' Then saidst
thou, 'Aunt, spring into that bucket that hangeth there, and ye
shall come anon to me. I did so; and I went downward, and
ye came upward. Tho was I all angry.' Thou saidst, 'Thus
fareth the world, that one goeth up and another goeth down.'
Tho sprang ye forth and went your way, and I abode there alone,
sitting an whole day sore and hungered and a cold; and thereto
had I many a stroke ere I could get thence."

"Auntie," said the Fox, "though the strokes did you harm, I
had liever ye had them than I, for ye may better bear them; for
one of us must needs have had them. I taught you good, will ye
understand it and think on it, that ye another time take better
heed and believe no man over hastily, is he friend or cousin, for
every man seeketh his own profit. They be now fools that do
not so, and specially when they be in jeopardy of their lives."

CHAPTER XXXIV.

A fair parable of the Fox and the Wolf.

"My Lord," said Dame Ersewynde, "I pray you hear how he can
blow with all winds, and how fair bringeth he his matters forth."

"Thus hath he brought me many time in scathe and hurt," said
the Wolf. "He hath once betrayed me to the She Ape, mine aunt,
where I was in great dread and fear, for I left there almost mine
one ear. If the Fox will tell it, how it befel, I will give him the fordele thereof, for I cannot tell it so well but he shall beryspe me."

"Well," said the Fox, "I shall tell it without stammering. I
shall say the truth. I pray you hearken me. He came into the

wood and complained to me that he had great hunger; for I saw him never so full but he would alway have had fain more. I have wonder where the meat becometh that he destroyeth. I see now on his countenance that he beginneth to grymme for hunger. When I heard him so complain, I had pity of him. And I said, I was also hungry. Then went we half a day together and found nothing. Tho whined he and cried, and said he might go no further. Then espied I a great hole, standing in the middis[1] under an hawe which was thick of brambles, and I heard a rushing therein, I wist not what it was. Then said I, 'Go therein and look if there be anything there for us; I wot well there is somewhat.' Tho said he, 'Cousin, I would not creep into that hole for twenty pound, but[2] I wist[3] first what is therein. Methinketh that there is some perilous thing. But I shall abide here under this tree, if ye will go therein tofore. But come anon again, and let me wete[4] what thing is therein. Ye can many a subtlety, and can well help yourself, and much better than I.' See my Lord the King, thus he made me, poor wight, to go tofore into the danger, and he, which is great, long, and strong, abode without and rested him in peace. Await if I did not for him there. I would not suffer the dread and fear that I there suffered, for all the good in earth, but if I wist how to escape. I went hardily in. I found the way dark, long, and broad. Ere I right in the hole came, so espied I a great light which came in from that one side. There lay in a great Ape with twain great wide eyen, and they glimmed as a fire; and she had a great mouth with long teeth, and sharp nails on her feet and on her hands; I weened it had be a mermouse, a baubyn, or a mercatte, for I saw never fouler beast. And by her lay three of her children, which were right foul, for they were right like the mother. When they saw me come, they gapeden wide on me and were all still. I was afraid and would well I had been thence; but I thought, I am therein, I must there through, and come out as well as I may. As I saw her, me thought she seemed more[5]

---

[1] *Middis*, midst. [2] *But*, except. [3] *Wist*, knew.
[4] *Wete*, know. [5] *More*, bigger.

than Isegrim the Wolf, and her children were more than I.   I
saw never a fouler meyne.[1]   They lay on foul hay which was all
bepissed.   They were beslabbed and beclagged to their ears too
in her own dung.   It stank that I was almost smothered thereof.
I durst not say but good, and then I said, 'Aunt, God give you
good day, and all my cousins, your fair children, they be of their
age the fairest that ever I saw.   O, Lord God, how well please
they me! how lovely! how fair be they!   Each of them for their
beauty might be a great king's son!   Of right we ought to thank
you, that ye thus increase our lineage.   Dear Aunt, when I
heard say that ye were delivered and laid down I could no
longer abide, but must come and friendly visit you.   I am sorry
that I had not erst knowen it.'

   "'Reynart, cousin,' said she, "ye be welcome.   For that ye
have found me, and thus come see me, I thank you.   Dear
cousin, ye be right true, and named right wise in all lands, and
also that ye gladly further and bring your lineage in great worship.
Ye must teach my children with yours some wisdom, that they
may know what they shall do and leave.   I have thought on you,
for gladly ye go and fellowship with the good.'

   "Oh how well was I pleased when I heard these words.   This
deserved I at the beginning when I called her aunt; howbeit
that she was nothing sybbe to me; for my right Aunt is Dame
Rukenawe that yonder standeth, which is wont to bring forth
wise children.

   "I said, 'Aunt, my life and my good is at your commandment,
and what I may do for you by night and by day.   I will gladly
teach them all that I can.'

   "I would fain have be thence for the stench of them; and also
I had pity of the great hunger that Isegrim had.

   "I said, 'Aunt, I shall commit you and your fair children to
God and take my leave.   My wife shall think long after me.'

   "'Dear cousin,' said she, 'ye shall not depart till ye have
eaten; for if ye did I would say ye were not kind.'

   Tho stood she up and brought me in another hole, whereas

---

[1] *Meyné*, household.

was much meat of harts and hinds, roes, pheasants, partridges, and much other venison, that I wondered from whence all this meat might come. And when I had eaten my bellyful, she gave me a great piece of an hind for to eat with my wife and with my household when I come home. I was ashamed to take it, but I might none otherwise do. I thanked her and took my leave. She bade me I should come soon again. I said I would, and so departed thence merrily that I so well had sped. I hasted me out, and when I came, saw Isegrim which lay groaning. And I asked him how he fared. He said, ' Nephew, all evil, for it is wonder that I live. Bring ye any meat to eat ? I die for hunger.' Tho had I compassion of him and gave him that I had, and saved him there his life ; whereof then he thanked me greatly, howbeit that he now oweth me evil will.

" He had eaten this up anon, tho said he, 'Reynart, dear cousin, what found ye in that hole ? I am more hungry now than I was tofore. My teeth ben now sharped to eat."

" I said then, ' Eme, haste you then lightly into that hole. Ye shall find there enough. There lieth mine Aunt with her children ; if ye will spare the truth, and lie great leasings, ye shall have there all your desire. But and ye say truth, ye shall take harm.'

" My Lord, was not this enough said and warned, who so would understand it, that all that he found, he should say the contrary. But rude and plump beasts cannot understand wisdom ; therefore hate they all subtle inventions, for they cannot conceive them. Yet nevertheless, he said he would go in, and lie so many leasings, ere he should mishap, that all men should have wonder of it ; and so went forth into that foul stinking hole, and found the marmosette. She was like the devil's daughter, and on her hung much filth clottered in gobbets.

" Tho cried he, 'Alas, me growleth of these foul nickers ! Come they out of hell ? Men may make devils afraid of them. Go and drown them, that evil might they fear ! I saw never fouler worms, they make all mine hair to stand right up.'

" ' Sir Isegrim,' said she, ' what may I do thereto ? They ben my children, and I must be their mother. What lieth that in

K

your way, whether they be foul or fair? They have you nothing cost. Here hath been one to-day before you which was to them nigh of kin, and was your better and wiser; and he said that they were fair. Who hath sent you hither with these tidings?'

"'Dame, will ye wit, I will eat of your meat. It is better bestowed on me than on these foul wights.'

"She said, 'Here is no meat.'

"He said, 'Here is enough.'

"And therewith he stert with his head toward the meat, and would have gone into the hole where the meat was. But mine aunt stert up with her children, and run to him with their sharp long nails so sore that the blood ran over his eyen. I heard him cry sore and howl, but I know of no defence that he made but that he ran fast out of the hole. And he was there scratched and beaten, and many an hole had they made in his coat and skin. His visage was all on a blood and almost he had lost his one ear. He groaned and complained to me sore : then asked I him if he had well lied. He said, 'I said like as I saw and found, and that was a foul beast with many foul wights.'

"'Nay, Eme,' said I, 'ye should have said Fair niece how fare ye and your fair children which ben my wellbeloved cousins?' The Wolf said, 'I had liefer that they were hanged ere I that said.'

"'Yea, Eme, therefore must ye receive such manner payment. It is better otherwile to lie than to say truth. They that ben better wiser and stronger than we be have done so tofore us.'

"See, my Lord the King, thus got he his red coif. Now standeth he all so simply as he knew no harm. I pray you ask ye him if it was not thus. He was not far off, if I wot it well."

CHAPTER XXXV.

How Isegrim proffered his glove for the Fox to fight with him.

THE Wolf said, " I may well forbear your mocks and your scorns and also your fell venomous words, strong thief that ye are. Ye said that I was almost dead for hunger, when ye help me in my need.

That is falsely lied, for it was but a bone that ye gave to me, ye had eaten away all the flesh that was thereon. And ye mock me and say that I am hungry, here where I stand. That toucheth my worship too nigh,—what many a spity word have ye brought forth with false leasings!—and that I have conspired the King's death, from the treasure that ye have said to him is in Hulsterlo,—and ye have also my wife shamed and slandered that she shall never recover it, and I should ever be disworshipped thereby if I avenged it not. I have forborne you long, but now ye shall not escape me. I can not make hereof great proof, but I say here tofore my lord and tofore all them that ben here that thou art a false traitor and a murderer, and that I shall prove and make good on thy body within lists in the field, and that body against body, and then shall our strife have an end. And thereto I cast to thee my glove, and take thou it up I shall have right of thee or die therefor."

Reynart the Fox thought, How come I on this campaign? we ben not both like. I shall not well conne stand against this strong thief. All my proof is now come to an end.

CHAPTER XXXVI.

How the Fox took up the glove. And how the King set to them day and field for to come and do their battle.

YET thought the Fox I have good advantage: the claws of his forefeet ben off, and his feet ben yet sore thereof, when for my sake he was unshoed. He shall be somewhat the weaker.

Then said the Fox, " Who that saith that I am a traitor or a murderer, I say he lieth falsely; and that art thou specially Isegrim. Thou bringest me there as I would be. This have I oft desired. Lo here is my pledge that all thy words ben false, and that I shall defend me and make good that thou liest."

The King received the pledges, and admitted the battle, and asked borowes[1] of them both that on the morn they should come

---

[1] *Borowes*, sureties.

and perform their battle, and do as they ought to do. Then the Bear and the Cat were borowes for the Wolf; and for the Fox were borowes Grymbart the Dasse and Byteluys.

CHAPTER XXXVII.

How Rukenawe the She Ape counselled the Fox how he should behave him in the field against the Wolf.

THE She Ape said to the Fox, "Reynart Nephew, see that ye take heed in your battle. Be cold and wise. Your Eme taught me once a prayer that is of much virtue to him that shall fight; and a great master and a wise clerk, and was abbot of Boudelo, that taught him, he said, who that said devoutly this prayer fasting shall not that day be overcomen in battle ne in fighting. Therefore, dear Nephew, be not afraid, I shall read it over you to-morrow, then may ye be sure enough of the Wolf. It is better to fight than to have the neck asunder."

"I thank you, dear aunt," said the Fox. "The quarrel that I have is rightful, therefore I hope I shall speed well, and that shall greatly be mine help."

All his lineage abode by him all the night and holp him to drive away the time.

Dame Rukenawe the She Ape, his aunt, thought alway on his profit and fordele. And she did all his hair from the head to the tail be shorn off smooth; and she anointed all his body with oil of olive; and then was his body also glat[1] and slipper that the Wolf should have none hold on him. And he was round and fat also on his body.

And she said to him, "Dear cousin, ye must now drink much that to-morrow ye may the better make your urine; but ye shall hold it in till ye come to the field. And when need is and time, so shall ye piss full your rough tail and smite the Wolf therewith in his beard. And if ye might hit him therewith in his eyen, then shall ye byneme him[2] his sight. That should much hinder him.

[1] *Glat*, smooth.   [2] *Byneme him*, take away from him.

But else, hold alway your tail fast between your legs that he catch you not thereby; and hold down your ears lying plat after your head that he hold you not thereby; and see wisely to yourself. And at beginning flee from his strokes, and let him spring and run after you, and run tofore where as most dust is, and stir it with your feet that it may flee in his eyen, and that shall much hinder his sight. And while he rubbeth his eyen, take your advantage and smite and bite him there as ye may most hurt him; and alway to hit him with your tail full of piss in his visage, and that shall make him so woe that he shall not wit where he is. And let him run after you for to make him weary. Yet his feet ben sore of that ye made him to lose his shoes, and though he be great he hath no heart. Nephew, certainly this is my counsel. The connyng goeth tofore strength; therefore see for yourself, and set yourself wisely at defence, that ye and we all may have worship thereof. I would be sorry if ye mishapped. I shall teach you the words that your Eme Martin taught me, that ye may overcome your enemy, as I hope ye shall do without doubt."

Therewith she laid her hand upon his head, and said these words: "Blaerde Shay Alphenio Kasbue Gorfons Alsbuifrio. Nephew, now be ye sure from all mischief and dread. And I counsel you that ye rest you a little, for it is by the day ye shall be the better disposed; we shall awake you in all in time."

"Aunt," said the Fox, "I am now glad. God thank you, ye have done to me such good I can never deserve it fully again. Methinketh there may nothing hurt me sith that ye have said these holy words over me."

Tho went he and laid him down under a tree in the grass, and slept till the sun was risen. Tho came the Otter and waked him, and bad him arise, and gave him a good young duck and said, "Dear cousin, I have this night made many a leap in the water ere I could get this young fat duck. I have taken it from a fowler. Take and eat it."

Reynart said, "This is good handsel. If I refused I were a fool. I thank you, cousin, that ye remember me. If I live I shall reward you."

The Fox ate the duck without sauce or bread. It savoured him well, and went well in. And he drank thereto four great draughts of water. Then went he to the battle ward, and all they that loved him went with him.

CHAPTER XXXVIII.

How the Fox came into the field and how they fought.

WHEN the King saw Reynart thus shorn and oiled he said to him, "Ey, Fox, how well can ye see for yourself!"

He wondered thereof; he was foul to look on.

But the Fox said not one word, but kneeled down low to the earth unto the King and to the Queen, and striked him forth into the field.

, The Wolf was there ready and spake many a proud word. The rulers and keepers of the field were the Leopard and the Losse.[1] They brought forth the book on which sware the Wolf that the Fox was a traitor and a murderer, and none might be falser than he was, and that he would prove on his body and make it good. Reynart the Fox sware that he lied as a false knave and a cursed thief, and that he would do good on his body.

When this was done, the governors of the field bade them do their devoir. Then roomed they all the field, save Dame Ruke-nawe the She Ape, she abode by the Fox and bade him remember well the words that she had said to him. She said, "See well to. When ye were seven years old ye were wise enough to go by night without lantern or moonshine where ye wist to win any good. Ye ben named among the people wise and subtle. Pain yourself to work so that ye win the prize, then may ye have ever honour and worship, and all we that ben your friends."

He answered, "My dearest aunt, I know it well. I shall do my best, and think on your counsel. I hope so to do that all my lineage shall have worship thereby, and mine enemies shame and confusion."

She said, "God grant it you."

---

[1] *Losse*, lynx (Dutch, *los*).

CHAPTER XXXIX.

How the Fox and the Wolf fought together.

THEREWITH she went out of the field and let them twain go together. The Wolf trode forth to the Fox in great wrath, and opened his forefeet, and supposed to have taken the Fox in them. But the Fox sprang from him lightly, for he was lighter to foot than he. The Wolf sprang after, and hunted the Fox sore. Their friends stood without the lists and looked upon them. The Wolf strode wider than Reynart did, and oft overtook him, and lift up his foot and weened to have smitten him. But the Fox saw to, and smote him with his rough tail, which he had all bepissed, in his visage. Tho weened the Wolf to have ben plat blind; the piss started in his eyen. Then must he rest, for to make clean his eyen. Reynart thought on his fordele, and stood above the wind scraping and casting with his feet the dust, that it flew the Wolf's eyenful. The Wolf was sore blinded therewith, in such wise that he must leave the running after him, for the sand and piss cleaved under his eyen, that it smarted so sore that he must rub and wash it away.

Tho came Reynart in a great anger and bote[1] him three great wounds on his head with his teeth, and said, " What is that, Sir Wolf! Hath one there bitten you? How is it with you? I will all otherwise on you yet. Abide. I shall bring you some new thing. Ye have stolen many a lamb, and destroyed many a simple beast, and now falsely have appealed me and brought me in this trouble. All this shall I now avenge on thee. I am chosen to reward thee for thine old sins, for God will no longer suffer thee in thy great raven and shrewdness. I shall now assoil thee, and that shall be good for thy soul. Take patiently this penance, for thou shalt live no longer. The hell shall be thy purgatory. Thy life is now in my mercy, but and if thou wilt kneel down and ask me forgiveness, and knowledge thee to be overcomen, yet though thou be evil, yet I will spare thee. For

---

[1] *Bote*, bit.

my conscience counselleth me I should not gladly slay no man."

Isegrim weened with these mocking and spiteous words to have gone out of his wits; and that dered[1] him so much that he wist not what to say, buff ne haff, he was so angry in his heart. The wounds that Reynart had given him bled and smarted sore, and he thought how he might best avenge it.

With great anger he lift up his foot and smote the Fox on the head so great a stroke that he fell to the ground. Tho stert the Wolf to, and weened to have taken him. But the Fox was light and wily, and rose lightly up, and met with him fiercely. And there began a fell battle which dured long. The Wolf had great spite on the Fox, as well it seemed. He sprang after him ten times each after other, and would fain have had him fast. But his skin was so slipper and fat of the oil, that alway he escaped from him. O, so subtle and snelle[2] was the Fox, that many times when the Wolf weened well to make sure of him, he stert then between his legs and under his belly, and then turned he again and gave the Wolf a stroke with his tail in his eyen, that Isegrim weened he should have lost his sight, and this did he often times. And alway when he had so smitten him, then would he go above the wind and raise the dust, that it made his eyen full of stuffs. Isegrim was woebegone, and thought he was at an afterdele;[3] yet was his strength and might much more than the Fox's. Reynart had many a sore stroke of him when he raught[4] him. They gave each other many a stroke and many a bite when they saw their advantage, and each of them did his best to destroy that other. I would I might see such a battle. That one was wily, and that other was strong. That one fought with strength, and that other with subtlety.

The Wolf was angry that the Fox endured so long against him. If his foremost feet had been whole, the Fox had not endured so long; but the sores were so open that he might not well run.

---

[1] *Dered*, injured.
[3] *At an afterdele*, about to pass away. Dutch, *dalen*, is to sink, as the sun when it is setting, *begint te dalen.*
[2] *Snelle*, quick.
[4] *Raught*, reached him.

And the Fox might better off and on than he, and also he swang his tail oft under his eyen, and made him that him thought that his eyen should go out.

At last he said to himself, I will make an end of this battle. How long shall this caitiff dure thus against me? I am so great, I should, if I lay upon him, press him to death. It is to me a great shame that I spare him so long. Men shall mock and point me with fingers to my shame and rebuke, for I am yet on the worst side. I am sore wounded; I bleed sore; and he drowneth me with his piss and casts so much dust and sand in mine eyen that hastily I shall not conne see, if I suffer him any longer. I will set it in adventure and seen what shall come thereof.

With that he smote with his foot Reynart on the head that he fell down to the ground, and ere he could arise he caught him in his feet and lay upon him as he would have pressed him to death. Tho began the Fox to be afraid, and so were all his friends when they saw him lie under. And on that other side all Isegrim's friends were joyful and glad. The Fox defended him fast with his claws as he lay upward with his feet, and gave many a clope.[1] The Wolf durst not with his feet do him much harm, but with his teeth snatched at him as he would have bitten him. When the Fox saw that he should be bitten and was in great dread, he smote the Wolf in the head with his foremost claws and tare the skin off between his brows and his ears, and that one of his eyen hung out; which did him much pain. He howled, he wept, he cried loud, and made a piteous noise, for the blood ran down as it had been a stream.

CHAPTER XI.

How the Fox, being under the Wolf, with flattering wordes glosed him, that the Fox came to his above again.

THE Wolf wiped his eyen, the Fox was glad when he saw that. He wrestled so sore, that he sprang on his feet while he rubbed his eyen. The Wolf was not well pleased therewithal, and smote

---

[1] *Clope*, blow (Dutch, *klop*).

after him ere he escaped, and caught him in his arms, and held him fast, notwithstanding that he bled.   Reynard was woe then. There wrestled they long and sore.   The Wolf waxed so angry that he forgat all his smarts and pain, and threw the Fox all plat under him, which came him evil to pass, for his one hand, by which he defended him stert in the falling into Isegrim's throat, and then was he afraid to lose his hand.

The Wolf said tho to the Fox, " Now choose, whether ye will yield you as overcome or else I shall certainly slay you. . Thy scattering of the dust, thy piss, thy mocking, ne thy defence, ne all thy false wiles, may not now help thee.   Thou mayest not escape me. Thou hast heretofore done me so much harm and shame, and now I have lost mine one eye and thereto sore wounded."

When Reynart heard that it stood so rowme[1] that he should choose to knowledge him overcomen and yield him or else to take the death, he thought the choice was worth ten mark, and that he must say that one or that other.   He had anon concluded what he would say, and began to say to him with fair words in this wise :

"Dear Eme, I will gladly become your man with all my good. And I will go for you to the holy grave, and shall get pardon and winning for your cloister of all the churches that ben in the holy land, which shall much profit to your soul and your elders' souls also.   I trow there was never such a proffer proffered to any king.   And I shall serve you like as I should serve our holy father the Pope.   I shall hold of you all that I have, and ever ben your servant, and forth I shall make that all my lineage shall do in like wise.   Then shall ye be a lord above all lords. Who should then dare do anything against you?   And furthermore whatsomever I take of polaille, geese, partridge, or plover, fish or flesh, or whatsomever it be, thereof shall ye first have the choice, and your wife and your children, ere any come in my body. Thereto I will alway abide by you, that where ye be there shall no hurt ne scathe come to you.   Ye be strong, and I am wily : let us abide together that, one with the counsel and that other

---

[1] *Rowme*, ruefully (Dutch, *rouw*, sorrow).

with the deed, then may there nothing misfall to usward. And we ben so nigh of kin each to other that of right should be no anger between us. I would not have foughten against you if I might have escaped. But ye appealed me first unto fight, tho must I do that I not do would gladly. And in this battle I have ben curtoys to you, I have not showed the utterest of my might on you like as I would have done if ye had been a stranger to me ; for the Nephew ought to spare the Eme, it is good reason and it ought so to be. Dear Eme, so have I now do, and that may ye mark well when I ran tofore you, mine heart would not consent thereto. For I might have hurt you much more than I did, but I thought it never; for I have not hurt you, ne done you so much harm that may hinder you, save only that mishap that is fallen on your eye. Ach ! therefore I am sorry, and suffer much sorrow in my heart. I would well, dear Eme, that it had not happed you, but that it had fallen on me, so that ye therewith had been pleased; howbeit that ye shall have thereby a great advantage. For when ye hereafter sleep ye need not to shut but one window where another must shut two. My wife and my children and my lineage shall fall down to your feet, tofore the King and tofore all them that ye will, desire and pray you humbly that ye will suffer Reynart, your nephew, live; and also I shall knowledge oft to have trespassed against you, and what leasings I have lied upon you. How might any lord have more honour than I proffer you. I would for no good do this to another. Therefore I pray you to be pleased herewithall. I wote well, if ye would, ye might have slew me ; but and ye so done had, what had ye won ? So must ye ever after this time keep you from my friends and lineage. Therefore he is wise that can in his anger measure himself, and not be over hasty, and to see well what may fall or happe afterward to him. What man that in his anger can well advise him, certainly he is wise. Men find many fools that in heat hasten them so much that after they repent them and then it is too late. But, dear Eme, I trow ye be too wise so to do. It is better to have praise, honour, rest, and peace, and many friends that be ready to help him, than to have shame,

hurt, unrest, and also many enemies lying in a wait to do him
harm. Also it is little worship to him that hath overcomen a man
then to slay him.   It is great shame, not for my life, though I
were dead that were a little hurt."

Isegrim the Wolf said, "Ay, thief, how fain wouldest thou be
loosed and discharged from me, that hear I well by thy words.
Were thou now from me on thy free feet thou wouldst not set by
me an egg shell.   Though thou promisedst to me all the world
of fine red gold, I would not let thee escape.   I set little by thee
and all thy friends and lineage.   All that thou hast here said is
but leasings and feigned falseness.   Weenest thou thus to deceive
me? it is long since that I knew thee.   I am no bird to be
locked, ne take by chaff.   I know well enough good corn.   O,
how wouldest thou mock me if I let thee thus escape.   Thou
mightest well have said this to one that knew thee not, but to me
thou losest thy flattering and sweet fluting, for I understand too
well thy subtle lying tales.   Thou hast so oft deceived me that
me behoveth now to take good heed of thee.   Thou false stinking
knave, thou sayest that thou hast spared me in this battle.   Look
hitherward to me.   Is not mine one eye out?   And thereto hast
thou wounded me in twenty places in my head.   Thou wouldest
not suffer me so long to rest as to take once my breath.   I were
over much a fool if I should now spare thee or be merciful to
thee.   So many a confusion and shame as thou hast done to me ;
and that also that toucheth me most of all, that thou hast disworshipped me and sklaundred Ersewynde my wife, whom I love
as well as myself, and falsely deceivedst her, which shall never out
of my heart : for as oft as it cometh to mine mind all mine anger
and hate that I have to thee reneweth."

In the meanwhile that Isegrim was thus speaking, the Fox
bethought him how he might help himself, and stuck his other
hand after between his legs, and grepe the Wolf fast.   And he
wrong him so sore that for woe and pain he must cry loud and
howl.   Then the Fox drew his other hand out of his mouth.
The Wolf had so much pain and anguish of the sore wringing,
that he spit blood.

CHAPTER XLI.

How Isegrim the Wolf was overcomen and how the battle was taken up and finished. And how the Fox had the worship.

THIS pain did him more sorrow and woe than his eye did that so sore bled, and also it made him to overthrow all in a swoon. Then Reynart the Fox leapt upon him with all his might, and caught him by the legs, and drew him forth through the field that they all might see it, and he stack and smote him sore. Then were Isegrim's friends all full of sorrow, and went all weeping unto their Lord the King, and prayed him that he would do cease the battle, and take it up into his hand.

The King granted it. And then went the keepers of the field the Leopard and the Lossem and said to the Fox and to the Wolf, "Our Lord the King will speak with you, and will that this battle be ended. He will take it into his hand. He desireth that ye will give your strife unto him, for if any of you here were slain it should be great shame on both sides. For ye have as much worship of this field as ye may have."

And they said to the Fox, "All the beasts give to you the prize that have seen this battle."

The Fox said, "Thereof I thank them, and what that shall please my lord to command that shall not I gainsay. I desire no better but to have won the field. Let my friends come hither to me. I will take advice of them what I shall do."

They said, "That they thought it good; and also it was reason in weighty matters a man should take advice of his friends."

Then came Dame Slopecade and Grymbart the Dasse her husband, Dame Rukenawe with her two sisters, Byteluys and Fulrompe her two sons and Hatenit her daughter, the Flyndermows [1] and the Weasel. And there came more than twenty which would not have come if the Fox had lost the field. So who that winneth and cometh to hys aboue, he getteth great loos and worship: and who that is overthrown and hath the worse, to

[1] *Flyndermows*, bat.

him will no man gladly come.   There came also to the Fox the
Beaver, the Otter and both their wives Panthecrote and Ordegale.
And the Ostrole, the Marten, the Fitchews, the Ferret, the Mouse,
and the Squirrel, and many more than I can name.   And all because he had won the field.   Yea some came that tofore had
complained on him, and were now of his next kin, and they
showed him right friendly cheer and countenance.   Thus fareth
the world now.   Who that is rich and high on the wheel, he hath
many kinsmen and friends that shall help to bear out his wealth :
but who that is needy and in pain or in poverty findeth but few
friends and kinsmen ; for every man almost escheweth his company and way.

There was then great feast.   They blew up trumpets and piped
with shalmoyses.

They said all, " Dear Nephew, blessed be God that ye have
sped well.   We were in great dread and fear when we saw you
lie under."

Reynart the Fox thanked all them friendly, and received them
with great joy and gladness.   Then he asked of them what they
counselled him.   If he should give the field unto the King
or no ?

Dame Slopecade said, " Yea hardily cousin.   Ye may with
worship well set it in to his hands, and trust him well enough."

Tho went they all with the keepers of the field unto the
King.   And Reynart the Fox went tofore them all, with trumpets
and pipes and much other minstrelsy.   The Fox kneeled down
tofore the King.

The King bad him stand up, and said to him, "Reynart ye
be now joyful.   Ye have kept your day worshipfully.   I discharge
you, and let you go freely quit where it pleaseth you.   And the
debate between you, I hold it on me, and shall discuss it by reason
and by counsel of noble men, and will ordain thereof that ought
be done by reason, at such time as Isegrim shall be whole.   And
then I shall send for you to come to me, and then by God's grace
I shall give out the sentence and judgment."

CHAPTER XLII.

An ensample that the Fox told to the King when he had won the field.

"My worthy and dear Lord the King," said the Fox, "I am well agreed and paid therewith. But when I came first into your Court there were many that were fell and envious to me, which never had hurt ne cause of scathe by me. But they thought that they might best over me, and all they crieden with mine enemies against me and would fain have destroyed me, because they thought that the Wolf was better withholden and greater with you than I was, which am your humble subject. They knew none other thing, why ne wherefore. They thought not as the wise be wont to do, that is what the end may happen.

"My lord these ben like a great heap of hounds which I once saw stand at a lord's place upon a dunghill, whereas they awaited that men should bring them meat. Then saw they an hound come out of the kitchen and had taken there a fair rib of beef ere it was given him. And he ran fast away withal; but the cook had espied or [1] he went away, and took a great bowl full of scalding water and cast it on his hips behind; whereof he thanked nothing the cook, for the hair behind was scalded off and his skin seemed as it had be through sodden. Nevertheless he escaped away and kept that he had won.

"And when his fellows the other hounds saw him come with this fair rib, they called him all and said to him, 'Oh how good a friend is the cook to thee, which hath given to thee so good a bone, whereon is so much flesh.'

"The hound said, 'Ye know nothing thereof. Ye praise me like as ye see me tofore with the bone. But ye have not seen me behind. Take heed, and behold me afterward on mine buttocks, and then ye shall know how I deserved it.'

"And when they had seen him behind on his hips how that his skin and his flesh was all raw and through sodden, tho

[1] *Or,* ere.

growled they all and were afraid of that syedyng water; and would not of his fellowship, but fled and ran away from him, and let him there alone.

"See, my Lord, this right have these false beasts. When they be made lords, and may get their desire, and when they be mighty and doubted,[1] then ben they extortioners and scatte and pylle the people and eaten them like as they were forhungred hounds. These ben they that bear the bone in their mouth. No man dare have to do with them, but preyse all that they bedrive.[2] No man dare say otherwise but such as shall please them, because they would not be shorn. And some help them forth in their un-righteous deeds because they would not have part, and lick their fingers, and strengthe them in their evil life and works. O, dear Lord, how little seen they that do thus after behind them, what the end shall be at last. They fall from high to low in great shame and sorrow, and then their works come to knowledge and be open in such wise that no man hath pity ne compassion on them in their mischief and trouble, and every man curse them and say evil by them to their shame and villainy. Many of such have been blamed and shorn full nigh, that they had no worship ne profit but lose their hair as the hound did, that is their friends which have help them to cover their misdeeds and extortions like as the hair covereth the skin. And when they have sorrow and shame for their old trespasses, then each body plucketh his hand from him, and flee, like as the hounds did from him that was scalded with the syedyng water, and let him these extortions in their sorrow and need.

My dear Lord King, I beseech you to remember this example of me; it shall not be against your worship ne wisdom. What ween ye how many ben there such false extortioners now in these days,—yea much worse than an hound that beareth such a bone in his mouth—in towns, in great lords' courts, which with great facing and bracing oppress the poor people with great wrong, and sell their freedom and privileges, and bear them on hand of things that they never knew ne thought, and all for to get good

---

[1] *Doubted*, feared.   [2] *Bedrive*, experience.

for their singular profit. God give them all shame, and soon destroy them, whosomever they be that so do!

"But God be thanked," said the Fox, "there may no man indite me, ne lineage, ne kin, of such works, but that we shall acquit us, and comen in the light. I am not afraid of any that can say on me any thing that I have done otherwise than a true man ought to do. Alway the Fox shall abide the Fox, though all his enemies had sworn the contrary. My dear Lord the King, I love you with my heart above all lords, and never for no man would I turn from you, but abide by you to the utterest. How well it hath been otherwise informed your highness, I have nevertheless alway do the best, and forth so will do, all my life that I can or may."

CHAPTER XLIII.

How the King forgave the Fox all things, and made him Sovereign and greatest over all his lands.

THE King said, "Reynart, ye be one of them that oweth me homage; which I will that ye alway so do. And also I will that, early and late, ye be of my council and one of my justices. See well to that ye not misdo ne trespass no more. I set you again in all your might and power, like as ye were tofore, and see that ye further all matters to the best right. For when ye set your wit and counsel to virtue and goodness, then may not our Court be without your advice and counsel, for here is none that is like to you in sharp and high counsel, ne subtler in finding a remedy for a mischief. And think ye on the example that ye yourself have told, and that ye haunt righteousness and be to me true. I will from henceforth work and do by your advice and counsel. He liveth not that if he misdid you, but I should sharply avenge and wreke it on him. Ye shall overall speak and say my words, and in all my land shall ye be, above all other, sovereign and my bayle.[1] That office I give you. Ye may well occupy it with worship."

All Reynart's friends and lineage thanketh the King highly.

[1] *Bayle,* bailiff, deputy, one who keeps in custody.

The King said, "I would do more for your sake than ye ween. I pray you all that ye remember him that he be true."

Dame Rukenawe then said, "Yes sykerly, my Lord, that shall he ever be, and think ye not the contrary. For if he were otherwise, he were not of our kin ne lineage, and I would ever mis-sake him, and would ever hinder him to my power."

Reynart the Fox thanked the King with fair courteous words, and said, " Dear Lord, I am not worthy to have the worship that ye do to me. I shall think thereon and be true to you all so long as I live, and shall give you as wholesome counsel as shall be expedient to your good grace."

Herewith he departed with his friends from the King.

Now hark how Isegrim the Wolf did. Bruin the Bear, Tybert the Cat, and Ersewynde and her children with their lineage drewen the Wolf out of the field, and laid him upon a litter of hay, and covered him warm, and looked to his wounds which were well twenty-five. And there came wise masters and surgeons which bound them and wash them. He was so sick and feeble that he had lost his feeling, but they rubbed and wryued[1] him under his temples and eyen, that he sprang out of his swound, and cried so loud that all they were afraid. They had weened that he had been wood.[2]

But the masters gave him a drink that comforted his heart and made him to sleep. They comforted his wife, and told to her that there was no death-wound ne peril of his life. Then the Court brake up; and the Beasts departed and went to their places and homes that they came from.

CHAPTER XLIV.

How the Fox with his friends and lineage departed nobly from the King and went to his castle Malperduys.

REYNART the Fox took his leave honestly of the King and of the Queen. And they bade him he should not tarry long, but shortly return to them again.

---

[1] *Wryued*, rubbed (Dutch, *wryven*, to rub).   [2] *Wood*, mad.

He answered and said, "Dear King and Queen, alway at your commandment I shall be ready, if ye need anything, which God forbid. I would alway be ready with my body and my good to help you, and also all my friends and lineage in likewise shall obey your commandment and desire. Ye have highly deserved it, God quite it you, and give you grace long to live. And I desire your license and leave to go home to my wife and children. And if your good grace will anything, let me have knowledge of it, and ye shall find me alway ready."

Thus departed the Fox with fair words from the King.

Now who that could set him in Reynart's craft, and could behave him in flattering and lying as he did, he should I trow be heard, both with the Lords Spiritual and Temporal. They ben many, and also the most part, that creep after his way and his hole. The name that was given to him abideth alway still with him. He hath left many of his craft in this world which alway wax and become mighty: for who that will not use Reynart's craft now is nought worth in the world, nor in any estate that is of might. But if he can creep in Reynart's net and hath been his scholar, then may he dwell with us, for then knoweth he well the way how he may arise, and is set up above of every man. There is in the world much seed left of the Fox which now overall groweth and cometh sore up. Though they have no red beards, yet there ben founden more foxes now than ever were heretofore. The righteous people ben all lost; Truth and Righteousness ben exiled and fordriven; and for them ben abiden with us Covetyse, Falsehood, Hate, and Envy; these reign now much in every country. For is it in the Pope's court, the Emperor's, the King's, Duke's, or any other lord's, wheresomever it be, each man laboureth to put other out from his worship, office and power, for to make himself to climb high, with lies, with flattering, with simony, with money, or with strength and force. There is nothing beloved ne known in the court nowadays but Money. The Money is better beloved than God. For men do much more therefor: for whosomever bringeth Money shall be well received, and shall have all his desire, is it of lords or of ladies or any other.   That Money doth much harm.   Money bringeth many in shame and dread of life, and bringeth false witness against true people for to get Money.   It causeth uncleanness of living, lying, and lechery. Now clerks gon to Rome, to Paris, and to many another place, for to learn Reynart's craft: is he clerk, is he layman, everiche of them treadeth in the Fox's path, and seeketh his hole.   The world is of such condition now, that every man seeketh himself in all matters.   I wot not what end shall come to us hereof.   All wise men may sorrow well herefor.   I fear that for the great falseness, theft, robbery, and murder, that is now used so much and commonly, and also the unshamefast lechery and avoultry,[1] bosted, blowen abroad with the avaunting of the same, that without great repentance and penance therefor that God will take vengeance and punish us sore therefor.   Whom I humbly beseech, and to whom nothing is hid, that he will give us grace to make amends to him therefor and that we may rule us to his pleasure.

And herewith will I leave; for what have I, to write of these misdeeds?   I have enough to do with mine own self.   And so it were better that I held my peace and suffer, and the best that I can, do, for to amend myself now in this time.   And so I counsel every man to do, here in this present life, and that shall be most our profit.   For after this life cometh no time that we may occupy to our advantage for to amend us.   For then shall every man answer for himself and bear his own burthen.

Reynart's friends and lineage to the number of forty have taken also their leave of the King, and went all together with the Fox, which was right glad that he had so well sped and that he stood so well in the King's grace.   He thought that he had no shame, but that he was so great with the King that he might help and further his friends, and hinder his enemies, and also to do what he would without he should be blamed; if he would be wise.

The Fox and his friends went so long together that they camen to his burgh to Malperduys, there they all took leave of each

---

[1] *Avoultry*, adultery.

other with fair and courteous words. Reynart did to them great reverence, and thanked them all friendly of their good faith and also worship that they had done and showed to him. And proffered to each of them his service, if they had need, with body and goods. And herewith they departed, and each of them went to their own houses.

The Fox went to Dame Ermelyne his wife, which welcomed him friendly. He told to her and to his children all the wonder that to him was befallen in the Court, and forgot not a word, but told to them every deal how he had escaped. Then were they glad that their father was so enhanced and great with the King. And the Fox lived forthon with his wife and his children in great joy and gladness.

Now who that said to you of the Fox more or less than ye have heard or read, I hold it for leasing. But this that ye have heard or read, that may ye believe well. And who that believeth it not, is not therefore out of the right belief; howbeit there be many if that they had seen it they should have none less doubt of it. For there ben many things in the world which ben believed though they were never seen : also there ben many figures, plays, founden that never were done ne shaped, but for an example to the people that they may there learn better to use and follow virtue and to eschew sin and vices. In like wise may it be by this book that who that will read this matter, though it be of japes and bourds, yet he may find therein many a good wisdom, and learnings by which he may come to virtue and worship. There is no one man blamed herein; it is spoken generally. Let every man take his own part as it belongeth and behoveth, and he that findeth him guilty in any deal or part thereof, let him repent and amend him. And he that is verily good, I pray God keep him therein. And if any thing be said or written herein that may grieve or displease any man, blame not me but the Fox, for they be his words and not mine.

Prayeng alle them that shal see this lytyl treatis/ to correcte and amende/ Where they shal fynde faute/ For I haue not added ne mysnusshed but hauc folowed as nyghe as I can my copye whiche was in dutche/ and by me william Caxton translated in to this rude and symple englyssh in thabbey of westmestre. fynysshed the vj daye of Juyn the yere of our lord ·M.CCCC.Lxxxj. and the xxj yere of the regne of kynge Edward the iiijth/

ROBERT THE DEUYLL.

II.

ROBERT THE DEUYLL.

Here begynneth the lyfe of the most myscheuoust Robert the Deuyll, which was afterwarde called the seruant of God.

𝔍𝔱 𝔟𝔢𝔣𝔢𝔩 𝔦𝔫 𝔱𝔶𝔪𝔢 past, there was a duke in Normandye which was called Ouberte, the which duke was passynge ryche of goodes, and also vertuous of lyuynge, and loued and dred God above all thynge, and dyde grete almesse dedes, and exceeded all other in ryghtwysnesse and justyce, and most cheualrouse in dedes of armes and notable actes doynge. This duke helde open house upon a Crystmasse daye, in a towne which was called Naverne, upon the Seyne, to the which courte came all the lordes and noble blode of Normandy. And because this noble duke was not maryed, his lordes nobles with one assente besought hym to marye and take a wyfe, to thentente that his lygnage might be multyplyed thereby, and that they myght have a ryght heyre to enherite his landes after his dysceyse. To the whyche request this good duke answered and sayd : " My lordes, what thynge that ye thynke best for me to do shall be done, upon a condycyon, in that ye wyll that I be maryed, that ye puruey me a wyfe accordynge to my myn estate, for and yf I shall coueyte ony heyre or noblyer of blode than I am myselfe, that myghte not stand with ryght, and yf I take one that is not of so noble an house as I am, that sholde be to me grete shame, and all my lygnage ; wherefore me thynke it were better that I kepe me as I am, than to do that thynge that sholde not be myne honeste, and afterwarde repente me." Whan these wordes were spoken, and well consydered by the lordes that

stode there present, then there rose up a wyse baron, and sayd to
the duke: "My lorde ye speke very wysely, and lyke a noble
prynce, but yf it please your hyeness to gyue audyence and here
me speke, I shall shewe you of a certayne persone of whome ye
shall enjoye yourselfe to here of her, and the whyche ye shall
obteyne I know well." Than answered the duke, and sayd:
"Shewe me then who that persone is." "Gracyous lorde," sayd
the baron unto the duke, "the duke of Bourgone hath a doughter
whyche excedethe al other in beaute, curteyse and deboynayre
wysdome and good maneres, the whiche ye may have yf ye wyll
desyre her, for I knowe well there wyll no man say naye thereto."
To the whiche the good duke answered and said, that lady playsed
hym ryght well, and that the baron had gyven hym good and wyse
counsell. And in short tyme after that, this lady was demaunded
of her fader, the duke of Bourgone, which gave hym her wyllyngly.
And then theyr bridale was kepte honourably, which were to
longe to write.

*How the duke of Normandye with grete royalte broughte his wyfe,
the doughter of the duke of Bourgone, in to Roan in Normandye,
after he had maryed her.*

AFTER that the forsayd duke had maryed the sayd ladye, he
brought her with a grete company of barons, knyghtes, and ladyes,
with grete tryumphe and glorye, into the land of Normandye,
and in the cyte of Roan,[1] in the which cyte she was honourably
receyued, and with grete melodye; and there was grete amyte
betwene the Bourgonyons and the Normans, which I lete passe
for to come the soner to my mater. The forsayd duke and
duchesse lyued togyder the space of xviii yere without any childe.
Whether it were Godde's wyl it sholde be so, or it were thrughe
theyr own defaulte, I can not juge, for it were better other whyle
that some people had no chylderne, and also it were better for
the fader and the moder to gete no chyldren, thenne to lacke of
chastysynge, the chyldren and fader and moder sholde al go to

[1] *Roan,* Rouen.

the deuyll : yet was this duke and duchesse deuout people, which loved and drede God, and gave grete almesse; and what tyme this duke wolde meddle with his lady, he euer prayed to God to sende hym a chylde, to honoure and serue God, and to multyply and fortyfy his lynage; but nother with prayer nor with almesse dedes this good duke and duchesse could gete no chyldren.

*How upon a tyme this duke and duchesse walked alone, sore com-
planynge the one to the other that they coude have no chylde
togyder.*

Upon a tyme this duke and duchesse walked, and the duke began to shewe his mynde to his ladye, saynge, "Madame, we be not fortunate in so much that we can gete noo chyldren; and they that made the maryage betwene us bothe they dyde grete synne, for I beleue and ye had been geuen to an other man, ye sholde haue had chyldren, and I also yf I had another ladye." This lady understood his sayenge : she answered softly, saynge thus : "Good lorde, we must thanke God of that which he sendeth us, and take it pacyently of what so euer it be."

*How Robert the Deuyll was conceyued, and how his moder gave him
to the deuyll in his concepcyon.*

This duke upon a tyme rode oute an hountyng in a grete angre and pensyfness, for thought that he coulde haue no chylde, sore complanynge, saynge to hymselfe, I see many women haue many fayre chyldren in whiche they enjoy gretely, by which I se wel that I am hated of God, and meruayle it is that I fall not in dyspare, for it greueth me so sore at my herte that I can gete no chyldren. The deuyll, which is alwaye redy to deceyue man-kynde, tempted the good duke, and troubled his mynde so that he wyst not what to do or say. Thus moued, he left his huntynge and wente home to his palayes, where he found his ladye also vexed and moued. As he came home he toke her in his armes, and kyssed her, and dyde his will with her, sayenge his prayers to our Lorde in this wyse: "O ! Lord Jhesu, I beseche the that I may get a chylde, at this houre, by the whiche thou mayst be honoured and served." But the ladye being so sore moued, spake thus folyshly, and said : "In the deuyle's name be it, in so muche as God hath not the power that I conceyue; and yf I be conceyued with chylde in this houre, I gyve it to the devyll, body and soule." And this same houre that this duke and duches were thus moued, the sayd lady was conceyued with a man chylde, whiche in his lyf wrought moche myschefe, as ye shall here after this, but afterwards he was converted, and dyde grete penance, and dyed a holy man, as is shewed here after.

How Robert the Deuyll was borne, and what great pain his moder suffered in hys byrthe.

THIS duchesse, as we haue herd before, was conceyued with the forsayd chylde, which she bare ix monethes as comonly women goo with chylde; and ye may well perceyue that this lady coude not be delyuered without grete payn, for she traueylled more than a moneth, and yf good prayers had not been, and almesse dedes, good werkes, and great penance done for her, she had deyed of chylde, for all the ladyes and gentylwomen that there were with her wened, she wold ·have perysshed and deyed in traualynge. Wherefore they were gretly abasshed and aferde with the merueylouse noise and tokens that they herde and se in the byrth of the said Robert the Deuyll, in that whan this chylde was borne, the sky waxed as darke as though it had been nyghte, as it is shewed in olde cronycles, that it thondred and lyghtened so sore, that men thought the firmament had been open, and all the worlde sholde haue perysshed. And there blewe soo moche wynde out of the iiii quarters of the worlde, and was such storme and tempest, that al the hous trembled so sore, that it shoke a grete pece of it to the earth, in so moche that all they that were in the house wened that the worlde had been at an ende, and that they, with the house and all, sholde haue sonken. But in shorte tyme it pleased God that all this trouble ceased, and the weder clered up, and the chylde was brought to chyrch to be crystened, whiche was named Robert. This childe was large of stature at his byrthe as he had been a yere old, whereof the people had grete wonder; and as this chylde was a berynge to the chirche to be crystned and home ayenst, it neuer ceased cryenge and houlynge. And in shorte space he had longe teeth wherwith he bote the norshes pappes in such wyse, that there was no woman durst gyue hym souke, for he bote off the hedes of theyr brestes; wherefore they were fayne to gyue hym souke and to brynge hym up with an horne. And whan he was twelve moneth olde, he coude speke and go alone better than other chyldrne that were thre yere old. And the elder that this chylde Robert waxed, more cursted; and there was no man that coude rule hym: and whan he founde or coude come by ony chyldrne he smote and bote and cast stones at them, and brake theyr armes and legges and neckes, and scratte out theyr eyen owt of theyr hedes, and therein was all his delyte and pleasure.

How all the chyldren with one assent named this chylde Roberte the Deuyll.

THIS chylde within fewe yeares grewe maruaylously, and more and more encresed of all, and boldness, and shrewdness, and set by no correccyon, but was euer smyttynge and tastynge, and cursed dedes doynge. And some tyme there gadred togyder all the boyes of the strete to fyghte with him, but whan they se hym they durst not abyde hym, but cryed one to another, " Here cometh the wode[1] Robert!" an other many cryed, " Here cometh the cursed madde Robert!" and some cryed, "Here cometh Robert the Deuyll!" and thus cryenge they voyded all the stretes, for they durst not abyde and loke hym in the face, and forthwith the chyldrne that knewe hym with one assente called hym Roberte the Deuyll, whiche name he kepte durynge his lyfe, and shall do as longe as the world standeth. Whan this chyld was seuen yere old or there aboute, the duke his fader seynge and

---

[1] *Wode*, mad.

consyderynge his wycked condycyons, called hym and sayd unto hym thus, " My sone me thyncke it necessary and tyme, for me to gete you a wyse scole mayster, to lerne vertues and doctrine, for ye be of age ynoughe," and whan the duke had thus sayd, he betoke [1] his sone to a good dyscreet and wyse scole mayster to rule and teche hym all good condycyons and maners.

How Robert kylled his scole mayster.

It fell upon a daye that his scole mayster sholde chastyse Robert and would have made hym to have lefte his cursed condycyons, but Robert gate a murderer or bodkin, and thrust his mayster in the bely that his guttes fell at his fete, and so fell downe deed to the erth, and Robert threw his boke ayenst the walles in despyte of his mayster saynge thus now haue I taughte the that never preste, nor clerke shal correct me, nor be my mayster. And from thens forth there coude no mayster be founde that was so bolde to take in hande to teche and correcte this Roberte, but were glad to let hym alone and have his owne wayes, and he put hymselfe to uyce and myschefe, and to no maner of vertue nor grace, nor wolde he lerne for no man lyuynge, but mocked both God and holy chyrche. And when he came to the churche and founde the prestes, and clarkes syngynge Goddes seruyce, he came preuely behind them, and caste ashes or duste in theyr mouthes in dyspyte of God. And when he sawe any body in the chyrche besy in their prayers he would come behynde them and gyue them a sowse in the necke that theyr hedes kyssed the ground, in so moche that euery body cursed hym for his wycked dedes doynge. And the duke his fader seynge his myscheuous dyspocysyon and cursed lyfe of his sone, he was so angry with hymselfe, that he wyshed hymself many tymes dede and out of the worlde. And the duchese in lykewyse was gretly moued and muche sorrowefull by cawse of the myscheuous lyfe of her sone, saynge in this wyse, " My lord our sone is nowe of sufficient age and able to bere armes, wherefore me thynke it were best that ye

---

[1] *Betoke*, entrusted.

máde hym knyght if than he wolde remembre thordre of knyghthode whereby he myght leve his wyckedness." The duke was
here withall content. And Robert had at that tyme but eyghtene
yere of age.

How Robert the Deuyll was made knyght by the duke his fader.

THIS duke assembled upon a hye feast of Whitsontyde, all his
barons and nobles of his lande, and the next of his kyn and frendes,
in the presence of whome he called his sone to hym saynge thus,
" Herke my sone Robert, and take hede what I shall tell you, it is
so that by thaduyce of my counsell and good frendes, I am now
aduysed to make you a knyght, to thentent that ye be with other
knyghtes to haunte chevalrye and knyghtes condýcions, to
thentente that ye shall leve and forsake your uyces and moost
hatfull lyf." Robert herynge this, answered his fader, " I shall
do your comandment, but as for the odre of knyghthode I set
nothynge thereby, for there is no degre shall cause me leve my
condycyons nor chaunge my lyfe, for I am not in that mynde to
do no better than I have done hetherto, nor to amende for no
man lyuynge." It was the costome of that lande, that on Whit-
sonyght the chyrche shold be watched, and tended with moche
people, and theder cam Robert like a madman, and overthrowynge
al them that came in his waye ferynge nother God nor the Deuyll,
and he was never styll of all the nyght, and in the mornynge whan
it was day Robert was made knyght. Then this duke comaunded
a tournament to be made in the which the said Robert wrought
maystryes, and dyde meruaylous dedes of armes, in kyllynge and
berynge downe hors and man, no man refusynge nor ferynge.
Of some he brake armes and some legges, and bare them thorowe
and kylled them out of hande ; from hym went none unmarked ; in
whiche iustynge Robert kylled x horses. The duke herynge how
his sone myscheued and murdred all that came in his handes he
went hymself into the tournament and comaunded upon a grete
payne to sease and ren no more. Then Robert rored for anger as
he had ben wode and wolde, not obeye his faders comaundement

but abode styl in the fylde smytynge some that he kylled of the moste valiauntes that thether were comen to tournaye. Than euery man cryed upon Robert to cease, but it auayled not, for he wolde not cease for no man, nor was there no man so bolde to encountre hym, for bycause that he was so stronge this Robert dyde so moche myschefe that all the people were in a rore, and assembled all with one assent in a great angre and ranne to the duke complaynynge, saynge thus : "Lorde, ye be gretely to blame that ye suffre your sone to do as he dothe ; we beseche yow for goddes sake to fynde some remedye for hym, to cause hym to cease or leue his mysrule."

How Robert the Deuyll rode about the countree of Normandy, robbynge, stelynge, morderynge, and brennynge chyrches, abbayes and other holy places of relygyon, and forsynge of women.

THAN whan Robert se there was no man more lefte in the felde, and that he coude do no more myschef there, than he toke his horse with the spores to seke his aventures, and began to do every day more harm than other one, for he forsed and rauysshed maydens and wyues without nombre, he kylled murdred so moche people, that it was pyte, also he robbed chyrches, abbayes, hermytages, and fermes, there was not an abbaye in all the countrey but he robbed and pylled them. These wycked dedes of Robert came to the eres of the good duke, and all they that were thus robbed and rebuked came to complayne of the grete outrage and suppressyon done by Robert, and styll was doynge thorowe out all the countree. One sayd, " My lorde, youre sone hathe forsed my wyfe," another sayd, " he hath rauyshed my doughter," the other sayd, "he hath stolen my goodes, and robbed my hous ; " and other sayd, "he hath wounded me to deth," with many semblable offences. Thus lay they greuously complanynge before the good duke, that grete pyte it was there for to se the good duke herynge the greuous and lamentable complayntes of the great murdre done by Robert his sone, thoroughout all the lande of Normande. Than his herte was suppressed with so grete sorrowe and thought, that the salt teres breste out of his eyen, and he wepte tenderly and sayd; "O ryght wyse God creatoure of heaven and erth, I haue so many tymes prayed ye to send me a chylde and all my delyte was to haue a son, to the entente that I myght of hym have grete joye, and solace. And now haue I one, the whiche doth my herte soo moche payne, sorowe and thought that I wote in no wyse what to begyn, nor doo, nor saye thereto, but good Lorde onely I crye upon the for helpe, and remedye to be a lytel released of my payne and sorowe."

How the duke sent out men of armes for to take Robert his sone, which Roberte toke them all, and put out theyr eyen in dyspyte of his fader, and sente them so home agayne.

THERE was a knyght of the Dukes hous, whiche perceyued that this good duke was uery sorrowfull and pensyfe, and knewe no remedy; then this knyght spake and sayd to hym: "My lorde, I wold aduyse you to sende for your sone Robert and let hym be brought to your presence, and there before your nobles, and nexte frendes to rebuke hym, and than commaund hym to leaue hys cursed lyf, and yf he wyll not, ye to do justice upon hym as on a straunge man." Hereto the duke consented, and thought the knyght gaue hym good counsell, and incontynent he sente out men to seke Robert, and in ony wyse they were to brynge hym to hys presence. This Robert, herynge of the complayntes made of all the people upon hym unto hys fader, and that his fader had sent out men to take hym, wherefore all them that he coude gete, he put out theyr eyen, and so he toke the men that his fader sende for hym, and put out theyr eyen in despyte of his fader. And whan he had thus blynded his fader's seruauntes, he sayd to them in mockynge, "Syrs, nowe shall ye slepe the better; go now home to my fader, and tell hym that I set lytel by hym, and bycause he sendeth you to brynge me to hym, therefore to hys dyspyte I have put out your eyen." These poore seruauntes whiche the duke had sent for Robert his sone, came home with great payne and in grete heuynesse saynge thus: "O good lorde se howe

M

youre sone Robert that ye dyde send us for hath arayed us, and
blynded us." The good duke seynge his men in this case, he
waxed very angry, and full of yre and began to compasse in his
mynde how and by what meanes he myght come by to take
Robert his sone.

*How the duke of Normandy made a proclamation throughout his
lande, how men sholde take Robert his sone, with al his company, and brynge them everychone to pryson.*

THAN spake a wyse lorde, sayinge thus, "My lorde take noo
more thought, for ye shall never se the day that Robert your sone
wyll come in your presence, in so moche as he hath done so great
and greuouse offences to your comons, and your owne messengers that ye sende for hym. But it were of necessite for you to
correct and punysshe hym for hys great offences, that he dayly
doth, and hath done, for we fynde it wryten, that the lawe
byndeth you therto." The duke, wyllynge to accomplyshe the
councel of his lordes, sende out messangers in all the hast, unto
all the portes, good townes and barons, throughout all his duke-
dome, commandynge on his behalfe all shryues, baylufes, or other
offycers to do theyr uttermoost dylygence to take Robert his sone
prysoner and to holde and kepe hym surely in pryson with all
his company and affinyte. Whan Roberte herde of this proclamation, he with all his company were sore aferde of the dukes
malyce and whan Robert se this he was almost out of his wyt for
wode angre, and wheted hys teeth lyke a bore, and sware a grete
othe saynge thus, "that he wolde have open war with his fader,
and subdewe and spyll all his lordshyppe."

*How Robert made hym a strong hous in a darke thycke wyldernes
where he wrought myscheff without comparyson and aboue al
mesure or natural reason.*

THEN whan Robarte herde and knewe of the forsayd thynges, he
lete make in a thycke wylde foreste a stronge house, wherein he
made his dwellynge place, and this place was wylde and strong,

and more meter for wylde beestes, than for any people to abyde
in, and there Robert assembled and gadered for his company, all
the moost myscheuouste and falsest theues that he coude fynde
or heere of in his faders lande, to wete morderers, theues, strete-
robers, rebelles, brenners of chyrches and houses, forsers of
women, robbers of chyrches, and the moost wyckeste and curseste
theues that were under the sone, Robert had gadered to doo hym
seruyce ; wherof he was Capytayne. And in the forsayd wyldernesse, Robert wyth his company dyde so moche myschefe,
that no tonge can tell. He mordred marchauntes, and all that
came by the waye, no man durst loke out nor come abrode for
fere of Robert and his company, of whome every man was aferde ;
for they robbed all the countree, in so moche, that no man durst
loke out, but they were kylled of Robert or his men. Also poore
pelgremes that went on pelgremage were murdered by Robert
and his company, in so moche, that euery man fledde from them,
lyke as the shepe fledde from the wolfe : for they were as
wolues warynge, sleyinge all that they coude come by, and thus,
Robert and his company ledde an ungracious lyfe. Also he was
a grete glotten of etynge and drynkynge, and neuer fastynge,
though it were neuer so great a fastynge daye. In Lente, or on
Ymber dayes, he ete flesshe, as well on Frydayes as on Sondayes ;
but after he had done all this myschefe, he suffred grete payne,
as hereafter ye shal here.

How Robert the Deuyll killed vii heremytes.

It befell upon a tyme that Robert, whiche euer imagyned and
studyed in his mynde howe and by what meane he might doo
moost myschefe and murdre, as he had ben euer accustomed
before he rode out of his hous or theuyshe neste to seke his
pray, and in the myddel of the wode he sawe vii hooly hermytes,
to whome he rode as faste as he coulde with his swerde redy
drawen, lyke a man oute of his mynde, and there he slewe this
vii heremytes, the whiche were bolde and good men, but they
were so vertuous and holy, that they suffred the marterdome for

the loue of God. And whan he had slayne these vii devout men, he spake in mockage, and said : " I haue founde here a neste of a many pope holy sons whome I haue shauen them crounes : I trowe they be dronke ; they were wonte to knele upon theyr knees, and now they lye upon theyr backes." There dyde Robert a cursed dede and blode shedynge, in despyte of God and holy chyrche ; and after that he hadde done this myscheuous dede he rode out of the wode lyke a deuyll out of helle, semynge worse thenne wode, and his clothes were all dyed rede with the blode of the people that he had murdred and slayne, and thus arayed he rode ouer the feldes, and clothes, handes, face, all were rede of the blode of the holy heremytes, whiche he had so pyteously murdred in the wyldernesse.

How Robert the Deuyll rode to his moder the duchesse of Normandye, beynge in the castell of Darques : she was come to a feste.

Robert rode so ferre and so longe, that he came to the castell of Darques ; but he mette before with a shypherde which had tolde him that his moder the duchesse should come of the said castell to dyner, and so he rode theder. But whan Robert came there, and the people see hym come, they ranne awaye frome hym, lyke the hare frome the houndes ; one ranne and shette hym in hys house, an other ranne into the chyrche for fere. Robert seynge this, that all the people fled from hym for fere, he began to sygh in his herte, and sayd to hymself,—" O ! Almyghty God, how may this be, that every man thus fleeth from me ! Nowe I perceyue that I am the moost myscheuouste and the moost cursedest wretche of this worlde, for I sente better to be a Jewe or a Sarasyne, than any Crysten man, and I se wel that I am worste of all yll. Alas ! sayd Robert the Deuyll, I may well hate and curse mine ungracyous and cursed lyfe, wherfore I am worthy to be hated of God and the worlde." In this minde and heuynesse came Robert to the castell gate, and lyghte downe from his horse, but there was no man that durste abyde about hym, nor come nyghe hym to holde his horse ; and he hadde no seruante to serue hym, but let his horse stande there at the gate, and drewe out his swerde, whiche was all blody, and incontynente toke the waye unto the halle, where the duchesse his moder was. Whan the duchesse sawe Robert her sonne come in this wyse, with a blody swerde in his hande, she was sore aferde, and wolde haue flede a way frome hym, for she knewe wel his condycyons. Robert, seynge that euery body dyde flee from hym, and that his owne moder wolde haue fledde in lykewyse, he called unto her pyteously afarre, and said : "Swete lady moder, be not aferde of me, but stande styl tyl I haue spoken with you, and flee not from me, in the worshyp of Crystes passyon !" Than Roberte's herte beynge full of thought and repentaunce, wente nygher her, saynge thus : " Dere lady moder, I praye and requyre you tell me how and by what manner or wherby cometh it that I am soo vycyous and curste, for I knowe wel I haue it other by you or of my fader ; wherefore incontynent I hertly desyre and praye you that ye shewe me the trouth hereof."

How the Duchesse desyred Robert her sone to smyte of her hede, and than she tolde him howe she had gyuen hym to the deuyll in his concepcyon.

THE duchesse had gretly meruaylynge whan she herde her sone speke these wordes; and piteously wepynge, with a sorrowful herte saynge thus to hym : "My dere sone, I requyre you hertly that ye wyll smyte of my heed." This sayd the lady, for very grete pyte that she had upon hym, for bycause she had gyuen hym to the deuyll in his concepcyon. Robert answerde his moder with an hevy and a pityeous chere, saynge thus : "O ! dere moder, why sholde I do so, that so moche myschefe have done, and this sholde be the worste dede that euer I dyde ; but I praye you to shewe me that I desyre to wete[1] of you." Then the duchesse, herynge his hertely desyre, tolde unto hym the cause why he was so vicious and full of myschefe, and how she gaue hym to the deuyll in his concepcyon, herselfe myspraysynge, said thus unto

[1] *Wete,* know.

Roberte: "O! sonne, I am the moost unfortunate woman lyu-ynge, and I knowledge that it is all my faute that ye be soo cursed and wycked a leuer."

How Robert the Deuyll toke leue of his moder.

ROBERT herynge his moders saynge he fell downe to the erthe into a swone, for very grete sorowe, and laye styll a longe whyle, than he remeued agayne and came to hymself and began bytterly to wepe, and complayne, saynge thus: "'The fendes of hell be with grete dylygence to applye theym to gete and haue my body and soule, but nowe from this tyme forthe, I forsake theym and all theyr werke, and wyll neuer do more harme but good, and amende my lyfe and leue my synes and do penaunce therefore." Than after this Robert spake to his moder, the whiche was in grete sorowe, and heuynesse saynge thus: "O moost reuerente lady moder, I hertely besecke and requyre you that it wilde please you to haue me recommaunded unto my fader; for I wyll take the waye to Rome to be assoyled of my synnes, which are innu-merable, and to abhomynable to recounte. Therefore I wyll neuer slepe one nyght there I slepe an other, tyll I come at Rome and god wyll."

How Robert departed from his moder, and rode into the wyldernesse where he founde his companye.

ROBERT in grete haste lyght upon his horse and rode to the wode where he had lefte his companye the whiche he founde. The duchesse made grete lamentacyon for her sone Robert, whiche had taken his leue of her, and sayd many tymes to herselfe, "Alas what shall I do, for it is all my faute that Roberte my sone hath done so moche myschefe:" and in the meane whyle that the duchesse made this sorowe and bewayllynge for her sone Robert, in came the duke into the chambre, and as soone as she sawe hym she began to tell hym of his sone Robert, pyteously wepynge; shewynge hym what he had sayd and done. Than the good duke axed whether Robert were disposed to leue his vycyous lyfe, and yf he were sory for his grete offences. "Ye my lorde," sayd she, "he is sore repentaunce:" then began the Duke sore to sygh, and sayd, "Alas it is all in vayne, that Robert thynketh to do, for I fere he shall neuer have power to make restytycyon of the hurtes and harmes the whiche he hathe doone in his lyfe. But I beseche Almyghty God to prolonge his lyfe, and sende hym a respyte that he may amende hys lyfe, and do penaunce for his synnes."

How Robert the Deuyll tolde his company he wolde goo to Rome for to be assoyled of his synnes.

Now is Robert come agayne to his companye which he founde syttynge at dyner, and whan they sawe hym they rose up and dyde hym reuerence; than Robert began to rebuke theym for theyr vycyous lyuynge sayynge thus, "My welbeloued felowes, I requyre you in the reuerence of God, that ye wyll herken, and take hede to this that I shall shewe you. Ye knowe well how that we haue ledde hetherto an ungracyous and moost uycyous lyfe, robbed and pylled chyrches, forced women, rauysshed maydens, robbed and kylled marchauntes. We have robbed and kylled nonnes, holy aunkers,[1] preestes, clerkes, and many other people without nombre haue we murdred and robbed, wherefore we be in the way of endles dampnacyon, except that God haue mercy upon us. Wherefore I requyre you everychone for goddes sake that ye wyll chaunge your opynyon, and leue your abhomynable synnes, and do penaunces therefor, for I wyll goo to Rome to be shryuen and to haue penaunce for my synnes." When Robert thus had sayd, one of the theues rose and sayd to his companye in mockage, "Nowe Syrs, take hede the Foxe wyll be an Aunker for he begynneth to preche. Robert mocketh fast with us, for he is our captayne, and doth more harme alone than all we do: how thynke ye wyll he be longe thus holy." Yet sayd Robert, "Gentyll felawes I praye you for goddes sake leue your con-

_____
[1] *Aunkers,* anchorites.

dycyons, and thynke on our soule, and do penaunce for your
moost fellest stynkynge synnes, and crye upon oure lorde for
mercy and forgeuenes, and he wyl forgeue you." Whan Robert
had sayd thus, than spake to hym one of the theues and sayd,
"I praye you mayster be in pease, for it auayleth not what ye
saye, ye do but spende your tyme in wast, for I nor my companye
wyll not amende our lyfe for no man lyuynge." And all his
companye commended his saynge, and sayden all with one voyce,
"He sayth trewe, for and we sholde dye, we wyll not leue our
olde condycyons and cursed lyfe, but and yf we haue done moche
hurte hetherto, we wyll do moche more hereafter."

How Robert the Deuyll killed all his companye.

ROBERT herynge the faste and wycked opynyon and myscheuous
purpose of his company waxed angry, and thought, yf they remayne
and abyde styll here, they wyl doo grete myschefe and murdre.
But he wente preuely unto the dore and shyte it fast, and gate a
grete staffe and layde one of the theues on the hede that he fell
downe and deed to the erth. And so he serued one after an
other, tyll he hadde kylled them everychone, thenne sayd he thus
to them, "Syrs, I haue rewarded you after your deserte, and by
cause ye have done me good seruyse, I haue gyuen you good
wages, for whosoeuer serueth a good mayster he is lyke to haue
good wages." Whan Robert thus had done he wolde have brente
the hous, but he consydered the great good that was therin,
wherfore he let it stande, shytte faste the dores about and locked
them, and brought awaye the keye with hym to his faders.

How Robert the Deuyll sente the keye of his chefe hous or theuysshe lodgynge to his faders the duke of Normandye, and how he wente to Rome.

THAN whan Robert had done all that said is, he tooke up his
hande and blessed hym, and rode through the forest the neere
waye to Rome. Robert rode that daye so long tyll that the nyght

came on, and was passynge sore and hongred, for he had eten
no mete of all that daye, and fortuned to come rydynge by an
Abbaye, whyche he had many tymes robbed, and the abbote was
his kynnessman. And Robert rode in to this abbaye and sayd
neuer a worde, but whan the monkes se Robert come they were
aferde, and ranne awaye, saynge one to another, "Here cometh
the ungracyous Robert, the Deuyll hath brought him hether."
Whan Robert herde this, and se them all renne awaye frome him,
than his sorrowe begun to renewe, and sayd in himself, in sore
syghynge and sorowfull herte : "I may well hate my cursed lyfe,
for euery man fleeth from me, and I haue spent my tyme un-
gracyously, and in euyll and cursed werkes." And there withall
he rode streyght in the chyrche dore and alyghte doun from his
horse, deuoutely sayinge his prayers to God in this wyse : "O
Lord Jhesu I moost synfull wretche and vessell of all stynkynge
synnes, I praye the that thou wylte haue mercy on me and
.preserue and kepe me from all daungers and peryll." And then
he wente and spoke to the abbotte and monkes so swetely and so
peteously and amyably that they began to go towarde hym, to
whom Roberte sayd peteously, wepynge knelynge on his knees :
"My lorde I knowledge myself that I haue greuously offended
you, and haue done grete harme and injurye unto your abbay.
Wherfore I requyre and praye you, in all the honoure of Crystes
passyon, of forgyuenesse." And than he spake to the Abbote
in thys wyse, "My Lorde abbott I praye you hertely haue me
recomaunded to my lorde my fader the duke of Normandye, and
delyuer hym this keye of the chefe hous where I haue dwelled
with my companye, the whiche I haue all slayne to thentent that
they sholde do no more harme. And in the hous lyeth all the
goodes and tresoure that I haue stolen from you and other men,
wherfore I am ryght sory, and I beseeche you of forgyuenesse,
and I pray you that this good may be rendred agene unto such
people as they haue belongynge to before." Robert abode that
nyght in the abbay, but in the mornynge erly he wente thens and
left behinde hym his horse and his swerde where withall he had
doone grete myschefe. And so he went alone towards Rome.

And on the same daye rode the Abbote to the Duke of Normandye, and gaue hym the keye that Robert had delyuered hym, and told the duke how he was gone to Rome. Than the duke gaue all the poor people theyr goodes agen that they lost befor, as ferre as it coude be founde in the hous. We wyll sease of the Duke and the Abbott, and speke of Robert whiche goth to Rome warde alone, with grete devocyon.

How Robert came to Rome for remyssyon of his synnes.

ROBERT went so longe ouer hylles and dales alone, tyll at last with grete payne and pouerte he came to Rome in to the cyte, upon a shere Thursdaye at nyght, and on the Frydaye after, the pope hymselfe sayd the deuyne seruyce, as the custom was in saint Peter's chyrche. And Robert presed fast to have comen to the pope, but the pope's seruantes se that Robert presed so sore to come to the pope, they smote hym, and bad hym goo back. But the more they smote hym, the more he presed and thronge to gette nygh the pope, and so at last he gate to hym, and fell doune on his knees at the feet of the pope, cryenge with a loud voyce, saynge thus: "O! holy fader, haue mercy on me!" and thus laye Robert cryenge longe, whyle the people that were by the pope were angry that Robert made suche a noyse, and wolde haue dryuen hym thens, but the pope seynge Robert's grete desyre, had pyte upon hym, and sayd to the people, " Late hym alone, for in all that I can se he hath grete deuocyon." Wherefore the pope commaunded them all to holde their pease, that he myght the better here and understande Robert. Then sayd Robert to the pope in this manner: "O! holy fader, I am the moost and the greteste syner of all the worlde!" The pope toke Robert up by the hande, and sayde to hym : " Good frende, what is your desyre, and what eleth you to make all this noyse?" Then sayd Robert: " O! holy fader, I beseche you to here my confessyon, for I be not by you assoyled, I am dampned worlde withouten ende, for it is meruayle that the deuyll bere me not awaye body and soule, seynge the foule innumerable synne that I am laden and bounden withall more than any man lyuynge. And in soo moche that ye are he that gyueth helpe and comforte to them that haue nede, therefore I humbly beseche you for the passyon of our Lorde Jhesu Cryst to here and purge me of my abhomynable synnes, wherby I am deceued and departed from al the joyes of heuen, and I am wors than a Jewe." The pope herynge this, demed and thought in hymselfe whether this were Robert the Deuyll, and axed hym, "Sone, be ye Robert the whiche I haue herde so moche spekynge of, the whiche is worst of all men." Then Robert answered and sayd, "Ye." Than the pope sayd : "I will assoyle you, but I conjure you in the name of God that ye do no man harme." The pope and all that were aboute hym were aferde to loke upon Robert. Robert fell on his knees with great deuocyon and repentaunce of hys synnes, saynge, "Holy fader, nay as longe as I lyue I promyse God and his blessed moder I will neuer hurte Crysten creature." Than incontynent the pope toke Robert aparte, and herde his confessyon, to whome Robert shrowe him deuoutly, shewynge how his moder had gyuen hym to the deuyll in his concepcyon, whereof the pope was sore aferde.

How the pope sente Robert thre myle without Rome to an holy heremyte.

THE pope this herynge was gretly abasshed, and blessyd him, and sayd to Robert : "My dere sone, ye muste goo thre myle without the towne, and there ye shall fynde an heremyte whiche is my goostly fader, and to hym ye shall confesse you, and say that I sende you to hym, and he shall asoyle you." Robert answered the pope : "I wyll go with a good wyll ;" and toke his leue of the pope saynge, "God gyue me grace to do that may be to the helth of my soule." Soo that nyght Robert abode in Rome, for it was late, and in the mornynge erly Robert went out of Rome towarde the place where he sholde fynde the heremyte ; and so he wente so longe over hylles and dales with grete desyre to be shryuen of his synnes, and at last he came where the heremyte dwelled, whereof he was glad, and came to the heremyte and told hym how the pope had sent hym theder to be confessed of hym. Than the heremyte sayd he was hertly welcome; and within a whyle Robert began to confesse and shewe his synne, and first he shewed the heremyte how his moder had gyuen hym to the deuyll in his concepcyon; and how he smote the chyldren in his youth or he coude goo alone; and how he kylled his scole master; and how many knyghtes he kylled at the iustynge whan his fader made hym knyght; and he rode thorowe his fader's land, robbynge and stelynge, forsynge of women, rauysynge of maydens; and how he thrast out the eyen of his fader's men in despyte of hym; and how he had kylled vii heremytes; and shortly showed hym all the offences that euer he dyde, sethen the houre of hys byrth tyll that tyme, whereof the heremyte had maruayle, but he was glad that Robert was repentaunt for hys synnes. Whan Robert had thus confessed hym, the heremyte sayd to hym: "Sone, thys nyght ye shall abyde here, and to morowe I shall gyue good councell of that ye haue to do." Robert that was so curst and myscheuous, ferful cruel, and proude as a lyon, is now as gentyll and curteys, and swete of wordes, and wyse in his dedes, as euer was ony duke or prynce lyuynge. Then Robert was so wery and ouercome with goynge, that he coude nother ete nor drynke, but went aparte and sayd his prayers to Almighty God, prayenge hym thrughe his endeles mercy, that he wolde kepe hym from the fendes temptacyon and deceyte. The heremyte made Robert to lye that nyght in a lytell chapell that stode nye his celle, and the heremyte prayed all the nyght to our lorde for Robert, which sawe that he had grete repentaunce for his synnes, and thus prayenge the heremyte fell a sleep.

How God sent an aungell to the heremyte to shewe him the penaunce
that he sholde gyue to Robert for his synnes.

THE heremyte being thus a slepe, ther cam to hym an aungell, saynge to hym in this wyse: "Holy fader, here and take hede of the message that God commaundeth the; yf that Robert wyll

be shryven of his synnes, he must kepe and counterfete the wayes
of a fole, and be as he were dombe; and he may ete no maner
of mete, but that he can take it from the dogges; and in this
wyse, without spekynge, and counterfetynge the fole, and no thynge
etynge but what he can take from the dogges, must he be tyll
tyme that it please God to shewe·hym that his synne be forgyuen." And with this vycyon the heremyte awoke out of his
slepe, and began to remembre hymselfe of this that sayd is, and
thanked our Lorde of his message done to hym. And whan the
day began to apere, the heremyte called Robert unto hym, with
fare and comfortable wordes saynge to him, "My frende, come
hether to me;" and incontynent Robert came to hym with grete
deuocyon, hym confessynge. And whan Robert had shryuen
him, the heremyte sayd thus unto hym: "Sone, I thought and
aduysed me of the penance that ye shall haue, to get remyssyon
of your synnes, in whiche ye gretly offended ayenst God, that is
to wete ye must counterfayte and playe the fole; and ye may ete
no mete but that ye can take it from the dogges whan men gyue
them ought; also you must kepe you dombe without speche, and
lye among dogges, for thus hath God thys nyght commaunded
me by a aungell to gyue you this for your penaunce, and ye may
offende no man the whyle your penaunce be a doynge; and this
penaunce ye must doo for your synnes in maner and forme as I
haue tolde you, tyll suche tyme as it shall please your Lorde to
sende you worde that your synnes be forgyuen." Robert beynge
mery and glad, thankynge our Lorde that he was assoyled of his
synnes, and had therfor so lyght penaunce as hym thought that
it was. Nowe taketh Robert leve of the heremyte, and goth to
do his sharpe penaunce, whiche he helde but lyghte, remembrynge
his grete abhomynable stynkynge synnes that he hath done all
the dayes of his lyfe. This was a fayre myracle, for he that
was so vycyous and so furyous a rebell, and proude a synner,
is now so full of uertues and fayre condycyons and tame as
a lambe.

*How Robert the Deuyll toke leve of the heremyte, and went agayne
to Rome to do his penaunce that the heremyte had gyuen him.*

ROBERT had taken leue of the heremyte, and is gone towarde
Rome, there for to do his penaunce. And whan he came into
the cyte he began to lepe and renne about the stretes, makynge
hymselfe as he had ben a fole. And the chyldren in the stretes se
Robert renne in this wyse, and they after hym shoutynge and
cryenge and castynge with myre and derte, and all suche fylth as
they founde in the stretes, and the burgeyses of the cyte laye in
theyr wyndowes and laughed and mocketh with Robert. Than
whan Robert had thus played the fole in Rome a certayne season,
he came on a tyme to themperour's courte and se the gate dyde
stande open and came streyght into the hall, and there jetted up
and downe from the one syde to the other; sometyme he went
faste and sometyme softely, and than he hopped and ran, and other
whyle stode styll, but he stode not longe in one place. The
emperour seynge Robert thus playenge the fole, he sayd to one
of his seruantes, se yonder is a fayre fauoured yonge man, me
thynke he is out of his mynde, the whiche is grete domage, for
he is fayre and a well made man, go and gyue hym mete. This
emperour's seruaunte dyde as he was commaunded, and called
Robert to hym and wolde haue gyuen hym some mete, but Robert
nolde ete nor drynke. And whyle Robert sate thus at the table,
the emperour sawe one of his houndes whiche was bytten with
an other dogge, wherefore, themperour cast hym a bone, and the
dogge caught the bone and began to gnawe there on, and Robert
seynge that lept from the table and toke it from hym, but the
dogge fought with Roberte for the bone, and helde faste the one
ende, and Robert the other ende, but Robert se it would be no
better, but set him downe on the grounde, and gnewe on the one
ende of the bone and the dogge on the other. Themperour and
they that loked there on laughed at Robert and the dogge, but.
Robert dyde so moche that he gate the bone alone, and laye and
gnewe it for he was sore enhongred. Themperour seynge that

Robert was so sore enhongred, he caste to an other dogge an hole lofe, but Robert toke it from hym and brake an two peces and gaue the dogge half, for bycause he gate it for the dogges sake. Themperour seynge this lough there at and sayd to his seruauntes ; "We haue here nowe the moste foolysshe fole, and the verayst nedy that euer I sawe, for he taketh the dogges mete from them, and eteth it himself; ther by a man may perfytely knowe that he is a natural fole." All that were in the hall gaue the dogges as moche mete as they might ete, to thentent that Robert myght fyll his belye with them, and whan he had fylled his belly, whyle he rose up, and walked up and downe in the hall with a staffe in his hande, smytynge upon stoles and benches lyke as and yf he had ben a very innocent fole. And thus walkynge he loked on euery syde, and sawe a dore where men wente in to a fayre gardyne, in the whiche gardyne there stode a fayre fontayne or well, and theder went Robert to drynke, for he was euyll a thurst. And whan nyght came on, Robert folowed the forsayd dogge where soo euer he wente, the whiche was accustomed to lye euery nyght under a steyre, and there he went and layde him downe; and Robert followed hym under the steyre and layde hym downe by the dogge. Themperour seynge this, had compassyon on Robert and commaunded that men sholde bere hym a bedde, that he myghte lye there upon to slepe; anone two seruantes brought Robert a bedde to slepe there on, but he poynted to bere it awaye ayene, for he had leuer to lye upon the floure and colde erth, than upon a softe bedde. Whereof themperour had grete meruayle, and commaunded that men sholde bere hym clene strawe, whiche they dyde. Than Robert whiche was feynte and wery of goynge, layde him downe to slepe on the strawe. Now haue this in your myndes, ye proude hertes and synners, thynke on Roberts grete penaunce and wylfull pouerte, and how he so grete a gentylman borne, forsoke his fader and his moder, and all his frendes, and his countree and lande, and all his dylycate metes and drynkes, and gaye raymentes and wordely pleasure, with all that of suche a state aperteyneth ; how wyllyngly he hathe all forsaken for the saluacyon of his soule; and is gone out of a duke's bedde to a dogges canell, and with dogges he ete and dranke and slepte, and rose whan they rose.   And in this penaunce lyued Robert vii yeres or there aboute, and the dogge that he communly slept withall perceyued that he foure the better, and had more mete for Robert's sake, than he was wonte to haue before, and that no man dyde bete hym, for his sake; wherfore he began to loue Robert passynge well, in so moche men myghte as soone haue kylled hym as dryuen hym from Robert.

How Robert threwe downe a bryde on a foule dongehyll, and how he put a lyuynge catte in an hole sethynge potte with podred befe.

It befel upon a tyme there was a bryde sholde goo to chyrche to be wedded, whiche was gayly apparelled, as unto a bryde apperteyned.   Robert seynge this bryde thus gayly arayed, toke her by the hande, and ledde her thorough a passynge foule donge hyll, and there made her fall and fouled her gaye araye, and than he ranne lyghtly awaye, shoutynge and laughynge, and ranne unto the brydes kytchen where her dyner was appereyled and caughte a lyuynge catte and caste her in the potte of pouldred befe.   The whiche incontynente was tolde to themperoure, whereat he and all his lordes laughed, and had grete game thereat; and they loued Robert passynge well, for he made moche myrth without harme.

How the Seneschall had gadred a grete armye of men of warre of Saresyns, and layde syege to Rome, by cause the emperoure wolde not gyue hym his doughter in maryage.

In the meane season whyle Robert was thus in Rome doynge his penaunce as a forsayd, which dured seuen yeres or there about in the emperoure's courte, the whiche emperour had a fayre doughter, but she was borne domb and neuer spoke. And the emperours senesshal dyuerse tymes had desyred his doughter in maryage of the emperoure, but he wolde neuer graunte hym her.   Wherfore the senesshall was gretly moued and angry ther with themperoure, for he thoughte he myght haue wonne of hym his empyre by force and myght; in soo moche the seneschall came upon a tyme with a grete hoost of Sarasyns, and layde syege to the cyte of Rome, wherof the emperour had grete maruayle and wondred. Than the emperour gadred and assembled all the lordes barons askinge of them counsell, saynge thus, "My lordes, gyue me good counseyl that we may withstande this Hethen dogges whiche haue layde syege here to our cyte; wherefore I take grete thought, for they kepe all my lande under theyr subieccyon and they wyll brynge us to confusyon yf that God out of his endles mercy helpe us not. Wherfore I praye you euerychone to go fyght with them with all our power and myght, and dryue them awaye." Than answered the lordes and knyghts all with one assent, saynge, "Souerayne lorde your counseyl is good and wyse, wherefore we be all ready to goo with you and gyue them batayle and defende our ryght bothe lande and cyte." The emperour thanked them of this answere and was glad therof, and made proclamacyon throughout all his landes and cytees that eury man old and younge that were able to bere armes sholde make them redy to fyght ayenst theyr moost cruell enmyes the Sarasyns which were come into his lande. And contynent whan this proclamation was done amonge the comyns euery man was wyllynge and redy to go with themperour to fyght and defende theyr ryght, and so they went forth in a fayre ordynaunce with themperour to fyght upon theyr mortall enmyes the Hethen dogges. And for all that themperour had moche mo people than the seneschall, yet the seneshall had wonne the felde, hadde not God of his grace sente theder Robert to resyste and helpe the Romaynes in theyr grete necessyte.

How our Sauyour Jhesu hauynge compassyon on the crysten blode, sent Robert by an aungell a whyte horse and harneys, commaundynge hym to go rescue and helpe the Romayns ayenst the Ethen dogges the Sarasyns.

THE emperour and the Romayns went to the batayle as sayd is ayenst the Sarasyns, and Robert was at home, where he

N

was accostomed to walke in the gardyne to a fountayne or well to drynke, and this was on the same daye that themperour with his hoste sholde gyue batayle ayenst the Sarasyns : than came there a uoyce out of Heuen sente from our Lorde, saynge in this maner : " Robert, God commaundeth you, by me, that ye incontynent arme you with this harneys, and lyght upon this horse that God hath sente you, and ryde in all the hast possyble and rescue the emperour and his people." Robert herynge the commaundement of God, was abasshed in his mynde, and durst not do ayenst goddes commaundement, but in continent he armed hym and lepte on the hors without tarynge and rode his waye. The emperour's doughter whiche I tolde you of before, stode at a wyndowe and sawe Robert thus armed on horsbacke, than if she coude haue spoken she wolde haue tolde it, but she coude not speke for she was dombe, but she remembred and bare it surely in her mynde. Robert thus horst and harnayst, rode into themperours hoost whiche he sawe sore ouer pressed with theyr enmyes the Turkes, in so moche, that had not God and Robert rescued them, the crysten had ben all slayne. But whan Robert was come into the hoost he put him in the moost prese of the Turkes and faughte and layde on eche syde on these cursed houndes ; there a man myght haue sene armes, legges, hedes tomble on the grounde, both horse and man that neuer rose after : it was a worlde to se the murdre that Robert dyde amonge the dampned dogges the Sarasyns. So to make shorte tale, Robert dyde so moche, that the Sarasyns were constraynced to flye awaye and themperour helde the felde and had the vyctorye of them.

How Robert turned agayne to the forsayd fountayne, and there un-armed hym, whan he had thus subdued and vaynquysshed the Sarasyns and put them to flyght.

Now hath the emperour gotten the felde and the honoure, thanked be God, and Robert is torned agayne to the sayd fountayne, and there unarmed hym and layde the harneys on the hors, whiche incontynent was vanyshed awaye that no man coude knowe nor perceyue where he become; and Robert bode styll standynge by the fountayne. Themperour's doughter seynge this had grete meruayll of this, and wolde haue told it forth but she was dombe and coude no speke. Robert had a race [1] in his face, whiche he gote in the batayll, but he was none otherwyse hurte; the emperour was glad, and thanked God of his victory ayenst the false dogges the Sarasyns; and thus beynge mery, he came home to his palays. And whan they were all set to dyner, Robert presented hymselfe before themperour as he was wonte to do, playnge the fole, and makynge him dombe as afore rehersed is. The emperour reioysed in hymselfe whan he se Robert, for he loued hym well; and whan he perceyued Robert's hurte in his face, and thought that some of his seruauntes had hurte hym whyle he was out, wherfore he was angry, and said : " Here in this court be some enuyous men, for whyle we haue ben out at batayle, they haue beten and hurte this poore innocent creature in his face, which is grete synne, for though he be a fole he dooth no man harme." So themperour commaunded them all upon a grete payne that no man sholde do hym harme, yf they dyde they sholde be punysshed, that all other sholde be ware by them. Than the emperoure began to axe his knyghtes yf there were any of them that coude telle of the knyght with the whyte hors that came preuely in to the felde, and so valyauntely rescued them. Themperour's doughter this herynge poynted themperour her fader that it was Robert ; but the emperour understode not what his doughter mente when she poynted, for she could not speke. Wherfore he called her maystres to hym, and axed her what his doughter mente by her poyntynge, and her maystres answered and sayd : " Your doughter menes by her poyntynge that this day ye haue goten the batayll and vyctorye thrughe the helpe of your fole Robert, and the race that is in his face he hath gotten it in the batayll." The emperour understandynge the mynde and intent of his doughter, he was angry and sayd to her maystres : " Ye sholde teche and lerne my doughter wysdome, and no folye ne

---

[1] *Race*, raze, graze.

peuysnesse wherewithall I am myscontent." The doughter seynge
that her fader was angry, pointed no more, notwithstandynge she
wyst well that it was trewe that she poynted and mente, for in as
moche as she had sene the aungell bring hym the hors and
harneys.   This remayned in this wyse a certayne season, and after
that the Sarasyns were put to flyght by the Romaynes, as sayd is,
yet came the senesshall agayne with moche more company, and
layde syege to Rome.   And the Romaynes sholde haue lost the
felde ayen, had not the knyghte on the whyte horse bene, to whome
God sent hors and harnays as he had done before.   To make
shorte tale, this knyght dyde so moche that the Sarasyns were put
to flyght, and the Romaynes won the felde and vyctorye as they
dyde before.   There were some of the emperour's meyny layde
wayte where this knyghte became, but as soon as the batayle was
done he was gone no man coude tell were he was become, saue
only the emperour's doughter which see hym at the fountayne
agayne unarmynge hym.

How Robert gatte the thyrde batalye as he dyde before which she
kepte secrete.

IN a short tyme after this the senesshall tourned agayne with a
moche greter power than he had before, and layde syege to Rome.
And when the emperour rode to the batayle, he commaunded his
knyghtes and barones to take good hede fro whens that knyght
came with the whyte horse, and what he was and where he
became, for he had grete desyre to knowe what he was.   The
knyghtes answered that it sholde be done.   The day came that
they must ryde forth to the batayle, and sertayne of the best
knyghtes rode pryuely into a wood that stode a lytell there besyde,
and there they wayted whiche waye the knyghte on the whyte
horse should come to the batayle ; but they loste theyr laboure,
for they coude not tell whens he come.   But when they sawe
hym in the batayle, they rode towarde hym to helpe hym and
receyue hym.   This same batayle was sore foughten on both
partyes, but the Sarasyns lost there courage, for Robert layde on

soo grete and myghty strokes, that no man myght stande under
his hande; so that in conclusyon Robert dyde so moche and so
valyantly, that the Sarasyns were put to the discomfyture wherof
themperour was gretly enioyed; the senesshall with the Sarasyns
were passynge angry and sore moued therewith all.

*How one of the Emperour's knyghtes hurte Robert in his thyghe
with a spere.*

THAN when this batayle was done, euery man rode home, and
Robert wolde haue tourned agayne to the fountayne to unarme
hym as he was was wonte to do before, but the forsayd knyghtes
were torned agayne to the wood, to awayte for the knyght with
the whyte hors; and whan they sawe hym come, they rode all at
ones out of the wood, and cryed with a loud voyce saynge unto
hym: "O noble knyght, tary and speke with us, who that ye be,
and whens and out of what lande ye come, to the entent that we
may shewe it to the emperour, whiche specyally he desyreth for to
knowe." Robert this herynge was sore ashamed, and smote his
white hors with his sporres, flyngynge ouer hylles and ouer valleyes,
for bycause he wolde not be knowen   But there followed hym a
bolde knyght, well horsed, with a spere, wenynge to haue kylled
his whyte horse, but he myste, and smote Robert in the thyghe
with his spere, and the spere heed brake of and stack styll in his
thyghe, but yet for all this he coude gete no knowlege of the
knyght with the whyte horse, for he rode from them all euerychone,
whereof they were passynge sory.   Robert rode so sore, tyll at the
laste he came unto the fountayne and unarmed hym, and layde
the harnays on the horse as he had done before, whiche in contynente was vanysshed awaye and gone; and he drew out the
spere hed out of his thyghe, and hyd it bytwene two grete stones
by the fountayne; than he layde grece and mosse upon his
wounde, for he durst let no man loke therto, for fere he sholde
haue ben knowen.   And all this sawe and marked the emperour's
doughter; for bycause she se that Robert was a fayre and well
fauoured yonge knyght, she began to cast her loue unto hym.

And whan Robert hadde dressed his wounde, he came in to the halle, to gete hym some mete, and he halted as lytell as he coude, and kept it secretly, that almoost no man coude perceyue it, and suffred moore payne a thousande tymes than it semeth by hym. Shortly after this, came home the knyght that had hurte Robert, and began to recounte to themperour how the knyght with the whyte horse had outryden hym, and how he had hurte hym sore ayenst his wyll, and sayd to the emperour : " I beseche you, my lorde emperour, here what I shall tell you, and in what maner ye shall knowe who is he that hath holpen you ; it is best ye make a proclamacyon and publyshe thrugheout your empyre, and yf there be ony knyght in whyte harnays and a whyte horse that he be brought to your presence, and that he brynge with hym the spere-heed where withall he was hurte in his thyghe, shewynge the wounde, and that ye gyve hym youre doughter to wyfe, and halfe youre empyre with her." Themperour this herynge, was of his counseyll very gladde, and incontynent all haste proclamed and publysshed thrugheout all the empyre, and thought that the knyght had gyuen hym good counseyll.

How the Senesschall thruste a spere-heed in to his thyghe, wenynge to have begyled the Emperour, and to haue wonne his doughter thereby.

IT befell in shorte tyme after, that the senesshall had knowlege and understandynge of the emperour's proclamation, and how he myght wynne themperour's doughter, whiche he had many tymes bene about. He dyde grete dylygence, and caused to be sought and gotten a whyte horse and white harnays, and thryste a spere heed in his thyghe, wenynge therby to deceyue themperour, and to gete his doughter to wyfe. And whan this was done he commanded all his men to arme them, and ryde wyth hym to the emperour. And he rode so sore tyll he came to Rome with great royalte and solace, and without any taryenge he rode streyght to the emperour, saynge to hym in this wyse : " My lorde I am he that you so valyauntly receyued : thre tymes I haue caused you to haue honoure and victorye ayenst the cursed Sarasyns." Themperour thynkynge upon no treason nor deceyte, sayd : "Ye be a valyaunt and a wyse knyght; but I had went the contrarye, for we haue taken you for a vylayne and a forsworne knyght." The senesshall was very angry and sore moued here withall, and answered the emperoure shortly and angerly ! " My lorde emperour, meruayll you nothynge here of, for I am not such a cowarde as ye wene that I be : " and thus saynge he toke out the spere-heed and shewed it the emperour, and uncouered the wounde the whiche he had made hymselfe in hys thyghe. The knyghte stode by whiche that hurt Robert before, and began to compasse in his mynde, for he se well that it was not the heed of the spere, but he durst saye nothynge for fere, lest the senesshall wolde haue kylled hym. We wyll leue nowe of the senesshall, and speke of Robert, which is among dogges, sore wounded, as ye have herde before.

How God sent an aungell to the heremyte that he sholde goo to Rome and seke Robert, for he had full doone his penaunce.

THE heremyte whiche ye haue herde of before, that shroue and sette Robert his penaunce, laye on a nyght in his selle and slepte, and thus slepynge there cam to hym a voyce, and bad hym lyghtly aryse and goo to Rome, to the place where Robert was doynge his penaunce ; and the aungell tolde the heremyte all the doynges of Robert, shewynge how that his penaunce was fully done, and that God hadde forgyuen hym his synnes, whereof the heremyte was uery gladde, and in the mornyng erly he arose and wente to Rome warde, and in lyke wyse in the same mornynge the senesshall rose be tyme and went to Rome to the emperoure to desyre and haue his doughter accordynge to the publycacyon and crye, to the whiche the emperoure consented her to hym without any long aduysement. But whan the doughter understode that she was gyuen to the senesshall she raylled and raged as though she hadde ben wood and madde ; she tare her hare from her heed, and all to tare her clothes, but it myght nothynge

auayle her, for she was constrayned, and must be arayed lyke a
bryde, and an emperour's doughter which shold be maryed, and
the emperour ladde her by the hande hymselfe to the chyrche
royally accompanyed with lordes and ladyes and gentylwomen,
but the doughter made the gretest sorowe of the worlde in so
moche that no man coude content her mynde.

*How the Emperour's doughter thrughe the grace of God began for to
speke the fyrste worde that ever she spake in her lyfe.*

THAN as the emperour with all his estate was come in to the
chyrche, the emperour's doughter whiche was dumbe, sholde
marye the senesshall; there dyde our lorde a fayre myracle, for
the loue of the holy man Robert, to the entente he sholde be
exalted, whome euery body helde fer a fole and with hym
mocked. Whan the preest sholde begyn the seruyce, and to
marye the senesshall and this yonge mayde togyder, the
doughter thrughe the grace of God began to speke to the emperoure her fader in this wyse: "Fader I holde you not wyse,
but fer ouer sene in that ye byleue that this proude folysshe
traytoure telleth you, for all that he telleth you is lyes; but here
in this towne is a holy and deuoute persone, for whose sake God
hath gyuen me my speche, wherfore I loue hym in my herte, for
I haue alwaye sene and marked his valyance and holynes, but
noo man wolde byleue me what poyntynge or sygnes that I
made." Thenne the emperoure this herynge, was almoost oute
of his mynde for joye, whan he herde his doughter thus speke,
the whiche neuer spake before, wherby he knewe well ynough
that the senesshall hadde betrayed and deceyued hym. The
senesshall this herynge, was wode angry and foule ashamed, and
lyghten upon his horse and rode awaye and all his companye.
The pope beyng presente axed the mayden who the man was
that she spoke of. Than the mayde ladde the pope and the emperour her fader to the fountayne where Robert was wonte to
arme and unarme hym, and there she toke out the spere heed
from bytwene the two stones where that Robert had hydde it,

and than she caused the spere to be brought forth, whereof the heed was broken, whiche was lyghtely brought to her, and that heed and the spere joyned togyder in one as cloes as thoughe they hadde not be broken. Than sayd the mayd to the pope, "We have hadde thre tymes vyctorye by his noble valyaunce ayenst the myscredaunte Sarasyns, for I haue thre tymes sene his horse and harnays wherwith he hath thre tymes armed and unarmed hym, but I can not tell who broughte hym horse and harnays, nor unto whom he delyuered it, but I knowe well that whan he hadde this done he layde hymselfe downe by the dogges." And the mayden sayd unto the emperoure her fader in this wyse, "This is he that hathe saued youre landes and youre honoure, and gate you vyctorye of the Hethen houndes the Sarasyns, wherfore ye ought of deute to rewarde hym, and yf it please you we wyll go all to hym and speke with hym." Than wente they for the fole, the emperour and the doughter with all the lordes and ladyes unto Robert, whome they founde lyenge among dogges, they folowed hym and dyde hym reuerence, but Robert answered them not.

How the heremyte found Robert, and commaunded hym to speke, saynge to hym, that his penaunce was full done and his synnes forgyuen.

THE emperour spake to Robert and said, "I praye you, swete frende, come to me and shewe me your thyghe I wyll nedes se." Whan Robert herde themperour say these wordes he wyst well ynoughe wherfore he was comen to hym, but he lete hym as thoughe he had not understonden hym. And Robert dyde many madde conceytes to make the pope and themperour to laughe and forgete that they spoke of. But the pope spake to Robert, and coniured hym in the name of God that on the crosse dyed for our redempcyon, that yf it be Goddes wyll that thou haste spoken that thou speke now unto us. And than Robert rose up lyke a fole and gaue the pope his blessynge. And here withall Robert loked be-hynde hym and saw the heremyte that set him his penaunce, and as soon as the heremyte se Robert whiche he had long sought, he cryed to hym with a loude voyce that every man myght here hym that were there : " My frende herken unto me, I knowe well that ye be Robert that men calle the Deuyll, but now ye be in grace and conceyte with Almyghty God, and for that foule and hydeous name ye shall haue a fayre name, and be called the Seruante of God. Ye be he that hath saued this lande from the Sarasyns, wherfore I praye you that ye serue and worshyp God as ye haue done hyderto, for oure Lorde sendeth me now to you commaundynge you to speke, and no more to counterfeyte the fole ; for it is Goddes wyll and commaundement, for he hath for-gyuen you all your synnes, for by caus ye haue made satysfacyon and full done your penaunce." Whan Robert herde this he fell lyghtely on his knees and lyfte up his handes towarde Heuen saygne thus, " I gyue laude and thankes to God, creator of Heuen and erthe, that it hath pleased the to forgyue me myne abhomynable and grete synnes thrughe so lytell and lyght penaunce that I haue done : " therefore, whan the pope, the emperour and the doughter, and all that were there present herde Robert speke thus swetely, they were all heerof gretely enioyed and had grete meruayll of. Themperoure seynge his noble valyaunce vertue and curtesye that in hym was and wolde haue gyuen hym his doughter to wyfe, but the heremyte wolde not it sholde be so ; wherfore euery man departed and wente home.

How Robert tourned agayne to Rome for to marye the Emperour's doughter by the commaundement and wyll of God.

Now the storye telleth as after that Robert had remyssyon of his synnes and was gone towarde his countre, than out of Rome God commaunded hym that he sholde tourne agayne to Rome and marye the emperour's doughter, which loued hym passyngly well, and he sholde haue by her a sone wherby the Crysten beleue sholde be encreased and fortefyed and defended. Robert at the commaundement of God turned agayne a Rome and maryed themperour's doughter with grete tryumphe and solace, for themperour and all the Romayns were therof very glad. This brydale was royally kepte and euery man that se Robert loued hym aboue all other; and the people sayd one to another, that they were gretely beholdynge to Robert, that he had redemed them from theyr mortall enmyes the Sarasyns. This feest was grete and notable and dured xiiij dayes, and whan the feest and brydale was done Robert wolde departe with his lady into Normandye to vysyte his fader and mother, and toke leue of themperour whiche gaue hym many royall and grete gyftes, as golde and siluer and precyous stones of diuerse colours. Also themperour gaue hym knyghtes and squyers to ryde and conduyte him in to his countree.

How Robert and his lady came to Rowane in Normandye with grete honour and worship.

ROBERT and his lady rode soo ferre they came into Normandye into the noble cyte of Rowane with grete myrth and solace, where they were receyued with grete tryumphe; for the comyntees of the countree were sorye and in grete heuyness that theyr duke Robert's fader was dyseased, for bycause that he was a wyse and a renomed prynce. A lytell besyde dwelled a cursed knyght, whiche hadde done the duchesse grete wronge and suppressed many knyghtes after her husbondes dysease. But whan Robert was come, euery man dradde hym and dyde hym grete reuerence and worshypp. Than some sayd we wende he had ben deed, and all the lordes and burgeys of Rowane, gadred them togyder and with grete honoure and reuerence they receyued Robert and helde hym as theyr lorde and souerayne. But whan they hadde receyued hym honourably, they shewed hym of this before sayd knyght; he hadde many tymes suppressed, and done wronge to his moder, sythen the deth of his fader. Than whan Robert herde and understode this, he sente lyghtely men of armes to take the sayd knyght, the whiche dyde so moche that they toke hym and brought hym to Robert whiche made hym to be hanged, wherfore the duches was ryght glad. But she was moche more gladder that Robert her sone was come home, for she wende he hadde ben deed. And whan Robert and his moder were thus togyder, he recounted unto her how the emperour had gyuen hym his doughter in maryage, and how he had done his penaunce. The duchesse herynge her sones wordes, she began to wepe very sore, for bycause he had suffred so grete pouerte and penaunce thrughe his defaute.

How the Emperour sent a messanger unto the Duke Robert, that he
sholde come and rescue hym ayenst the Senesshall.

In the meane season, whyles Robert was thus at Rowane with his moder and his lady in grete joye and solace, there came a messanger fro the emperour unto Robert whiche dyde hym reuerence, and saynge thus unto hym : "My lorde duke, the emperour hathe sente me hyther to you, and he prayeth you for to come and rescue hym ayenst the false traytoure the senesshall with the Sarasyns, which haue layde syege to Rome." Whan Robert herde these wordes, he was sorye in his mynde for themperour, and shortly assembled as many men of armes as he coulde get in his lande of Normandye, and forth withall rode with them towarde Rome, to helpe and socoure the emperour. But before he coude come thyder the false traytour the senesshall had slayne the emperour, which was grete pyte. But Robert wente streyght into Rome, and lyghtly with all his power and myght went ayenst the senesshall. And whan Robert aspyed the false traytoure, he descryed hym, saynge thus : "Abyde, thou false traytour, now thou shalte neuer escape my handes yf thou abyde me in the felde, for thou art now nygh thy lyve's ende. Thou dydest putte ones a spere-heed in thy thygh for to haue deceyued the Romayns, defende now thy lyue ayenst me, for thou shalte neuer escape myn handes, and thou hast also slayne my lorde themperoure, wherefore thou shalt be well rewarded after that thou hast deserued." And with these wordes Robert, with grete desyre and myghty courage, rode unto the senesshall and gaue hym suche stroke on the helmette, that he cloue helmet and heed unto the teeth, and in contynente the traytour fell downe deed unto the erth. And Robert made hym to be brought in to Rome, to the entente that he sholde there be slayne to reuenge the Romayns, the whiche was done in the presence of all the people that were in Rome; and in this wyse fenysshed that traytour the senesshall his lyfe, and had a shameful death, wherby men may make and take hede that it is grete folye to coveyte or desyre thynges passynge theyr degre; for and the senesshall had not desyred the emperoure's doughter, the whiche passed and exceeded ferre aboue his degree, he had not dyed this shameful deth, but myght haue lyued and the emperour also, and haue dyed good frendes.

How that the Duke Robert tourned agayne to Rowayne after he had made the Senesshall to be slayne.

ROBERT the duke defended the cyte from theyr enemyes, and than he retourned agayne with all his companye unto Rowane to his wyfe, whiche was passynge sorrowfull and pensyfe. But whan she herde that the traytour the senesshall had slayne her fader, she was almoost out of her mynde; but Robert's moder comforted her in the best maner that she coude or myght. And for to make shortely an ende of our mater, and so to fenysshe this boke we wyll lette passe to wryte of the grete dole and sorowe of the yonge duchesse, and speke of the young duke Robert, whiche in his youth was about to all myschefe and vyce, and all ungracyousnes, without ony measure or reason, for he was a greter devourer, and a more vengeable, than any lyon, nothynge sparynge, nor on no man hauying mercy nor pyte. And after this he lyued xii yere in grete penaunce, like a wylde man, without ony speche, and lyke a dumbe beest etynge and drynkynge with dogges, and there after was he exalted and honoured of them whiche before dyde holde hym for a fole or an innocente, and mocked with hym. This Robert lyued longe in vertue and honoure with that noble ladye his wyfe, and he was beloued and dradde of hyghe and lowe degre, for he dyde ryght and justyce,

as well ouer the ryche as ouer the poore, kepynge his land in reste
and in pease, and begote a chylde with her, and whiche he called
Rycharde, whiche dyde afterwarde many noble actes and dedes
of armes with grete Charlemayne kynge of Fraunce, for he dyde
helpe hym for to gere and fortefye the Crysten fayth, and he
made alwayes grete warre upon the Sarasyns. And he lyued in
his land in rest and pease, and was beloued of poore and ryche,
and all his comente loued hym in lykewyse as Robert his fader
was loued, for they lyued bothe deuoutly and in vertue. Wherfore I praye God that we may so lyue in this lyfe we may optayne
and come to euerlastynge lyfe. To the whiche brynge us he that
bought us and al mankynde with his preecyous blode and bytter
passyon. Amen.

Thus endeth the lyfe of Robert the Deuyll,
That was the seruaunt of the Lorde,
And of his condycyons that was full euyll,
Emprynted in London by Wynken de Worde.

Here endeth the lyfe of the most feerfullest and unmercyful-
lest and myscheuous Robert the Deuyll, whiche was afterwarde
called the Seruaunt of our Lorde Jhesu Cryste. Emprynted in
Flete-strete in the sygne of the sonne, by WYNKYN DE WORDE.

VIRGILIUS.

III.

VIRGILIUS.

How Romulus cam within the fayer towne of Reynes that he destroyed, and how he slewe his broder Remus that was lorde of Raynes.

As Romulus harde say of his broder Remus, and of the towne of Raynes, than he was uery heauy; for the walles of Raynes was so hygh that a man that stode in the deche myght nat schote ouer well with a hande bowe; and the walles of Rome was so lowe that a man myght wel lepe ouer, and with no deches.

It fortuned that Remus went to see his broder Romulus at Rome, and toke with hym manye folke after his estate and . byrthe, and left his wyfe in abydynge, in the towne of Raynes in Champanion, with a lytyll chylde or yonge son named Remus after his owne name. And whan he was com before Rome, and sawe the walles, he sayd three tymes that the walles were to lowe ; moreouer he sayde, with a ronne he wolde lepe ouer them ; and bye and bye he take a ronne and lept klene ouer.

And whan his broder Romulus had harde this, howe his broder had lepte ouer, he sayd that he had done yll, and therefore he shuld lese his hed. And as Romulus dyd enter into his broders palayce, then he toke Remus, and he with his owne handes smote of his broders hed, and slew hym.

And it was nat longe tyme after that he raysed a great armey of people thorowghe all his contreye, and prepared hym towarde the towne of Raynes in Champanien, and began to set his ordinaunce towarde the walles of the towne, and dyd destroye the

O

palayce, towers, and other places to the erthe, in so muche that
he lefte but a few standynge or none : but he coulde nat fynd
the wyfe of Remus, his suster, for she was fled away out of the
towne, under the erthe at a false porte to hyr frendes and kyn-
ffolke, for she was one of the greatest borne women that was
than there aboute. And as Romulus had destroyed the lande and
towne of Raynes, he departed and went home toward the cytie
of Rome with all his hooste, where he was receyued rychelye.

*Howe the son of Remus, that also was named Remus after his fader,
dyd slewe his unkell Romulus and afterwarde was made emperoure, and so reyned emperoure.*

Than was the wyfe of Remus very sadde and morned very sore
when she knewe of the dethe of hyr husbond, and also of the
destructyon of the towne of Raynes destroyed by the handes of
hys brother. And she caused workemen shulde make the walles
ageyne after hyr broders departyng fro it, insomoche that she
made the towne of Raynes more stronger and fayrer than it was
euer afore, and renewed it rychely after hyr myght and power :
for she was not of so great myght as she was when her husbonde
was alyue.

And also this noble ladye norysshed her chylde well, and within a lyttyl space he began to wexe bygge and stronge, and myghty
anoughe to bere armure. Than sayd his moder to hym :

" My dere son, when wyll you wreke your faders dethe that
your unkell slewe ? "

And he answered to his moder : " Within this iij moneythes."

And forthewith he caused his kynsffolke to reyse theyr people ;
and when they were gathered they departed.

He cam with a great power towarde Rome, and when he cam
to Rome he entered in thereat, no maner of bodye ayenste sayinge. And when he was within, he made a crye that no man
should do no comons harme. Than went he to the Emperours
palayce. And when the Emperour knewe that he was come, he
asked counsayl ; and the senyatours answered, that there was no

remedy but deth : bycause ye slewe his fader, so shall he ageyne slee you. And with that cam in Remus into the palayce of his unkle Romulus, no body ayenst sayinge ; and there he saw his unkell afore him stand in his emperly stole. Than was he in-flamed with yre and drewe out his swerde, and toke his uncle by the here, and smote of his hed. And whan it was done, he asked the lordes and senyatours of Rome, or they wolde thereforre warre ? and they answered all, "nay :" and gaue to hym the hole empyre and crowned hym as ryght heyer; and whan he was Emperour he sent for his moder and she came to hym.

And than was Rome made with stronge walles and deches, and than gatte Rome name ; and there haunted many dyuerse nacyons, and they dyd buylde and edefye many fayre dwellynge places in Rome. This Remus was a stronge man of bodye, ryche of good, wyse in counsayll, and had under hym many landes and lord-shyppes.

This Remus had a knyght of his moders behalfe, that was ryght hardy and bolde in batayle, and he toke or maryed a wife in the cytie of Rome, that was one of the greatest senyatours dawghters of Rome and hyghest of lynage. And Remus reyned not long after, but dyed, and his sone was made Emperoure and reygned after hym. And this knyght of Champanien, that had maryed the senyatours dawghter, he made great warre with hym, and dyd hym very muche harme.

This knyght had one son by his wyfe, that with great travalynge of laboure was bourne, and there was he named Virgilius of Vigilo, for by cause that he was a great space of tyme watched so with men,

Howe Virgilius was sette to schole.

As Virgilius was borne, than the towne of Rome quaked and trembled. And in his youthe he was wyse and subtell, and was put to schole.

And shortly after dyed his fader, and than Virgilius moder wolde no more marye ayen, for she loued her lord so well. And after the decese of hyr husbond, hyr kynsfolke wold haue put her fro hyr enherytaunce that she had lyinge within and without Rome, and one of the fayreste castels and strongest in all the towne or there abowt that could be emagined or made by any man. And she complayned often to the Emperoure, that was nere of kynne unto hyr husbonde; but the Emperoure was a angery man and wolde nat here hyr complayntes, also he was nat beloued of the lordes nor of the comon people.

Within short tyme after, he decesyd and his sone and heyer Persydes was emperoure after his faders dethe, and ruled after his own mynde all the lande. And he had all the Romans under hym, insomuche that he ruled them so strayghtly that they were sore adrad of hym.

And Virgilius was at scole at Tolenten, where he stodyed dyligently, for he was of great understandynge. Upon a tyme the scholers hadde lycence to goo to play and sporte them in the fyldes after the vsaunce of the holde tyme: and there was also Virgilius therby also, walkynge amonge the hylles all about. It fortuned he spyed a great hole in the syde of a great hyll, wherin he went so depe that he culde not see no more lyght. And then he went a lytell ferther therin, and then he saw som lyght agayne, and then wente he fourth streyghte. And with in a lytyll wyle after, he harde a voice that called, "Virgilius, Virgilius;" and he looked aboute and he colde nat see no bodye. Than Virgilius spake and asked, "Who calleth me!" than harde he the voyce agayne, but he sawe no body; than sayd he, "Virgilius, see ye not that lytyll bourde lyinge besyde you there marked with that worde?" Than answered Virgilius, "I see that borde well enough."

The voyce sayd, "Doo a waye that bourd, and lette me oute ther atte."

Than answered Virgilius to the voyce that was under the lytell borde, and sayd, "Who art thow that talkest me so!"

Than answered the deuyll: "I am a deuyll coniured out of the body of a certeyne man, and banysshed here tyll the day of iugement, without that I be delyuered by the handes of men. Thus, Virgilius, I pray the delyuer me out of this payn, and I shall shewe unto the many bokes of nygromancy, and howe thow shalt cum by it lyghtly and knowe the practyse therein, that no man in the scyence of negromancy shall pass the. And moreouer I shall showe and informe you so that thou shalt haue all thy desyre, wherby my thynke it is a great gyfte for so lytyll a doynge, for ye may also thus all your power [1] frendys helpen, and make rythe your ennemyes unmyghty."

Thorowgh that great promyse was Virgilius tempted ; he badde the fynd showe the bokes to hym that he myght haue and occupy them at his wyll. And so the fynde shewed hym, and than Virgilius pulled open a bourde, and there was a lytell hole, and therat wrange the deuyll out lyke a yeel, and cam and stode by fore Virgilius lyke a bygge man. Therof Virgilius was astoned and meruelyed greatly therof that so great a man myght come out at so lytell a hole.

Than sayd Virgilius, "Shulde ye well passe into the hole that ye cam out of?"

" Ye, I shall well," sayd the deuyll.

" I holde the beste plegge that I have, ye shall not do it."

" Well," said the deuyll, " thereto I consent."

And than the deuyll wrange hym selfe into the lytell hole ayen, and as he was therein Virgilius kyuered the hole ageyn with the bourd close, and so was the deuyll begyled and myght not there come out ayen, but there abydeth shytte styll therin.

Then called the deuyll dredefully to Virgilius, and sayd, " What haue ye done ? "

Virgilius answered, "Abyde there styll to your day apoynted." And fro thensforth abydeth he there.

And so Virgilius becam very connynge in the practyse of the blacke scyence.

It was so that the moder of Virgilius wexed olde, in so muche that she lost her herynge. Than called she one of hyr seruauntes, and sayd to hym, "Ye must to Tolleten, and tell Virgilius my sone that he come and redresse his enherytaunce within and

---

[1] *Power*, poor.

without Rome, and gyue up the schole, for he shulde be by ryght one of the greateste of all **Rome.**"

The messenger departed and wente toward Tolleten where Virgilius was, and whan he cam there, he founde Virgilius teychyng and lernynge the greattest lordes of the lande, and other landes also : for I ensure ye, he was a fayr and a wyse yonge man, and conynge in the scyence of negromancy aboue all men than lyuynge.

He salued Virgilius, and shewed unto hym all the mater that he cam for ; and whan Virgilius harde all the matter howe it was, he was very heuy, not for the good, but for his moder ; for Virgilius had good anough.   He rewarded the messenger, and also sende his moder iiij somers[1] laden with money, and with other costely iewels, and sende hyr also one whyte horse ; and so the messengre took his leue of Virgilius, and so departed.

And Virgilius abydyng styll in Tolenten emagened in his mynde howe he myght best conuey the rest of his good to Rome and that he myght followe.   And whan he ordeyned and set in order all the rest, he toke his leue and departed fro Tolenten toward Rome, with many of his scholers with him.

Whan he cam to Rom to his moder, he salewed his moder, and she hym ; for she was glad of his commynge, for she saw hym not afore by the space of xij years a fore.

How Virgilius did make his complaynt to the Emperour as he was com to Rome.

As Virgilius was com to Rome he was receyued ryght worshypfullye of his power kynsfolke, and not of the ryche, for they withhelde his landes oute of his hande ; for that cause was he nat welcome to them, but were angery of his comyng, for they wolde nat ete with hym nor drynk with hym.

Than was Virgilius angery, and than gaue he to all his power kyndsfolke that with helde nothynge fro his moder, landes, harneyse, horses, siluer and golde and other thynges.   And

---

[1] *Somers,* sumpter horses.

he gaue to his naybours great thankes for the kyndnes that
they showed to his moder in his absence. After this dyd Virgilius abyde longe tyme with hys moder, tyll the tyme that the
Emperour ieysed a newe custom or taxe. Than went all the
lordes to the Emperour that helde any lande of hym, and also
Virgilius with all his company and many kynsfolke and frendes.
And whan he cam before hym, he salewed hym, and shewed unto
hym howe he was enheryted of his landes and tenementes, and
of those that with helde it, and desyred that he myght haue it
ageyne. Than answered the Emperour, that he shulde take
thereof counsayll. And forthwith he went to counsayll with them
that loued not Virgilius : and they answered to the Emperour;
" Me thynketh that the land is well deuyded to them that hath it,
for they may helpe you in your nede. What nedeth you for to
care for the dysherytynge of one schole mayster? and byd hym
take hede and loke of his schole, for he hath no ryght to any
lande here aboute the citie of Rome." And thus the Emperour
sayd that he must take pacyence by the space of iiij. or v. yere
that we myght examyne with in our selfe whether ye be ryght
eyer or no. And with that answere was Virgilius very angry, and
sayd that he shulde be auenged.

And whan he cam home he sende for all his poor kynsfolke
and fryndes, and put them in his houses and dwellynge places
that he hadde within Rome, and purueyed them of mete and
drynke, and byd them make mery tyll Julio, that the corne and
frute is rype. And whan it was rype, Virgilius by his negromancy
dyde caste the ayer ouer all the frute and corne of his landes that
his enemyes hylde fro hym, and caused it to be gathered and
brought in to his howses, that none of his enemyes had none
thereof. In this maner of wyse dyd Virgilius deseyue his enemyes
of all the frute and corne, insomuch that they had not on pennys
worth of that goods that they witheld fro hym.

And whan Virgilius enemyes sawe the frute so gathered, they
assembled a great power, and cam towarde Virgilius to take hym
and smyte of his hed. And when they were assembled, they
were so stronge, that the Emperour for fere fled out of Rome, for

they were xij. seniatours that had all the worlde under them ; and Virgilius had had ryght he had ben one of the xij. but they had dysheryted hym and his moder. And whan Virgilius knewe of theyr commynge, he closed all his landes with the ayer rounde about all his lande, that none lyuynge creature myght there come in to dwelle ayenst his wyll or pleasure.

Howe the Emperoure of Rome beseged Virgilius beynge in his castell.

As Virgilius enemyes cam to destroye and take hym, and when they cam before his castell, he closed theym with the aeyer that they had no myght to gowe nor for warde nor back ward, but abyde styll, where of they merueyled. And than Virgilius answered, " Ye cum to dysheryt me, but ye shall nat ; and knowe ye well that you shall haue no profyte of the frutes as longe as I lyue ; and ye maye tell to the Emperour that I shall tarry iiij. or v. yeres tyll he take counsayll. I desyne not to plete in the lawe, but I shall take my good where I fynde it ; and also tell the Emperour I care nat for all his warre nor all that he can do to me." Than returned Virgilius and made ryche all his poure kynsfolke. And, whan Virgilius was returned, than wente they home and knewe nat what they shoulde do.

Than cam they to the Emperour and complayned of Virgilius, and sayde, that Virgilius sayde, that he set nat by the Emperoure and all that he coude make. And when the Emperoure harde this, he was greatly amoued and sore anangered, and sayd, that I shall brynne and set on fyer all his howses, and also I shall smyte of his hedde. And there with all not longe taryinge, he caused his lordes and knyghtes that helde lande of hym, that they shulde reyse all theyr men of armes that they had under them, to be redy at a day at his commaundement ; and at the day apoynted the Emperour and all his hooste were assembled. They tooke theyr way towarde the place of Virgilius, that was rounde aboute well walled and closed with aeyr ; that whan the Emperour cam before the walles with all his hoste, they myght not gowe nor forwarde nor backwarde. And than went fro his castell fourthe Virgilius, and with his negromancy he made also a lyght in suche maner that they coulde nat goo forwarde nor returne, but stande styll. And he made also by his cunnyn, that the Emperour thought that he was closed rounde aboute with a great water, in so muche that they myght nat come to the castell, nor for to come fro the castell, but stode styll; and thus dyd Virgilius serue the Emperoure and all hys hooste.

And moreouer cam Virgilius to the emperoure, and sayde, "Lorde Emperoure, ye have no power with all your strength to do me harme nor my landes also; for be ryght ye shulde make of me as one of your greatest lordes and nearest of your kynred, for I at your nede maye helpe you more than al your other folke."

Than answered the Emperour to Virgilius, "You begyler, may I ons get you under my handes, I wyll geue the that thow hast deserued."

Than answered Virgilius, and sayd, "Lorde Emperour, I fere you nat. But thynke you well, that I shall tame you well a nowghe, that ye shall be glad to know me for one of your kynsfolke and of your blode; but ye wolde dysheryte me, but ye shall not."

Than caused Virgilius muche mete to be dressed bytwene his howse and the hoste, that the Emperour and his folke myght se it, and howe they dressed it; but they myght haue none thereof but the smoke or reke, for they of the hoste was shyt in with the aeyr as thowghe it hadde ben a great water. And so dyd Virgilius serue the Emperour and his folke, nor was there no body in his hoste that coulde fynde any remedy to helpe them there agayn.

Upon a tyme as they were in that thraldome afore the castell, there cam a man that colde skyll in the scyence of negromancy, and cam afore the Emperoure, and sayd, that he wolde by hys practyce make slepe all Virgilius folke; and so he dyd, in so muche that Virgilius his selfe myght scant withdrawe hym fro slepynge. Than was he sorye and wyste nat what to do, for the Emperours folke was delyuered, and began to come upon Virgilius walles.

And whan Virgilius saw that, he loked in his boke of negromancye where in he was very parfeyte, and there he founde in what maner he myght delyuer his folke fro slepe. And than he cungered that he made the Emperoure stand styll agene, that he myght nat remeue out of his place, nor all his folke, nor the mayster of negromancy myght nat remeue nor styrre, as thowgh they were deed : and they that were upon the ladders, one fote uppe, another downe, and so stode styll, and also some stode with one foot on the lader, and a nother upon the wall, and so for to stand styll till it pleased Virgilius.

Whereof the Emperour was sore auexed and angery, and asked his mayster if they shulde stand styll in that maner ? and he gaue hym no answere, but he spake to Virgilius and sayd that he wulde showe upon hym his cunnynge.

And than Virgilius answered, and bad hym do his beste, "for I set nat a strawe by you nor all that you can do to me."

And thus helde Virgilius the Emperour and all his folke closed in this maner with the ayer, by space of a day. And in the nyght came Virgilius to the Emperour and sayd ; " It is a shame for so noble a prynce thus to stop the way, and take upon hym that he can nat do."

Than sayd the Emperour to Virgilius : " Helpe me oute of this daunger, and I shall restore ageyne to you all your landes and tenementes, and haue all thynges at your owne wyll."

Than answered Virgilius to the Emperour, " I wyll delyuer you out of this daunger, so that ye wyll gyue me grace."

" Ye, by my crowne ; and I knowe you for on of my kynred and I dessyre to haue you with me in my felawshyp."

And than Virgilius put a waye the closynge, and reseyued the Emperour and all his folke into his castell, where golde and ryches were plenty, and serued them with mete and drynke ryght plentyously, after theyr degre, of the deyntyest and strangest that myght be gotte, that they saw neuer afore. And the Emperour was there more rychely serued than euer he was before or after. And Virgilius rewarded euery persone after his degree, and with manye costely and meruelouse gyftes.

Howe the Empervur restored ageyne unto Virgilius all his enheryt-
aunce and gooddes, and gaue to hym many other thynges.

THAN toke they leue of Virgilius and retourned home ageyne.
And whan they were returned home, the Emperour gaue to Virgilius his land ageyn and all that he asked, and was the greattest
lorde of the Emperours counsayll.

After that it hapenyd that Virgilius was enamoured of a fayre
ladye, the fayrest in all Rome. Virgilius made a crafti negromancy that tolde hir all his mynde : when the lady knewe his
mynde, she thowght in hyr selfe to deseyue hym, and saydc, if
he wyll come at mydnyght to the castell walle, she shulde lette
downe a basket with stronge cordes, and there to drawe hym
vppe at hyr wyndowe. And with this answere was Virgilius very
glad, and sayd, he shudde doo it with a good wyll.

Howe the gentyl woman pulled vppe Virgilius, and howe she let
hym hange in the basket when he was halfe way vp to hyr
wyndowe, and howe the people wondered and mocked hym.

A DAY was set that Virgilius sholde come to a tower that stode
in the market place of Rome, and in all the towne was none so
hygh. And at the day apoynted Virgilius cam to the tower, and
the gentyl woman was thereat waytynge, and as she sawe hym
there stande, she let downe the basket at the wyndowe. And
when it was downe Virgilius went in ; and whan he was therein,
she pulled hym up tyll that he came half waye ; and there she let
him hange, and made the corde faste.

Than the gentylwoman spake : "Ye be deceyued, and I shall
let you hange tyll to morowe, for it is market day, that all the
folke may wonder of you and your dyshoneste that you wolde
haue do." And therewithall she shyt her wyndowe, and let hym
hang tyll the mornynge that it was daye, tyll all the men in Rome
wyst it, and also the Emperour, that was ashamed, and sent for
the gentylwoman, and bad hyr let hym downe, and so she dyd.
And whan he was downe, he was ashamed, and sayd, that shortly

after he wolde be auenged on hyr; and so went home to his
gardayne that was the fayrest that stode within Rome. Than
toke he his bokes, and by his connynge put out all the fyer that
was in Rome, and none of them without myght bryng in fyer into
the cytie; and this dured for the space of a daye and a nyght.
But Virgilius had anowghe, and no body els had, nor myght not
make no fyer within Rome.

Howe Virgilius put out all the fyer of Rome.

THE Emperoure and all his barons and the comons of Rome
merveyled that there was no fyer in al the cytie; and than they
thowght in theyr myndes that Virgilius had put it out. Than the
Emperour sent for Virgilius, and prayd hym of his counsayll that
men myght have fyer ageyne. Than he must cause a scaffolde
to be made in the mydle of the market-place, and there ye muste
set the gentylwoman in hyr smocke that hynge me in the basket
yesterday; and than lett make a crye thorowgh all the cytie of
Rome, who so wyll haue ony fyer must come to the scaffolde in
the market-place, and of the gentylwoman there they shuld haue
fyer, or otherwyse none : and knowe that one the other can gyve
none, nor sell none; and thus ye must do if ye wyll haue ony
fyer. When they harde this, they cam with great multytude to
the scaffolde.

Howe the gentylwoman was put upon the scaffolde, and howe the folke of the towne went and fetched fyer.

THE Emperoure and all his lordes sawe that there was no other
remedye but they muste nedes do after Virgilius counsayll. He
did cause a scaffolde to be made in the market-place, and caused
the gentyll woman to be set there on in hyr smocke; and there
men fetche fyer; the pore men with candels and strawe, and the
ryche men lyghted they theyr torches. Thre dayes must the
gentylwoman stande in that manere or els they shulde haue no
fyer. And after the thyrde day went the gentylwoman home

sore ashamed, for she knewe well that Virgilius had done that violence to hyr.

. Within a whyle after maryed Virgilius a wyfe : and when that was done, Virgilius made a merueylous paleyce with iiij corners : and as it was made, he layed the Emperoure therin in one of the corners, and herde that all the men did say in that quarter. And in lykewise dyd he bryng him in the other iij quarters, and so he harde what they sayde in the other quarters of Rome, and thus gowyng by the iiij quarters harde he what they sayde thorowe all Rome; they myght nat speke so secretly but he harde it.

Howe Virgilius made saluatio Romæ.

THE Emperour asked of Virgilius howe that he myght make Rome prospere and haue many landes under them, and knowe when any lande wolde ryse agen theym.

And Virgilius sayd to the Emperoure, " I woll within short space that do." And he made vpon the Capitolium, that was the towne house, made with caruede ymages, and of stone, and that he let call *Saluacio Romæ ;* that is to say, this is the Saluacyon of the cytie of Rome. And he made in the compace all the goddes that we call mamettes and ydolles, that were under the subiection of Rome; and euery of the goddes that there were had in his hande a bell; and in the mydle of the godes made he one god of Rome. And when so euer that there was any lande wolde make ony warre ageynst Rome, than wolde the godes tourne theyr backes towarde the god of Rome; and than the god of the lande that wolde stande up ageyne Rome clynked his bell so longe that he hathe in his hand, tyll the senatours of Rome hereth it, and forthwith they go there and see what lande it is that wyll warre a gaynst them ; and so they prepare them, and goeth a geyne them and subdueth theym.

This forsayde token knewe the men of Carthago, that was sore a greued for the great harme that the Romans had done them. And they toke a pryuay counseyll in what manner they myght destroy that worke. Than thought they in there mynde to sende iij men out and gaue them great multytude of golde and syluer. And these iij men toke theyr leue of the lordes and went towarde the cytie of Rome. And when they were come to Rome they reported themselfe sothesayers and trewe dremers.

Vpon a tyme wente these iij men to a hyll that was within the cytie, and there they buryed a great potte of money very depe in the erthe, and when that was done and kyuered ageyne, they went to the brygge of Tyber and let fall in a certayne place a great barell with golden pens.

And when this was done these thre men went to the seniatours of Rome and said :

"Worshypfull lordes, we haue this nyght dremed, that with in the fote of a hyll here with in Rome is a great pot with money. Wyll ye lordes graunt to us, and we shall do the coste to seke there after ?"

And the lordes consented and than they toke laberours and delued the money out of the erthe.

And when it was done, they went a nother tyme to the lordes, and sayde :

"Worshypful lordes, we haue also dremed that in a certeyne place of Tyber lyeth a barell full of golden pens ;[1] if that you wyll graunte to us that we shall go seke it : "

And the lordes of Rome thynkyng no dyscepte, graunted to those sothesayers, and badde them do that that they shulde do there best. And than the sothe sayers was glad. And than they hyred shyppes and men, and went toward the place where it was ; and when they were come they sowght in everye place there about, and at the laste founde the barelfull of golden pens, whereof they were glade ; and than they gaue to the lordes costely gyftes.

And than to come to theyr purpose, they cam to the lordes a geyne, and sayde to them :

"Worshypfull lordes, we haue dremed a geyne that under the foundacyon of Capitolium, there where Saluatio Romæ standeth, be xij barelles full of golde ; and pleasyeth you lordes that you wolde graunt us lycence, it shall be to your great auantage."

---

[1] *Pens,* pence, coins.

And the lordes, styrred with couytayse, graunted them, bycause ij tymes a fore they told trewe. Whereof they were glad, and gatte laberours, and began to dygge under the fundacyon of Saluatio Romæ. And when they thought that they had dygged a noughe they departed fro Rome, and the next daye folowynge fell that house downe, and all the worke that Virgilius had made. And so the lordes knew that they were deseyued, and were sorowfull, and after that hade nat no fortune as they had a fore tymes.

How the Emperour asked counsayll of Virgilius howe the nyght ronners and yll doers myght be ryd out of the stretes.

The Emperour had manye complayntes of the nyght ronners and theues, and also of great murderynge of people in the nyght, in so muche that the Emperour asked counsayll of Virgilius, and sayd that he hath great complayntes of the theues that ronnyth by nyght, for they kyll many men; "what counsayll Virgilius is best to be done?"

Than answered Virgilius to the Emperour, "Ye shall make a horse of coper, and a coper man apon his backe, hauynge in his handes a flayll of yron, and that horse ye shall do brynge a fore the towne howse, and then ye shall lett crye that a man fro henseforth at x. of the clocke shulde ryng a bell, and he that after the bell ronge was in the strete should be slayne, no worke thereof be done."

And whan this crye was made the roffyans set nat a poynt, but kept the streetes as they dyd a fore, and wolde nat let therfore; and as sone as the bell was ronge at x. of the clocke, then lept the horse of coper with the coper man thorowgh the stretes of Rome, insomuche that he lefte nat one strete in Rome unsowght. And as sone as he found any man or woman in the strete he slewe them starke deed, insomuche that he slewe a boue CC. persons or more.

And this seyeng, the theues and nyght ronners howe they might fynde a remedy therefore thought in theyr myndes to make a dragge with a ladder theron; and as they wolde gowe out be nyght they toke theyr ladders with them, and when they harde the horse come, than caste they the dragge upon the howses, and so went up a pon theyr ladders to the top of the howses, so that the coper man myght nat toche them; and so abyd they styll in theyr wycked doyng.

Than came they a gene to the Emperoure and complayned, and than the Emperoure asked counsayll of Virgilius; and Virgilius answered and sayd, "that he muste get to coper houndes and set them of eyther syde of the coper horse, and let crye a geyne that no body after the bell is ronge shulde departe oute of theyr howse that wolde lyue."

But the nyght walkers carede not a poynt for that crye; but when they harde the horse comynge, with theyr ladders clymed upon the howse, but the dogges lept after, and tered them all to peces; and thus the noyse went thorowgh Rome, in so muche that no body durst in the nyght go in the strete, and thus all the nyght walkers were destroyed.

How Virgilius made a lampe that at all tymes brenned.

For profeyte of the comon people, Virgilius on a great myghty marbell pyller, dyd make a brygge that cam vp to the paleyce, and so went Virgilius well vp the pyller oute of the paleyce. That paleyce and the pyller stode in the mydde of Rome; and vpon this pyller made he a lampe of glasse that allwaye byrned without gowyng out, and no body myght put it out. And this lampe lyghtened ouer all the cytie of Rome fro the one corner to the other, and there was nat so lytell a strete but it gaue suche lyght that semed ij torches there had stande. And vpon the walles of the palayce made he a metall man that helde in his hande a metall bowe that poynted euer upon the lampe for to shote it out; but alway burned the lampe and gaue lyght ouer all Rome. And vpon a tyme went the burgeyses daughters to play in the paleyse and beheld the metall man; and one of them asked in sporte, Why he shat nat? And than she cam to the man and with hyr hande toched the bowe, and than the bolte flew oute, and brake the lampe that Virgilius made. And it was wonder that the mayden went nat out of her mynde for the great fere she had, and also the other burgeyses daughters that were in hyr companye, of the great stroke that it gaue when it hyt the lampe, and when they sawe the metall man so swyftly ronne his waye. And neuer after was he no more sene. And this forsayd lampe was abydynge byrnyng after the deth of Virgilius by the space of C.C.C. yeres or more.

How Virgilius made a orcharde by the fountayne, the fayrest and goodlyest that euer culde be founde in all the worlde.

GREAT wonder dyd Virgilius in his tyme ; for after that palayce he made an horcharde wherin he set all maner of trees berynge frute, and also many herbes growynge in that yarde. And as the tyme was, sawe men dayly, rype frute, fayre blossoms, full plentyous. In the myddell of the orcharde was a fayer clere fountayne, the fayrest that euer was sene ; and in this orchard was many dyuers of byrdes syngyng, for they myght well cum in, but they culde no more flye out ageyne, for it was closed in such with the ayer ; and men harde also theyr byrdes syng that was within, and culde not goo forth. Also he had in his orcharde all maner of tame bestes that were profitable for men. Also he made of the water that ran out of the fountayn a standynge water about the trees, the clerest that myght be, and there in was of all maner of fysshe that culde be thought. Also in this orcharde all maner of joyfulnes, both of trees, herbes, fowles, and bestes thereof that men myght thynke, or be immagened by mannes reasons. Also he dyd make greater thynges than all this ; for he made a vaute or seller in the orcharde, the fayreste that myght be made or thought by mannes reason, which seller he made for to put in his money and ryches that he had ; for he was so ryche, and so great multitude that he knewe no ende. And he set ij metall men before the dore to kepe it, and in eche hande a great hamer, and therwith they smyte vpon a anuilde, one after the other, inso-

P

muche that the byrdes that flye ouer hereth it, and by and bye
falleth there down deed; and otherwyse had Virgilius not his
good kepte.

Howe Virgilius made his wyfe a ymage.

A IMAGE made Virgilius a hye in the ayer that myght nat fall; and
the people of Rome myght nat open noder wyndowe nor doer but
they must nedes see it.   And this image had this properte, that
no woman after she had seen the image had no luste to do bodely
lust; and therefore the women had great enuy, and they com-
pleyned them to Virgilius' wyfe that they theyr sporte and dalyinge
had loste and prayed hyr that she wolde destroy that image and
make it fall.   And than wayted Virgilius' wyfe hir tyme, and went
vp the brigge of the ayer and cast down the image.   And when
Virgilius cam and founde his image downe, he was very angery,
and sayd to his selfe, that it shulde nat auayll them, for he wolde
set it up ageyne : and swore that he shulde know who had cast it
downe.   And he set it ageyne, and asked his ladye, and she had
caste downe it? and she sayd, " Naye."

And than cam the women ageyne to Virgilius' wyfe, and sayd,
" That it was worse than it was before, and prayed hyr, that she
shulde caste it downe ageyne."

And than Virgilius went pryuyley into a corner, and wayted his
wyfe, for he had sene before howe the women had complayned
them to hyr.   And than went Virgilius' wyfe and caste downe the
image; and Virgilius, that had hyd hym, sawe howe his wyfe had
caste it downe, and with a anger wold haue cast her after with
the ymage; and he sayd, " The deuyll satisfye you, for I dyd it for
the beste.   But I shall neuer more medyll, but I shall let the
women do theyr wyll."   And fro thenseforthe began Virgilius to
hate his wyfe.

Howe Virgilius went to the Sodans daughter.

OFTEN tymes herde Virgilius tell of the fayrnes of the Sodans
dawghter, insomuche that he was enamoured of hyr, thoughe he
neuer sawe hyr; than by his connynge made he a brygge in the

ayer, and went ouer to hyr, and when he had spoke with hyr, and showed hyr his mynde, than she consented to hym, notwithstandyng she neuer sawe hym aforc.

And she sayde on a time that she wolde departe with hym into his countre, and knowe what maner a man he were, and what dwellyng he had. Than answered Virgilius, and sayde to hyr : "What wyll I doo : but ye shall passe ouer many landes, and you shall not trede in them." Than caryed he hyr ouer into his owne lande, ouer the brygge that he had made in the ayer, and so browght hyr to Rome ; and when he was at home, he asked hyr "If she sawe no body?" and she said, "No, but hym alone."

And thanne showed Virgilius to hyr hys palayce and orchard, and the metall men, that stode styll a pece smytynge : and he shewed to hyr also all his treasur, and he presented it to hyr ; and she wolde nat reseyue it, sayinge, "That she had to muche of hyr faders to kepe." And Virgilius helde her in his orcherde as longe as it please hym. And as the Soudan founde nat is dawghter he was sorofull, for because he woste nat where she was become. And they sowght all about, but in no place culde theye fynde hyr.

Howe Virgilius brought agene the Sodans daughter into hyr faders lande, and how he founde hyr slepynge vpon hyr bedde.

WHEN the Sodans dawghter had byd longe with Virgilius in his orcharde, than desyred she to goo home to hyr faders lande. And than toke Virgilius the Sodans dawghter in his hannes, and caste hyr vpon the brygge in the ayer, and he his selfe brought hyr to hyr faders palayce, and put hyr in hyr chamber vpon hyr bed ; and than he betoke hyr to the goddes, and so returned he home to his place towarde Rome.

And in the begynnynge of the day arose the Sodan that was sore vexed for the lesynge of his dawghter ; and than cam one of hyr chamberlaynes to the Emperoure, and tolde hym howe his dawghter was come ageyne, and lay vpon hyr bed and slepte.

Than cam he to hyr hastely and asked hyr where she had bene, and howe she was come there ageyne?

"Fader," sayd she, "there was a fayre man of a straunge land, and he brought me thorowgh the ayer to his paleyce and orcharde; but I haue nat spoke to man nor woman but to hym alone, and I knowe nat what lande it is."

The Sodan answered and sayde to hyr, "That she shulde brynge some of the frute of that cuntrey with hyr:" and she sayde she wolde.

And within a wyle came Virgilius to Babylone, and toke the Sodans daughter with hym ageyne, and so departed ageyne to his cuntrey with hyr, and kepte hir longe as pleased hym; and when she departed ageyne she toke with hir walnottes and other frute.

And when she was come home she shewed her father the walnuttes and other frutes of the lande. "Ha, ha," sayde he, "it is on the syde of France that so often (he) hath borne you away."

Howe Virgilius was taken there.

THE Sodan cam upon a tyme to his dawter and sayde; "My daughter, when he commethe agene to you that was wonte to careye you awaye, gyue to hym this drynke that I shall gyue to you, but drynke ye none thereof, I warne you : for when he hath drunkyn thereof he shall slepe, and when he is a slepe let me know therof : than shall we take hym, and know fro whens he is."

And the lady dyd as she was commaunded. And whan Virgilius was com, she gaue hym to drynke of the drynke that hir fader gaue hyr : and when he had drunke, he slepte, and so was taken.

Than was Virgilius brought to the Sodan, and the lordes, and also the dawter of the Sodan. And than the Sodan showed his knyghtes that that was the man that had stolen his dawghter away : and than he sayd to Virgilius : "Ye be welcome; for your pleasure that ye haue had, ye shall suffer dethe."

Than answered Virgilius to the Sodan : "I wolde that I had

neuer sene hir, and if that ye wyll let me gowe I shall neuer come
ageyne : "

Than answered the Sodan and the lordes : " That shall we nat
do ; but for youre myssedede ye shall suffer a shamefull dethe."

Than answered the Sodans dawghter, " Yf ye put hym to deth
I shall suffer deth with hym."

Than answered the Sodan : " Therto I consente, for ye shall
be burned with hym."

Than answered Virgilius, " That shall you nat do, with all the
strength and myght that ye can do, thoughe ye be of so great
power."

*Howe Virgilius cam out and led with hym the fayer lady the Sodans
daughter, and how he founded the towne of Naples.*

WHAN Virgilius harde of this, he made with his cunnynge than
the Sodan and all his lordes (thynk) that the great ryuer of Babylon
was in the myddell among them ranne, and that they swemed,
and laye, and spronge lyke duckes. And thus toke Virgilius with
hym the fayre lady upon the brygge in the ayer. And when they
were bothe upon the brygge, he delyuered the Sodan fro the
ryuere, and all the lordes. And than they sawe Virgilius caray
awaye his dawghter ouer the see upon a brygge in the ayer, wher
of he merueyled and was very sorye, and wyste nat what to do,
for he culde nat remedy it. And in this maner dyd he conuey
the Sodans dawghter ouer the see to Rome.

And Virgilius was sore enamored of that lady. Than he
thought in hys mynde, howe he myght mareye hyr, and thoughte
in his mynde to founde in the myddes of the see a fayer towne
with great landes belongyng to it ; and so he dyd by his cunnynge,
and called it Napells. And the fundacyon of it was of egges. And
in that towne of Napells he made a tower with iiij corners, and in
the toppe he set a napyll upon a yron yarde, and no man culde
pull away that apell without he brake it : and thorowghe that yron
set he a botel, and on that botel set he a egge ; and he henge
the apell by the stauke upon a cheyne, and so hangyth it styll.

And whenne the egge styrreth so shulde the towne of Napels quake, and whan the egge brake than shulde the towne synke. When he had made an ende he lette call it Napels.

And in this towne he layde a part of his treasur that he had, therin: and also set therin his louer, the fayer lady the Sodans dawghter: and he gaue to her the towne of Napels and all the landes therto belongynge, to hir use and hyr chyldren. And within short whyle after, he maryed her to a sertayne lorde or knyght of Spayn.

Within shorte wyle after, it fortuned that the Emperour had a great fantasy to the towne of Napells, for it bare the name in the tyme for one of the fayrest in the world: and it lay also in the fayrest market place aboute Rome. Than secretly sende the Emperour letters to all his lordes that were under hym, that they shoulde, as shortely as they myght, rayse theyr folke, and to come to Rome for to besege the towne of Napels. And so they dyd, insomuche that they assembled a great companye, and wente towarde the towne of Napels and destroyed all afore hym. And when he was come to Napels he beseiged it. And the knyght that maryed the lady that was within Napels defended the towne nobely ageynste the Emperoure and all his hoste. And in the meane wyle sente this knyght a messengere to Virgilius, whiche tolde hym all howe the Emperour beseged the towne of Napels: wherwith Virgilius was angery, and sent worde that the knyght shulde nat set be hym nat all his hoste, for I shall prouyde well a nough for you: and so departed the messenger to Napels.

Howe the Emperour beseged the towne of Napels.

AND when Virgilius knewe that the Emperour beseged Napels, than made he all the fresshe water to be lyke rayne, in suche maner that the Emperours folke had neuer a drop of water and they of Napels had a noughe; and in the meane season reysed Virgilius his hoste, and cam towarde the Emperoure to Napels. But the Emperour myght no lenger taray, for the horse and men dyed for faute of water, and so he loste a great parte of theym.

Than the Emperoure seynge this, departed home ageyn to the cytie of Rome, all eschamed and dyscumfyt ; and as he returned homewarde, in the waye, he met with Virgilius comynge with all his companye towarde Napels.

And when Virgilius sawe the Emperoure, he cam to hym, and salued hym in this manere : " O noble Emperoure, howe fortuned this to you, that be so nooble a prynce as you be, to gyue up the seage of Napels, and to returne home agene to the cytie of Rome, all dyscumfit, without doynge any harme at all so schortly ? "

Than wyste the Emperoure well that Virgilius mocked hym, and he was therwith very angery.

And than went Virgilius to Napeis, and he caused the lordes of the towne to make a othe that they shulde beyre no Romans within the forsayde towne.

Howe Virgilius dyd strengthe the towne of Napels with scholers and merchauntes.

As Virgilius rescyued the othes of the lordes of Napels than returned he ageyne to Rome, and feched his bokes and other mouable goodes, and browght it to Napels, and let his good a lone that he had shet in the seller. And his dwellynge he gaue to his frendes to kepe, and his dwellynge places, and so departed to Napels. There he made a schole and gaue therto much landes, that euery scholer a hydynge and gowyng to schole had lande to lyue on of the towne ; and they that gaue up the schole they loste the lande : and there cam many fro Tuleten to schole. And when he had ordeyned the towne well with scholers, than made he a warme bath that euery man myght bathe hym in that wolde ; and that bathe is there to this tyme, and it was the fyrste bathe that euer was. And after this made he a brygge the fayrest that euer man sawe, and there myght men se all maner of fayer shyppes that belonged to merchaun-sedyse, and all other thynges of the see. And the towne in those days was the fayrest and noblest in all the worlde. And in this schole aforesayde dyde Virgilius rede the great conynge and scyaunce of egromancy, for he was the conyngest that euer was a fore, or after, in that scyence. And within schorte space his wyfe dyed, and she had neuer no chyldren by hym. And moreouuer aboue all men he loued scholers, and gave much moneye to bye bokes with all. And thus he ruled them ryght nobely, for he myght do it ryght well, for he was one of the greatest borne men of all the world, and had beene the greateste lorde of all Rome.

Howe Virgilius made in Rome a metall serpente.

THAN made Virgilius at Rome a metall serpente with his cunnynge, that who so euer put his hande in the throte of the serpente, was to swere his cause ryght and trewe; and if hys cause were false he shulde nat plucke his hande out a geyne : and if it were trewe they shulde plucke it out a geyne without any harme doynge. So it fortuned that there was a knyght of Lumbardye that mystrusted his wyfe with one of his men that was moost set by in the conseyte of his wyfe : but she excused hyr selfe ryght noblye and wysely. And she consented to goo with hym to Rome to that serpent, and there to take hyr othe that she was not gylty of that, that he put apon hyr. And therto consented the knyght.

And as they were bothe in the carte, and also hyr man with hyr, she sayd to the man; that when he cam to Rome, that he shulde clothe hym with a foles-cote, and dysgyse hym in suche maner that they shulde nat knowe hym, and so dyd he. And when the day was come that he shulde come to the serpent, he was there present.

And Virgilius knewe the falsenes of the woman by his cunnynge of egromancy. Than sayd Virgilius to the woman : " With drawe your othe and swere nat."

But she wolde nat do after hym, but put hyr hande into the serpentes mouthe. And when hyr hande was in, she sware before hyr husbande that she had no more to do with hym than with that fole, that stode hyr by ; and by cause that she sayd trowthe she pulled out hyr hande a geyne out of the throte of the serpent nat hurt. And than departed the knyght home and trusted hyr well euer after.

And Virgilius hauyng therat great spyte and anger that the woman had so escaped, destroyed the serpent : for thus scaped the lady a waye fro that great daunger. And then spake Virgilius, and sayde : that the women be ryght wyse to enmagen ungracyousenes, but in goodness they be but innocentes.

Howe Virgilius dyed.

THUS as Virgilius in his life had done many maruylous and sotyll thynges, and also had promysed to the Emperour many other dyuerse thynges and meruylouse : for he promysed to make the trees and spyces to bere frute thre tymes in a yere : and euery tree shulde haue rype frute and also blossomes at one tyme thereon growynge : also he shulde maken the shyppes for to sayle a geynste the streme as with the streme at all tymes ; and he wolde haue made the peny to be as lyghtely gat as spente. And these thynges afore sayde promysed Virgilius to the Emperour for to do, and many other dyuerse thynges that were to longe for to reherse here, if that it fortuned hym nat to dye in the mene wyle.

And after this made Virgilius a goodly castell that hadde but one goying in thereto, and no man myght nat enter in therto, but at the one gate, or els nat. And also aboute the same castell flowed there a water and it was unpossyble for any man there to haue anye enterynge. And this castell stode without the cytie of Rome and this enteringe of this gate was made with xxiiij yron flayles, and on euery syde was there xij men on eche syde, styll a pece smytynge with the flayles neuer seasynge, the oon after the other ; and no man myght cum in, without the flayles stood styll, but he was slayne. And these flayles was made with such a gyn that Virgilius stopped them when he lyst to enter in therat, but no man els culde fynde the way. And in this castell put Virgilius parte of his treasure ther in pryuyly ; and when this was done he imagyned in his mynde by what meane he myght make his selfe yonge ageyn, bycause he thought to lyve longer many yeres, to do manye wonders and marueylouse thynges.

And vpon a tyme went Virgilius to the Emperoure, and asked hym, of lycence by the space of iij wekes. But the Emperoure in no wyse wold graunte unto hym, for he wold haue Virgilius at all tymes by hym.

Than harde he that Virgilius went to his house and toke with hym one of his men that he aboue all men trusted, and knewe well that he wolde best kepe his counsayll; and they departed to his castell that was without the towne, and when they were afore the castell there sawe the man men stande with yron flayles in theyr handes sore smytyng.

Than sayd Virgilius to his man: "Enter you fyrste into the castell."

Than answered the man and sayd, "If I shulde enter the flayles wolde slee me."

Than shewed Virgilius to the man of eche syde the enterynge in and all the vyces that therto belonged; and when he had shewed hym all the wayes, he made scase the flayles and went into the castell. And when they were bothe in, Virgilius turned the vyces ageyne, and so went the yron flayles as they dyd a fore.

Then sayde Virgilius, "My dere beloued frende, and he that I aboue all men truste, and knowe moost of my secret;" and than led he the man into the seller where he had made a fayer lampe at all seasons burnynge. And than sayd Virgilius to the man: "Se you the barell that standeth here?" and he sayde, "ye there muste put me. Fyrst ye muste slee me, and hewe smalle to peces, and cut my head in iiij peces, and salte the heed under in the bottum, and then the peces there after, and my herte in the myddel, and then set the barell under the lampe, that nyght and daye therin may droppe and leke : and ye shall ix dayes longe, ones in the daye fyll the lampe, and fayle nat. And when this is all done, than shall I be renued and made yonge ageyn, and lyue longe tyme and maney wynters mo, if that it fortune me nat to be taken of a boue and dye."

And when the man harde his master Virgilius speke thus, he

was sore abasshed, and sayd : "That will I neuer whyle I lyue, for in no maner wyll I slee you."

And then sayd Virgilius : "Ye at this tyme must do it, for it shall be no grefe unto you."

And at the last Virgilius treated his man so muche, that he consented to hym : and then toke the seruant Virgilius, and slewe hym, and when he was thus slayn, he hewe hym in peces and salted hym in the barell, and cut his heed in iiij. peces as his master bad hym, and than put the herte in the myddell and salted them wele : and when all this was done, he hynge the lampe ryght ouer the barell, that it myght at all tymes droppe in therto. And when he had done all this, he went out of the castell and turned the vyces, and then went the coper men smyghtynge with their flayles so strongly upon the yron anueldes as they dyd afore, that there durst no man enter : and he came euery day to the castell and fylled the lampe, as Virgilius had bad hym.

And as the Emperoure myssed Virgilius by the space of seuen dayes, he merueyled greatly where he shulde be by come ; but Virgilius was kylled and layed in the seller by his seruaunte that he loued so well.

And than the Emperour thought in his mynde to ask Virgilius seruaunte, where Virgilius his master was : and so he dyd, for he knewe well that Virgilius loued hym above all men in the worlde. Than answered the seruaunte to the Emperoure, and sayde, "Worschypfull lorde, and it please your grace I wot nat where he is, for it is seuen dayes past that I sawe hym laste ; and than wente he forthe I cannot tell whyther, for he wulde nat let me goo with hym."

Than was the Emperoure angery with that answere, and sayd : "Thou lyest falce thefe that thou art ; but without thou showe me shortly where he is, I shall put the to dethe."

With those wordes was the man abashed, and sayde : "Worshypfull lorde, seuen dayes a goo I went with hym without the towne to the castell, and there he went in, and there I left hym, for he wold nat let me in with hym."

Then sayd the Emperour, "Goo with me to the same castell,"

and so he dyd; and whan they cam a fore the castell and wolde haue entered, they myght nat, bycause flayles smyt so faste.

Than sayde the Emperoure : "Make pease this flayles, that we may cum in."

Than answered the man : "I knowe nat the way."

Than sayd the Emperour, "Than shalt thou dye;" and than thorowgh the fere of dethe he turned the vyce and made the flayles stande styl, and then the Emperoure entered into the castell with all his folke, and soughte al a bout in euery corner after Virgilius; and at the laste they sowghte so longe that they cam into the seller where they sawe the lampe hang ouer the barell, where Virgilius lay in deed. Than asked the Emperoure the man : "Who had made hym so herdey to put his mayster Virgilius to dethe?" And the man answered no worde to the Emperoure. And than the Emperour, with great anger, drewe out his swerde, and slewe he there Virgilius man.

And when all this was done, than sawe the Emperoure and all folke a naked chylde, iij. tymes rennynge a boute the barell, saynge the wordes : "cursed be the tyme that ye cam euer here;" and with those wordes vanyshed the chylde away, and was neuer sene a geyne : and thus abyd Virgilius in the barell, deed.

Then was the Emperour very heuy for the dethe of Virgilius, and also all Virgilius kynred, and also all the scholers that dwelled aboute the towne of Napels, and in especyall all the towne of Napels, for by cause that Virgilius was the founder therof, and made it of great worshypp. Than thought the Emperoure to haue the good and ryches of Virgilius, but there were none so harday that durste cum in to fetche it, for fere of the coper men, that smote so faste with theyr yron flayles : and so abyd Virgilius treasure in the seller. And Virgilius dyd many other merueylouse thynges that in this boke is not wryten. And thus (God) gyue us grace that we may be in the boke of euer lastynge blysse. Amen.

Thus endethe the lyfe of Virgilius with many dyuers consaytes that he dyd. Emprynted in the cytie of Anwarpe By me Johnn Doesborcke dwellynge at the camer porte.

THE HISTORY OF HAMLET

PRINCE OF DENMARK.

IV.

THE HISTORY OF HAMLET
PRINCE OF DENMARK.

CHAPTER I.

How Horvendile and Fengon were made Governors of the Province
of Ditmarsh, and how Horvendile married Geruth, the
daughter to Roderick, chief K. of Denmark: by whom he had
Hamlet: and how after his marriage his brother Fengon slew
him traitorously, and married his brother's wife, and what
followed.

You must understand, that long time before the Kingdom of
Denmark received the faith of Jesus Christ, and embraced the
doctrine of the Christians, that the common people in those days
were barbarous and uncivil, and their Princes cruel, without faith
or loyalty. They sought nothing but murder, and deposing or
(at the least) offending each other; either in honours, goods, or
lives; not caring to ransom such as they took prisoners, but
rather sacrificing them to the cruel vengeance, naturally imprinted
in their hearts. They lived in such sort, that if they were sometimes a good prince, or king among them, who being adorned
with the most perfect gifts of nature, would addict himself to virtue,
and use courtesy, although the people held him in admiration (as
virtue is admirable to the most wicked), yet the envy of his neighbours was so great, that they never ceased until that virtuous man
were dispatched out of the world.

King Roderick, as then reigning in Denmark, after he had

appeased the troubles in the country, and driven the Sweath-landers and Slaveans from thence, he divided the kingdom into divers Provinces, placing Governors therein. Such Governors after (as the like happened in France) bare the names of Dukes, Marquises, and Earls, giving the government of Jutie (at this present called Ditmarsh) lying upon the country of Cimbrians, in the straight or narrow part of land, that sheweth like a point or cape of ground upon the sea, which neithward bordereth upon the country of Norway.

The governors appointed by King Roderick were two valiant and warlike Lords, Horvendile and Fegon, sons to Gervendile, who likewise had been governor of that Province.

Now the greatest honour that men of noble birth could at that time win and obtain, was in exercising the art of piracy upon the seas ; assailing their neighbours, and the countries bordering upon them : and how much the more they used to rob, pill, and spoil other Provinces, and Islands far adjacent, so much the more their honours and reputation increased and augmented. Herein Horvendile obtained the highest place in his time, being the most renowned pirate that in those days scoured the seas, and havens of the North parts. His great fame, so moved the heart of Collere, King of Norway, that he was much grieved to hear that Horvendile surmounted him in feats of arms, thereby ob-scuring the glory by him already obtained upon the seas. Honour more than covetousness of riches, was (in those days) the reason that provoked those barbarian princes, to overthrow and vanquish one the other ; not caring to be slain by the hands of a victorious person. This valiant and hardy king, having challenged Hor-vendile to fight with him body to body, the combat was by him accepted, with conditions, that he which should be vanquished, should lose all the riches he had in his ship, and that the vanquisher should cause the body of the vanquished, that should be slain in the combat, to be honourably buried, death being the prize and reward of him that should lose the battle.

Collere, King of Norway, although a valiant, hardy, and courageous prince, was in the end vanquished and slain by

Horvendile: who presently caused a tomb to be erected, and therein, with all honourable obsequies fit for a prince, buried the body of King Collere, according to their ancient manner, and superstitions in those days. The conditions of the combat were fulfilled, bereaving the King's ships of all their riches; and having slain the King's sister, a very brave and valiant warrior, and over-run all the coast of Norway, and the Northern Islands, Horvendile returned home again laden with much treasure. He sent the most part thereof to his sovereign, King Roderick, thereby to procure his good liking, and so to be accounted one of the greatest favourites about his majesty.

The King, allured by those presents, and esteeming himself happy to have so valiant a subject, sought by a great favour and courtesy, to make him become bounden unto him perpetually, giving him Geruth his daughter to his wife, of whom he knew Horvendile to be already much enamoured. The more to honour him, King Roderick determined himself in person to conduct his daughter Geruth into Jutie, where the marriage was celebrated according to the ancient manner. Of this marriage proceeded Hamlet, of whom I intend to speak.

Fengon, brother to this Prince Horvendile, fretting and despiteing in his heart at the great honour and reputation won by his brother in warlike affairs, was solicited and provoked by a foolish jealousy to see him honoured with royal alliance. He feared thereby to be deposed from his part of the government: or rather desiring to be only governor, thereby to obscure the memory of the victories and conquests of his brother Horvendile, determined whatsoever happened to kill him. This he did in such sort, that no man once so much as suspected him, every man esteeming that from such and so firm a knot of alliance and consanguinity, there could proceed no other issue than the full effects of virtue and courtesy. But as I said before, the desire of bearing sovereign rule and authority, respecteth neither blood nor amity, nor careth for virtue as being wholly without respect of laws, or majesty divine: for it is not possible that he which invadeth the country and taketh away the riches of another man

Q

without cause or reason, should know, or fear God. Was not this a crafty and subtle counsellor? but he might have thought that the mother, knowing her husband's case, would not cast her son into the danger of death.

Fengon, having secretly assembled certain men, and perceiving himself strong enough to execute his enterprise, Horvendile his brother being at a banquet with his friends, suddenly set upon him, where he slew him as traitorously, as cunningly he purged himself of so detestable a murder to his subjects. Before he had any bloody or violent hands, or once committed parricide upon his brother, he had incestuously abused his wife, whose honour he ought as well to have sought and procured, as traitorously he pursued and effected his destruction. And it is most certain, that the man that abandoneth himself to any notorious and wicked action, whereby he becometh a great sinner, he careth not to commit much more heinous and abominable offences.

Fengon covered his boldness and wicked practice with so great subtilty and policy, and under a veil of mere simplicity, that he was favoured for the honest love that he bare to his sister-in-law, for whose sake he affirmed he had in that sort murdered his brother, so that his sin found excuse among the common people, and of the nobility was esteemed for justice.

For Geruth being as courteous a Princess as any then living in the North parts, and one that had never once so much as offended any of her subjects, either commons or courtiers, this adulterer and infamous murderer slandered his dead brother, that he would have slain his wife, and that he by chance finding him upon the point ready to do it, in defence of the lady had slain him, bearing off the blows which as then he struck at the innocent Princess, without any other cause of malice whatsoever. Herein he wanted no false witnesses to approve his act, which deposed in like sort as the wicked calumniator himself protested, being the same persons that had borne him company and were participants of his treason. Instead of pursuing him as a parricide and an incestuous person, all the courtiers admired and flattered him in his good fortune : making more account of false witnesses and detestable wicked reporters, and more honouring the calumniators, than they esteemed of those that sought to call the matter in question, and admiring the virtues of the murdered Prince, would have punished the massacrers and bereavers of his life. This was the cause that Fengon, emboldened and encouraged by such impunity, durst venture to couple himself in marriage with her whom he used as his concubine during good Horvendile's life, in that sort spotting his name with a double vice, and charging his conscience with abominable guilt and twofold impiety. The unfortunate and wicked woman, that had received the honour to be the wife of one of the valiantest and wisest Princes in the North, abased herself in such vile sort, as to falsify her faith unto him, and which is worse, to marry him that had been the tyrannous murderer of her lawful husband : which made divers men think that she had been the causer of the murder, thereby to live in her adultery without control. But where shall a man find a more wicked and bold woman than a great personage once having loosed the bands of honour and honesty? This Princess, who at the first, for her rare virtues and courtesies, was honoured of all men, and beloved of her husband, as soon as she once gave ear to the tyrant Fengon, forgot both the rank she held among the greatest dames, and the duty of an honest wife on her behalf.

But I will not stand to gaze and marvel at women : for that there are many which seek to blaze and set them forth : in which their writings, they spare not to blame them all for the faults of some one or few women. But I say that either nature ought to have bereaved men of that opinion to accompany with women, or else to endow them with spirits as that they may easily support the crosses they endure, without complaining so often and so strangely, seeing it is their own beastliness that overthrows them. For if it be so, that a woman is so imperfect a creature as they make her to be : and that they know this beast to be so hard to be tamed as they affirm : why then are they so foolish to preserve them, and so dull and brutish as to trust their deceitful and wanton embracings. But let us leave her in this extremity of lasciviousness, and proceed to show you, in what sort the young Prince Hamlet behaved himself, to escape the tyranny of his uncle.

CHAPTER II.

How Hamlet counterfeited the madman, to escape the.tyranny of his uncle, and how he was tempted by a woman (through his uncle's procurement), who thereby thought to undermine the Prince, and by that means to find out whether he counterfeited madness or not: and how Hamlet would by no means be brought to consent unto her; and what followed.

GERUTH having, as I said before, so much forgotten herself, the Prince Hamlet perceived himself to be in danger of his life, as being abandoned of his own mother, and forsaken of all men. Assuring himself that Fengon would not detract the time to send him the same way his father Horvendile was gone, to beguile the tyrant in his subtleties (that esteemed him to be of such a mind, that if he once attained to man's estate, he would not long delay the time to revenge the death of his father) he counterfeited the madman with such craft and subtle practices that he made shew as if he had utterly lost his wits. Under that veil he covered his pretence, and defended his life from the treasons and practices of the tyrant his uncle. And although he had been at the school of the Roman Prince, who because he counterfeited himself to be a fool, was called Brutus, yet he imitated his fashions and his wisdom. For every day being in the Queen's Palace (who as then was more careful to please Fengon, than ready to revenge the cruel death of her husband, or to restore her son to his inheritance) he rent and tore his clothes, wallowing and lying in the dirt and mire, his face all filthy and black; he ran through the streets like a man distraught, not speaking one word, but such as seemed to proceed from madness and mere frenzy. All his actions and gestures were no other than the right counten-ances of a man wholly deprived of all reason and understanding: in such sort that as then he seemed fit for nothing but to make sport to the pages and ruffling courtiers that attended in the court of his uncle and father-in-law.   But the young Prince noted them well enough, minding one day to be revenged in such manner that the memory thereof should remain perpetually to the world.

Behold, I pray you, a great point of a wise and brave spirit in a young Prince, by so great a show of imperfection in his person for advancement, and his own embasing and despising, to work the means and prepare the way for himself to be one of the happiest kings in his age.   In like sort, never any man was reputed by any of his actions more wise and prudent than Brutus, dissembling a great alteration in his mind, for that the occasion of such his device of foolishness proceeded only of a good and mature counsel and deliberation; not only to preserve his goods and shun the rage of the proud tyrant, but also to open a large way to procure the banishment and utter ruin of wicked Tarquinius, and to enfranchise the people (which were before oppressed) from the yoke of a great and miserable servitude. And so did not only Brutus, but this man and worthy Prince, to whom we may also add King David, that counterfeited the madman among the petty kings of Palestina, to preserve his life from the subtle practices of those kings.   I show this example unto such as, being offended with any great personage, have not sufficient means to prevail in their intents, or revenge the injury by them received.   But when I speak of revenging any injury received upon a great personage or superior, it must be understood by such an one as is not our sovereign, against whom we may by no means resist, nor once practise any treason nor conspiracy against his life.   He that will follow this course, must speak and do all things whatsoever that are pleasing and acceptable to him whom he meaneth to deceive, practise his actions, and esteem him above all men, clean contrary to his own intent and meaning.   For that is rightly to play and counterfeit the fool, when a man is constrained to dissemble, and kiss his hand, whom in his heart he could wish an hundred foot deep under the earth, so he might never see him more, if it were not a thing wholly to be disliked in a Christian, who by no means ought to have a bitter gall, or desires infected by revenge.

Hamlet in this sort counterfeiting the madman, many times did divers actions of great and deep consideration, and often made such and so fit answers, that a wise man would have judged from what spirit so fine an invention might proceed. Standing by the fire and sharpening sticks like poinards and pricks, one in smiling manner asked him wherefore he made those little staves so sharp at the points. "I prepare," saith he, "piercing darts, and sharp arrows to revenge my father's death." Fools, as I said before, esteemed those his words as nothing; but men of quick spirits, and such as had a deeper reach, began to suspect somewhat, esteeming that under that kind of folly there lay hidden a great and rare subtlety such as one day might be prejudicial to their prince. They said that under colour of such rudeness he shadowed a crafty policy, and by his devised simplicity, he concealed a sharp and pregnant spirit; for which cause they counselled the King to try and know, if it were possible, how to discover the intent and meaning of the young Prince.

But they could find no better, nor more fit invention to entrap him, than to set some fair and beautiful woman in a secret place, that with flattering speeches and all the craftiest means she could use, should purposely seek to allure his mind. To this end certain courtiers were appointed to lead Hamlet into a solitary place within the woods, whither they brought the woman. And surely the poor Prince at this assault had been in great danger, if a gentleman that in Horvendile's time had been nourished with him had not shown himself more affectioned to the bringing up he had received with Hamlet, than desirous to please the Tyrant, who by all means sought to entangle the son in the same nets wherein the father had ended his days. This gentleman bare the courtiers, appointed as aforesaid of this treason, company; more desiring to give the Prince instructions what he should do than to entrap him. He made full account that the least show of perfect sense and wisdom that Hamlet should make would be sufficient to cause him to lose his life: and therefore by certain signs, he gave Hamlet intelligence in what danger he was like to fall if by any means he seemed to obey. This much abashed the Prince, as then wholly being in affection to the Lady. But by her he was likewise informed of the treason, as being one that from her infancy loved and favoured him, and would have been exceeding sorrowful for his misfortune, whom she loved more than herself. The Prince in this sort having both deceived the courtiers and the lady's expectation, every man thereupon assured themselves that without all doubt he was distraught of his senses; that his brains were as then wholly void of force, and incapable of reasonable apprehension, so that as then Fengon's practice took no effect. But for all that he left not off: still seeking by all means to find out Hamlet's subtilty, as in the next chapter you shall perceive.

CHAPTER III.

How Fengon, uncle to Hamlet, a second time to entrap him in his politic madness, caused one of his counsellors to be secretly hidden in the Queen's chamber, behind the arras, to hear what speeches passed between Hamlet and the Queen, and how Hamlet killed him and escaped that danger, and what followed.

AMONG the friends of Fengon, there was one that above all the rest, doubted of Hamlet's practises, in counterfeiting the madman. He for that cause said, that it was impossible that so crafty a gallant as Hamlet that counterfeited the fool, should be discovered with so common and unskilful practices, which might easily be perceived, and that to find out his politic pretence it were necessary to invent some subtle and crafty means, more attractive, whereby the gallant might not have the leisure to use his accustomed dissimulation. To effect this he said he knew a fit way and a most convenient mean to effect the King's desire, and thereby to entrap Hamlet in his subtilties, and cause him of his own accord to fall into the net prepared for him, and thereby evidently show his secret meaning.

His device was thus, that King Fengon should make as though

he were to go some long voyage, concerning affairs of great importance, and that in the meantime Hamlet should be shut up
alone in a chamber with his mother.   Wherein some other should
secretly be hidden behind the hangings, unknown either to him
or his mother, there to stand and hear their speeches, and the
complots by them to be taken, concerning the accomplishments
of the dissembling fool's pretence.   He assured the King that if
there were any point of wisdom and perfect sense in the gallant's
spirit, that without all doubt he would easily discover it to his
mother, as being devoid of all fear that she would utter or make
known his secret intent, being the woman that had borne him in
her body, and nourished him so carefully.   He withal offered
himself to be the man that should stand to hearken, and bear
witness of Hamlet's speeches with his mother; that he might not
be esteemed a counsellor in such a case wherein he refused to be
the executioner, for the behoof and service of his Prince.

This invention pleased the King exceeding well.   He esteemed
it as the only and sovereign remedy to heal the Prince of his
lunacy, and to that end making a long voyage, issued out of his
palace, and rode to hunt in the forest.   Meantime the counsellor
entered secretly into the Queen's chamber, and there hid himself
behind the arras, not long before the Queen and Hamlet came
thither.   Hamlet being crafty and politic, as soon as he was within
the chamber, doubting some treason, and fearing if he should
speak severely and wisely to his mother touching his secret practices he should be understood, and by that means intercepted,
used his ordinary manner of dissimulation.   He began to come
like a cock beating with his arms in such manner as cocks use
to strike with their wings, upon the hangings of the chamber,
whereby, feeling something stirring under them, he cried, "A rat,
a rat," and presently drawing his sword thrust it into the hangings.
This done, he pulled the counsellor, half dead, out by the heels,
made an end of killing him, and being slain, cut his body in
pieces, which he caused to be boiled and then cast it into an
open vault, that so it might serve for food to the hogs.

By this means, having discovered the ambush, and given the

inventor thereof his just reward, he came again to his mother, who in the meantime wept and tormented herself, to see all her hopes frustrate, for that, what fault soever she had committed, yet was she sore grieved to see her only child made a mere mockery, every man reproaching her with his folly. One point thereof she had as then seen before her eyes, which was no small prick to her conscience, esteeming that the Gods sent her that punishment for joining incestuously in marriage with the tyrannous murderer of her husband. He likewise ceased not to invent all the means he could, to bring his nephew to his end, accusing his own natural indiscretion, as being the ordinary guide of those that so much desire the pleasures of the body, who shutting up the way to all reason respect not what may ensue of their lightness and great inconstancy. For a pleasure of small moment is sufficient to give them cause of repentance, during their lives, and make them curse the day and time that ever any such apprehensions entered into their minds, or that they closed their eyes to reject the honesty requisite in Ladies of her quality, and to despise the holy institution of those dames that had gone before her both in nobility and virtue. Geruth called to mind the great praises and commendations given by the Danes to Rinde, daughter to King Rothere, the chastest Lady in her time, and withal so shamefast that she would never consent to marriage with any prince or knight whatsoever; surpassing in virtue all the ladies of her time, as she herself surmounted them in beauty, good behaviour, and comeliness.

While in this sort the Queen sat tormenting herself, Hamlet entered into the chamber, who having once again searched every corner of the same, distrusting his mother as well as the rest, and perceiving himself to be alone, began in sober and discreet manner to speak unto her saying,—

"What treason is this, O most infamous woman, of all that ever prostrated themselves to the will of an abominable man, who under the veil of a dissembling creature covereth the most wicked and detestable crime that man could ever imagine, or was committed. How may I be assured to trust you, that like a vile wanton adulteress, altogether impudent and given over to her pleasure, runs spreading forth her arms joyfully to embrace the traitorous villainous tyrant, that murdered my father, and most incestuously receivest the villain into the lawful bed of your loyal spouse, impudently entertaining him instead of the dear father of your miserable and discomforted son, if the gods grant him not the grace speedily to escape from a captivity so unworthy the degree he holdeth, and the race and noble family of his ancestors. Is this the part of a queen, and daughter to a king? to live like a brute beast, to follow the pleasure of an abominable king, that hath murdered a far more honester and better man than himself in massacring Horvendile, the honour and glory of the Danes, who are now esteemed of no force nor valour at all, since the shining splendour of knighthood, was brought to an end by the most wickedest, and cruelest villain living upon earth. I for my part will never account him for my kinsman, nor once know him for mine uncle, nor you my dear mother for not having respect to the blood that ought to have united us so straitly together, and who neither with your honour nor without suspicion of consent to the death of your husband could ever have agreed to have married with his cruel enemy. O Queen Geruth, it is licentiousness only that hath made you deface out of your mind the memory of the valour and virtues of the good King your husband and my father! It was an unbridled desire that guided the daughter of Roderick to embrace the Tyrant Fengon, and not to remember Horvendile, unworthy of so strange entertainment; neither that he killed his brother traitorously, and that she being his father's wife betrayed him, although he so well favoured and loved her, that for her sake he utterly bereaved Norway of her riches and valiant soldiers, to augment the treasures of Roderick, and make Geruth wife to the hardiest prince in Europe. It is not the part of a woman, much less of a Princess, in whom all modesty, courtesy, compassion and love ought to abound, thus to leave her dear child to fortune in the bloody and murderous hands of a villain and traitor. Brute beasts do not so: for lions, tigers, ounces, and leopards fight for the safety and defence of their

whelps; and birds that have beaks, claws, and wings, resist such
as would ravish them of their young ones; but you to the contrary expose and deliver me to death, whereas ye should defend
me. Is not this as much as if you should betray me, when you,
knowing the perverseness of the tyrant and his intents, full of
deadly counsel as touching the race and image of his brother,
have not once sought nor desired to find the means to save your
child and only son by sending him into Swethland, Norway, or
England, rather than to leave him as a prey to your infamous
adulterer? Be not offended, I pray you, Madame, if transported
with dolour and grief I speak so boldly unto you, and that I
respect you less than duty requireth, for you having forgotten me,
and wholly rejected the memory of the deceased King my father,
must not be abashed if I also surpass the bounds and limits of
due consideration. Behold into what distress I am now fallen,
and to what mischief my fortune and your over great lightness,
and want of wisdom have induced me, that I am constrained to
play the madman to save my life, instead of using and practising
arms, following adventures, and seeking all means to make myself known to be the true and undoubted heir of the valiant and
virtuous King Horvendile. It was not without cause, and just
occasion, that my gestures, countenances, and words seem all to
proceed from a madman, and that I desire to have all men
esteem me wholly deprived of sense and reasonable understanding, because I am well assured, that he who hath made no conscience to kill his own brother (accustomed to murders, and
allured with desire of government without control in his treasons)
will not spare to save himself with the like cruelty, in the blood
and flesh of the loins of his brother, by him massacred: and
therefore, it is better for me to fain madness than to use my right
senses as nature hath bestowed them upon me. The bright
shining clearness thereof I am forced to hide under this shadow
of dissimulation, as the sun doth her beams under some great
cloud, when the weather in summer time overcasteth. The face
of a madman serveth to cover my gallant countenance, and the
gestures of a fool are fit for me, to the end that guiding myself

wisely therein I may preserve my life for the Danes, and the memory of my late deceased father. For the desire of revenging his death is so engraven in my heart that if I die not shortly, I hope to take such and so great vengeance, that these countries shall for ever speak thereof. Nevertheless I must stay the time, means, and occasion; lest by making over great haste I be now the cause of mine own sudden ruin and overthrow, and by that means, end, before I begin to effect my heart's desire. He that hath to do with a wicked, disloyal, cruel, and discourteous man, must use craft, and politic inventions, such as a fine wit can best imagine, not to discover his enterprise: for seeing that by force I cannot effect my desire, reason alloweth me by dissimulation, subtilty, and secret practices to proceed therein. To conclude, weep not, Madame, to see my folly, but rather sigh and lament your own offence, tormenting your conscience in regard of the infamy that hath so defiled the ancient renown and glory that (in times past) honoured Queen Geruth: for we are not to sorrow and grieve at other men's vices, but for our own misdeeds, and great follys. I desire you, for the surplus of my proceedings, above all things, as you love your own life and welfare, that neither the King, nor any other, may by any means know mine intent, and let me alone with the rest, for I hope in the end to bring my purpose to effect."

Although the Queen perceived herself nearly touched, and that Hamlet moved her to the quick, where she felt herself interested, nevertheless she forgot all disdain and wrath, which thereby she might as then have had, hearing herself so sharply chidden and reproved, for the joy she then conceived, to behold the gallant spirit of her son, and to think what she might hope, and the easier expect, of his great policy and wisdom. But on the one side she durst not lift up her eyes to behold him, remembering her offence, and on the other side she would gladly have embraced her son, in regard of the wise admonitions by him given unto her. They quenched the flames of unbridled desire that before had moved her to affect King Fengon, and engrafted in her heart the virtuous actions of her lawful spouse, whom inwardly she much lamented, when she beheld the lively image and portraiture of his virtue and great wisdom in her child, representing his father's haughty and valiant heart. So overcome and vanquished with this honest passion, and weeping most bitterly, having long time fixed her eyes upon Hamlet, as being ravished into some great and deep contemplation, and as it were wholly amazed, at the last embracing him in her arms, with the like love that a virtuous mother may or can use, to kiss and entertain her own child, she spake unto him in this manner.

"I know well, my son, that I have done thee great wrong in marrying with Fengon, the cruel tyrant and murderer of thy father and my loyal spouse. But when thou shalt consider the small means of resistance, and the treason of the palace, with the little cause of confidence we are to expect or hope for of the courtiers, all wrought to his will, as also the power he made ready, if I should have refused to like of him, thou wouldst rather excuse, than accuse me of lasciviousness or inconstancy, much less offer me that wrong, to suspect that ever thy mother Geruth once consented to the death and murder of her husband. I swear unto thee by the majesty of the Gods that if it had lain in my power to resist the tyrant, although it had been with the loss of my blood, yea and my life, I would surely have saved the life of my Lord and husband with as good a will and desire, as since that time, I have often been a means to hinder and impeach[1] the shortening of thy life, which being taken away, I will no longer live here upon earth : for seeing that thy senses are whole and sound, I am in hope to see an easy means invented for the revenging of thy father's death. Nevertheless, mine own sweet son, if thou hast pity of thyself, or care of the memory of thy father, although thou wilt do nothing for her that deserveth not the name of a mother in this respect, I pray thee carry thine affairs wisely ; be not hasty, nor over furious in thy enterprises ; neither yet advance thyself more than reason shall move thee to effect thy purpose. Thou seest there is almost no man wherein thou mayest put thy

---

[1] *Impeach*, hinder ; a sense in which the word was once frequently used, and the original sense.

trust, nor any woman to whom I dare utter the least part of my secrets, that would not presently report it to thine adversary. He, although in outward show he dissembleth to love thee, the better to enjoy his pleasures of me, yet he distrusteth and feareth me for thy sake, and is not so simple to be easily persuaded that thou art a fool or mad. If thou chance to do anything that seemeth to proceed of wisdom or policy, how secretly soever it be done, he will presently be informed thereof, and I am greatly afraid that the devils have showed him what hath past at this present between us—Fortune so much pursueth and contrarieth our ease and welfare—or that this murder that now thou hast committed, be not the cause of both our destructions, which I by no means will seem to know, but will keep secret both thy wisdom and hardy enterprise. I beseech the Gods, my good son, that they guide thy heart, direct thy counsels, and prosper thy enterprise, so that I may see thee possess and enjoy that which is thy right, and wear the crown of Denmark, by the Tyrant taken from thee. May I rejoice in thy prosperity, and therewith content myself, seeing with what courage and boldness thou shalt take vengeance upon the murderer of thy father, as also upon all those that have assisted and favoured him in his murderous and bloody enterprise."

"Madame," said Hamlet, "I will put my trust in you, and from henceforth mean not to meddle further with your affairs, but beseech you, as you love your own flesh and blood, that you will from henceforth no more esteem of the adulterer mine enemy, whom I will surely kill, or cause to be put to death in despite of all the devils in hell. Have he never so many flattering courtiers to defend him, yet will I bring him to his death; and they themselves also shall bear him company therein, as they have been his perverse counsellors in the action of killing my father, and his companions in his treason, massacre, and cruel enterprise. Reason requireth, that even as traitorously they then caused their Prince to be put to death, that with the like, nay well much more justice they should pay the interest of their felonious actions.

"You know, Madame, how Hother your grandfather, and father to the good King Roderick, having vanquished Guimon, caused him to be burnt, for that the cruel villain had done the like to his lord Gevare, whom he betrayed in the night time. And who knoweth not that traitors and perjured persons deserve no faith nor loyalty to be observed towards them. Conditions made with murderers, ought to be esteemed as cobwebs, and accounted as if they were things never promised nor agreed upon. If I lay hands upon Fengon, it will neither be felony nor treason, he being neither my King nor my Lord; but I shall justly punish him as my subject, that hath disloyally behaved himself against his Lord and sovereign Prince. And seeing that glory is the reward of the virtuous, and the honour and praise of those that do service to their natural Prince, why should not blame and dishonour accompany Traitors, and ignominious death all those that dare be so bold as to lay violent hands upon sacred Kings, that are friends and companions of the gods, as representing their majesty and persons. To conclude, glory is the crown of virtue, and the price of constancy, and seeing that it never accompanieth with infelicity, but shunneth cowardice and spirits of base and traitorous conditions, it must necessarily follow, that either a glorious death will be mine end, or with my sword in hand, laden with triumph and victory, I shall bereave them of their lives that made mine unfortunate, and darkened the beams of that virtue which I possessed from the blood and famous memory of my Predecessors. For why should men desire to live, when shame and infamy are the executioners that torment their consciences. Villainy is the cause that withholdeth the heart from valiant enterprises, and diverteth the mind from honest desire of glory and commendation, which endureth for ever? I know it is foolishly done to gather fruit before it is ripe, and to seek to enjoy a benefit not knowing whether it belong to us of right: but I hope to effect it so well, and have so great confidence in my fortune that hitherto hath guided the action of my life, that I shall not die without revenging myself upon mine enemy, and that himself shall be the instrument of his own decay, and execute that which of myself I durst not have enterprised."

After this Fengon, as if he had been out some long journey,

came to the Court again and asked for him that had received the charge to play the intelligencer, to entrap Hamlet, in his dissembled wisdom. He was abashed to hear neither news nor tidings of him, and for that cause asked Hamlet what was become of him, naming the man. The Prince, that never used lying, and who in all the answers that ever he made during his counterfeit madness never strayed from the truth, as a generous mind is a mortal enemy to untruth, answered and said, that the counsellor he sought for was gone down through the privy; where, being choked by the filthiness of the place, the hogs meeting him had filled their bellies.

CHAPTER IV.

How Fengon the third time devised to send Hamlet to the King of England, with secret letters to have him put to death; and how Hamlet, when his companions slept, read the Letters, and instead of them, counterfeited others, willing the King of England to put the two Messengers to death, and to marry his daughter to Hamlet, which was effected, and how Hamlet escaped out of England.

A MAN would have judged anything rather than that Hamlet had committed that murder. Nevertheless Fengon could not content himself, but still his mind gave him, that the fool would play him some trick of legerdemain, and willing would have killed him. But he feared King Roderick, his father-in-law, and further durst not offend the Queen, mother to the fool, whom she loved and much cherished, showing great grief and heaviness to see him so transported out of his wits. And in that conceit, seeking to be rid of him, Fengon determined to find the means to do it by the aid of a stranger, making the King of England minister of his massacring resolution. He chose rather that his friend should defile his renown, with so great a wickedness, than himself to fall into perpetual infamy, by an exploit of so great cruelty. To the King of England Fengon purposed to send

Hamlet, and by letters desire the King of England to put Hamlet to death.

Hamlet understanding that he should be sent into England, presently doubted the occasion of his voyage. For that cause, speaking to the Queen, he desired her not to make any show of sorrow or grief for his departure, but rather counterfeit a gladness, as being rid of his presence, whom, although she loved, yet she daily grieved to see him in so pitiful estate, deprived of all sense and reason. He desired her further, that she should hang the hall with tapestry, and make it fast with nails upon the walls, and keep the brands for him which he had sharpened at the points then when as he said he made arrows to revenge the death of his father. Lastly, he counselled her, that the year after his departure being accomplished, she should celebrate his funerals : assuring her, that at the same instant, she should see him return with great contentment and pleasure unto her for that his voyage. Now to bear him company, were assigned two of Fengon's faithful ministers, bearing letters engraved in wood, that contained Hamlet's death, in such sort as he had advertised the King of England. But the subtle Danish prince, being at sea, whilst his companions slept, read the letters, and knew his uncle's great treason, with the wicked and villainous minds of the two courtiers that led him to the slaughter. He razed out the letters that concerned his death, and instead thereof graved others, with commission to the King of England to hang his two companions. Not content to turn the death they had devised against him upon their own necks, he wrote further, that King Fengon willed him, to give his daughter to Hamlet in marriage. So arriving in England, the messengers presented themselves to the King, giving him Fengon's letters ; who having read the contents, said nothing as then, but staid convenient time to effect Fengon's desire. Meantime he used the Danes familiarly, doing them that honour to sit at his table, for that kings as then were not so curiously nor solemnly served as in these our days. For in these days mean kings and lords of small revenue are as difficult and hard to be seen, as in times

R

past the monarchies of Persia used to be : or as it is reported of
the great King of Ethiopia, who will not permit any man to see
his face, which ordinarily he covereth with a veil.   And as the
messengers sat at the table with the King, subtle Hamlet was so
far from being merry with them, that he would not taste one
bit of meat, bread, nor cup of beer whatsoever, as then set upon
the table.   It was not without great wondering of the company,
abashed to see a young man and a stranger not to esteem of the
delicate meats and pleasant drinks served at the banquet, rejecting them as things filthy, evil of taste, and worse prepared.   The
King who for that time dissembled what he thought, caused his
guests to be conveyed into their chamber, willing one of his
secret servants to hide himself therein, and so certify him what
speeches passed among the Danes at their going to bed.

Now they were no sooner entered into the chamber, and those
that were appointed to attend upon them gone out, but Hamlet's
companions asked him why he refused to eat and drink of that
which he found upon the table, not honouring the banquet of so
great a king, that entertained them in friendly sort, with such
honour and courtesy as it deserved.   They said further, that he
did not well, but dishonoured him that sent him, as if he sent
men into England that feared to be poisoned by so great a king.
The Prince, that had done nothing without reason and prudent
consideration, answered them and said : "What I think you, that
I will eat bread dipt in human blood, and defile my throat with
the rust of iron, and use that meat that stinketh and savoureth of
man's flesh, already putrified and corrupted, and that scenteth like
the savour of a dead carrion long since cast into a vault I   And
how would you have me to respect the King, that hath the
countenance of a slave, and the Queen who, instead of great
majesty, hath done three things more like a woman of base
parentage, and fitter for a waiting Gentlewoman than beseeming
a Lady of her quality and estate."   Having said so, he used
many injurious and sharp speeches as well against the King
and Queen, as others that had assisted at the banquet for the
entertainment of the Danish Ambassadors.   But therein Hamlet

said truth, as hereafter you shall hear; for that in those days, the
North parts of the world living as then under Satan's laws, were
full of enchanters, so that there was not any young gentleman
whatsoever that knew not something therein sufficient to serve
his turn, if need required. As yet in those days in Gothland and
Biarmy, there are many that knew not what the Christian religion
permitteth, as by reading the histories of Norway and Gothland
you may easily perceive. And so Hamlet, while his father lived,
had been instructed in that devilish art, whereby the wicked
spirit abuseth mankind, and advertiseth him (as he can) of things
past.

It toucheth not the matter herein to discover the parts of
divination in man, and whether this Prince by reason of his over
great melancholy, had received those impressions, divining that
which never any but himself had before declared. The Philo-
sophers discoursing of divers deep points of philosophy attribute
the force of those divinations to such as are Saturnists by complexion, who oftentimes speak of things which, their fury ceasing,
they then already can hardly understand who are the pronouncers.
For that cause Plato saith, many diviners and many poets, after
the force and vigour of their fire beginneth to lessen, do hardly
understand what they have written, although entreating of such
things while the spirit of divination continueth upon them, they
do in such sort discourse thereof that the authors and inventors
of the arts themselves by them alleged commend their discourses
and subtle disputations. Likewise I mean not to relate that
which divers men believe, that a reasonable soul becometh the
habitation of a meaner sort of devils, by whom men learn the
secrets of things natural. Much less do I account of the supposed governors of the world feigned by magicians, by whose means
they brag to effect marvellous things. It would seem miraculous
that Hamlet should divine in that sort which after proved so true,
if, as I said before, the devil had not knowledge of things past.
But to grant that he knoweth things to come I hope you shall
never find me in so gross an error, nor will compare and make
equal derivation and conjecture with those that are made by the

spirit of God and pronounced by the holy prophets that tasted of that marvellous science, to whom only were declared the secrets and wondrous works of the almighty. Yet there are some imposturous companions that impute so much divinity to the Devil the father of lies, that they attribute unto him the truth of the knowledge of things that shall happen unto men. They allege the conference of Saul with the witch, although one example out of the Holy Scriptures specially set down for the condemnation of wicked man, is not of force to give a sufficient law to all the world. For they themselves confess that they can divine, not according to the universal cause of things, but by signs borrowed from such like causes, which are always alike ; and by those conjectures they can give judgment of things to come. But all this being grounded upon a weak support, which is a simple conjecture, and having so slender a foundation, as some foolish or late experience, the fictions being voluntary, it should be a great folly in a man of good judgment, specially one that embraceth the preaching of the gospel and seeketh after no other but the truth hereof, to repose upon any of these likelihoods or writings full of deceit.

As touching magical operations, I will grant them somewhat therein ; finding divers histories that write thereof, and that the Bible maketh mention and forbiddeth the use thereof. Yea the laws of the Gentiles and ordinances of Emperors, have been made against it, in such sort, that Mahomet the great Heretic and friend of the Devil, by whose subtleties he abused most part of the East countries, hath ordained great punishments for such as use and practise those unlawful and damnable arts. Which for this time leaving off, let us return to Hamlet, brought up in these abuses, according to the manner of his country, whose companions hearing his answer reproached him of folly, saying that he could by no means show a greater point of indiscretion than in despising that which is lawful, and rejecting that which all men received as a necessary thing. They said that he had grossly forgotten himself, as in that sort to accuse such and so excellent a man as the King of England, and to slander the Queen, being then as famous and wise a princess, as any at that day reigning in the Islands thereabouts, who would cause him to be punished, according to his deserts. But he continuing in his dissimulation, mocked, saying that he had not done anything that was not good and most true. On the other side the King being advertised thereof by him that stood to hear the discourse, judged presently that Hamlet speaking so ambiguously was either a perfect fool, or else one of the wisest princes in his time, answering so suddenly, and so much to the purpose, upon the demand by his companions made touching his behaviour. The better to find the truth he caused the babbler to be sent for, of whom he inquired in what place the corn grew whereof he made bread for his table, and whether in that ground there were not some signs or news of a battle fought whereby human blood had therein been shed? The babbler answered that not far from thence there lay a field full of dead men's bones, in times past slain in a battle, as by the great heaps of wounded skulls, might well appear, and for that the ground in that part was become fertiler than other grounds, by reason of the fat and humours of the dead bodies, that every year the farmers used there to have in the best wheat they could find to serve his majesty's house. The King perceiving it to be true, according to the young Prince's words, asked where the hogs had been fed that were killed to be served at his table? Answer was made him, that those hogs getting out of the said field wherein they were kept, had found the body of a thief that had been hanged for his demerits, and had eaten thereof. Whereat the King of England being abashed, would needs know with what water the beer he used to drink of, had been brewed? which having known, he caused the river to be digged somewhat deeper, and therein found great store of swords and rusty armours, that gave an ill savour to the drink.

It were good that I should here dilate somewhat of Merlin's prophesies which are said to be spoken of him before he was fully one year old. If you consider well what hath already been spoken, it is no hard matter to divine of things past, although the minister of Satan therein played his part, giving sudden and prompt answers to this young Prince, for that herein are nothing but natural things, such as were well known to be true, and therefore not needful to dream of things to come. This known, the King was greatly moved with a certain curiosity to know why the Danish Prince said that he had the countenance of a slave, suspecting thereby that he reproached the baseness of his blood and that he would affirm that never any Prince had been his sire. Wherein to satisfy himself, he went to his mother, and leading her into a secret chamber, which he shut as soon as they were entered, desired her of her honour to show him of whom he was engendered in this world. The good Lady, well assured that never any man had been acquainted with her love touching any other man than her husband, sware that the King her husband only was the man, but the King her son, already convinced with the truth of the Danish Prince's answers, threatened his mother to make her tell by force, if otherwise she would not confess it. She for fear of death, acknowledged that she had given herself to a slave, and made him father to the King of England. Whereat the King was abashed and wholly ashamed. I give them leave to judge who esteem themselves honester than their neighbours, and suppose that there can be nothing amiss in their houses, whether they would make more inquiry than is requisite to know that which they would rather not have known. Nevertheless, dissembling what he thought, and biting upon the bridle, rather than he would deprive himself, by publishing the lasciviousness of his mother, this King of England thought better to leave a great sin unpunished than thereby to make himself contemptible to his subjects, who peradventure would have rejected him, as not desiring to have a bastard to reign over so great a kingdom.

But as he was sorry to hear his mother's confession, on the other side he took great pleasure in the subtilty and quick spirit of the young Prince, and for that cause went unto him to ask him why he had reproved three things in his Queen convenient for a slave, and savouring more of baseness than of royalty, and far unfit for the majesty of a great Prince. The King, not content to have received a great displeasure by knowing himself to be a bastard, and to have heard with what injuries he charged her whom he loved best in all the world, would not content himself until he

·also understood that which displeased him as much as his own proper disgrace. This was that his Queen was the daughter of a chambermaid, and withal Hamlet noted certain foolish countenances she made, which not only showed of what parentage she came, but also that her humours savoured of the baseness and low degree of her parents, whose mother, he assured the King, was as then yet holden in servitude. The King admiring the young Prince, and beholding in him some matter of greater respect than in the common sort of men, gave him his daughter in marriage, according to the counterfeit letters by him devised, and the next day caused the two servants of Fengon to be executed, to satisfy, as he thought, King Fengon's desire. But Hamlet, although the sport pleased him well, and that the King of England could not have done him a greater favour, made as though he had been much offended, threatening the King to be revenged. The King, to appease him, gave him a great sum of gold, which Hamlet caused to be molten, and put it into two staves, made hollow for the same purpose, to serve his turn therewith as need should require. Of all other the King's treasures he took nothing with him into Denmark but only those two ·staves. As soon as the year began to be at an end, having somewhat before obtained licence of the King, his father-in-law, to depart, Hamlet went for Denmark. Then with all speed that he could he should return again into England to marry the King of England's daughter, and so set sail for Denmark.

CHAPTER V.

How Hamlet, having escaped out of England, arrived in Denmark the same day that the Danes were celebrating his funerals, supposing him to be dead in England; and how he revenged his father's death upon his uncle and the rest of the courtiers; and what followed.

HAMLET in that sort sailing into Denmark, being arrived in the country, entered into the palace of his uncle the same day that they were celebrating his funerals. Going into the hall, he procured no small astonishment and wonder to them all, no man thinking other but that he had been dead. Among the which many cf them had rejoiced not a little, for the pleasure which they knew Fengon would conceive for so pleasant a loss ; and some were sad, as remembering the honourable King Horvendile, whose victories they could by no means forget, much less deface out of their memories that which pertained unto him. These greatly rejoiced to see a false report spread of Hamlet's death, and that the tyrant had not as yet obtained his will of the heir of Jutie. They rather hoped God would restore him to his senses again for the good and welfare of that province. Their amazement at the last being turned into laughter, all that as then were assistant at the funeral banquet of him whom they esteemed dead, mocked at each other for having been so simply deceived. Wondering at the Prince, that in his so long a voyage he had not recovered any of his senses, they asked what was become of them that had borne him company into Great Britain, to whom he made answer (showing them the two hollow staves, wherein he had put his molten gold, that the King of England had given him to appease his fury, concerning the murder of his two companions) and said, here they are both. Whereat many that already knew his humours, presently conjectured that he had played some trick of legerdemain, and to deliver himself out of danger, had thrown them into the pit prepared for him. So fearing to follow after them and light upon some evil adventure, they went presently out of the court, and it was well for them that they did so, considering the tragedy acted by him the same day. It had been accounted his funeral, but in truth their last day that as then rejoiced. For when every man busied himself to make good cheer, and Hamlet's arrival provoked them more to drink and carouse, the Prince himself at that time played the butler and a gentleman attending on the tables. He did not suffer the pots nor goblets to be empty, whereby he gave the noblemen such store of liquor, that all of them being full laden with wine and gorged with meat, were constrained to lay themselves down in the same

place where they had supped, so much their senses were dulled,
and overcome with the fire of over great drinking, a vice common
and familiar among the Almaines, and other nations inhabiting
the north parts of the world. When Hamlet perceived this, and
found so good opportunity to effect his purpose and be revenged
of his enemies, and by that means to abandon the actions, gestures, and apparel of a madman, occasion so fitly finding his turn,
and as it were effecting itself, he failed not to take hold thereof.
Seeing those drunken bodies, filled with wine, lying like hogs,
upon the ground, some sleeping, others vomiting the over great
abundance of wine which without measure they had swallowed
up, Hamlet made the hangings about the hall to fall down and
cover them all over, which he nailed to the ground, being boarded,
and at the ends thereof he stuck the brands whereof I spake before
by him sharpened, which served for pricks, binding and tying the
hangings, in such sort, that what force soever they used to loose
themselves, it was impossible to get from under them. And
presently he set fire in the four corners of the hall, in such sort
that of all that were as then therein not one escaped away. They
were forced to purge their sins by fire, and dry up the great
abundance of liquor by them received into their bodies, all of
them dying in the inevitable and merciless flames of the hot and
burning fire.

The Prince perceiving this, became wise, and knowing that his
uncle before the end of the banquet had withdrawn himself into
his chamber, which stood apart from the place where the fire
burnt, he went thither, and entering into the chamber laid hand
upon the sword of his father's murderer, leaving his own which,
while he was at the banquet, some of the courtiers had nailed
fast into the scabbard. Then going to Fengon, Hamlet said, "I
wonder, disloyal king, how thou canst sleep here at thine ease
when all thy palace is burnt. The fire thereof has burnt the
greatest part of thy courtiers and ministers of thy cruelty and
detestable tyrannies. What is more, I cannot imagine how thou
shouldst well assure thyself and thy estate, as now to take thy
ease, seeing Hamlet so near thee armed with the shafts by him

prepared long since and at this present ready to revenge the traitorous injury by thee done to his Lord and Father."

Fengon then knew the truth of his nephew's subtle practice, and heard him speak with stayed mind. What is more, he perceived a sword naked in his hand, which he already lifted up to deprive him of his life. He leaped then quickly out of the bed, taking hold of Hamlet's sword, that was nailed into the scabbard, which as he sought to pull out, Hamlet gave him such a blow upon the chin of the neck, that he cut his head clean from his shoulders, and as he fell to the ground said: "This just and violent death is a first reward for such as thou art. Now go thy ways, and when thou comest in hell, see thou forget not to tell thy brother, whom thou traitorously slewest, that it was his son that sent thee thither with the message, to the end that being comforted thereby, his soul may rest among the blessed spirits, and quit me of the obligation which bound me to pursue his vengeance upon mine owne blood, that seeing it was by thee that I lost the chief thing that tied me to this alliance and con-sanguinity."

This was a man, to say the truth, hardy, courageous, and worthy of eternal commendation, who arming himself with a crafty, dissembling and strange show of being distract out of his wits, under that pretence deceived the wise, politic, and crafty: thereby not only preserving his life from the treasons and wicked practices of the tyrant, but, which is more, by a new and unexpected kind of punishment revenged his father's death many years after the act committed. He directed his courses with such patience, and effected his purposes with so great boldness and constancy, that he left a judgment to be decided among men of wisdom which was more commendable in him, his constancy, or magnanimity, or his wisdom in ordering his affairs, according to the premeditable determination he had conceived.

If vengeance ever seem to have any show of justice, it is then, when piety and affection constrain us to remember our fathers unjustly murdered, as the things whereby we are dis-

pensed withal, and which seek the means not to leave treason
and murder unpunished : seeing David a holy and just king, and
of nature simple, courteous, and debonaire, yet when he died he
charged his son Solomon, that succeeded him in his throne, not
to suffer certain men that had done him injury to escape unpunished. Not that this holy king, as then ready to die, and to give
account before God of all his actions, was careful or desirous of
revenge, but to leave this example unto us, that where the Prince
or country is interested, the desire of revenge cannot by any
means (how small soever) bear the title of condemnation, but is
rather commendable and worthy of praise : for otherwise the good
kings of Judah, nor others, had not pursued them to death that had
offended their predecessors, if God himself had not inspired and
engraven that desire within their hearts. Hereof the Athenian
laws bear witness, whose custom was to erect images in remembrance of those men that, revenging the injuries of the common-
wealth, boldly massacred tyrants and such as troubled the peace
and welfare of the citizens.

Hamlet having in this manner revenged himself, durst not
presently declare his action to the people, but to the contrary
determined to work by policy, so to give them intelligence what
he had done, and the reason that drew him thereunto. Being
accompanied with such of his father's friends that then were
rising, he stayed to see what the people would do, when they
should hear of that sudden and fearful action. The next morning the towns bordering thereabouts desiring to know from
whence the flames of fire proceeded which they had seen the
night before, came thither, and perceiving the King's palace burnt
to ashes and many bodies, most part consumed, lying among the
ruins of the house, all of them were much abashed, nothing being
left of the palace but the foundation. But they were much more
amazed to behold the body of the King all bloody, and his head
cut off lying hard by him. Thereat some began to threaten revenge, yet not knowing against whom. Others, beholding so
lamentable a spectacle, armed themselves. The rest rejoiced,
yet dare not to make any show thereof. Some detested the

cruelty, others lamented the death of their Prince ; but the greatest part, calling Horvendile's murder to remembrance, acknow-
ledging a just judgment from above, that had thrown down the
pride of the tyrant. In this sort the diversities of opinions among
the multitude of the people being many, yet every man ignorant
what would be the issue of that tragedy, none stirred from thence,
neither yet attempted to move any tumult, every man fearing his
own skin and distrusting his neighbour, esteeming each other to
be consenting to the massacre.

CHAPTER VI.

How Hamlet, having slain his Uncle and burnt his palace, made
an oration to the Danes, to show them what he had done ; and
how they made him King of Denmark ; and what followed.

HAMLET then seeing the people to be so quiet, and most part of
them not using any words, all searching only and simply the cause
of this ruin and destruction, not minding to lose any time, but
aiding himself with the commodity thereof, entered among the
multitude of people, and, standing in the middle, spake unto
them as followeth :—

"If there be any among you, good people of Denmark, that as
yet have fresh within your memories the wrong done to the valiant
King Horvendile, let him not be moved, nor think it strange to
behold the confused, hideous, and fearful spectacle of this present
calamity. If there be any man that affecteth fidelity, and alloweth
of the love and duty that man is bound to show his parents, and
find it a just cause to call to remembrance the injuries and
wrongs that have been done to our progenitors, let him not be
ashamed beholding this massacre, much less offended to see so
fearful a ruin both of men and of the bravest house in all this
country. For the hand that hath done this justice could not effect
it by any other means, neither yet was it lawful for him to do it
otherwise than by ruinating both sensible and insensible things,
thereby to preserve the memory of a just vengeance.

"I see well, my good friends, and am very glad to know so good attention and devotion in you, that you are sorry before your eyes to see Fengon so murdered, and without a head, which heretofore you acknowledged for your commander. But I pray you remember, this body is not the body of a king, but of an execrable tyrant, and a parricide most detestable. O Danes, the spectacle was much more hideous when Horvendile your King was murdered by his brother. What, should I say a brother? Nay, rather by the most abominable executioner that ever beheld the same. It was you that saw Horvendile's members massacred, and that with tears and lamentations accompanied him to the grave. His body disfigured, hurt in a thousand places, and misused in ten times as many fashions. And who doubteth, seeing experience hath taught you, that the tyrant, in massacring your lawful King, sought only to infringe the ancient liberties of the common people? It was one hand only that murdering Horvendile, cruelly despoiled him of life, and by the same means unjustly bereaved you of your ancient liberties, and delighted more in oppression than to embrace the pleasant countenance of prosperous liberty, without adventuring for the same? And what mad man is he, that delighteth more in the tyranny of Fengon, than in the clemency and renewed courtesy of Horvendile? If it be so, that by clemency and affability, the hardest and stoutest hearts are mollified and made tractable, and that evil and hard usage causeth subjects to be outrageous and unruly: why behold you not the debonair carriage of the first, to compare it with the cruelties and insolences of the second, in every respect as cruel and barbarous as his brother was gentle, meek, and courteous. Remember, O you Danes, remember, what love and amity Horvendile showed unto you, with what equity and justice he swayed the great affairs of this kingdom, and with what humanity and courtesy he defended and cherished you, and then I am assured that the simplest man among you will both remember and acknowledge, that he had a most peaceable, just, and righteous King taken from him, to place in his throne a tyrant and murderer of his brother. Fengon hath perverted all right, abolished the ancient Laws of our fathers, contaminated the memories of our ancestors, and by his wickedness polluted the integrity of this kingdom, upon the neck thereof having placed the troublesome yoke of heavy servitude. He has abolished that liberty wherein Horvendile used to maintain you, and suffer you to live at your ease. And should you now be sorry to see the end of your mischiefs, and that this miserable wretch, pressed down with the burden of his offences, at this present payeth the usury of the parricide committed upon the body of his brother. Who would not himself be the revenger of the outrage done to me, whom he sought to deprive of mine inheritance, taking from Denmark a lawful successor, to plant a wicked stranger, and bring into captivity those that my father had enfranchised, and delivered out of misery and bondage? And what man is he that having any spark of wisdom, would esteem a good deed to be an injury, and account pleasures equal with wrongs and evident outrages? It were then great folly and temerity in Princes and valiant commanders in the wars, to expose themselves to perils and hazards of their lives for the welfare of the common people, if that for a recompense they should reap hatred and indignation of the multitude. To what end should Hother have punished Balder, if instead of recompense, the Danes and Swethlanders had banished him to receive and accept the successors of him that desired nought but his ruin and overthrow? What is he that hath so small feeling of reason and equity, that would be grieved to see treason rewarded with the like, and that an evil act is punished with just demerit, in the party himself that was the occasion? Who was ever sorrowful to behold the murderer of innocents brought to his end? or what man weepeth to see a just massacre done upon a Tyrant, usurper, villain, and bloody personage?

"I perceive you are attentive, and abashed for not knowing the author of your deliverance, and sorry that you cannot tell to whom you should be thankful for such and so great a benefit as the destruction of a tyrant, and the overthrow of a place that was the storehouse of his villainies and the true receptacle of all the thieves and traitors in this kingdom. But behold here in your presence him that brought so good an enterprise to effect. It is I, my good friends, it is I, that confess I have taken vengeance for the violence done unto my lord and father, and for the subjection and servitude that I perceived in this Country, whereof I am the just and lawful successor. It is I alone, that have done this piece of work whereunto you ought to have lent me your hands and therein have aided and assisted me, I have only accomplished that, which all of you might justly have effected, by good reason, without falling into any point of treason or felony. It is true that I hope so much of your good wills towards the deceased King Horvendile, and that the remembrances of his virtues is yet so fresh within your memories, that if I had required your aid herein you would not have denied it, specially to your natural Prince. But it liked me best to do it myself alone, thinking it a good thing to punish the wicked without hazarding the lives of my friends and loyal subjects, not desiring to burthen other men's shoulders with this weight, for that I made account to effect it well enough without exposing any man into danger, and by publishing the same should clean have overthrown the device which at this present I have so happily brought to pass. I have burnt the bodies of the courtiers to ashes, being companions in the mischiefs and treasons of the tyrant, but I have left Fengon whole, that you might punish his dead carcass, seeing that when he lived you durst not lay hands upon him, to accomplish the full punishment and vengeance due unto him, and so satisfy your choler upon the bones of him that filled his greedy hands and coffers with your riches, and shed the blood of your brethren and friends. Be joyful then, my good friends, make ready the nosegay for this usurping King, burn his abominable body and cast the ashes of him that hath been hurtful to all the world, into the air; drive from you the sparks of pity, to the end that neither silver, nor crystal cup, nor sacred tomb may be the restful habitation of the relics and bones of so detestable a man. Let not one trace of a parricide be seen, nor your country defiled with the presence of the least member of this tyrant without pity, that your neighbours may not smell the contagion, nor our land the polluted infection of a body condemned for his wickedness. I have done my part, to present him to you in this sort, now it belongs to you to make an end of the work and put to the last hand of duty, whereunto your several functions call you. For in this sort you must honour abominable princes : and such ought to be the funeral of a tyrant, parricide, and usurper both of the bed and patrimony that no way belonged unto him, who having bereaved his country of liberty, it is fit that the land refuse to give him a place for the eternal rest of his bones.

"O my good friends, seeing you know the wrong that hath been done unto me, what my griefs are and in what misery I have lived since the death of the King, my lord and father, and seeing that you have both known and tasted these things then whenas I could not conceive the outrage that I felt : what need I recite it unto you? What benefit would it be to discover it before them that knowing it would burst as it were with despite to hear of my hard chance, and curse Fortune for so much abasing a royal Prince as to deprive him of his majesty, although not any of you durst so much as show one sight of sorrow or sadness? You know how my stepfather conspired my death, and sought by divers means to take away my life, how I was forsaken of the Queen my mother, mocked of my friends, and despised of mine own subjects. Hitherto I have lived laden with grief, and wholly confounded in tears, my life still accompanied with fear and suspicion, expecting the hour when the sharp sword would make an end of my life and miserable anguishes. How many times counterfeiting the madman, have I heard you pity my distress, and secretly lament to see me disinherited, and yet no man sought to revenge the death of my father, nor to punish the treason of my incestuous uncle, full of murders and massacres? This charity ministered comfort, and your affectionate complaints made me evidently see your goodwills, that you had in memory the calamity of your Prince, and within your hearts engraven the desire of vengeance for the death of him that deserved a long life. What heart can be so hard and untractable, or spirit so severe, cruel and rigorous, that would not relent at the remembrance of my extremities, and take pity of an orphan child, so abandoned of the world? What eyes were so void of moisture, but would distil a field of tears, to see a poor prince assaulted by his own subjects, betrayed by his mother, pursued by his uncle, and so much oppressed that his friends durst not show the effects of their charity and good affection? O, my good friends, show pity to him whom you have nourished, and let your hearts take some compassion upon the memory of my misfortunes. I speak to you that are innocent of all treason, and never defiled your hands, spirits, nor desires with the blood of the great and virtuous Horvendile. Take pity upon the Queen some time your sovereign lady, and my right honourable mother, forced by the tyrant, and rejoice to see the end and extinguishing of the object of her dishonour, which constrained her to be less pitiful to her own blood so far as to embrace the murderer of her own dear spouse, charging herself with a double burden of infamy and incest, together with injuring and disannulling of her house, and the ruin of her race. This hath been the occasion that made me counterfeit folly, and cover my intents under a veil of mere madness, which hath wisdom and policy thereby to enclose the fruit of this vengeance which that it hath attained to the full point of efficacy and perfect accomplishment you yourselves shall be judges, for touching this and other things concerning my profit, and the managing of great affairs, I refer myself to your counsels, and thereunto am fully determined to yield, as being those that trample under your feet the murderers of my father, and despise the ashes of him that hath polluted and violated the spouse of his brother, by him massacred, that hath committed felony against his Lord, traitorously assailed the majesty of his King, and odiously thralled his country under servitude and bondage, and you his loyal subjects from whom he bereaved your liberty, and feared not to add incest to parricide, detestable to all the world, to you also it belongeth by duty and reason commonly to defend and protect Hamlet, the minister and executor of just vengeance, who being jealous of your honour and reputa-

S

tion, hath hazarded himself, hoping you will serve him for fathers, defenders, and tutors, and regarding him in pity, restore him to his goods and inheritances. It is I that have taken away the infamy of my country, and extinguished the fire that embraced your fortunes, I have washed the spots that defiled the reputation of the Queen, overthrowing both the tyrant and the tyranny and beguiling the subtleties of the craftiest deceiver in the world, and by that means brought his wickedness and impostures to an end. I was grieved at the injury committed both to my father, and my native country, and have slain him that used more rigorous commandments over you, than was either just or convenient to be used unto men that have commanded the valiantest nations in the world. Seeing then he was such a one to you, it is reason, that you acknowledge and think well of the benefit for the good I had done your posterity, and admiring my spirit and wisdom, choose me your King, if you think me worthy of the place. You see I am the author of your preservation, heir of my father's kingdom, not straying in any point from his virtuous action, no murderer, violent parricide, nor man that ever offended any of you but only the vicious. I am lawful successor in the kingdom, and just revenger of a crime above all others most grievous and punishable. It is to me, that you owe the benefit of your liberty received, and of the subversion of that tyranny that so much afflicted you. I have trodden under feet the yoke of the tyrant, and overwhelmed his throne, and taken the sceptre out of the hands of him that abused a holy and just authority: but it is you that are to recompense those that have well deserved, you know what is the reward of so great desert, and being in your hands to distribute the same, it is of you, that I demand the price of my virtue and the recompense of my victories."

This oration of the young Prince so moved the hearts of the Danes, and won the affections of the nobility, that some wept for pity other for joy, to see the wisdom and gallant spirit of Hamlet. Having made an end of their sorrow, all with one consent proclaimed him King of Jutie and Chersonese, at this present the proper country of Denmark. Having celebrated his coronation, and received the homages and fidelities of his subjects, he went into England to fetch his wife, and rejoiced with his father-in-law touching his good fortune. But it wanted little that the King of England had not accomplished that which Fengon with all his subtilties could never attain.

CHAPTER VII.

How Hamlet after his coronation went into England, and how the King of England secretly would have put him to death, and how he slew the King of England: and returned again to Denmark with two wives, and what followed.

HAMLET being in England showed the King what means he had wrought to recover his kingdom. But when the King of England understood of Fengon's death, he was both abashed and confused in his mind, at that instant feeling himself assailed with two great passions, for that in times past, he and Fengon having been companions together in arms, had given each other their faith and promises, by oath, that if either of them chanced to be slain by any man whatsoever, he that survived, taking the quarrel upon him as his own, should never cease till he were revenged, or at the least do his endeavour. This promise incited the barbarous king to massacre Hamlet. But the alliance, presenting itself before his eyes, and beholding the one dead, although his friend, and the other alive, and husband to his daughter, made him deface his desire of revenge. But in the end the conscience of his oath and promise obtained the upper hand, and secretly made him conclude the death of his son-in-law, which enterprise, after that, was cause of his own death and overrunning of the whole country of England by the cruelty and despight conceived by the King of Denmark. I have purposely omitted the discourse of that battle, as not much pertinent to our matter, as also, not to trouble you with too tedious a discourse, being content to show you the end of this wise and valiant King Hamlet, who revenging himself upon so many enemies, and discovering all the treasons practised against his life, in the end served for a sport to fortune, and an example to all great personages, that trust overmuch to the felicities of this world, that are of small moment and less continuance.

The King of England, perceiving that he could not easily effect his desire upon the King his son-in-law, as also not being willing to break the laws and rites of hospitality, determined to make a stranger the revenger of his injury, and so accomplish his oath made to Fengon without defiling his hands with the blood of the husband of his daughter, and polluting his house by the traitorous massacring of his friend. In reading of this history it seemeth Hamlet should resemble another Hercules, sent into divers places of the world, by Euristheus, solicited by Juno, where he knew any dangerous adventure, thereby to overthrow and destroy him ; or else Bellerophon sent to Ariobatus to put him to death; or, leaving profane histories, another Urias by King David appointed to be placed in the forefront of the battle, and the man that should be first slain by the barbarians. For the King of England's wife being dead not long before (although he cared not for marrying another woman) desired his son-in-law to make a voyage for him into Scotland, flattering him in such sort, that he made him believe that his singular wisdom caused him to prefer him to that embassage, assuring himself that it were impossible that Hamlet, the subtlest and wisest prince in the world, should take anything in the world in hand without effecting the same.

Now the Queen of Scots being a maid and of a haughty courage, despised marriage with all men, as not esteeming any worthy to be her companion, in such manner that by reason of this arrogant opinion there never came any man to desire her love but she caused him to lose his life. But the Danish King's fortune was so good that Hermetrude, for so was the Queen's name, hearing that Hamlet was come thither to entreat a marriage between her and the King of England, forgot all her pride, and despoiling herself of her stern nature, being as then determined to make him, being the greatest Prince as then living, her husband, and deprive the English Princess of her spouse, whom she thought fit for no one but herself. And so this Amazon without love, disdaining Cupid, by her free-will submitted her haughty mind. The Dane arriving in her Court, she desired to see the old King of England's letters, and mocking at his fond appetites, whose blood as then was half congealed, cast her eyes upon the young and pleasant Adonis of the North, esteeming herself happy to have such a prey fall into her hands, whereof she made her full account to have the possession. She that never had been overcome by the grace, courtesy, valour, or riches of any prince nor lord whatsoever, was as then vanquished with the only report of the subtleties of the Dane. She, knowing that he was already affianced to the daughter of the King of England, spake unto him and said, " I never looked for so great a bliss, neither from the Gods, nor yet from fortune, as to behold in my countries the most complete Prince in the North, and he that hath made himself famous and renowned through all the nations of the world, as well neighbours as strangers, for the only respect of his virtue, wisdom, and good fortune, serving him much in the pursuit and effect of divers things by him undertaken. I think myself much beholden to the King of England, although his malice seeketh neither my advancement nor the good of you, my Lord, to do me so much honour as to send me so excellent a man to entreat of a marriage (he being old and a mortal enemy to me and mine) with me that am such a one as every man seeth is not desirous to couple with a man of so base quality as he, whom you have said to be the son of a slave. But, on the other side, I marvel that the son of Horvendile, and grandchild to King Roderick, he that by his foolish wisdom and feigned madness surmounted the forces and subtleties of Fengon, and obtained the kingdom of his adversary, should so much abase himself, having otherwise been very wise and well advised in all his actions, touching his bedfellow, and he that for his excellency and valour surpasseth human capacity, should stoop so low as to take to wife her that, issuing from a servile race, hath only the name of a king for her father, for that the baseness of her blood will always cause her to show what are the virtues and noble qualities of her ancestors. And you, my Lord," said she, "are you so ignorant as not to know that marriage should not be measured by any foolish opinion of an outward beauty, but rather by virtues and antiquity of race, which maketh the wife to be honoured for her prudence, and never degenerating from the integrity of his ancestors? Exterior beauty also is nothing, where perfection of the mind doth not accomplish and adorn that which is outwardly seen to be in the body, and is lost by an accident and occurrence of small moment. As also such toys have deceived many men, and drawing them like enticing baits, have cast them headlong into the gulf of their ruin, dishonour, and utter overthrow. It was I to whom this advantage belonged, being a Queen, and such a one as for nobility may compare myself with the greatest princes in Europe, being nothing inferior unto any of them neither for antiquity of blood, nobility of parents, nor abundance of riches. I am not only a Queen, but such a one as that, receiving whom I will for my companion, can make him bear the title of a King, and with my body give him possession of a great kingdom and goodly province. Think then, my Lord, how much I account of your alliance, who being accustomed with the sword to pursue such as durst embolden themselves to win my love, it is to you only to whom I make a present both of my kisses, embracings, sceptre, and crown. What man is he, if he be not made of stone, would refuse so precious a pawn as Hermetrude with the kingdom of Scotland? Accept, sweet King, accept this Queen, who with so great love and amity desireth your so great profit, and can give you more contentment in one day than the Princess of England would yield you pleasure during her life. Although she surpass me in beauty, her blood being base, it is fitter for such a King as you are to choose Hermetrude, less beautiful, but noble and famous, rather than the English lady with great beauty, but issuing from an unknown race, without any title of honour."

Now, think if the Dane hearing such forcible reasons, and understanding that by her which he half-doubted, as also moved without choler for the treason of his father-in-law, that purposely sent him thither to lose his life, and being welcomed, kissed, and played withal by this Queen, young and reasonable fair, if he were not easy enough to be converted, and like to forget the affection of his first wife, with this to enjoy the realm of Scotland, and so open the way to become King of all Great Britain?

To conclude, he married her and led her with him to the King of England's Court, which moved the King from that time forward much more to seek the means to bereave him of his life. He had surely done it, if his daughter, Hamlet's other wife, more careful of him that had rejected her than of her father's welfare, had not discovered the enterprise to Hamlet, saying, "I know well, my Lord, that the allurements and persuasions of a bold and altogether shameless woman, being more lascivious than the chaste embracements of a lawful and modest wife, are of more force to entice and charm the senses of young men: but for my part I cannot take this abuse for satisfaction to leave me in this sort, without all cause, reason, or precedent fault once known in me your loyal spouse, and take more pleasure in the alliance of her who one day will be the cause of your ruin and overthrow. And although a just cause of jealousy and reasonable motion of anger dispense with me at this time to make no more account of you than you do of me, that am not worthy to be so scornfully rejected, yet matrimonial charity shall have more force and vigour in my heart than the disdain which I have justly conceived to see a concubine hold my place and a strange woman before my face enjoy the pleasures of my husband. This injury, my Lord, although great and offensive, which to revenge, divers ladies of great renown have in times past sought and procured the death of their husbands, cannot so much restrain my good-will, but that I may not choose but advertise you what treason is devised against you, beseeching you to stand upon your guard for that my father's only seeking is to bereave you of your life, which if it happen, I shall not long live after you. Many reasons induce me to love and cherish you, and those of great consequence, but specially and above all the rest, I am and must be careful of you, when I feel your unborn child; for which respect, without so much forgetting yourself, you ought to make more account of me than of your concubine. Her I will love because you love her, contenting myself that your son hateth her, in regard to the wrong she doth to his mother. For it is impossible that any passion or trouble of the mind whatsoever can quench those fierce passions of love that made me yours, neither that I should forget your favours past, when loyally you sought the love of the daughter of the King of England. Neither is it in the power of that thief that hath stolen your heart, nor my father's choler, to hinder me from seeking to preserve you from the cruelty of your dissembling friend (as heretofore, by counterfeiting the madman, you prevented the practices and treasons of your uncle Fengon), the complot being determined to be executed upon you and yours."

Without this advertisement the Dane had surely been slain, and the Scots that came with him. For the King of England, inviting his son-in-law to a banquet with the greatest courtesies that a friend can use to him whom he loved as himself, had the means to entrap him, and cause him dance a pitiful galliard, to celebrate the marriage between him and his new lady. But Hamlet went thither with armour under his clothes, and his men in like sort, by which means he and his escaped with little hurt; and so after that happened the battle before spoken of, wherein the King of England losing his life, his country was the third time sacked by the barbarians of the islands and country of Denmark.

CHAPTER VIII.

How Hamlet, being in Denmark, was assailed by Wiglerus, his uncle, and after betrayed by his last wife, called Hermetrude, and was slain: after whose death she married his enemy, Wiglerus.

HAMLET having obtained the victory against the King of England, and slain him, laden with great treasures and accompanied with his two wives, set forward to sail into Denmark. But by the way he had intelligence, that Wiglerus, his uncle, and son to Roderick, having taking the royal treasure from his sister Geruth, mother to Hamlet, had also seized upon the kingdom, saying that neither Horvendile nor any of his held it but by permission, and that it was in him, to whom the property belonged, to give the charge thereof to whom he would. But Hamlet, not desirous to have any quarrel with the son of him from whom his predecessors had received their greatness and advancement, gave such and so rich presents to Wiglerus, that he, being contented, withdrew himself out of the country and territories of Geruth's son. But within certain time after, Wiglerus, desirous to keep all the country in subjection, enticed by the conquest of Scanie and Sialandie, and also that Hermetrude, the wife of Hamlet, whom he loved more than himself, had secret intelligence with him, and had promised him marriage so he would take her out of the hands of him that held her, sent to defy Hamlet, and proclaimed open war against him. Hamlet, like a good and wise Prince, loving especially the welfare of his subjects, sought by all means to avoid that war. But again, refusing it, he perceived a great spot and blemish in his honour; and accepting the same, he knew it would be the end of his days. The desire of preserving his life was on the one side, and his honour on the other side, pricking him forward; but at the last, remembering that never any danger whatsoever had once shaken his virtues and constancy, he chose rather the necessity of his ruin than to lose the immortal fame that valiant and honourable men obtained in the wars. There is as much difference between a life without honour and an honourable death, as glory and renown is more excellent than dishonour and evil report.

But the thing that spoiled this virtuous Prince was the overgreat trust and confidence he had in his wife Hermetrude, and the vehement love he bare unto her. He did not once repent the wrong in that case done to his lawful spouse, and but for the which peradventure that misfortune had never happened unto him. He never thought that she whom he loved above all things would have so villainously betrayed him, he not once remembering his first wife's speeches, who prophesied unto him that the pleasures he seemed to take in his other wife would in the end be the cause of his overthrow. They had ravished him of the best part of his senses, and quenched in him the great prudence that made him admirable in all the countries in the ocean seas and through all Germany. Now, the greatest grief that this King (besotted on his wife) had, was the separation of her whom he adored, and assuring himself of his overthrow, he was desirous either that she might bear him company at his death, or else to find her a husband that should love her, he being dead, as well as ever he did. But the disloyal Queen had already provided herself of a marriage, to put her husband out of trouble and care for that. He perceiving him to be sad for her sake, when she should have absented herself from him, she to blind him the more, and to encourage him to set forward to his own destruction, promised to follow him whithersoever he went, and to take the like fortune that befell to him, were it good or evil, and that so she would give him cause to know how much she surpassed the English woman in her affection towards him, saying, that woman is accursed that feareth to follow and accompany her husband to the death. To hear her speak, men would have said that she had been the wife of Mithridates, or Zenobia Queen of Palmyra, she made so great a show of love and constancy. But by the effect, it was after easily perceived how vain the promise of this inconstant and wavering Princess was, and how incomparable the life of this Scottish Queen was to the vigour of her chastity, being a maid before she was married. For that Hamlet had no sooner entered into the field but she found means to see Wiglerus, and the battle began, wherein the miserable Danish Prince was slain. But Hermetrude presently yielded herself, with all her dead husband's treasures, into the hand of the tyrant, who, more than content with that metamorphosis so much desired, gave order that presently the marriage, bought with the blood and treasure of the son of Horvendile, should be celebrated.

Thus you see that there is no promise or determination of a woman but that a very small discommodity of fortune mollifieth and altereth the same, and which time doth not pervert; so that the misfortunes subject to a constant man shake and overthrow the natural slippery loyalty of the variable steps of women, wholly without any faithful assurance of love or true unfeigned constancy; for, as a woman is ready to promise, so is she heavy and slow to perform and effect that which she hath promised, as she that is without end or limit in her desires, flattering herself in the diversity of her wanton delights, and taking pleasure in diversity and change of new things, which as soon she doth forget and grow weary of. And, to conclude, such she is in all her actions; she is rash, covetous, and unthankful, whatsoever good or service be done unto her. But now I perceive I err in my discourse, vomiting such things unworthy of this sex; but the vices of Hermetrude have made me say more than I meant to speak, as also the Author from whence I take this history hath almost made me hold his course, I find so great a sweetness and liveliness in this kind of argument: and the rather because it seemeth so much the truer, considering the miserable success of poor King Hamlet.

Such was the end of Hamlet, son of Horvendile, Prince of Jutie, to whom, if his fortune had been equal with his inward and natural gifts, I know not which of the ancient Grecians and Romans had been able to have compared with him for virtue and excellency. But hard fortune followed him in all his actions, and yet he vanquishing the malice of his time, with the vigour of constancy, hath left us a notable example of haughty courage, worthy of a great Prince, arming himself with hope in things that were wholly without any colour or show thereof, and in all his honourable actions made himself worthy of perpetual memory, if one only spot had not blemished and darkened a good part of his praises. For that the greatest victory that a man can obtain is to make himself victorious and lord over his own affections, and that restraineth the unbridled desires of his concupiscence. For if a man be never so princely, valiant, and wise, if the desires and enticements of his flesh prevail and have the upper hand, he will abase his credit, and, gazing after strange beauties, become a fool, and, as it were, incensed, dote on the presence of women. This fault was in the great Hercules, Samson, and the wisest man that ever lived upon the earth, following this train, therein impaired his wit; and the most noble, wise, valiant, and discreet personages of our time, following the same course, have left us many notable examples of their worthy and notable virtues.

But I beseech you that shall read this history not to resemble the spider that feedeth of the corruption that she findeth in the flowers and fruits that are in the gardens, whereas the bee gathereth her honey out of the best and fairest flowers she can find. For a man that is well brought up should read the lives of whoremongers, drunkards, incestuous, violent, and bloody persons, not to follow their steps, and so to defile himself with such uncleanness, but to shun paliardise,[1] abstain the superfluities and drunkenness in banquets, and follow the modesty, courtesy, and continency that recommendeth Hamlet in this discourse, who, while other made good cheer, continued sober; and where all men sought as much as they could to gather together riches and treasure, he, simply accounting riches nothing comparable to honour, sought to gather a multitude of virtues, that might make him equal to those that by them were esteemed as gods, having not as then received the light of the Gospel, that men might see among the barbarians and them that were far from the knowledge of one only God, that nature was provoked to follow that which is good and those forward to embrace virtue, for that there was never any nation, how rude or barbarous soever, that took not some pleasure to do that which seemed good, thereby to win praise and commendations, which we have said to be the reward of virtue and good life. I delight to speak of these strange histories, and of people that were unchristened, that the virtue of the rude people may give more splendour to our nation, who, seeing them so complete, wise, prudent, and well advised in their actions, might strive not only to follow—imitation being a small matter—but to surmount them, as our religion surpasseth their superstition, and our age more purged, subtle, and gallant than the season wherein they lived and made their virtues known.

---

[1] *Paliardise, paillardise,* immodesty.

THE FAMOUS HISTORIE OF
FRYER BACON.

V,

THE FAMOUS HISTORIE OF FRYER BACON.

Of the Parents and Birth of Fryer Bacon, and how he addicted himselfe to Learning.

𝔍𝔫 𝔪𝔬𝔰𝔱 𝔪𝔢𝔫'𝔰 𝔬𝔭𝔦𝔫𝔦𝔬𝔫𝔰 he was borne in the west part of England and was sonne to a wealthy farmer, who put him to schoole to the parson of the towne where hee was borne : not with intent that he should turne fryer (as he did), but to get so much understanding, that he might manage the better that wealth hee was to leave him. But young Bacon tooke his learning so fast, that the priest could not teach him any more, which made him desire his master that he would speake to his father to put him to Oxford, that he might not lose that little learning that hee had gained : his master was very willing so to doe : and one day meeting his father, told him, that he had received a great blessing of God, in that he had given him so wise and hopefull a child, as his sonne Roger Bacon was (for so was he named), and wished him withall to doe his duty, and to bring up so his child, that hee might shew his thankfulnesse to God, which could not better be done then in making of him a scholler; for he found by his sodaine taking of his learning, that hee was a child likely to prove a very great clerke : hereat old Bacon was not well pleased (for he desired to bring him up to plough and to the cart, as hee him-selfe was brought), yet he for reverence sake to the priest, shewed not his anger, but kindly thanked him for his paines and counsell, yet desired him not to speake any more concerning that matter ;

for hee knew best what best pleased himselfe, and that he would doe : so broke they off their talke, and parted.

So soone as the old man came home, he called to his sonne for his bookes, which when he had, he lock'd them up, and gave the boy a cart whip in the place of them, saying to him : Boy, I will have you no priest, you shall not be better learned than I, you can tell now by the almanack when it is best sowing wheat, when barly, pease, and beane : and when the best libbing [1] is, when to sell graine and cattell I will teach thee ; for I have all faires and markets as perfit in my memory, as Sir John our priest has masse without booke : take mee this whip, I will teach thee the use of it, it will be more profitable to thee then this harsh Latin : make no reply, but follow my counsell, or else by the masse thou shalt feele the smart hand of my anger.   Young Bacon thought this but hard dealing, yet would he not reply, but within sixe or eight dayes he gave his father the slip, and went to a cloyster some twenty miles off, where he was entertained, and so continued his learning, and in small time came to be so famous, that he was sent for to the University of Oxford, where he long time studied, and grew so excellent in the studies of art and nature, that not England onely, but all Christendome admired him.

How the king sent for Fryer Bacon, and of the wonderfull things he shewed the king and queene.

THE king being in Oxfordshire, at a Noblemans house, was very desirous to see this famous fryer, for he had heard many times of his wondrous things that he had done by his art : therefore hee sent one for him to desire him to come to the court.   Fryer Bacon kindly thanked the king by the messenger, and said, that he was at the kings service, and would suddenly attend him : but sir, saith he (to the gentleman), I pray make you haste, or else I shall be two houres before you at the court.   For all your learning (answered the gentleman) I can hardly beleeve this, for schollers, old-men and travellers, may lye by authority.   To

---

[1] *Libbing,* gelding (Dutch, *lubben*).

strengthen your beliefe (said Fryer Bacon) I could presently
shew you the last wench that you kissed, but I will not at this
time. One is as true as the other (said the gentleman) and I
would laugh to see either. You shall see them both within these
foure houres, quoth the fryer, and therefore make what haste
you can. I will prevent that by my speed (said the gentleman),
and with that rid his way : but he rode out of his way, as it
should seem ; for he had but five miles to ride, and yet was he
better than three houres a riding them ; so that Fryer Bacon
by his art was with the king before he came.

The king kindly welcommed him, and said that hee long time
had desired to see him ; for he had as yet not heard of his life.
Fryer Bacon answered him that fame had belide him, and given
him that report that his poore studies had never deserved, for hee
beleeved that art had many sonnes more excellent then himselfe
was. The king commended him for his modesty, and told him,
that nothing could become a wise man lesse than boasting : but
yet withall he requested him now to be no niggard of his knowledge, but to shew his queene and him some of his skill. I
were worthy of neither art or knowledge (quod Fryer Bacon),
should I deny your maiestie this small request : I pray seat
yourselves, and you shall see presently what my poore skill can
performe : the king, queene, and nobles sate them all down.
They having so done, the fryer waved his wand, and presently
was heard such excellent musicke that they were all amazed,
for they all said they had never heard the like. This is, said
the fryer, to delight the sense of hearing, I will delight all your
other sences ere you depart hence : so waving his wand againe,
there was lowder musicke heard, and presently five dancers
entred, the first like a court-laundresse, the second like a foot-
man, the third like an usurer, the fourth like a prodigall, the
fift like a foole : these did divers excellent changes, so that
they gave content to all the beholders, and having done their
dance, they all vanished away in their order as they came in.
Thus feasted he two of their sences ; then waved he his wand
againe, and there was another kind of musicke heard, and whilest

T

it was playing, there was sodainly before them a table richly
covered with all sorts of delicates : then desired he the king and
queene to taste of some certaine rare fruits that were on the
table, which they and the nobles there present did, and were
very highly pleased with the taste ; they being satisfied, all
vanished away on the sodaine.   Then waved he his wand againe,
and sodainly there was such a smell, as if all the rich perfumes
in the whole world had bin there prepared in the best manner
that art could set them out : whilst hee feasted thus their smelling, he waved his wand againe, and there came divers nations in
sundry habits (as Russians, Polanders, Indians, Armenians), all
bringing sundry kinds of furres, such as their countries yeelded :
all which they presented to the king and queene : these furres
were so soft in the touch, that they highly pleased all those that
handled them, then after some odde fantasticke dances (after
their countrey manner) they vanished away : then asked Fryer
Bacon the king's majesty, if that hee desired any more of his
skill ? the king answered that hee was fully satisfied for that time,
and that hee onely now thought of something that hee might
bestow on him, that might partly satisfie the kindnesse that hee
had received.   Fryer Bacon said, that hee desired nothing so
much as his maiesties love, and if that he might be assured of
that, hee would thinke himselfe happy in it : for that (said the
king) be thou ever sure of it, in token of which receive this jewell,
and withall gave him a costly jewell from his necke.   The fryer
did with great reverence thanke his maiestie, and said : as your
maiesties vassall you shall ever finde me ready to do you service,
your time of neede shall finde it both beneficiall and delightfull.
But amongst all these gentlemen, I see not the man that your
grace did send for me by, sure he hath lost his way, or else met
with some sport that detaines him so long.   I promised to be
here before him, and all this noble assembly can witnesse I am
as good as my word : I heare him comming : with that entered the
gentleman all bedurted (for he had rid through ditches, quag-
mires, plashes, and waters, that hee was in a most pittifull case)
he seeing the fryer there looked full angerly, and bid a plague on

all his devils, for they had led him out of his way, and almost drowned him. Be not angry sir (said Fryer Bacon) here is an old friend of yours that hath more cause: for she hath tarried these three houres for you (with that hee pulled up the hangings, and behinde them stood a kitchen-mayde with a basting-ladle in her hand) now am I as good as my word with you: for I promised to helpe you to your sweetheart, how do you like this? So ill, answered the gentleman, that I will be revenged of you. Threaten not (said Fryer Bacon) least I do you more shame, and doe you take heed how you give schollers the lye againe: but because I know not how well you are stored with money at this time, I will bear her charges home: with that she vanished away: the king, queene, and all the company laughed to see with what shame this gentleman indured the sight of his greasie sweetheart: but the gentleman went away discontented. This done Fryer Bacon tooke his leave of the King and Queene, and received from them divers gifts (as well as thankes) for his art he shewed them.

How Fryer Bacon deceived his Man, that would fast for his conscience sake.

FRYER BACON had one onely man to attend on him and he too was none of the wisest, for he kept him in charity, more then for any service he had of him. This man of his (named Miles) never could indure to fast as other religious persons did, for alwayes hee had in one corner, or another, flesh which hee would eate when his maister eat bread only, or else did fast and abstaine from all things. Fryer Bacon seeing this, thought at one time or other to be even with him, which he did one Fryday in this manner. Miles on the Thursday night had provided a great blacke-pudding for his Frydayes fast: this pudding put he in his pocket (thinking belike to heate it so, for his maister had no fire on those dayes) on the next day, who was so demure as Miles, hee looked as though hee would not have eat any thing: when his maister offerd him some bread, hee refused it, saying his sinnes deserved

a greater penance then one dayes fast in a whole weeke: his
maister commended him for it, and bid him take heed that he
did not dissemble: for if he did, it would at last be knowne;
then were I worse then a Turke said Miles: so went he forth
as if he would have gone to pray privately, but it was for nothing
but to prey upon his blacke pudding; that pulled he out, (for it
was halfe roasted with the heate) and fell to it lustily; but he
was deceived, for having put one end in his mouth, he could
neither get it out againe nor bite it off, so that hee stamped
out for helpe: his maister hearing him, came; and finding him
in that manner, tooke hold of the other end of the pudding,
and led him to the hall, and shewed him to all the schollers,
saying: see here my good friends and fellow students what a
devout man my servant Miles is, he loveth not to break a fast
day, witnesse this pudding that his conscience will not let him
swallow: I will have him to be an example for you all, then tyed
hee him to a window by the end of the pudding, where poore
Miles stood like a beare tyed by the nose to a stake, and indured many floutes and mockes: at night his maister released
him from his penance; Miles was glad of it, and did vow never
to breake more fast dayes whilst that he lived.

How Fryer Bacon saved a Gentleman that had given himselfe to the Devill.

IN Oxfordshire there lived a gentleman, that had through his
riotous expences wasted a faire inheritance that was left him by
his father: after which hee grew so poore, that he had not wherwith to buy himselfe so much bread as would mainteine his miserable life: the memory of his former state that hee had lived in,
and the present want that he now sustained, made him to grow
desperate and regardlesse both of his soule and bodies estate:
which gave the devill occasion to worke upon his weaknesse in
this maner following.

On a time, hee being alone full of griefe and care, (griefe
for his folies past, and care how to get a poore living for the

remainder of his dayes) the Devill came to him and asked him what hee wanted (hee came not in a shape terrible, but like an old penny-father). This gentleman was amazed at his sodaine presence, but hearing him demand of his wants, hee tooke to him courage and said: I want all things, I want money to buy my apparrell, money to buy mee meat, money to redeeme my land and money to pay my debts: can or will you helpe mee in this misery? I will, answered the Devill, on some conditions helpe you to money for to supply all these wants and that sodainly. On any condition, said the Gentleman, helpe mee, and I sweare for to performe them: I take no oathes (answered the Devill) I must have bonds, if you will doe so, meet mee by the woods side to morrow morning, and there I will have the moneys ready: I will, said the gentleman (for hee poore man was glad of it on any conditions, as he said before). The next day hee went to the wood where the Devill had promised to meet him: long had he not been there, but he beheld the Devil comming, and after him two other like servingmen with bagges of money: this reioyced the poore gentlemans heart to thinke that hee should once again live like a man. The Devill comming to him said: sonne I will performe my promise unto you if that you will seale to the conditions that I have here already drawne: willingly, said the gentleman, I will, I pray read them. The Devill read them to this effect: that he lent him so much money as he should have need of, to be imployed to these uses following: First, to redeeme his mortgaged land: next to pay his debts: lastly, to buy him such necessaries as hee wanted: this to be lent on this condition, that so soone as he had paid all debts, that he should be at the lenders disposing, and his without any delay, freely to yeeld himselfe to him upon the first demand of the aforesaid lender. To this the gentleman sealed, and had the money carried to his chamber, with which money hee in short time redeemed his land, and bought such things as he needed, and likewise payed all his debts, so that there was not any man that could aske him one penny.

Thus lived this gentleman once againe in great credit, and grew

so great a husband that he increased his estate, and was richer
then ever his father before him was : but long did this joy of his
not continue, for one day hee being in his studie the Devil
appeared unto him, and did tell him that now his land was
redeemed, and his debts paid, and therefore the time was come
that hee must yeeld himselfe to his mercy, as hee was bound by
bond. This troubled the gentleman to heare, but more to thinke
how that he must become a slave to a stranger that hee did not
know (for hee knew not as yet that he was the Devill) but being
urged to answer for himselfe (by the devill) hee said that hee had
not as yet paid all his debts, and therefore as yet hee was not
liable to the bonds strait conditions.   At this the Devill seemed
angry and with a fearefull noyse transfformed himselfe to an ugly
shape, saying, alas poore wretch, these are poore excuses that
thou framest, I know them all to be false, and so will prove
them to thy face to morrow morning, till when I leave thee to
despaire : So with great noyse he went his way, leaving the
gentleman halfe dead with feare.

When he was gone, the gentleman reviving bethought himselfe
in what a miserable state he was now in, then wished he that
he had lived and died poorely, then cursed he all his ambitious
thoughts, that led him first to desire againe that wealth which he
had so vainly by his riot lost : then would hee curse his prodigall
expences that were the originall of all his misery : thus was he
tormented a long time in his minde, at last he fully resolved to
end his wretched life by some violent death, and to that end he
went forth thinking to kill himselfe, which he had done, had it
not beene for the Fryer: for as he was falling upon his sword,
Fryer Bacon came by and called to him to hold, which he did.
Fryer Bacon demanded of him the cause why he was so desperate that he would run headlong to hell? O sir, said he, the
cause is great, and the relation is so terrible to me, that I would
intreat you not to trouble me any more, but to leave me to my
owne will ; his answer filled the Fryer with amazement and pitty
both at once, which made him to urge him in this manner. Sir,
should I leave you to this wilfull damnation, I were unfit ever

hereafter to weare or touch any robe that belongeth unto the
holy order, whereof I am a brother: you know (I doubt not)
that there is given power to the church to absolve penitent
sinners, let not your wilfulnesse take away from you that benefit
which you may receive by it: freely confesse your selfe (I pray
you) unto me, and doubt not but I shall give your troubled conscience ease: Father (said this Gentleman) I know all that you
have spoken is truth, and I have many times received comfort
from the mother church, (I dare not say our, for I feare that
shee will never receive me for a childe) I have no part in her
benediction, yet since you request so earnestly the cause, I will
tell you, heare it and tremble. Know then that I have given my
selfe to the Devill for a little wealth, and he to morrow in this
wood must have me: now have you my griefe, but I know not
how to get comfort. This is strange (quoth Fryer Bacon,) yet
be of good comfort, penitentiall teares may doe much, which see
you doe not spare; soone I will visit you at your house, and give
you that comfort (I hope) that will beget you againe to goodnesse: the Gentleman with these words was somewhat comforted and returned home. At night Fryer Bacon came to him,
and found him full of teares for his haynous offences, for these
teares he gave him hope of pardon, demanded further what
conditions hee had made with the Devill; the gentleman told
him, how that he had promised himselfe to him so soone as hee
had paid all his debts: which he now had done, for he owed
not one peny to any man living. Well said Fryer Bacon, continue thy sorrow for thy sinnes, and to morrow meete him without feare, and be thou content to stand to the next mans iudgement that shall come that way, whether thou doest belong to
the Devill or no: feare not, but do so, and be thou assured that
I will be he that shall come by, and will give such iudgement
on thy side, that thou shalt be free from him: with that Fryer
Bacon went home, and the gentleman went to his prayers.

In the morning the gentleman (after that hee had blessed himselfe) went to the wood where he found the Devill ready for him.
So soone as he came neere, the Devill said, Now, deceiver, are you

come: now shall thou see that I can and will prove that thou hast paid all thy debts, and therefore thy soule belongeth to me. Thou art a deceiver (said the gentleman) and gavest me money to cheat me of my soule, for else why wilt thou be thy own judge? let me have some other to iudge between us. Content, said the Devill, take whom thou wilt. Then I will have (said the gentleman) the next man that commeth this way. Hereto the Devill agreed. No sooner were these words ended, but Fryer Bacon came by, to whom this gentleman speake, and requested, that he would be iudge in a waighty matter betweene them two: the Fryer said, he was content, so both parties were agreed: the Devill said they were, and told Fryer Bacon how the case stood between them in this manner.

Know Fryer, that I seeing this prodigall like to starve for want of food, lent him money, not onely to buy him victuals, but also to redeeme his lands and pay his debts, conditionarily that so soone as his debts were paid, that hee should give himselfe freely to mee, to this, here is his hand (shewing him the bond) now my time is expired, for all his debts are paid, which he cannot denie. This case is plaine, if it be so that his debts are paid: his silence confirmes it, said the Divell, therefore give him a iust sentence. I will, said Fryer Bacon: but first tell me (speaking to the gentleman) didst thou never yet give the Devill any of his mony backe, nor requite him any wayes. Never had hee any thing of me as yet (answered the gentleman). Then never let him have any thing of thee and thou art free. Deceiver of mankind, said he (speaking to the Devill) it was thy bargaine, never to meddle with him so long as hee was indebted to any, now how canst thou demand of him any thing, when he is indebted for all that hee hath to thee, when hee payeth thee thy money, then take him as thy due; till then thou hast nothing to doe with him: and so I charge thee to be gone. At this, the Devill vanished with great horror, but Fryer Bacon comforted the gentleman, and sent him home with a quiet conscience, bidding him never to pay the Devils money backe as he tendred his owne safety: which he promised for to observe.

How Fryer Bacon made a Brasen head to speake, by the which hee would have walled England about with Brasse.

FRYER BACON reading one day of the many conquests of England, bethought himselfe how he might keepe it hereafter from the like conquests, and so make himselfe famous hereafter to all posterities. This (after great study) hee found could be no way so well done as one; which was to make a head of brasse, and if he could make this head to speake (and heare it when it speakes) then might hee be able to wall all England about with brasse. To this purpose hee got one Fryer Bungey to assist him, who was a great scholler and a magician, (but not to bee compared to Fryer Bacon) these two with great study and paines so framed a head of brasse, that in the inward parts thereof there was all things like as in a naturall mans head : this being done, they were as farre from perfectione of the worke as they were before, for they knew not how to give those parts that they had made motion, without which it was impossible that it should speake : many bookes they read, but yet could not finde out any hope of what they sought, that at the last they concluded to raise a spirit, and to know of him that which they could not attaine to by their owne studies. To do this they prepared all things ready and went one evening to a wood thereby, and after many ceremonies used, they spake the words of coniuration, which the Devill straight obeyed and appeared unto them, asking what they would ? Know, said Fryer Bacon, that wee have made an artificiall head of brasse, which we would have to speake, to the furtherance of which wee have raised thee, and being raised, we will here keepe thee, unlesse thou tell to us the way and manner how to make this head to speake. The Devill told him that he had not that power of himselfe. Beginner of lyes (said Fryer Bacon) I know that thou dost dissemble, and therefore tell it us quickly, or else wee will here bind the to re- maine during our pleasures. At these thretnings the Devill consented to doe it, and told them, that with a continuel fume of the six hotest simples it should have motion, and in one month space speak, the Time of the moneth or day hee knew not: also hee told them, that if they heard it not before it had done speaking, all their labour should be lost: they being satisfied, licensed the spirit for to depart.

Then went these two learned fryers home againe, and prepared the simples ready, and made the fume, and with continuall watching attended when this Brasen head would speake. Thus watched they for three weekes without any rest, so that they were so weary and sleepy, that they could not any longer refraine from rest. Then called Fryer Bacon his man Miles, and told him, that it was not unknown to him what paines Fryer Bungy and himselfe had taken for three weekes space, onely to make, and to heare the Brasen-head speake, which if they did not, then had they lost all their labour, and all England had a great losse thereby: therefore hee intreated Miles that he would watch whilst that they slept, and call them if the head speake. Feare not, good master (said Miles) I will not sleepe, but harken and attend upon the head, and if it doe chance to speake, I will call you: therefore I pray take you both your rests and let mee alone for watching this head. After Fryer Bacon had given him a great charge the second time: Fryer Bungy and he went to sleepe, and Miles, alone to watch the brasen head: Miles, to keepe him from sleeping, got a tabor and pipe, and being merry disposed, sung this song to a Northren

TUNE OF CAM'ST THOU NOT FROM NEW-CASTLE.

> To couple is a custome,
>   all things thereto agree:
> Why should not I then love?
>   since love to all is free.
>
> But Ile have one that's pretty,
>   her cheekes of scarlet die,
> For to breed my delight,
>   when that I am her by.
>
> Though vertue be a dowry,
>   yet Ile chuse money store:
> If my love prove untrue,
>   with that I can get more.

The faire is oft unconstant,
    the blacke is often proud.
Ile chuse a lovely browne,
    come fidler scrape thy crowd.

Come fidler scrape thy crowd,
    for Peggie the brown is she
Must be my Bride, God guide
    that Peggie and I agree.

With his owne musicke and such songs as these spent he his time, and kept from sleeping at last. After some noyse the head spake these two words, TIME IS. Miles hearing it to speake no more, thought his master would be angry if hee waked him for that, and therefore he let them both sleepe, and began to mocke the head in this manner: Thou brazen-faced head, hath my master tooke all this paines about thee, and now dost thou requite him with two words, TIME IS: had hee watched with a lawyer as long as he hath watched with thee, he would have given him more, and better words then thou hast yet, if thou canst speake no wiser, they shal sleepe till doomes day for me: TIME IS; I know TIME IS, and that you shall heare goodman Brazenface.

TO THE TUNE OF DAINTIE COME THOU TO ME.

Time is for some to plant,
Time is for some to sowe;
Time is for some to graft
The horne as some doe know.

Time is for some to eate,
Time is for some to sleepe,
Time is for some to laugh,
Time is for some to weepe.

Time is for some to sing,
Time is for some to pray,
Time is for some to creepe,
That have drunke all the day.

Do you tell us copper-nose, when TIME IS, I hope we Schollers know our times, when to drinke drunke, when to kiss our hostes, when to goe on her score, and when to pay it, that time comes seldome. After halfe an houre had passed, the head did speake againe, two wordes, which were these: TIME WAS. Miles respected these words as little as he did the former, and would not wake them, but still scoffed at the brazen head, that it had learned no better words, and have such a tutor as his master, and in scorne of it sung this song.

TO THE TUNE OF A RICH MERCHANT MAN.

Time was when thou a kettle
    wert fill'd with better matter .
But Fryer Bacon did thee spoyle,
    when he thy sides did batter.

Time was when conscience dwelled
    with men of occupation :
Time was when Lawyers did not thrive,
    so well by mens vexation.

Time was when kings and beggers
    of one poor stuffe had being :
Time was when office kept no knaves :
    that time it was worth seeing.

Time was a bowle of water,
    did give the face reflection ;
Time was when women knew no paint,
    which now they call complexion.

TIME WAS : I know that brazen-face, without your telling, I know Time was, and I know what things there was when Time was, and if you speake no wiser, no master shall be waked for mee. Thus Miles talked and sung till another halfe houre was gone, then the brazen head spake again these words; TIME IS PAST : and therewith fell downe, and presently followed a terrible noyse, with strange flashes of fire, so that Miles was halfe dead with feare : at this noyse the two Fryers awaked, and wondred to see the whole roome so full of smoake, but that being vanished they might perceive the brazen head broken and lying on the ground : at this sight they grieved, and called Miles to know how

this came. Miles halfe dead with feare, said that it fell downe
of itselfe, and that with the noyse and fire that followed he was
almost frighted out of his wits : Fryer Bacon asked him if hee
did not speake? yes (quoth Miles) it spake, but to no purpose,
Ile have a parret speake better in that time that you have been
teaching this brazen head. Out on thee villaine (said Fryer
Bacon) thou hast undone us both, hadst thou but called us when
it did speake, all England had been walled round about with brass,
to its glory, and our eternal fames : what were the wordes it spake?
very few (said Miles) and those were none of the wisest that I
have heard neither: first he said, TIME IS. Hadst thou call'd us
then (said Fryer Bacon) we had been made for ever. Then (said
Miles) half an hour after it spake againe and said, TIME WAS.
And wouldst thou not call us then? (said Bungey) Alas (said
Miles) I thought he would have told me some long tale, and then
I purposed to have called you : then half an houre after he cried,
TIME IS PAST, and made such a noyse, that hee hath waked you
himselfe mee thinkes. At this Fryer Bacon was in such a rage
that hee would have beaten his man, but he was restrained by
Bungey : but neverthelesse for his punishment, he with his art
strucke him dumbe for one whole months space. Thus the greate
worke of these learned Fryers was overthrown (to their great
griefes) by this simple fellow.

*How Fryer Bacon by his art took a towne, when the King had lyen
before it three months, without doing to it any hurt.*

In those times when Fryer Bacon did all his strange trickes, the
Kings of England had a great part of France, which they held a
long time, till civill warres at home in this land made them to
lose it : it did chance that the King of England (for some cause
best knowne to himselfe) went into France with a great armie,
where after many victories, he did beseige a strong towne and lay
before it full three moneths, without doing to the towne any great
damage, but rather received the hurt himselfe. This did so
vexe the King, that he sought to take it in any way, either by

policy or strength : to this intent hee made proclamation, that whosoever could deliver this towne into his hand, hee should have for his paines ten thousand crownes truely paid.   This was proclaimed, but there was none found that would undertake it. At length the newes did come into England of this great reward that was promised.   Fryer Bacon hearing of it, went into France, and being admitted to the kings presence, hee thus spake unto him : Your maiestie I am sure hath not quite forgot your poore subject Bacon, the love that you shewed to mee being last in your presence, hath drawn mee for to leave my countrey, and my studies, to doe your maiestis service : I beseech your grace, to command mee so farre as my poore art or life may doe you pleasure.   The king thanked him for his love, but told him, that hee had now more need of armes than art, and wanted brave souldiers more than learned schollers.   Fryer Bacon answered, Your grace saith well ; but let mee (under correction) tell you, that art oftentimes doth those things that are impossible to armes, which I will make good in some few examples.   I will speak onely of things performed by art and nature, wherein shall be nothing magical : and first by the figuration of art, there may be made instruments of navigation without men to rowe in them, as great ships to brooke the sea, only with one man to steere them, and they shall sayle far more swiftly than if they were full of men : also chariots that shall move with an unspeakable force, without any living creature to stirre them.   Likewise, an instrument may be made to fly withall, if one sit in the midst of the instrument, and doe turne an engine, by which the wings being artificially composed, may beat ayre after the manner of a flying bird.   By an instrument of three fingers high, and three fingers broad, a man may rid himself and others from all imprisonment : yea, such an instrument may easily be made, whereby a man may violently draw unto him a thousand men, will they, nill they, or any other thing.   By art also an instrument may be made, wherewith men may walke in the bottome of the sea or rivers without bodily danger : this Alexander the Great used (as the ethnick philosopher reporteth) to the end he might behold the secrets of the seas.

But physicall figurations are farre more strange ; for by that may
be framed perspects and looking-glasses, that one thing shall
appeare to be many, as one man shall appeare to be a whole
army, and one sunne or moone shall seem divers. Also perspects
may be so framed, that things farre off shall seem most nigh unto
us : with one of these did Iulius Cæsar from the sea coasts in
France marke and observe the situation of the castles in England.
Bodies may also be so framed that the greatest things shall
appeare to be the least, the highest lowest, the most secret to
bee the most manifest, and in such like sort the contrary. Thus
did Socrates perceive, that the dragon which did destroy the citie
and countrey adioyning, with his noisome breath, and contagious
influence, did lurke in the dennes between the mountaines : and
thus may all things that are done in cities or armies be discovered
by the enemies. Againe, in such wise may bodies be framed,
that venemous and infectious influences may be brought whither
a man will : in this did Aristotle instruct Alexander; through
which instruction the poyson of a basiliske, being lift up upon
the wall of a citie, the poison was convayd into the citie, to the
destruction thereof : also perspects may be made to deceive the
sight, as to make a man beleeve that hee seeth great store of
riches, when that there is not any. But it appertaineth to a
higher power of figuration, that beams should be brought and
assembled by divers flexions and reflexions in any distance that
we will, to burne any thing that is opposite unto it, as it is
witnessed by those perspects or glasses that burne before and
behinde; but the greatest and chiefest of all figurations and
things figured, is to describe the heavenly bodies, according to
their length and breadth in a corporall figure, wherein they may
corporally move with a daily motion. These things are worth a
kingdom to a wise man. These may suffise, my royall lord, to
shew what art can doe : and these, with many things more, as
strange, I am able by art to performe. Then take no thought for
winning this towne, for by my art you shall (ere many dayes be
past) have your desire.

The king all this while heard him with admiration : but hearing him now, that hee would undertake to win the towne, hee burst out in these speeches : most learned Bacon, doe but what thou hast said, and I will give thee what thou most desirest, either wealth, or honour, choose which thou wilt, and I will be as ready to performe, as I have been to promise.

Your maiesties love is all that I seeke (said the fryer) let mee have that, and I have honour enough, for wealth, I have content, the wise should seek no more : but to the purpose. Let your pioniers raise up a mount so high, (or rather higher) than the wall, and then shall you see some probability of that which I have promised.

This mount in two days was raised : then Fryer Bacon went with the king to the top of it, and did with a perspect shew to him the towne, as plainly as if hee had beene in it : at this the king did wonder, but Fryer Bacon told him, that he should wonder more, ere next day noone : against which time, he desired him to have his whole army in readinesse, for to scale the wall upon a signal given by him, from the mount. This the king promised to doe, and so returned to his tent full of joy, that he should gain this strong towne. In the morning Fryer Bacon went up to the mount and set his glasses, and other instruments up : in the meane time the king ordered his army, and stood in a readinesse for to give the assaults : when the signal was given, which was the waving of a flagge : ere nine of the clocke Fryer Bacon had burnt the state-house of the towne, with other houses only by his mathematicall glasses, which made the whole towne in an uprore, for none did know how it came : whilest that they were quenching of the same Fryer Bacon did wave his flagge : upon which signall given, the king set upon the towne, and tooke it with little or no resistance. Thus through the art of this learned man the king got this strong towne, which hee could not doe with all his men without Fryer Bacons helpe.

How Fryer Bacon over-came the German coniurer Vandermast,
and made a spirit of his owne carry him into Germany.

THE king of England after hee had taken the town shewed great mercy to the inhabitants, giving some of them their lives freely, and others he set at liberty for their gold: the towne hee kept at his owne, and swore the chiefe citizens to be his true subiects. Presently after the king of France sent an ambassadour to the king of England for to intreat a peace betweene them. This ambassadour being come to the king, he feasted him (as it is the manner of princes to doe) and with the best sports as he had then, welcomed him. The ambassadour seeing the king of England so free in his love, desired likewise to give him some taste of his good liking, and to that intent sent for one of his fellowes (being a Germane, and named Vandermast) a famous coniuror, who being come, hee told the king, that since his grace had been so bountiful in his love to him, he would shew him (by a servant of his) such wonderfull things that his grace had never seene the like before. The king demanded of him of what nature those things were that hee would doe: the ambassadour answered that they were things done by the art of magicke. The king hearing of this, sent straight for Fryer Bacon, who presently came, and brought Fryer Bungey with him.

When the banquet was done, Vandermast did aske the king, if he desired to see the spirit of any man deceased: and if that hee did, hee would raise him in such manner and fashion as he was in when that he lived. The king told him, that above all men he desired to see Pompey the Great, who could abide no equall. Vandermast by his art raised him, armed in such manner as hee was when he was slaine at the battell of Pharsalia; at this they were all highly contented. Fryer Bacon presently raised the ghost of Iulius Cæsar, who could abide no superiour, and had slaine this Pompey at the battell of Pharsalia: at the sight of him they were all amazed, but the king who sent for Bacon: and Vandermast said that there was some man of art in that presence, whom he desired to see. Fryer Bacon then shewed himselfe, saying; it was I Vandermast, that raised Cæsar, partly to give content to this royall presence, but chiefely for to conquer thy Pompey, as he did once before, at that great battell of Pharsalia, which he now againe shall doe. Then presently began a fight between Cæsar and Pompey, which continued a good

U

space, to the content of all, except Vandermast. At last Pompey
was overcome and slaine by Cæsar: then vanished they both
away.

My lord ambassadour (said the king) me thinks that my Englishman has put down your German: hath he no better cunning than
this? Yes, answered Vandermast, your grace shall see me put
downe your Englishman ere that you goe from hence; and therefore Fryer prepare thy selfe with thy best of art to withstand me.
Alas, said Fryer Bacon, it is a little thing will serve to resist thee
in this kind. I have here one that is my inferior (shewing him
Fryer Bungey) try thy art with him; and if thou doe put him to
the worst, then will I deale with thee, and not till then.

Fryer Bungey then began to shew his art: and after some
turning and looking in his booke, he brought up among them
the Hesperian Tree, which did beare golden apples: these apples
were kept by a waking dragon, that lay under the tree: He having
done this, bid Vandermast finde one that durst gather the fruit.
Then Vandermast did raise the ghost of Hercules in his habit
that he wore when that he was living, and with his club on his
shoulder: Here is one, said Vandermast, that shall gather fruit
from this tree: this is Hercules, that in his life time gathered of
this fruit, and made the dragon crouch: and now againe shall
hee gather it in spight of all opposition. As Hercules was going
to plucke the fruit, Fryer Bacon held up his wand, at which
Hercules stayed and seemed fearful. Vandermast bid him for
to gather of the fruit, or else he would torment him. Hercules
was more fearfull, and said, I cannot, nor I dare not: for great
Bacon stands, whose charms are farre more powerfull than thine,
I must obey him Vandermast. Hereat Vandermast curst Hercules, and threatned him: But Fryer Bacon laughed, and bid
not to chafe himself ere that his journey was ended: for seeing
(said he) that Hercules will doe nothing at your command, I will
have him doe you some service at mine: with that he bid Hercules
carry him home into Germany. The Devill obeyed him, and tooke
Vandermast on his backe, and went away with him in all their
sights. Hold Fryer, cried the ambassadour, I will not loose Van-

dermast for half my land. Content yourself my lord, answered Fryer Bacon, I have but sent him home to see his wife, and ere long he may returne. The king of England thanked Fryer Bacon, and forced some gifts on him for his service that he had done for him : for Fryer Bacon did so little respect money, that he never would take any of the king.

How Fryer Bacon through his wisdom saved the endangered lives of three Brethren.

THE peace being concluded betweene the King of England and the King of France, the King of England came againe into his country of England, where he was received very ioyfully of all his subjects : But in his absence had happened a discord betweene three brethren, the like hath not beene often heard. This it was : A rich gentleman of England dyed, and left behind him three sonnes. Now for some reason (which was best known to himselfe) he appointed none of them by name to be his heyre, but spake to them all after this manner : You are all my sonnes, and I love you all as a father should doe, all alike, not one better than the other ; and cause I would alwayes doe rightly so neere as I can, I leave all my lands and goods to him that loves me best : These were his last words that he spake concerning any worldly affaires.

After he was dead and buried, there arose a great controversie betwixt them, who should inherit their fathers goods and lands, every one pleading for himselfe, how that he loved his father best. All the cunning lawyers of the kingdome could say nothing to the purpose, concerning this case, so that they were inforced to begge of the king a grant for a combat : for they would not share the lands and goods among them, but every one desired all or else nothing. The king seeing no other way to end this controversie, granted a combat : the two eldest being to fight first, and the conqueror to fight with the youngest, and the survivor of them was to have the land.

The day being come that was set for these combatants, they

all came in armed for the fight.   Fryer Bacon being there present,
and seeing such three lustie young men like to perish, and that
by their owne flesh and bloode, grieved very much, and went to
the king desiring his maiestie that he would stay the fight, and
he would finde a meanes without any bloodshed to end the
matter: the king was very glad hereof, and caused the combatants to be brought before him, to whom he said : gentlemen,
to save the blood of you all, I have found a way, and yet the
controversie shall be ended that is now amongst you : Are you
contented to stand to his iudgment that I shall appoint?   They
all answered, that they were.   Then were they bid to returne
three days after.   In that time Fryer Bacon had caused the
body of their deceased father to be taken out of the ground, and
brought to the court: the body hee did cause to be bound to
a stake, naked to the middle upwards and likewise prepared
three bowes and shafts for the three brethren: all these kept hee
secretly.

The third day being come, came these three brethren, to whom
Fryer Bacon in the presence of the king gave the three bowes
and shafts, saying, be not offended at what I have done, there is
no other way but this to judge your cause : See here is the body
of your dead father, shoot at him, for he that cometh nearest to
his heart, shall have all the lands and goods.

The two eldest prepared themselves, and shot at him, and
stucke their arrowes in his breast.   Then bid they the youngest
to shoot: but he refused it, saying, I will rather lose all, then
wound that body that I so loved living : Had you ever had but
halfe that love (in you) to him that I have, you would rather have
had your own bodies mangled, than to suffer his lifelesse corps
thus to be used ; nay, you doe not onely suffer it, but you are the
actors of this act of shame : and speaking this, he wept.

Fryer Bacon seeing this, did give the iudgement on his side,
for he loved his father best, and therefore had all his lands and
goods : the other two brothers went away with shame for what
they had done.   This deed of Fryer Bacons was highly commended of all men : for he did not onely give true judgement,

but also saved much blood that would have beene shed, had they beene suffered to have fought.

How Fryer Bacon served the Theeves that robbed him, and of the sport that his man Miles had with them.

It was reported about the countrey how that the king had given Fryer Bacon great store of treasure. The report of this wealth made three theeves plot to rob Fryer Bacons house, which they put in practise one evening in this fashion. They knockt at the doore and were let in by Miles: No sooner were they in, but they took hold of him, and led him into the house, and finding Fryer Bacon there, they told him that they came for some money, which they must and would have ere they departed from thence. He told them, that he was but ill stored with money at that time, and therefore desired them to forbeare him till some other time. They answered him againe, that they knew that hee had enough, and therefore it was but folly to delay them, but straight let them have it by faire means, or else they would use that extremitie to him that hee would bee loth to suffer. Hee seeing them so resolute, told them that they should have all that hee had, and gave to them one hundred pounds a man. Herewith they seemed content, and would have gone their wayes. Nay, said Fryer Bacon, I pray gentlemen at my request tarry a little, and heare some of my mans musicke: you are hyred reasonable well already, I hope in courtesie you will not deny mee so small a request. That will wee not, (said they all).

Miles thought now to have some sport with them, which hee had, and therefore played lustily on his tabor and pipe. So soone as they heard him play (against their wills) they fell a dauncing, and that after such a laborious manner, that they quickly wearied themselves (for they had all that while the bagges of money in their handes.) Yet had Fryer Bacon not revenge enough of them, but bid his man Miles lead them some larger measure as hee thought fitting, which Miles did. Miles straight ledde them out of the house into the fields, they followed him, dauncing after a

wildé anticke manner : then led hee them over a broad dike full
of water, and they followed him still, but not so good a way as he
went (for he went over the bridge, but they by reason of their
dauncing, could not keepe the bridge, but fell off, and dauncing
through the water) then led hee them through a way where a
horse might very well have been up to the belly : they followed
him, and were so durtie, as though they had wallowed in the myre
like swine : sometimes gave hee them rest onely to laugh at them :
then were they so sleepie when hee did not play, that they fell to
the ground.   Then on a sudden would hee play againe, and make
them start up and follow him.   Thus kept hee them the better
part of the night.   At last hee in pittie left playing, and let them
rest.   They being asleep on the bare ground he tooke their money
from them, and gave them this song for their farewell, to the tune
of, "Oh doe me no harme good man."

> You roaring boyes, and sturdy theeves,
>   you pimpes, and aples squires :
> Lament the case of these poor knaves,
>   and warme them by your fires.

> They snorting lye like hogs in stie.
>   but hardly are so warme :
> If all that cheat, such hap should meet,
>   to true men 'twere no harme.

> They money had, which made them glad,
>   their ioy did not indure :
> Were all theeves serv'd as these have beene,
>   I thinke there would bee fewer.

> When that they wake, their hearts will ake,
>   to thinke upon their losse :
> And though the gallows they escape,
>   they goe by weeping crosse.

They were scarce any thing the better for this song, for they
slept all the while : so Miles left them at their rest : but they had
small cause to sleepe so soundly as they did, for they were more
wett than ere was scold with cucking.   Miles gave his master his
money againe, and told the story of their merry pilgrimage : he

laughed at it, and wisht all men had the like power to serve all such knaves in the like kind. The theeves waking in the morning and missing their money, and seeing themselves in that plight, thought that they had been served so by some divine power, for robbing a church-man, and therefore they swore one to the other, never to meddle with any churchman againe.

How Vandermast, for the disgrace that he had received by Fryer Bacon sent a souldier to kill him ; and how Fryer Bacon escaped killing, and turned the souldier from an Atheist to be a good Christian.

FRYER BACON sitting one day in his study, looked over all the dangers that were to happen to him that moneth, there found he, that in the second week of the moneth between sunne rising and setting, there was a great danger to fall on him, which without great care of prevention take away his life. This danger which he did foresee, was caused by the Germane coniurer Vandermast, for he vowed a revenge for the disgrace that he had received. To execute the same, hee hyred a Walloon souldier, and gave him one hundred crownes to do the same, fifty beforehand, and fifty when hee had killed him.

Fryer Bacon, to save himselfe from this danger that was like to happen to him, would alwayes when that he read, hold a ball of brasse in his hand, and under that ball would he set a bason of brasse, that if hee did chance to sleepe in his reading, the fall of the ball out of his hand into the bason, might wake him. Being one day in his study in this manner, and asleepe, the Walloon souldier was got in to him, and had drawne his sword to kill him : but as hee was ready for to strike, downe fell the ball out of Fryer Bacon's hand, and waked him. Hee seeing the souldier stand there with a sword drawne, asked him what hee was ? and wherefore hee came there in that manner ? The souldier boldly answered him thus : I am a Walloon, and a souldier, and more then this, a villaine : I am come hither, because I was sent ; I was sent, because I was hyred ; I was hyred, because I durst do it :

the thing I should doe, is not done : the thing to be done, is to kill thee : thus have you heard what I am and why I came. Fryer Bacon wondered at this man's resolution ; then asked hee of him, who set him on worke to bee a murderer? Hee boldly told him, Vandermast the Germane coniurer : Fryer Bacon then asked him what religion he was of? He answered, of that which many doe professe, the chief principles of which were these : to goe to an ale-house, and to a church with one devotion, to absteine from evil for want of action, and to doe good against their wills. It is a good profession for a devil (said Fryer Bacon.) Doest thou believe hell? I believe no such thing, answered the souldier. Then I will shew thee the contrary, said the Fryer : and presently raised the ghost of Iulian the Apostate, who came up with his body burning, and so full of wounds, that it almost did affright the souldier out of his wits. Then Bacon did command this spirit to speake, and to shew what hee was, and wherefore hee was thus tormented? Then spake hee to it in this manner : I sometimes was a Roman Emperor : some count greatnesse a happinesse : I had happinesse beyond my empire, had I kept that, I had beene a happy man : would I had lost my empire when I lost that. I was a Christian, that was my happiness ; but my selfe love and pride made me to fall from it ; for which I now am punished with never ceasing torments, which I must still endure : the like which I enioy is now prepared for unbeleeving wretches like myself, so vanished he away.

All this while the souldier stood quaking, and sweat as he had felt the torments himselfe ; and falling downe on his knees desired Fryer Bacon to instruct him in a better course of life, then he had yet gone in. Fryer Bacon told him, that he should not want his helpe in any thing, which he performed, instructing him better : then gave he him money, and sent him to the warres of the holy land, where he was slain.

How Fryer Bacon deceived an old Usurer.

Not farre from Fryer Bacon, dwelt an olde man that had great store of money which hee let out to use, and would never doe

any good with it to the poore, though Fryer Bacon had often put
him in minde of it, and wished him to do some good whilest he
lived. Fryer Bacon seeing this, by his art made an iron pot,
which seemed full of gold. This being done, he went to this
rich usurer, and told him, that he had some gold which he had
gathered in his time that he had lived; but it being much in
quantity, hee feared that if it were knowne, it would be taken
from him, because it was unfitting a man of his coat should have
so much: now he desired him that hee would let him have some
hundred pounds, which was not the sixth part of his gold, and he
should kepe it for him. The usurer was glad to heare of this,
and told him that he should have it, and that he would keep his
gold as safe as himself would: Fryer Bacon was glad to heare
of this, and presently fetcht the pot: at the sight of which the
usurer laughed, and thought to himself, how all that gold was his
owne, for hee had a determination to gull the fryer, but he gulled
himselfe. So here is the gold (said Fryer Bacon) now let me
have of you one hundred pounds, and keep you this gold till I
pay it backe again. Very willingly (said the usurer) and told him
one hundred pounds out, which Fryer Bacon tooke and delivered
him the note, and so went his way. This mony did Fryer Bacon
give to divers poore schollers, and other people and bid them pray
for old Good-gatherers soules health (so was this usurer call'd)
which these poor people did, and would give him thankes and
prayers when they met him, which he did wonder at, for he never
deserved the praires of any man. At last this old Good-gatherer
went to looke on this pot of gold, but instead of gold he found
nothing but earth, at which sight he would have died, had not
his other gold hindred him, which hee was to leave behind him:
so gathering up his spirits, hee went to Fryer Bacon, and told
him he was abused and cheated; for which he would have the
law of him, unlesse he made him restitution. Fryer Bacon told
him, that he had not cheated him, but bin his faithful steward to
the poore, which he could not chuse but know, either by their
prayers, or their thanks; and as for the law he feared it not, but
bid him doe his worst. The old man seeing Fryer Bacon's

resolution, went his way, and said, that hereafter hee would be his owne steward.

How Miles, Fryer Bacons man did coniure for meat, and got meate for himselfe and his hoast.

MILES chanced one day upon some businesse, to goe some six miles from home, and being loth to part with some company that he had, he was be-lated, and could but get halfe way home that night; to save his purse hee went to ones house that was his masters acquaintance : but when he came, the good man of the house was not at home, and the woman would not let him have lodging. Miles seeing such cold entertainment wished he had not troubled her, but being now there, he was loth to goe any further and therefore with good words he perswaded her for to give him lodging that night. She told him that she would willingly doe it, if her husband were at home, but he being now out of towne, it would be to her discredit to lodge any man. You neede not mistrust me, (said Miles) : locke me in any place where there is a bed, and I will not trouble you till to morrow that I rise. She thinking her husband would be angry if she should deny any of his friends so small a request, consented that he should lye there, if that he would be locked up : Miles was contented and presently went to bed, and she locked him into the chamber where he lay.

Long had not he beene a bed, but he heard the doore open; with that he rose and peeped through a chinke of the partition, and saw an old man come in : this man set down his basket that he had on his arme, and gave the woman of the house three or four sweet kisses : then did hee undo his basket, and pulled out of it a fat capon ready roasted, and bread, with a bottle of good olde sacke; this gave hee unto her, saying, Sweetheart, hearing thy husband was out of towne, I thought good to visite thee, I am not come emptie handed, but have brought some thing to be merrie withal : lay the clothe sweete hony, and let us to banquet. She kindly thanked him, and presently did as he bad her : they were not scarce set at the table, but her husband returning backe, knockt at the doore. The woman hearing this was amazed, and knew not what to doc with her old lover: but looking on her apron strings, she straight found, (as women used to doe) a trick to put herself free from this feare; for shee put her lover under the bed, the capon and bread she put under a tub, the bottle of wine shee put behinde the chest, and then she did open the doore, and with a dissembling kisse welcomed her husband home, asking him the reason why that he returned so quickly. He told her, that hee had forgot the money that he should have carried with him, but on the morrow betimes hee would be gone. Miles saw and heard all this: and having a desire to taste of the capon and the wine, called the goodman. He asked his wife who that was? She told him, an acquaintance of his, that intreated lodging there that night. He bid her open the door, which she did, and let Miles out. Hee seeing Miles there, bid him welcome, and bade his wife to set them some meate on the table: she told him that there was not any ready, but prayed him to kepe his stomacke till morrow, and then she would provide them a good breakefast. Since it is so Miles (said the goodman) wee must rest contented, and sleepe out our hunger. Nay stay said Miles, if that you can eate, I can find you good meat; I am a scholler, and have some art. I would faine see it (said the goodman). You shall quoth Miles, and that presently. With that Miles pulled forth a booke out of his bosome, and began his coniuration in this fashion:

> From the fearefull lake below,
> From whence spirits come and goe;
> Straightway come one and attend
> Fryer Bacons man, and friend.

Comes there none yet? quoth Miles: then I must use some other charme.

> Now the owle is flowne abroad,
> For I heare the croaking toade;
> And the bat that shuns the day,
> Through the darke doth make her way,

Now the ghosts of men doe rise,
And with fearful hideous cryes,
Seeke revengement (from the good)
On their heads that spilt their blood,
Come some spirit, quicke I say
Night's the Devils holy-day :
Where ere you be, in dennes, or lake,
In the ivy, ewe, or brake :
Quickly come and me attend,
That am Bacons man and friend.
But I will have you take no shape
Of a bear a horse, or ape :
Nor will I have you terrible,
And therefore come invisible.

Now is he come, (quoth Miles) and therefore tell me wnat meat you will have mine hoast? Any thing Miles, (said the goodeman) what thou wilt. Why then (said Miles) what say you to a capon? I love it above all meat (said the goodman). Why then a capon you shall have, and that a good one too. Bemo my spirit that I have raised to doe mee service, I charge thee, seeke and search about the earth, and bring me hither straight the best of capons ready roasted. Then stood hee still a little, as though he had attended the comming of his spirit, and on the sudden said : It is well done, my Bemo, hee hath brought me (mine hoast), a fat capon from the King of Tripolis owne table, and bread with it. Aye but where is it Miles (said the hoast) I see neither spirit nor capon. Looke under the tub (quoth Miles) and there you shall finde it. He presently did, and brought (to his wives griefe) the capon and bread out. Stay (quoth Miles) we do yet want some drinke that is comfortable and good; I think mine hoast a bottle of Maliga sacke were not amisse, I will have it: Bemo, haste thee to Maliga, and fetch me from the governours a bottle of his best sacke. The poore woman thought that hee would have betrayed her and her lover, and therefore wished that he had beene hanged, when that hee came first into her house. Hee having stood a little while, as before, saide, Well done, Bemo, looke behinde the great chest (mine hoast). Hee did so, and brought out the bottle of sacke. Now (quoth hee) Miles sit downe, and welcòme to thine owne cheere : You may see wife (quoth he) what a man of art can doe, get a fatte capon, and a bottle of good sacke in a quarter of an houre, and for nothing, which is best of all : Come (good wife) sit downe, and bee merry; for all this is paid for, I thanke Miles.

Shee sate, but could not eat a bit for anger, but wished that every bit they did eate might choake them : Her old lover too that lay under the bed all this while still looked when that Miles would discover him. When they had eaten and drunke well, the good man desired Miles that hee would let him see the spirit that fetched them this good cheere : Miles seemed unwilling, telling him that it was against the laws of art, to let an illiterate man see a spirit, but yet, for once hee would let him see it : and told him withall, that hee must open the door, and soundly beat the spirit, or else hee should bee troubled hereafter with it, and because he should not feare it, hee would put it in the shape of some one of his neighbours. The good man told him, that hee neede not to doubt his valour, he would beat him soundly, and to that pur-pose hee took a good cudgell in his hand, and did stande ready for him. Miles then went to the bed side, under which the old man lay, and began to coniure him with these words,

> Bemo quickly come, appeare,
> Like an old man that dwells neere ;
> Quickly rise, and in his shape,
> From this house make thy escape ;
> Quickly rise, or else I sweare,
> Ile put thee in a worser feare.

The old man seeing no remedy, but that hee must needes come forth, put a good face on it, and rose from under the bed : Behold my spirit (quoth Miles) that brought me all that you have had ; now bee as good as your word and swaddle him soundly. I protest (said the goodman) your Devill is as like Goodman Stumpe the tooth-drawer, as a pomewater is like an apple : is it possible that your spirits can take other mens shapes : Ile teach this to keepe his owne shape ; with that hee beat the old man soundly, so that Miles was faine to take him off, and put the old man out of doore, so after some laughing, to bed they all went: but the woman could not sleepe for griefe, that her old lover had had such bade usage for her sake.

How Fryer Bacon did helpe a young man to his Sweetheart, which Fryer Bungye would have married to another; and of the mirth that was at the wedding.

AN Oxfordshire gentleman had long time loved a faire mayde, called Millisant; this love of his was as kindly received of her, as it was freely given of him, so that there wanted nothing to the finishing of their ioyes, but the consent of her father, who would not grant that she should bee his wife (though formerly he had been a meanes to further the match) by reason there was a knight that was a suitor to her, and did desire that hee might have her to his wife: but this knight could never get from her the least token of good wil: so surely was her love fixed upon the gentleman. This knight seeing himselfe thus despised, went to Fryer Bungye, and told him his mind, and did promise him a good piece of money if he could get her for him, either by his art, or counsell.

Bungye (being covetous) told him, that there was no better way in his mind, than to get her with her father to go take the air in a coach: and if hee could doe so, he would by his art so direct the horses, that they should come to an old chappell, where hee would attend, and there they might secretly be married. The knight rewarded him for his counsell, and told him that if it tooke effect, he would be more bountifull unto him, and presently went to her father, and told him of this. Hee liked well of it, and forced the poore maid to ride with them. So soone as they were in the coach, the horses ran presently to the chappell, where they found Fryer Bungye attending for them: at the sight of the church and the priest, the poore maid knew that she was betraid, so that for griefe shee fell in a swound: to see which her father and the knight, were very much grieved, and used their best skill for her recovery.

In this time, her best beloved, the gentleman, did come to her fathers to visit her, but finding her not there, and hearing that shee was gone with her father and the knight, he mistrusted some foul play: and in all hast went to Fryer Bacon, and desired of him some help to recover his love againe, whom he feared was utterly lost.

Fryer Bacon (knowing him for a vertuous gentleman) pittyed him; and to give his griefes some release, shewed him a glasse, wherein any one might see any thing done (within fifty miles space) that they desired: so soone as he looked in the glasse, hee saw his love Millisant with her father, and the knight, ready to be married by Fryer Bungye: at the sight of this hee cryed out that he was undone, for now should he lose his life in losing of his love. Fryer Bacon bids him take comfort, for he would prevent the marriage; so taking this gentleman in his armes, he set himselfe downe in an enchanted chaire, and suddenly they were carried through the ayre to the chappell. Just as they came in, Fryer Bungye was ioyning their hands to marry them: but Fryer Bacon spoyled his speech, for he strucke him dumbe, so that he could not speake a worde. Then raised he a myst in the chappell, so that neither the father could see his daughter, nor the daughter her father, nor the knight either of them. Then tooke he Millisant by the hand, and led her to the man she most desired: they both wept for ioy, that they so happily once more had met, and kindly thanked Fryer Bacon.

It greatly pleased Fryer Bacon to see the passion of these two lovers, and seeing them both contented, he marryed them at the chappell doore, whilest her father, the knight, and Fryer Bungye went groping within, and could not find the way out. Now when he had married them, he bid them get lodging at the next village, and he would send his man with money: (for the gentleman was not stored, and he had a great way to his house) they did as he bad them. That night hee sent his man Miles with money to them; but he kept her father, the knight, and Fryer Bungey till the next day at noon in the chappell, ere he released them.

The gentleman and his new married wife made that night a

great supper for ioy of their marriage, and bid to it most of the
village : they wanted nothing but musicke, for which they made
great moane.　This want, Fryer Bacon (though he was absent)
supplied : for after supper there came such a maske, that the like
was never seene in that village : for first, there was heard most
sweet still musicke, then wind musicke : then came three apes,
and three monkeys, each of them carrying a torch : after them
followed sixe apes and monkeys more, all dressed in anticke
coats : these last sixe fell a dancing in such an odde manner,
that they moved all the beholders to much laughter : so after
divers antick changes, they did reverence to the bridegroome and
bride, and so departed in order as they came in.　They all did
marvell from whence these should come : but the bridegroome
knew that it was Fryer Bacons art that gave them this grace to
their wedding.　The next daye he went home to his owne house
with his bride : and for the cost he had bestowed on them, most
part of the townes-folke brought them on their way.

　　Miles made one amongst them too ; he for his masters sake
was so plyed with cups, that he in three dayes was scarce sober :
for his welcome, at his departure he gave them this song : to the
tune of, "I have been a fiddler," &c.

> And did you heare of a mirth that befell,
> 　the morrow after a wedding day :
> At carrying a bride at home to dwell,
> 　and away to Twiver, away, away !
>
> The Quintin was set, and the garlands were made,
> 　'tis a pity old custome should ever decay :
> And woe be to him that was horst on a iade,
> 　for he carried no credit away, away.
>
> We met a consort of fiddle-de-dees,
> 　we set them a cock-horse, and made them to play
> The winning of Bullen, and Upsie-frees,
> 　and away to Twiver, away, away.
>
> There was ne'er a lad in all the parish,
> 　that would goe to the plow that day :
> But on his fore-horse his wench he carries,
> 　and away to Twiver, away, away.

The butler was quicke, and the ale he did tap,
    the maidens did make the chamber full gay :
The serving-men gave me a fuddling cap,
    and I did carye it away, away.

The smithe of the towne his liquor so tooke,
    that he was perswaded the ground look'd blue,
And I dare boldly to sweare on a booke,
    such smiths as he there are but a few.

A posset was made, and the women did sip,
    and simpering said they could eate no more :
Full many a maid was laid on the lip ;
    Ile say no more, but so give o're.

They kindly thanked Miles for his song, and so sent him home with a foxe at his tayle. His master asked him, where he had beene so long? He told him at the wedding. I know it, (said Fryer Bacon) that thou hast beene there, and I know also (thou beast) that thou hast beene every day drunke. That is the worst that you can say by me, master, for still poore men must be drunke, if that they take a cup more than ordinary; but it is not so with the rich. Why how is it with the rich then? I will tell you (said Miles) in a few words,

    Lawyers they are sicke ;
    And Fryers are ill at ease ;
    But poore men they are drunke ;
    And all is one disease.

Well sirrah (said Fryer Bacon) let me not heare that you are infected any more with this disease, lest I give you sowre sawce to your sweet meat. Thus did Fryer Bacon helpe these poore lovers, who in short time got the love of the old man, and lived in great ioy: Fryer Bungey's tongue was againe let loose, and all were friends.

How Vandermast and Fryer Bungye met, and how they strived who should excel one another in their coniurations: and of their deaths.

VANDERMAST thinking that Fryer Bacon had beene dead, came into England, and in Kent met with Fryer Bungey: he owing

        X

him no good will for Fryer Bacons sake, took his horse out of
the stable, and instead of it, left a spirit like unto it. Fryer
Bungye in the morning rose, and mounting this spirit, (which he
thought had beene his horse) rode on his iourney : but he riding
through a water, was left in the midst of it by this spirit; and
being thus wet, hee returned to his inne. At the inne doore,
Vandermast met him, and asked him, if that were swimming time
of the year? Bungye told him, if that he had been so well
horsed as he was, when Fryer Bacon sent him into Germany, he
might have escaped that washing. At this Vandermast bit his
lip, and said no more, but went in. Bungye thought that he
would be even with him, which was in this manner. Vandermast loved a girl well, which was in the house, and sought many
times to winne her for gold, love, or promises. Bungye knowing
this, did shape a spirit like her, which he sent to Vandermast.
Vandermast appointed the spirit to come to his chamber that
night, and was very ioyful : but his ioy turned into sorrow, and
his wanton hopes into a bad nights lodging : for Fryer Bungye
had by his art spread such a sheet on his bed, that no sooner was
he laid with the spirit on it, but it was carryed through the ayre,
and let fall into a deepe pond, where Vandermast had been
drowned, if he had not had the art of swimming : He got quickly
out of the pond, and shaked himselfe like a rough water-spaniel :
but being out, he was as much vexed as before, for he could not
tell the way home, but was glad to keepe himselfe in heat that
night with walking. Next day he coming to his inne, Fryer
Bungye asked him how he did like his wash ? He said, so well,
that he wished him such another. Thus did they continually
vexe each other, both in words, and ill actions. Vandermast
desiring to do Fryer Bungey a mischiefe, did challenge him to
the field (not to fight at sword and dagger, single rapier, or case
of poinyards, but at worser weapons farre, it was at that diabolical
art of magicke) there to shew which of them was most cunning,
or had most power over the Devill : Bungye accepted of his
challenge, and both provided themselves of things belonging to
the art, and to the field they went.

There they both spred their circles some hundred foot from one another: and after some other ceremonies did Vandermast begin: hee by his charmes did raise up a fiery dragon, which did runne about Fryer Bungyes circle, and did scorch him with his heat so that he was almost ready to melt. Fryer Bungye tormented Vandermast in another element: for he raised up the sea-monster that Perseus killed, when he did redeem the faire Andromeda. This sea-monster did run about Vandermast, and such flouds of water did he send out of his wide mouth, that Vandermast was almost drowned. Then did Fryer Bungye raise a spirit up like saint George, who fought with the dragon, and killed it: Vandermast (following his example) raysed up Perseus, who fought also with his sea-monster, and killed it, so were they both released from their danger.

They being not contented with this tryall of their skill, went further in their coniurations, and raised up two spirits, each of them one. Bungye charged his spirit for to assist him with the greatest power hee had, that by it he might be able to overcome Vandermast. The Devill told him he would, if that he from his left arme would give him but three drops of blood; but if that he did deny him that, then should Vandermast have power over him to doe what he would: the like told Vandermasts Devill to him: to this demand of the spirits, they both agreed, thinking for to overcome each other; but the Devill overthrew them both.

They having given the Devill this bloud, as is before spoken of, they both fell againe to their coniurations: first, Bungye did rayse Achilles with his Greekes, who marched about Vandermast and threatned him. Then Vandermast raised Hector with his Troians, who defended him from Achilles and the Greekes. Then began there a great battell between the Greekes and Troians, which continued a good space: at last Hector was slaine, and the Troians fled. Then did follow a great tempest, with thundring and lightning, so that the two coniurers wished that they had been away. But wishes were in vaine: for now the time was come, that the Devill would be paid for the knowledge that he had lent them, he would not tarry any longer, but then tooke them in the height of their wickednesse, and bereft them of their lives.

When the tempest was ended, (which did greatly affright the townes there by) the townesmen found the bodies of these two men, (Vandermast and Bungey) breathlesse, and strangely burnt with fire. The one had Christian buriall, because of his order sake : the other, because he was a stranger. Thus was the end of these two famous coniurers.

How Miles would coniure for money, and how he broke his legge for feare.

MILES one day finding his Masters study open, stole out of it one of his coniuring-bookes : with this booke would Miles needes coniure for some money : (for he saw that his master had money enough, and he desired the like, which did make him bold to trouble one of his masters devils :) in a private place he thought it best to doe it : therefore he went up to the top of the house, and there began to reade : long had he not read, but a devill came to him in an ugly shape, and asked him what he would have? Miles being affrighted, could not speake, but stood quaking there like an aspin leafe : the devill seeing him so, (to increase his feare) raised a tempest, and hurled fire about, which made Miles leape from off the leades, and with his fall broke his legge.

Fryer Bacon hearing this noyse, ranne forth, and found his man Miles on the ground, and the Devill hurling fire on the house top. First laid he the Devill againe : then went he to his man and asked how hee got that broken legg? Hee told him his Devill did it : for he had frighted him, and made him leape off from the house top. What didst thou there? (said his Master.) I went to coniure, Sir (said Miles) for money ; but I have got nothing but a broken legge ; and I now must beg for money to cure that, if you be not the more pittifull to me. I have often-times given you warning not to meddle with my bookes (said his Master) and yet you will still be doing : take heed, you had best, how you deale with the Devill againe : for he that had power to breake your legge will breake your necke, if you againe doe meddle with him : for this I doe forgive you : for your legge breaking hath paid for your sawcinesse : and though I gave you not a broken head, I will give you a plaister : and so sent him to the chirurgions.

How two young Gentlemen that came to Fryer Bacon, to know how their fathers did, killed one another; and how Fryer Bacon for griefe, did breake his rare Glasse, wherein he could see any thing that was done within fifty miles about him.

IT is spoken of before now, that Fryer Bacon had a glasse, which was of that excellent nature, that any man might behold any thing that he desired to see within the compasse of fifty miles round about him : with this glasse he had pleasured divers kinds of people : for fathers did oftentimes desire to see (thereby) how their children did, and children how their parents did; one friend how another did; and one enemy (sometimes) how his enemy did : so that from far they would come to see this wonderfull glasse. It happened one day, that there came to him two young gentlemen, (that were countrey men, and neighbors children) for to know of him by his glasse, how their fathers did : Hee being no niggard of his cunning, let them see his glasse, wherein they straight beheld their wishes, which they (through their owne follies) bought at their lives losse, as you shall heare.

The fathers of these two gentlemen, (in their sonnes absence) were become great foes : this hatred betweene them was growne to that height, that wheresoever they met, they had not onely wordes but blowes. Just at that time, as it should seeme, that their sonnes were looking to see how they were in health, they were met, and had drawne, and were together by the eares. Their sonnes seeing this, and having been alwayes great friends, knew not what to say to one another, but beheld each other with angry lookes. At last, one of their fathers, as they might per-ceive in the glasse, had a fall, and the other taking advantage, stood over him ready to strike him. The sonne of him that was downe, could then containe himselfe no longer, but told the other young man, this his father had received wrong. He answered againe, that it was faire. At last there grew such foule words betweene them, and their bloods were so heated, that they presently stabbed one the other with their daggers, and so fell downe dead.

Fryer Bacon seeing them fall, ranne to them, but it was too late, for they were breathlesse ere he came. This made him to grieve exceedingly: he iudging that they had received the cause of their deaths by this glasse, tooke the glasse in his hand, and uttered words to this effect:

Wretched Bacon, wretched in thy knowledge, in thy understanding wretched; for thy art hath beene the ruine of these two gentlemen. Had I been busied in those holy things, the which mine order tyes me to, I had not had that time that made this wicked glasse: wicked I well may call it, that is the causer of so vile an act: would it were sensible, then should it feele my wrath; but being as it is, Ile ruin it for ruining of them: and with that he broke his rare and wonderfull glasse, whose like the whole world had not. In this grief of his, came there newes to him of the deaths of Vandermast and Fryer Bungey: This did increase his griefe, and made him sorrowfull, that in three days he would not eate any thing but kept his chamber.

Howe Fryer Bacon burnt his books of Magick, and gave himselfe to the study of Divinity only; and how he turned Anchorite.

In the time that Fryer Bacon kept his chamber, hee fell into divers meditations: sometimes into the vanity of arts and sciences: then would hee condemne himselfe for studying of those things that were so contrary to his order and soules health; and would say, that magicke made a man a Devill: sometimes would hee meditate on divinity; then would he cry out upon himselfe, for neglecting the study of it, and for studying magick: sometime would he meditate on the shortnesse of mans life then would he condemne himselfe for spending a time so short, so ill as he had done his : so would he goe from one thing to another and in all condemne his former studies.

And that the world should know how truly he did repent his wicked life, he caused to be made a great fire ; and sending for many of his friends, schollers, and others, he spake to them after this manner : "My good friends and fellow students, it is not unknowne unto you, how that through my art I have attained to that credit, that few men living ever had : of the wonders that I have done, all England can speak, both king and commons : I have unlocked the secret of art and nature, and let the world see those things, that have layen hid since the death of Hermes, that rare and profound philosopher : my studies have found the secrets of the starres ; the bookes that I have made of them, doe serve for presidents to our greatest doctors, so excellent hath my judgment beene therein. I likewise have found out the secrets of trees, plants and stones, with their several uses ; yet all this knowledge of mine I esteeme so lightly, that I wish that I were ignorant, and knew nothing : for the knowledge of these things, (as I have truly found) serveth not to better a man in goodnesse, but onely to make him proud and thinke too well of himselfe. What hath all my knowledge of natures secrets gained me? Onely this, the losse of a better knowledge, the losse of divine studies, which makes the immortall part of man (his soule) blessed. I have found, that my knowledge has beene a heavy burden, and has kept downe my good thoughts : but I will remove the cause, which are these bookes : which I doe purpose here before you all to burne." They all intreated him to spare the bookes, because in them there were those things that after-ages might receive great benefit by. He would not hearken unto them, but threw them all into the fire, and in that flame burnt the greatest learning in the world. Then did he dispose of all his goods ; some part he gave to poor schollers, and some he gave to other poore folkes : nothing left he for himselfe : then caused he to be made in the church-wall a cell, where he locked himselfe in, and there remained till his death. His time hee spent in prayer, meditation, and such divine exercises, and did seeke by all means to perswade men from the study of magicke. Thus lived he some two yeeres space in that cell, never comming forth : his meat and drink he received in at a window, and at that window he did discourse with those that came to him ; his grave he digged with his owne nayles, and was laid there when he dyed.   Thus was the Life and Death of this famous Fryer, who lived most part of his life a Magician, and dyed a true Penitent Sinner, and an Anchorite.

THE HISTORY OF GUY EARL
OF WARWICK.

THE HISTORY OF GUY EARL OF WARWICK.

CHAPTER I.

An account of his parents, birth, and youthful exploits; and how he fell in love with Earl Roband's beautiful daughter, who despised his suit.

I SHALL not trouble the reader with a long genealogy of the descent of our famous Guy of Warwick (the subject of our ensuing history); it shall therefore suffice to tell the reader, that in the sixth year of the reign of King Edgar the Great, this, our famous Guy, was born in the city of Warwick. His father was a gentleman of Northumberland, in which country he had been (in the time of the Mercian kings) the possessor of a fair estate: but the arms of King Edgar prevailing over the King of Mercia, as well as the rest of the Saxon kings that constituted the heptarchy, Guyraldus Cassibilanus (for that was the name of Guy's father), being engaged on the behalf of the King of Mercia, whose subject he was, lost his estate in the quarrel: and afterwards seeking to mend his fortune in our most southern climates, he came to Warwick, and was so well received of the gentry there, but especially of Earl Roband, who was then the King's governor, both of the town and castle, that he made him his steward; in which place he so well acquitted himself, that he married the daughter of an eminent knight in that town; and by her he had a son, who at his very birth looked like a hero, and whom his father named Guy, and who, in process of time, became Earl of Warwick, whose life and noble actions are the subject of our present history. There were not wanting some presages of his future greatness, even before he was born; particularly, his mother, during her pregnancy, dreamed that she saw Mars descend in a bloody chariot, drawn by two fiery dragons; and telling her, "That the infant contained in her womb, should so excel in arms, that he should be the glory of this nation, and the terror of the Pagan world:" which dream she discovered to the Countess of Warwick, above a month before she was delivered of him. And indeed, being born, he gave early proofs of his being an extraordinary man; for he was scarce come to be eight years old, before he gave the world some early prognostics of his great strength and martial genius, by beginning to practise running, wrestling, throwing stones, and other exercises, even above what his young years were capable of; exceeding those that were both older and bigger than himself; and for which he was observed by all spectators. And as he grew more towards maturity, he delighted in. hardships, and such exercises as required both strength and labour; so that at sixteen there were but few that durst encounter with him; for then he would use to enter the lists, and always came off victorious. Which coming to Earl Roband's ears, he sent for him, and entertained him at dinner with himself, and several of the gentry of the country, who were very well pleased with his conversation; after which he played several prizes before the Earl, carrying the day, whatever he played with.

But by being at the Earl's house, he came to have a sight of fair Phælice, his beautiful daughter, with whom he was so extremely taken, that nothing but she could satisfy him. She was indeed so fair, that she could not be seen without being loved. She was so fair, Venus herself could never boast more beauty; and had she but been present at the famous contest between Juno, Pallas, and Venus, about the golden apple, on which was writ, "Let it be given to the fairest," she had certainly borne away the prize from them all. And some have affirmed, that all the odds between Venus and her was, that Venus had a mole, and she had none: for she had most directly Venus's hair, the same high forehead and attractive eyes: the roses and the lilies in her cheeks were mixed with that equality, that none could say which of them had the ascendant; her lips were of a perfect coral dye, nor could the ivory match her teeth for whiteness. She was indeed from head to foot the mirror of all comeliness, an English phœnix, the only supreme fair; of whom it was the general opinion, beauty could nowhere but in•Phælice's face be found in its perfection; but these perfections were so many daggers, sticking poor Guy to the heart; for he imagined these charming looks of hers did unto him dart nothing but disdain; and that which his eyes looked on with delight, did nothing else but fill his heart with pain. One while her smiles gave him encouragement; another time the sternness of her looks tossed him upon the billows of despair. He would often sigh at the capriciousness of Fortune, that she should deal so very strangely by him, to give a wound that beauty would not heal. Then, recollecting himself, he would say, "Fond man, why will not beauty heal thy wound? Thou wrongest thyself and thy fair goddess too, for who can know a woman's heart by her looks? And looking on her is all that thou hast done. Well, now I will take a course shall be more resolute: I will speak, or let her know my mind by writing. But if I should, can I have any hopes that she should hear my words, or read my lines? She is Earl Roband's heir, and born too high to listen to such poor designs as mine. For, though I am a gentleman by birth, yet I have no earldoms, nor lordships neither; and women are exceedingly ambitious, and mounting up upon the wings of pride, do oftener match themselves for worldly treasure, than for that sacred love that is far more precious; which makes some rather wish there were no gold, than love should be so basely sold for it. And if my Phælice should be such a one, what will my words, or tears, or sighs prevail? I only strive against the wind and tide, and heap continual torments on my soul. Why should I then attempt with waxen wings to fly where Phœbus's chariot burns so brightly? But hold," said he again, "thou timorous lover, and banish fear, or let thy passion go; be resolute, and thou shalt have success; for Phælice, doubtless, has a tender heart; and he that shoots Love's darts may well befriend thee, because thy love is so like his mother's picture. I am resolved to go to Phælice's bower, and from as true a heart as flesh can yield, entreat her in a happy hour to hear me, and with kind pity to remove my sorrows; to look upon me with a tender breast, since as her love is inclined, I hold my life."

This said, he unto Warwick Castle goes, where the rich jewel of his heart remained. Earl Roband bids him welcome, and prepares to entertain him with a match of hunting, but he to that lends an unwilling ear, and to prevent it pretends sudden sickness. The Earl was grieved at this alteration, and sent his own physician to him, who told him, that the only remedy consisted in his being presently let blood, and that his body, under that distemper, was very difficult and hard to cure.

To which Guy thus replied, "Doctor, I do applaud your judgment, and know full well that what you say is true. I find myself exceeding ill. But there is a flower, which, if I might but touch, would heal me better far than all the skill of Galen and Hippocrates to boot: it is called by a pretty pleasing name, and I think Phælix soundeth something like it."

"I know it not," replied the doctor to him, "nor is there in the herbal any flower that beareth such a name as I remember."

"Yes, yes," said Guy, "I am sure there is such a flower, and that it is to be got within this castle; nor doth it grow far from yonder tower. But, doctor, I can find it out myself, and therefore will not give you so much trouble." On which the doctor left him. Whilst Guy, bemoaning his unhappy state, sat sighing by a window all alone, which window had a very curious prospect into a pleasant and delightful garden; in which, as suddenly he cast his eye, he saw the adored empress of his thoughts, which did so much exhilarate his soul, that he despised physicians and their potions. Fear now was banished, and Hope reigned as king. "This is a lucky time," said Guy to himself, "which I so long have waited for. Now the bright sun of fortune shines upon me. Now may I end the grief that Love began, and court my

Destiny while thus she smiles. Now I will enter into yonder shade to court the only paragon of beauty. Phælice, I come: now Cupid, now assist me : prepare an arrow ready for thy bow, and send it to the heart of her I love. And since I never went a wooing yet, be now propitious to me. Give such prevailing rhetoric to my tongue, that Phælice's heart may hang upon my lips. But above all, grant this, O gentle Cupid, that when I make most solemn protestations of my sincere and ever constant love, that she may believe my words."

Then down with speed he goes unto the garden, where softly knocking, he was soon let in by a young maid that waited upon Phælice; who seeing him, and thinking he had been sent thither by her father, as he was coming towards her, rose up to meet him; whom Guy, with Love's enchanting eye beholding, with a becoming mien, accosts her thus :

" Fairest of all the curious works of nature, whose equal never breathed in common air, more wonderful than any earth can yield, the bright idea of celestial beauty. Eternal honour wait upon thy name. The suit I have to thee is much like that which once Leander came to Hero with, hoping thereby to reap more lovely fruit than ever Mars gained from the queen of Love, when he outwitted Vulcan. The present which I bring, is a heart filled with love, and love can only satisfy my soul. Incline then, madam, to my humble motion : compassionate the griefs that I endure, and let that life that rests at your devotion be regarded. With pity take my dying heart in cure, and let it not expire in groaning torments, nor burst with griefs, because too well it loves thee. I know, dear Phælice, that great princes love thee, and deeds of honour for thy sake have done. But neither king nor prince can love thee more, no, nor so much as I, though but the son of thy great father's steward ; for so inestimable is my love, that whatsoever all others shall pretend, can never countervail it."

Whilst thus poor Guy was making protestations, Phælice thus interrupted him :

" O gentle youth, speak not of love, I pray thee, for that is a thing I have no mind to hear of : virginity with me shall live and die. Love is composed of play and idleness, and leadeth only unto vain delight. Besides, it is in thee too great a boldness, for thou art far inferior to my degree: and should thy love be to my father told, I know it would procure thee a reproof. And therefore learn instruction from the proverb, 'That princely eagles scorn to catch flies.' Then, if thou in thy suit wouldst have success, let thy desires be equal to thy fortune, and aim not at those things that are above it. Thou ownest, thyself, princes have courted me; then why should I, that have refused their courtship, stoop down so low as to my father's steward; nay, lower yet, unto his steward's son? My youth and beauty is but in its bloom, and I have no mind to throw it away on one that is so much inferior to me." And with this answer she departed from him, leaving poor Guy more troubled now than ever: for now, almost hopeless in love, he never does expect its comforts more :—

> But all his time he does to sorrow give,
> Wishing each day the last that he may live.

CHAPTER II.

How Guy, after his being despised by Phœlice, grew almost distracted, till she, being admonished by a vision, shews herself more favourable to him.

LOADED with grief, poor Guy could take no rest, distracted in his melancholy mind, refusing all things that delightful seemed, as harsh, distasteful, and abhorred by him. Phælice denies him love, and slights his suit; and then what comfort can the world afford him? He looks like one, whom faith had doomed to death. And like Orestes, in his frantic fits, he tears the golden tresses from his head; or mad Orlando, when of sense deprived, from whom the use of reason is departed: so fares it with this love-tormented man, whose ranging thoughts run all into disorder. Society he shuns, and keeps alone, accusing Destiny, and cursing Beauty. He is a friend to none, but hates himself beyond the bounds of nature and of love. "Venus," cries he, "how are thy laws forgot, to punish him who never did offend thee? what is the cause that I am thus rejected? who interrupts my love to Beauty's mirror? I will drag him hence to roaring Erebus, there to be plagued with never ceasing tortures. I will to the court of Jove, where my loud shouts shall, with their clamour, rend the very skies. Shall I be cozened, as Orpheus was? Assist me, Thersus, to revenge this wrong. Where is Rhadamant, that Justice cannot pass? Eurydice even for a song is sold; fiends, furies, goblins, hydras, for a fall I am prepared to manage every one of you. - I will mount upon the back of Pegasus, and in bright Phœbus's flames I will wrap myself. Then will I tumble windy Æolus to sleep in Thetis's watery crystal lap. From thence I will post unto the torrid zone, to find which way fair Phælice's love is fled. Jason had luck to win the golden fleece : I like the skin, but care not for the horns. Fair Helen was a wanton Grecian wench. Bold Mars will venture ; Venus cannot help it. Trust a fair face ! not I ; let him that list. What is Hercules without a club in his hand ? "

Thus of his senses was poor Guy deprived ; thus did he rave and say he knew not what, being left by Love as blind as Cupid's eyes, till reason reassumed her rule again, and wild disordered passions ceased to tyrannise: for in nocturnal visions Phælice saw the power of Love, and gave to Guy her heart.

When Morpheus, drowsy serjeant of the night, had with his leaden key lockèd up the sense, and laid on Phælice's eyes his sable mace, the heart-tormentor Cupid, he that wounds, and makes poor lovers buy their bargains dear, sends from his bow a golden-headed shaft, and wounded Phælice in her maiden bed ; and to her sight presents a martial man, in armour clad, and fit for all encounters. "Give him thy heart," said he, "for he deserves it. For comely shape and limbs, courage, and valour, the world hath not a champion that is like him. Great honour, lady, thou shalt thereby gain, to adorn thy birth, that is noble and renowned. He shall aspire to such a height of fame, that kings and princes shall his friendship covet. He shall the glory of his country be, and by the sword perform such wondrous things, that kings shall

Y

court him to become their champion. Be not ambitious then that thou art high born, nor be disdainful of a mean estate. Be not defiled then with a scornful soul, nor lifted up, because Heaven has made thee fair! for it is in vain against my bow to strive. If I say love, it must and shall be so. Fix not thy thoughts then upon worldly wealth, for coin has no affinity to love, although by stealth it draws away the heart. Nor can these money matches ever be happy; for as the goods of fortune do decay, so does that Love which they beget consume. I know the sway that golden treasures bear, by false illusions, and by base deceits, and see how women's humours now-a-days run after riches to their own confusion. I see that every abject country peasant, with gold enough, can buy a dainty wife. But, Phælice, if thou knewest as well as I, how much displeased Heaven is at such abuses, thou wouldst scorn that ever virgins should be sold for gold and silver, as your cattle are. Love must be simple, harmless, plain, and pure, and grounded upon sincere affection; and it must likewise be reciprocal, or else it is not as it ought to be. Love's inward thoughts too, must in outward deeds (such as from sacred truth proceed) concur. Thy lover comes not for advancement to thee, because thy father is a worthy Earl; nor for Arabian spice, nor Indian gems; but as great Jupiter to Leda came, it is only to enjoy thy love and beauty. Therefore, sweet virgin, use him well and kindly; make much of him, embrace him for thy own, and let him in thy heart have a chief place: let him no longer for thee moan and grieve, but when thou seest him next, give him encouragement; and in the arms of thy affection let him be embraced." And with that word EMBRACED, he shot and hit the very centre of her tender heart. Feeling the wound, she starts, and then awaked, being thereby taught to pity smarting lovers; for Cupid to the head his arrow drew, because he would be sure it should hit home. With that she fetched a very grievous sigh, and from her eyes a shower of tears did fall. "Where is," quoth she, "the gentle love-god gone, whose power I find so powerful over all? Oh! call him back, my fault I do confess; I have in love been too, too void of pity. Sweet boy, solicit for me to thy mother; for at her altars

now will I sacrifice; and from henceforth no other I will adore.
No goddess in my ears shall gracious be, but she who hath the
all-subduing power of conquering with delight obdurate hearts.
Compassion now hath worthy conquest made of that strong fort
that did resistance make. To make a league, one shaft had
been sufficient; a league for life, a truce that lasts till death."

Guy, more than life, prefers his Phælice's love: Phælice loves
him as dear as he doth her; but it is, alas! to him as yet unknown,
though he made his apparent long before; that now she is his, he
does not yet understand; his wound still bleeds, and there is no
salve applied: till forced by his passion, and the pain he feels, he
boldly thus his second suit begins :—

"Phælice, I have been long ago arraigned, and now I from
your hand expect my judgment. I have been a prisoner in a gaol
of woe, so long that now I do demand my sentence. Oh! speak
unto me either of life or death, for I am quite grown weary of my
life. In that fair form of thine, if kindness dwell, express it with,
'I love;' if none there be, then say, 'I cannot unto love incline.'
Thus thou with me mayst make a quick despatch. Let then thy
frowns or smiles declare my fate. For, for this kingdom's crown,
I would not long endure these racking pains that now I undergo."

Phælice replied, "It is not at my dispose for to yield to love
without my friends' consent, for then I should be guilty of the
crime of being disobedient to my parents. You know my father's
greatness in the land, and if he should (as probably he will) refuse
the love of one he thinks too mean, how could we bear the stroke
disgrace would strike? No remedy but death could ease my
sorrow, and shame would soon become my winding-sheet."

"O doubt not of your father in this case," replied Guy, "for
Warwick's noble Earl shall see such deeds of valour done by me,
he neither will, nor can deny the match. Enjoin me what adventures thou thinkest fit, that wounds and scars may let my body
blood."

"Why then," quoth Phælice, "make thy valour shine, throughout the world as glorious as the sun; and I will give to thee my
heart, soul, and life, and which shall crown the rest, my truest

love : let deeds of honour by thy hands be done ; and by a martial life enhance thy fame ; and for a recompense of all thy toil, take Phælice for thy true and lawful wife."

" To gain thy love," said Guy, " I ask no more, and shall esteem it bought at an easy rate.   O that I were at work, my task to prove with some such churlish man as Hercules."

> " Phælice, this kiss is all that now I crave,
> And till I have purchased fame no more I'll have."

CHAPTER III.

How Guy, taking leave of Phælice, took shipping for France, and landed in Normandy, where he fought with three champions, delivering a fair lady who was condemned to die.

GUY, now by Phælice freed from Sorrow's thrall, arms his great thoughts with Honour's enterprise, and so embarking, sails away from France, leaving behind him England, and his joy.   He seeks for enemies, he longs for foes, and desires nothing more than a fair opportunity to signalise the glory of his arms.   And being safe arrived in Normandy, and having escaped the fury of a storm, Guy and the Captain of the vessel both went ashore, and there refreshed themselves ; but they had not long been there, before their ears were deafened with the loud shouts of a multitude of people, and with the louder noise of drums and trumpets ; this warlike noise extremely pleased our Guy, for now he thought there would be work for him, who wanted nothing more than some encounter.   Therefore inquiring of his host the cause of those loud noises that he heard without, he told him, " That a beautiful young lady, whose name was called Dorinda, having been ravished by the Duke of Blois's son, and charged him with the crime, she was committed by the Duke his father unto prison, as one that had accused him falsely of the crime ; and that three ruffians were suborned to swear she laid that crime to him on purpose to prevent his marriage with the Princess of Parma, that she might be revenged for his breach of promise

made to her; which so incensed the old Duke, that he condemned her to be burned, unless she had a champion to vindicate
her innocence, by fighting with her three accusers. This news
much pleased Guy, who was resolved to vindicate the innocent,
and lay here a foundation for his future fame. So that inquiring
farther into it, and finding that the cause he was about to undertake was just, he presently gave order for his horse and arms to
be got ready; and so accoutring himself in his warlike habili-
ments, he then took his leave of his host, and also of the Captain,
who had in vain endeavoured to dissuade him from it: and
having desired the Captain (who would willingly have gone along
with him) to wait for his return, he rode unto the place of combat,
where he saw the lady fastened to the stake, with several friends
about her, lamenting for her hard fate. Guy scarce had time for
to take a view of her, before those villains who had falsely accused
her, entered the lists well armed and mounted, and proudly
wheeling to the right and left, they made a stand; one of them
demanded in a very haughty manner, whether any there present
durst enter the lists to vindicate the innocence of that condemned
criminal: "Let him come forth, and I shall soon," said he,
"make him repent his rash and unadvised undertaking." This
set Guy all on fire, who thereupon entering the lists, rode up, and
said, "Yes, here is a man, thou perjured villain, that dares to
vindicate a wronged lady's honour; and know, that I so little
fear you, that I will revenge her quarrel, not singly, with one
only, but with you all together; that so the matter may be the
sooner ended." This speech of Guy's so much enraged his
adversary, that giving order for the trumpets sounding, both
couched their spears, and so encountered each other, and with so
much fury, that the earth trembled under them; but Guy had so
much the advantage, that coming with his spear directly on his
adversary's breast, he found a passage through it to his heart, so
that he straight fell down, and with one groan expired.

The remaining combatants, vowing revenge for their companion's death, charged both with desperate fury upon Guy, who
thereupon drew out his massy and well-tempered blade, and

brandishing it in his hand, soon made them feel it was like the sword of fate, which there was no withstanding; so that one falling dead by his companion, and the other being wounded, begged on his knees that life he had so justly forfeited; which, that he might more easily obtain, he made a free confession of his crime, and showed how they had all been hired to accuse the lady, by Philbertus, the Duke's son, who really was guilty; and for a thousand crowns had hired them all to bear false witness for him, against that lady whom he had abused.

This full discovery caused through all the field an universal shout; each magnifying the valour and generosity of Guy; and we may be assured the lady was not behindhand in sounding out the praise of her deliverer; but who this generous stranger was, was what all wished to know, but none could tell. When he alighted and unbound her, she joyfully embraced his knees, imploring a thousand blessings on his head, offering what rewards he pleased to have: but he refused them all, telling her, "What he did was out of love to virtue and to honour. But wished her to take care of her own safety, by timely getting out of the Duke's power, lest he should use some other means to take away her life." So bidding her farewell, he rode back to the ship, and there related to the Captain what befell him, who with no little joy heard the relation. Yet after some consideration, it was judged best to stay no longer in that harbour; and so they weighed their anchors, and sailed out to sea.

> Then did brave Guy a treble victory win,
> Or else the lady in bad plight had been.

CHAPTER IV.

How Philbertus, the Duke of Blois's son, hearing what Guy had done, followed him to the sea, where a dreadful fight happened between them, in which Philbertus and his men were taken prisoners.

As much haste as Guy and the Captain made to get out of the harbour, yet they were not got altogether out of danger; for

Philbertus being informed that one Guy, a native of England, had
not only overcome his knights of the post, but that his villainy
was also thereby discovered, and the injured lady freed and got
out of his reach; it made his anger boil up to the utmost pitch of
rage, threatening to wreak his malice on the head of Guy, for
doing him so great an injury; and therefore he secretly armed
sixty of his servants and his attendants, and with them made all
the haste imaginable to the port where he had information Guy's
ship lay, thinking to surprise him and the lady there together.
But finding himself disappointed, and that Guy had set sail three
hours before his coming, his disappointment made his rage boil
higher, especially believing Guy fled for fear of him, and that he
was also conveying the lady away with him. Whereupon going
on board a stout vessel that lay in the harbour, he commanded
them to weigh anchor, and make all the sail they could after the
English ship, which by a small boat just come into port, he
was informed was sailed to the eastward. The mariners immediately got ready, and having a fair wind, and the ship being a
very good sailer, in the running of a glass and a half they came
within sight of the ship wherein Guy was. No sooner was the
French ship come in sight, but the mariners gave notice of it to
their Captain, who viewing of the ship with his prospect glass,
told Guy, that he was sure they were pursued, and that the enemy
being treble their number, their best way was to hoist up all their
sails, and to make the best of their way; and that then, by the
help of the evening, he did not doubt but to get clear of them.
"Why, how many ships," said Guy, "are they that chase us?"
"Why," said the Captain, "I discern no more than one at present, but it is a good stout ship, and carries thrice the men on
board that we do."—"Well, well," said Guy, "if that be all be
of good courage; and the first thing we do, let us tack about,
and meet them like courageous Englishmen; I will bear the
brunt of war myself alone. I would not for the crown of
France, I will swear it, have it reported that Guy ever fled."
This speech had the effect upon the seamen, that one and all
cried, "Let us engage them straight." Nor did the Captain now

appear less willing. And so they cried, "All hands aloft," to put
them in a posture of defence; which they had no sooner done,
but up the French ship comes, and grapples them; this Guy
was glad to see, hoping he should be with them presently, and
therefore he gave orders to let the French board them without
much difficulty; who, by that means supposing they had been
victorious, gave such a shout as victors do at land. This insolence
made Guy so lay about him, each blow he struck had more than
human force, and in a few moments all the deck was nothing but
a scene of blood and slaughter; no armour was of proof against
his sword, for at each blow fresh streams of blood ran down.
Philbertus was amazed at the dismal sight, and wished himself
in his own ship again; and ordered those few that were left
alive, if possible, to get to his own ship, and then immediately
ungrapple; which Guy perceiving, having cleared his deck, he
soon leaped on board of the French ship, and singly there maintained a bloody fight, hewing them down with so much fury, that
many of them, to escape his sword, leaped into the sea. Philbertus seeing this, gave all the encouragement to his men that
was possible; and as one now grown desperate, charged on Guy's
helmet with such force, as made it sparkle fire; at which undaunted
Guy returned him such a blow, as at his feet made him fall down
for dead; which made the soldiers all throw down their arms,
and cry aloud for quarter. And thereupon Guy, who was always
merciful to conquered foes, ended the battle, commanding all his
men to fight no more: in which time Philbertus came to himself
again, and with a low submission, begged his life, which Guy as
freely gave him. And having removed him and the rest into his
own ship, set fire to that of Philbertus, and sailed on his intended
voyage, coasting along the shore, until they touched upon that
part of Normandy that borders upon Germany; where Guy, with
an undaunted courage, landed; and there was welcomed with
the pleasing news, that a great tilt and tournament was to be
held for Blanch the Emperor's daughter, a beautiful and an
accomplished lady, who was to be the victor's prize, who thereby
had a right to marry her, and to have with her a brace of grey-

hounds, a falcon, and a milk white steed. Upon this welcome news, Guy discharges the Captain of the vessel, leaving the prisoners with him, to dispose of at his pleasure; who putting them to their ransom, they obtained their liberty, while Guy, with eager haste, rode to his royal tilting.

> And flushed with victory already won,
> Thought greater things might by him now be done.

CHAPTER V.

How Guy triumphed over all the German princes, and won the beauteous Blanch, the Emperor's daughter, and after leaving her, returned for England.

GUY of the Captain having took his leave, goeth where there was more business to be done: for hearing that there was to be a meeting of valiant knights from divers Christian lands, that did intend to run a race of valour, for which a great advantage was propounded, it was charming music to his greedy ear. The prize that drew them all unto this place, was the daughter to the Almain Emperor, fair Blanch, whose wondrous face had that attractive power, that it united all the graces in her. It was thither all the worthies posting came: who won the damsel (for so was the law) by manly courage, and victorious might, should have her mounted on a milk white steed, attended with two greyhounds and a falcon, all of the same colour (if white may be so called); this was his lot that could obtain the day, to bear away the honour, and the maid. Our English knight prepares him for the field, where kings and princes also present were, and dukes and earls a very great assembly held, about that wondrous fair, and beauteous prize. Though only one must speed, and hundreds miss, yet there each man imagines Blanch his own. The spacious field wherein they were assembled, hardly afforded room for the armed knights. The golden glittering armour that was there darted the sunbeams back into the clouds. The pampered horses proudly pranced about, to hear the clangour of the trumpets sound.

A German Prince of an undaunted spirit did the first onset and encounter give unto an Earl, whose valour did requite him with blow for blow, as resolutely brave, till by a stroke on his head the Earl received, he was unhorsed, falling on the ground for dead.

Next, Guy with courage to the Prince comes forth, and fights just like another Hercules; like force he never felt before nor since; nor never was put into such hard extremes. Just where himself had laid the Earl before, there down comes he, both horse and man to the ground.

Duke Otton seeing this, was in a rage, and with such wrathful humours was incensed, he vowed by heaven that nothing should appease his fury, but the death of that proud foe. "Prepare thee now," quoth he, "to breathe thy last, monster or devil, whatsoever thou be." They join together in a dreadful fight, the clattering armour sounds, the splinters fly, and the ascending dust will not let them see: their blood allays it, streaming from their wounds. Both their swords break; they alight, and with main force Guy threw the Duke to the ground, that his bones did crack.

Duke Rainer would revenge his cousin then, and for the encounter next of all prepares: "I see," quoth Guy, "that you are less than men, that with a blow or fall are vexed so soon. But come and welcome, I am ready for you. We say in England, THE WEAKEST MUST GO TO THE WALL." Then they together rushed, and shook the ground, whilst animating trumpets sound the alarm. In Rainer's shoulder Guy made such a wound, that he soon lost the use of his right arm; who thereupon yielded himself as vanquished.

Then, for a while, all stood amazed at Guy, none being forward to encounter him, till Lovain's Duke resolved to try his fortune, having good hope that he might better speed. Then sitting fair on a proud steed that ill endured the bit, well mounted and well armed, "I think," quoth he, "thou some enchanter art, that in thine arm the force of magic hast." "I will teach thee to believe ere I have done," quoth Guy, "for thou shalt feel that I can charm. I will conjure with no other spell but iron, by which

I will send thee unto heaven or to hell." With that he gave him such a cruel stroke, that he could but a weak reply return : then with a second and a third he broke his helmet. With that, " Hold, hold," cried he, " I have enough, I will rather yield than die. Let them fight for a woman that desire it ; I think the devil scarce can deal with thee."

Then not a man more would encounter him, they all were terrified and stood in fear, and against Guy were all filled with rage : " What," said they, "shall a stranger bear the honour of this great day ? what cursed fortune is this, that he should have the glory of the field ? " Amongst themselves they cursed his happiness, and could have killed him, but that no man dared put his own life in hazard by so doing. If wishes might have done it, he had died ; but there was no man durst attempt to fight him.

The Emperor then sent a knight for Guy, and asked his name, and of his birth and country, which he told him. " Then," said his Majesty, " I must commend thy haughty courage, resolutely bold : brave Englishman, thou art thy country's pride : in Europe lives not such another man. I do admire thy worth, great is thy valour ; my tongue cannot suffice to speak thy praise. Ascend to honour's just deserved seat, thou art a second Hector in mine eyes. This day thy worthy hand has showed me more than in my life before I ever saw. Come and receive thy due desert of me ; my daughter's love is free at thy dispose ; the greyhounds, steed, and falcon, take unto thee ; thy worthiness does merit more than these : hold, here is a jewel, wear it for my sake, which shall be as a witness of my love."

Guy thanked his highness for his gracious favours, and vowed him service whilst his life did last. Then to the Princess, with a mild behaviour, he cast a reverent, humble, modest look, saying, " Fair lady, fortune is my friend, that such a beauty to my lot is given. Madam, accept your loyal English knight, to do you service when you shall command it ; who, while he hath a drop of blood to spend, will sacrifice it all on your behalf, against whosoever shall dare to contradict you. Too high it is for me to be your husband; it is enough to be your servant Guy. In England doth my marriage-love remain, to whom I must and will be true for ever; about whose face, such pains hath nature took, I durst have sworn, flesh never could have matched it. But now I find, and ever shall acknowledge it, there is a phœnix in the world besides her, and that is yourself: and I dare all mankind to say one tittle that shall contradict it; but which is fairest there is no eye can tell; no human judgment in the world can try it, or positively say which hath most beauty, Blanch or my fair bride. I dare be bold to call your beauties twins; and that compared unto either of you, Venus herself was but a black Moor. Oh Phælice! here is thy picture in this Princess. Methinks thou art present in her lovely looks. Thou that of my soul's faculties art mistress, recorded in Time's brazen-leafed book, if I to thee prove false, even in thought, and much more in my actions, Jove's fearful vengeance light upon my head."

Quoth Blanch, "Thy constancy," and then she sighed, "is highly to be praised, and thou applauded. He that Love's promise will not faithfully keep, in horrors and in torments let him dwell. But I suppose thy vows are yet unmade, and so what thy sword won thy heart may take."

"Madam," said Guy, "what I avouch is true, and I dare call even Heaven to witness it: my protestations are above the skies; and he who made them, knows I speak the truth. Madam, the sun declines, and the day grows ancient, I will therefore humbly take my leave of you, for now my body is to repose inclined, although my troubled mind can take no rest; my restless mind is now in Warwick Castle, although my body be in Normandy. Here I make others bend, but there I bow, and lie as low as the humble ground; even at Love's feet to the ground I cast myself. Though victory my temples here have crowned, I cannot stay, I must to England back. My mind misgives me that Phælice is not well. Like my sad thoughts, my armour shall be black, and in a mournful iron shell it will suit me. For where the mind suspicious cares does meet with, distrust is ever dealing doubtful snares. Yet I have much good fortune on my side, that know

the means how to attain my bliss ; for Phælice ties her love to my
conditions, and she for this, I trust, will be my own. By this she
may, but if she more request, there is nothing in the world that I
will deny her."

With hasty journey therefore home he goes, leaving the vulgar
unto nine days' wonder. And being safe arrived on English
ground, he unto Phælice posted; for too long he thought each
minute that he stayed away. And coming to her presence, he
beholds her with greater joy, and with more cheerful looks than
pen can write, or can by tongue be told.

> What tongue can tell, what pen can write, how sweet
> Are absent lovers' joys when once they meet.

CHAPTER VI.

How Guy returning to Warwick was received by Phælice ; by
whom he was sent forth again to seek new adventures ; but
before he went destroyed a monstrous dun cow upon Dunsmore
Heath.

PHÆLICE having received the news of Guy's arrival upon the
English shore, and of the mighty fame he had acquired, by all
the warlike deeds his hands had done, expected soon to see him
at her father's castle, preparing to receive him according to his
worth, and to the great affection she had for him. Nor did her
expectations fail her, for Guy made all the haste a man could
make, to lay the prize of all his glorious conquests at her feet.
Where being come, after salutes, and mutual embraces, Guy thus
bespoke her :

"Fair foe," said he, "I come to challenge thee; for there is no
man that I can meet will fight me. I have been where a crew of
cowards are, but none that dare maintain the right of ladies ; good,
proper, and well spoken men, indeed, but let me win a Princess from
them all. Phælice, this sword hath won an Emperor's daughter,
as sweet a wench as any lives in all Europe. I bought her at the
price of blood and wounds ; well worth my bargain : but thy better
face hath made me leave her to some other's lot; for I protest,

by Heaven, I could not love her. This stately steed, this falcon, and these hounds I took, as in full payment of the rest; for I have always kept my love to thee enclosed within the centre of my heart. My constancy to thee I have still preserved, leaving all other women as they are. But say, my Phælice, shall I now obtain thee? wilt thou consent that Hymen tie our hands? art thou resolved to keep still to thy vow, that none but I shall ever have thy heart? canst thou forsake the world, change thy condition, and now become thy true and faithful lover's wife?"

To whom fair Phælice thus replied again : "Know, worthy knight, my joys have been enlarged at the report of thy great deeds abroad : some were, I hear, in such a bloody sweat, their valour, fame, and reputation bleeds. Therefore, my Guy, I give thee humble thanks, that thou for me so much didst undergo, and for my sake such hard adventures made. To win a Princess, was a precious prize : but sure, methinks, if I Sir Guy had been, she greater favour from me should have found than take a horse, and turn a lady by. What! is a horse, a falcon, and a hound more worthy than so beautiful a lady? Perhaps you will say, it was done for love of me; I do imagine, nay, believe it is : and though I jest, I will do more for thee, than thou, or any but myself doth know; I will never marry while life's glass doth run, but only to thyself. But, give me leave, my love, to speak my mind; let me lock up my secrets in thy breast. I had a vision did affection move : Cupid came to me, whilst I slumbering lay, and in my mother's name commanded me to love thee. And whilst he was to this persuading me, an armed man just as I see thee now, he set before my eyes, and thus he spake : 'Phælice, be gentle hearted, bow and yield, and do not the sovereign power of love oppose; but all thy loyalty, thy truth, and thy love, bestow them freely on this matchless youth : throughout the world his fame admired shall be; and mighty men shall tremble at his wrath; to end the quarrels of great kings shall he be often courted. His worthiness no common path shall tread; but actions to be feared he shall effect, and to pass bring things of the greatest moment.' This, in effect, he did to me relate, and to his will I have obedient been. Now how to hate thee if I would, I know not: for I have of perfect kindness learned the skill. Believe me, Guy, for if it were not thus, this secret of my heart thou shouldst not know. But now, my love, before thou dost possess thy constant Phælice in her marriage bed, thou must far greater and more worthy deeds perform than what thou hast already done: the winning of a lady and her steed are.but small things to what thou yet must do. I will ever love thee, though thou never dost more, but cannot grant the use of love till then."

Quoth Guy, "Not grant the use of love, fair Phælice! then I perceive, I must again go travel and see what fate has for me still to do. I will content thee, love, one way or other, and either slay, or else be slain myself, ere I into this realm again return; and thou confess I have thy dream fulfilled. Assist me, Heaven, as I sincerely mean, for I protest by all the powers above, no unjust quarrel ever shall make me fight, nor yet to wrong the wronged will I ever incline: for those that by oppression fall, I will stand; in honour's cause my life I will freely venture. Come, my Bellona, my sword do thou girt on, and in thy ivory arms embrace my armour, and such kind kisses as thou canst afford bestow upon me in the stead of charms. Upon Ulysses's loving wife I think, and how thou now her life doth imitate. Farewell, my Phælice, health and happiness attend thee to thy heart's desire for ever; and like success I beseech God to grant me, as I my love to thee shall keep entire. When war's stern looks abroad I have performed, at my return Hymen will make amends."

Unto Earl Roband next does Guy repair, and tells him he is come to take his leave; for he must go where honour finds him work, and there receive the just rewards of virtue. "At home, my honourable lord," said he, "I find that valour has no stage for action, I will therefore search what is to be done abroad; from kingdom to kingdom I will go, and find out work, for no good comes of idleness; it only bringeth men up to sloth and cowardice, and I hate cowards as I hate the devil."

To which the Earl returned, "Dear Guy, thou makest me

grieve at this sad news ; and more because thou hast disappointed me. The news is more than I can well endure. I hoped I should enjoy thy wished for company, and thou wouldest go no more abroad ; and now thou speakest of new adventures. O ! change thy mind, brave Guy, and stay with me ; no longer trust to fortune's treacherous smiles ; though now she hath so kindly dealt with thee, yet she may leave thee to an unlucky hour, and turn her many favours into frowns. O ! do not over rashly hazard thy glory : lost honour is not easily got again."

To this Guy answered thus, "My noble Lord, that man of dangers must not be afraid, that to adventures doth himself dispose, but must supported be with resolution, and for his foes still think himself too good. I will never fear I shall be overcome, whilst I have hands to fight, or legs to stand. Therefore I will leave your honour, wishing all health unto your happy state. If fortune means to frown, yet she shall see that I will disdain her hate. What star soever swayed when I was born, I have a mind will laugh at all misfortunes."

The Earl perceiving him resolved to go, told him, "That he would be no hindrance to his proceedings, and only would ask one request of him before he went : " Guy told him, "Whatsoever he asked that was within his power to perform, he should not be denied." Then said the Earl, "It is this, that when you are once again come safe to England, you will go abroad no more, but live at home with me." Which Guy having promised him, prepared for his departure, and soon after took his leave, going to the seaside, there to embark for France.

Being come there, and ready to embark, the wind proved contrary, and so continued for six days together ; during which time fame through each corner of the land had made a mighty noise of an exceeding great and monstrous cow, lurking within the woods not many miles from Warwick, making most dreadful devastations, destroying man and beast, and putting all their keepers unto flight, being so mighty strong, that it was thought not possible to destroy it ; and some affirm, that she was at least four yards in height and six in length, and had a head propor-

tionable, with two sharp horns growing direct, with eyes resemb-
ling lightning for their fierceness; and was of a dun colour, and
from thence named the dun cow; and the place where she lay,
being on the borders of a great heath, was from thence called
Dunsmore Heath, which name it retains to this day.

Upon notice which was given to the King (who was then at
York) of the havoc and slaughter which was made by this
monstrous creature, he offered knighthood, and several other
privileges, to any one that would undertake to destroy it. But
such was the terror she had spread throughout the country, that
none was found so hardy as to adventure himself on such a
dangerous enterprise ; and the absence of Guy (who by this time
was supposed to be in France) was generally lamented ; all
believing he would undertake it.

Guy (who was all this while waiting for a fair wind) hearing the
discourse of the country, and hating to be idle, resolved privately
to go and engage with this destroyer of his country; and so
taking his sword, a strong battle-axe, and his bow and quiver
with him, he rid *incognito* to the place where this monster used to
lodge, which was in a great thicket of trees, which grew on the
side of a heath, near a pool of standing water; finding, as he rid
along, the cottages and houses everywhere thereabouts deserted,
and the carcases of men and beasts lie scattered round about ;
which filled him with great pity and compassion for his country,
and extreme resentment against that monstrous destroyer.

Being come at last within bow-shot of the place, the monster
espied him, and thrusting her head through the thicket, her
dreadful eyes were enough to fill any heart with terror but that of
the courageous Guy, who notwithstanding her horrid roaring soon
bent his bow of steel, and as he was one of the expertest archers
England then could boast of, drawing his arrow to the head, let
fly ; which striking on the monster's hide, rebounded back as
from an adamantine wall, without the least impression being made :
at which, whilst Guy was in some admiration, the dreadful beast,
swift as the eastern winds, came running towards him, with her
sharp pointed horns, aiming directly at him, which he observing,

lifted his battle-axe on high, and on the forehead struck her such a blow as made her to recoil, and roar most hideously, and yet enraged more, she came on again; and clapping her horns upon his breast, dinted his armour, though of highest proof, before he could avoid her, but wheeling his warlike steed about, he met her again, and with redoubled strokes, gave her a desperate wound under the ear, the only place she could be wounded in so sensibly; whereat she again roared, snorted, and stamped on the ground: and by this, Guy perceiving she was mortal, followed that stroke, with others no less forcible, by which at last she fell upon the ground; and Guy, alighting from his horse, hewed her so long, till with a horrid groan she breathed her last.   Then leaving her almost deluged in her own blood, he rid to the next town that was inhabited, and there made known the monster's death, to the great joy of the inhabitants: the people loaded him with presents, and honoured him with thanks; and all the country came in to see that monster dead, which when alive they stood so much afraid of.[1]

And, though Guy thought to get away before the King had notice of it, yet fame was swifter far than Guy, and he was sent for by the King before he could get on shipboard, and so was forced to go to York; where he was no sooner arrived, but the King embraced him, and after a splendid entertainment he gave him the order of knighthood, and many rich gifts, causing one of the ribs of the said monster to be hanged up in Warwick Castle. And Guy having departed from the King very well satisfied with his entertainment, and the wind now serving, he goes on board to seek fresh adventures in foreign lands.

> Where he so many wondrous things did do,
> As stagger'd faith, and nonpluss'd reason too.

---

[1] To this adventure Butler alludes in his *Hudibras*, when he describes Talgol the butcher, "mortal foe to cows:"

> " He many a boar and huge dun cow
> Did, like another Guy, o'erthrow;
> But Guy with him in fight compared,
> Had like the boar or dun cow fared;
> With greater troops of sheep he'd fought
> Than Ajax, or bold Don Quixote."

CHAPTER VII.

How Guy, with Herand and two other knights, were assaulted by sixteen villains that lay in ambuscade for him in a wood, whom he destroyed; having killed two, and wounded the other of the knights: and afterwards assisted the Duke of Lovain, who was besieged by the Emperor, &c.

Now Guy expects a favourable gale, and has it even to his heart's desire, and with a speedy passage doth he sail to seek new adventures once again in France, where finding none, from thence away he goes to Lovain, where the Emperor besieged the Duke thereof, because he had the misfortune to kill the Emperor's cousin, whom he greatly loved, and therefore took his death exceeding ill; and thereupon a quarrel did arise, and wars ensued between two mighty foes. Thither goes Guy to lend the Duke his aid. But in the way a plot to take away his life was, by the false Duke Otton, basely laid, although it was not effected; for Guy so well about him laid, that it succeeded not: the matter was, Otton before in France by Guy disgraced, had vowed, wherever he met him, he should die. And to that end, sixteen appointed were to lie in ambush, that they might surprise him, who in a forest slily hid themselves, and on a sudden all surrounded Guy, who only was attended with three knights, and never before was Guy in like distress. But seeing how it was, "Now, friends," said he, "show yourselves right bred English gentlemen. Here is indeed some odds, sixteen to three, but I, the fourth, will stand you in some stead; you three shall combat six, that is two to one, and leave the other ten alone to me." With that he drew his sword and laid so about him, that in the air their rattling armour echoed, and down they quickly dropped on every side. Guy quickly made dispatch of his half score. But there remained half a dozen more, who had slain two of his beloved knights, which he no sooner knew, but straight he stamped upon the ground, and with a fearful tone, he uttered forth these words: "Ah, villains! how my soul abhors this sight; for these how my revengeful passions strive! this bloody deed with blood I will repay; you die, though you had each a thousand lives. Two you have slain outright and wounded Heraud, which is the last cursed act you shall do." And then, with force almost exceeding all that human arm could ever boast, he lays upon them blows which made them reel, and quickly brought them breathless to the ground. At length, cut all in piecemeals for the fowls : "Lie there," quoth Guy, "and feast the hungry crows, or feed the savage beast that hither come. But for these worthy gentlemen that have lost their lives in the defence of me, and for my sake left England's pleasant soil, them will I inter in honourable wise, with what solemnity the place affords, and be myself a mourner at their funeral."

From thence unto a hermit not far off he rid, and did with care that charge to him commit, who did that office carefully perform, and bare home wounded Heraud to his cell, who was not dead (though Guy supposed him slain), but quickly by the hermit was recovered.

Now forth goes Guy, sad, pensive, and perplexed, grieving that destiny had dealt so hardly, to take away his dearly beloved company, and leave him as he travelled all alone, that none could ease the torments of his mind. But in his lonely solitary travel, at last his fortune brought him to a place that was for honour very much renowned, and there he met with tilts and tournaments, which entertained him with delight and glory. And there kind fortune gave him her consent to win the prize from every valiant knight; of all the worthy men that hither came, not one could match him in Duke Reyner's court.

Then to the Duke of Milan he repairs, where he is admired of all for his great worth ; and understanding some affairs of weight fell out betwixt Duke Segwin of Lovain, and the Emperor, he from the Duke of Milan went his way, and forthwith took his journey to Lovain. But as he passed through the way, he met a pilgrim that with travel seemed faint, whom he greets, and with some news entreats him to refresh his longing ear. He with a sigh or two, said : "Sir, with news I have but little business;

there is but one thing in the world I care for, and only that and nothing else I mind : I in despair do seek a man, because I have long sought, but cannot find him ; a man more to me than all the men in the world beside."

"Thou speakest," said Guy, "like one that hast some gratitude. But tell me, pray, what man art thou ? And what is he for whom thou hast expressed so great a kindness ? "

"I am an Englishman, of knight's degree," quoth Heraud, "and the subject of my grief is the loss of one Sir Guy, my countryman."

Guy then, with tears of joy, embraces him : "And art thou living, Heraud, my dear friend ? " said Guy, and kindly took him in his arms. "Then here I bid my sorrows all adieu ; pray, who thy wounds did cure ? "

Heraud, no less surprised with joy and wonder to find Sir Guy his countryman again, cried out, "And have I found thee thus, my friend ! my pains and travel have been well rewarded. It was the good old hermit that saved me, by the medicine he applied." Then each embraced and both renewed their joys at this so good and happy meeting. No angry star with inauspicious rays befell them then, but both were well content.

Then, mounting on their steeds, they bend their course, with easy pace, unto Duke Lovain's court, where they his city find in great distress, straitly besieged by the Emperor's forces. But Segwin was extremely satisfied that worthy Guy was come unto his aid ; "for now," quoth he, "I dare be bold to say we have an honourable valiant man : advise me, warlike knight, what is to be done to free me from the danger I am in ? "

"My lord," quoth Guy, "great as the danger seems, myself will find a way to set you free : let us presently upon them issue forth ; our courage will make the cowards fly."

"The counsel," quoth the Duke, "I do approve, and to thy project give my free consent. Let life, limb, blood be lost, I will follow thee. So let all do that come to me in love."

Then suddenly they rush out of the city, and on the Almains suddenly set, where they did such a bloody slaughter make that many thousand lives were soon cut off: of thirty thousand that besieged the town, there scarce was three thousand that escaped.

The Emperor at this was much perplexed, but with new forces gave a fresh assault, as knowing well they could not be relieved, and so their strength must weaken by degrees. And therefore coming with a new supply, believed he in short time might famish them. Guy and the Duke appear upon the walls, and tell him, " he shall never win the town, for they can spare his soldiers what provision they can desire," and so flung down abundance of victuals from the walls, and withal told them, "That if they wanted he could spare them more." "And now," quoth Guy, "that we have fed your bodies, I hope your stomachs will be up to fight; but I am afraid you are not rightly bred, but like some dunghill cocks, will crow and run away. But still, when cowards do a fray begin, before the battle ends away they run, and so yourselves have lately done, we see. Your tongues we heard, but could not feel your hands; your words were hot, but actions cool enough; though I confess your heels are wondrous nimble. We did believe that when you first came hither we should have found you men of strength and courage, but, having tried you, find it is no such matter, unless you could surprise us while we sleep; for waking we will encounter one for ten, and never wished to have a better match. And if you can do better, let us see it; therefore prepare, for we will be with you presently." And then upon their foes forthwith they flew, fighting like men that laughed pale Death to scorn; for they resolved they would their city free or never live to see another morning. Much blood was shed, and many lives it cost; but in the end the Almains lost the day. The Duke, with Guy, swiftly pursued their foes, who, like so many hares, fled away.

The victors to the city back repaired, with trophies of the glory they had gained, and all that heard the action much admired the great exploit so resolutely done. But unto Guy the Duke returned his thanks; "For thou," quoth he, "art Cæsar of our field."

"My lord," quoth Guy, "I take not so much joy that I have by my sword your freedom wrought, as I should glory, if it were

my hap to make the Emperor and you good friends. Give me
but leave, and I will do my endeavour, and put good will to a
blunt soldier's wit."

The Duke consented, and desires Sir Guy to take a guard of
soldiers from the town.

Then Guy forthwith went to the Emperor, and being by his
officers conducted into his presence, he bespeaks him thus :

"All health to your imperial majesty, and peace to thee, if
thou to us say peace ; and love to thee, if thou wilt love embrace.
As we are Christians, let us war no more, but fight against those
that are foes to Heaven. We do not sue thee in a servile manner,
as fearing any force or power thou hast ; for victory on our side
displays its banner, and to our view yields a delightful prospect ;
no cause doth move us but the cause of conscience, to bring the
heathen to religion's law : and therefore now, most noble Emperor,
declare thy mind. Shall we be Christian foes, or Christian friends ?
shall we among ourselves divide the name, or challenge them that
have that name denied ? "

Guy having ended what he had to say, the Emperor to him
made this reply :

"Brave Englishman, hadst thou spoke thus before, thousands
had lived, that now the sword has slain ; but those must in the
bowels of the earth remain, until the general resurrection : but,
for the future, wars betwixt us shall cease, and I will embrace
thee as my friend. Thy motion, honoured knight, to honour tends,
and thou shalt live in fame's immortal praise ; and when thou art
buried in eternal night, thy name unto the end of days shall last."

"Come, go, great Prince," quoth Guy, "into the town, and
with Duke Segwin there a league renew. Our end shall be to
pull down pagans, those foes to religion."

The Emperor being brought by Guy into the city, the Duke of
Lovain from his castle came, and after mutual salutations past,
the Emperor was conducted to the castle, where, by the mediation
of Sir Guy, there was a league between them soon concluded, to
the great joy of all the people ; which was, with feasting and
rejoicing, welcome on every side.

CHAPTER VIII.

How after Guy had made peace between the Emperor and the Duke of Lovain, he was furnished with two thousand men, and ten ships of war, for the relief of Bizantium; and being scattered from the rest of the fleet, is set upon by three pirates, two of which he destroys and forces the third to fly.

GUY having thus accomplished his end of making peace between two contenders, the Emperor and the Duke of Lovain, they both entreat Guy to stay amongst them, to enjoy that peace he had procured. But by no means could they prevail upon him. He was for seeking out new scenes of action, but would no more employ his arms against Christians; and therefore earnestly entreated them to furnish him with forces to go against the faithless Saracens, who had broke in upon the Grecian empire, and besieged Bizantium. They both agreed, and left it to himself to take what force he thought sufficient, and they would furnish him with all things necessary for the war. Guy, after having returned thanks to both for their kind and generous offer, assured them he would so employ their forces as should be for the honour of all Christendom. And thereupon immediately selected two thousand of the choicest soldiers present; one of the Emperor's forces, and the other of them belonging to the Duke of Lovain, who with equal willingness went with him, as proud of being those whom he had chosen. Next, he embarked them on ten ships of war, and then took leave of the Emperor and the Duke, promising, that at his return he would present them with such trophies and evidences of his soldiers' courage as the fortune of war should yield him: and so departed with a prosperous gale.

Guy being now ploughing the briny ocean, almost a month, and meeting no adventure, thought fortune dealt a little hardly by him. But by a wind, common enough to those that sail upon the Lovain seas, disjoined from his fleet, she gave him new occasion for his valour; for he was met by three Turkish men of war (and three to one you will say is odds at football), who being of the Sallee rovers, supposed they had got a prize, as judging him a merchantman, and thereupon came boldly up, thought straight to have boarded him ; which Guy perceiving, could not choose but smile, and tell his men they had now an occasion to exercise their valour, and thereupon drew out his flaming sword, so often tried in war, and charged on the assailing infidels with such a martial fury, that Mars himself could hardly have done more, glutting the gaping jaws of hungry Death, not only cutting down the men, but also spoiling all their shrouds and tackle ; whilst valiant Heraud, and the rest remained not idle on the other side ; for they having prepared hemp, tar, resin, and other like combustible materials, set them on fire, and threw them into the Turk's ship that engaged them : this was a stratagem till then unknown ; which catching hold of the decks, masts, and rigging, soon set the ship on fire, which they being utterly unable to extinguish, soon quit their flaming castle, and rather chose to perish in the ocean ; which the other ships beholding, and being much surprised to meet with such resistance, now found too late they had caught a tartar, and so hoisted their sails, preparing to be gone; which one of them had the good hap to do, but Guy resolving to make sure of the other, so closely grappled with her, that he soon leapt on board her, and there made such a slaughter, that all the deck was covered with the carcases of those that fell as victims to his sword; which so amazed the Turks, that they cried in vain to Mahomet to come and save them from those inhuman devils that assaulted them. But although Mahomet knew nothing of the matter, yet Guy, out of compassion, spared their lives. Then putting forty of his men on board, he sent the ship, with the remaining prisoners, to his friend the Duke, as the first fruits of what his valour purchased. No sooner had this brisk engagement ended, but Guy's nine ships came up with him again, which had by reason of a fog been separated from him. And the night coming on, Guy ordered they should stand off to the southeast, for fear of running fowl upon the rocks, too often met with in those parts.

No sooner was the longed for morning come, but from the

main topmast, a seaman calling unto Guy, told him, he made the land; which ere the sun had run out half his race, the whole ship's crew beheld as well as he. And as unto the land they nearer drew, they could discover famed Bizantium's shore, which then was by the Turks and Saracens infested almost round. Guy thereupon ordered his forces to be landed at the next convenient harbour, and from thence sent Heraud with two other captains, to learn, if possible, how things then stood, both with respect to the besieged, and the besiegers. In five hours' time Heraud returned again, and from a Turk whom they had met without, and taken prisoner, they understood the city was besieged by fifty thousand men, who were most Turks and Saracens, and that it had been so for three months' time, but that it was defended by the Christians, commanded by Albertus, a very worthy Saxon.

This news was very welcome unto Guy, who now thought he had a fair opportunity to show his valour, and serve the Christian interest, by the destruction of the infidels. And there he immediately despatched Heraud his trusty friend, and one knight more, unto the Lord Albertus, to let him know that he was come from Germany, and lay ready now in such a port, with two thousand Christians under his command, ready to serve him; and if he would in the evening make a sally out at the gate that looks towards the sea, he would be ready with his men to force his way through the enemy's camp, and join him, and so come into the city to assist him.

Heraud and his companion undertook to deliver this message to Albertus; and by the help of Turkish habits, passed all the guards, without the least suspicion; and coming to the gates, declared they had a message to Albertus, whereupon they were let in, and straight conducted to the castle, where Albertus and his chief officers were sitting in council of war, to whom after due reverence paid, they gave an account of their business; but having declared this only by word of mouth, Albertus and his officers seemed somewhat doubtful, as not knowing but it might be a stratagem, contrived by the enemy, to take the city; but when Heraud had delivered Albertus a letter under Guy's own hand, to whose great fame for martial deeds Albertus was no stranger, they quickly changed their sentiments, and treated them as they deserved, for such a welcome message, to which they gave a ready and cheerful compliance; entertaining them with all imaginable civility and kindness, promising not to fail sallying out at the time and gate appointed. Heraud and his friend returning back to Guy, acquainted him with all that passed, who being very joyful that things succeeded so well, landed his men with all imaginable silence and dexterity, drawing them up in battalia upon the shore, and giving orders to those that continued on board, to stand off at sea, till he should signify his pleasure to them to come into harbour. After which he marched towards the city with all the privacy and silence that could be. But for all his caution the enemy had perceived them and taken the alarm; so that, gathering together from all quarters, they were ready to receive him: Guy, no wit discouraged, made a short speech to his soldiers, telling them of the goodness of their cause, and the assistance they should have from their friends in the city, bid them fall on undauntedly, and the day was their own: upon which they gave a great shout, and Guy, drawing his flaming sword, fell on his foes with such undaunted fury, that they soon bore down all that were before them; so that wherever they came, the mangled bodies of their foes overspread the crimson plain. Guy, with redoubled blows, slaughtering wherever it was he turned himself: thus the dispute continued for more than two hours' space; in which Guy had so well improved his time, that he and his small forces, with the assistance of three thousand from the city, who sallied out according to their promise, had destroyed almost thirty thousand men. So that the Pagan army, finding themselves thus worsted on all sides, retreated to their camp in much confusion; which filled the Soldan with revengeful thoughts, which he resolved forthwith to execute; and presently after gave orders to his soldiers, early next morning, to assault the city, which he supposed, wearied with the last night's fatigue, would scarce be able to make much resistance. Guy suffered their retreat that night, not thinking it convenient to pursue them, and with his soldiers entered the town, where, by Albertus and his officers, and all the citizens beside, he and his men were joyfully received, and kindly welcomed.   Albertus in his arms embracing Guy, conducted him to his own lodgings, and kindly thanked him for his brave assistance ; then gave him a most noble treat, where they drank healths to the Emperor, and all the German Princes, to whom Sir Guy professed himself a subject ; whom they thought happy above other Princes, in having such a subject as Sir Guy.   And after they had ate and drank sufficiently, they all retired to rest their weary limbs, after the great fatigue they had undergone.

Early next morning, as the Soldan ordered, the army was prepared for the assault, the drums all rattling, and the trumpets sounding; at which the army gave so great a shout, as made the hills resound the echo back, the noise whereof awaked our warlike Guy from the sweet sleep which he till then had taken ; who, rising, straight ascended to the tower, and there beheld the army of the enemies, who, with their scaling ladders, were marching towards the walls.   Then he instantly gave order unto Heraud to get his forces in readiness ; which being done, he turned to Albertus, and bespoke him thus : "My lord, the honour of all Christendom lies now at stake, and therefore it concerns us now to make a brave defence.   They intend to scale our walls ; but in my opinion, we had much better meet them in their march, without the walls, than tarry for them here.   Our forwardness will bring a damp upon them, and quite confound and break their measures too : fortune does always favour bold attempts : and victory, you see, has on our side declared herself already; which will both encourage our soldiers and dishearten those of our enemies."

Albertus readily approved of what Sir Guy had said, commending his high courage, and rendering thanks to Heaven, that had sent so stout a champion to defend the town.   And then, because the enemy was near, each went to their respective posts in order to attack them : and opening the gates, all sallied out to meet them, according to the order Guy proposed; he with his Germans marching in the front.   By this bold march of theirs to meet them, the enemy started, and believed they should have harder work of it than they thought of: and therefore, throwing down their scaling engines, they put themselves into battalia; which Guy perceiving, gave orders to his archers in the front to begin first, who, drawing their strongbows, poured in amongst them such a shower of arrows as almost darkened the sun itself, and, galling the Turkish horse, put them into disorder; whereupon Guy and Heraud broke into the main body, killing and wounding all that durst oppose them, still pressing them both to the right and left, with flights of arrows, which struck a mighty terror into the infidels. The Bizantines, led by Albertus, and encouraged by the warlike Guy, in a short time routed the left wing of the enemy; while Guy fought the main body, hewing the Pagans down on every side, and like the hand of fate dealt death at every blow; until at last, he came to the squadron by Colbron led, one of the Pagans' generals; who being newly to the battle come, began to wonder at the mighty havoc that Guy had made in the army; and therefore, coming forwards towards Guy, he, in his haughty way, spoke to him thus: "Thou makest a show of valour, I perceive; but if thou any real valour hast, let us have a little sport between thee and I, only to see which of our swords cuts best : thou hast a weapon there that is much too small, and is, methinks, too blunt to make one bleed."—"Too blunt?" said Guy, "I tell thee, Pagan, thou shalt find it otherwise : I will whet it, ere we part, upon thy bones, and make thee quickly tell another tale. If it should fail me now, I should much wonder, for it has never failed me yet, I am sure; but often cut such lubbers down as thou art. Come, art thou ready? Bid thy friends adieu, for thou art never like to see them more." Then did they lend each other such hard blows, that sparks of fire did from their helmets fly : the numerous Pagans round about them flock, expecting all in the end the death of Guy; for Colbron was not only very strong, but had been long time champion to the Pagans. At length Guy gave him such a blow, that down comes Colbron and his strength to the ground. "Pagan," said Guy, "is my sword sharp, or no? For even now thou blamedst it as too blunt : rise up, for if thou canst not feel thy legs, off goes thy head, as sure as this is steel;" and thereupon he gave him such a blow, as forthwith made him shorter by the head; which, when the amazed infidels beheld, they were with wonder all astonished; for they so confident of Colbron were, they durst have ventured goods, and life, and limb, on any combat that by him was fought.

Then Heraud (to give Guy some breathing time) challenged a Pagan, called Elendant, and dared and defied him to his face (for valiant Heraud did no courage want). The Pagan, somewhat hot, with fury filled, engaged Heraud, and soon was overcome, and to the lake below sent after Colbron : then Guy unto another champion goes, Morgade called, whom Guy so well belaboured, he quickly sent him after his two fellows : the Pagans seeing thus their champions slain, forsook the field, and fled unto their camp. Where when they came, they told all to the Soldan ; who, filled with rage, and cursing all his gods, ordered his troops to rally once again ; which, when they durst not do for fear of Guy, the Soldan rather than not be revenged, sent Guy a formal challenge, demanding him to fight a single combat with him ; and by the event of that to end the war. Guy joyfully accepted of his terms ; and all things being ready for the combat, they both met with such martial rage and fury as even made the earth itself to quake ; the Soldan being prompted by despair, and Guy courageous for the Christians' honour, redoubled on him such resistless blows, as made his gilded armour soon give way ; and by that means Guy quickly found a passage to his heart, which so soon as with his trusty sword he had pierced, not able longer to support himself, cursing his gods, the Soldan fell down dead. This fatal sight being seen by Eskeldort, a bloody and tyrannic Turkish Prince, he straightway vowed revenge, and rides up armed to the place where Guy then stood; "Villain," quoth he, "whom like a dog I hate, I will make thee curse the time that thou wast born : know, therefore, I am come to fetch thy head ; for to my mistress I have promised it. My dogs shall feed upon thy English flesh ; they must devour thy body every bit. Come, I have vowed by Mahomet thou diest. Thy trusting in thy Saviour shall not save thee."

"And thou hast given away my head," said Guy, "unto a lady?

It is a noble gift. An honest man will do what he has said, and never promise more than he designed. Come on thy ways, and take it quickly off, or else the lady will suppose you jeer her."

Then straight with disdain they rush together, laying on as hard as they could drive; but Guy's keen sword did so hew Eskeldort, that for his head he durst no longer strive; but on a sudden, for to save his own, puts spurs to his horse, and in all haste is gone.

After this rout, the plunder of the field was by the victors taken; and then Guy returns in warlike triumph to the city, where they received him with the greatest pomp and truest joy, that they knew how to show; while as he rid triumphant through the streets, the people, from the houses' tops and windows, threw garlands down before him, and strewed his way with flowers, echoing along the streets, "Long live brave Guy, the noble and renowned English champion, our fortunate and great deliverer:" in memory whereof, they afterwards set up his statue in the market-place, which has been since destroyed by the Turks.

Guy, after this deliverance of the city, having been treated as he well deserved, stayed with Albertus there about ten days, and then desired to return to England; and leaving half his men there, as Albertus had requested him, that to the city they might be a guard, he with the rest embarked on his ships, and, with great presents, sailed back for Germany.

> Thus having wrought the Pagans' overthrow,
> He made the world his worth and valour know.

CHAPTER IX.

How Guy, being in a Forest, seeing a Lion and a Dragon fighting, took the Lion's part, and killed the Dragon: also how Guy and Heraud found Earl Terrey wounded, and his Lady taken from him by sixteen villains, most of whom he killed, and restored the Lady to her Husband.

GUY and his ships, being becalmed at sea, put into harbour to refresh themselves, where Guy and his friend Heraud went ashore; and it so happening that a pleasant forest lay bordering near the place they landed at, they entered it, and walked a little way, to see if they could light of any venison; observing, as they went, how shady trees embraced each other in their green-leafed arms, and how famed echo keeps her dwelling there, and little birds there fearless sing their notes; they chanced to find a silver streaming spring, which there they looked on as a rarity; and with those crystal streams they cooled their heats, and quenched that thirst they had so long endured; and there to satisfy their craving stomachs, they made of herbs and roots a pleasant meal: when, on a sudden, an unusual noise (which seemed to be at no great distance off) invades their listening ears; but it resembled most a lion roaring. "Hark, hark," said Guy, "I am almost affrighted at this strange uncouth noise. Heraud, let us straight take horse, that we may be prepared for all events: I never heard a sound that scared me more in all my life. I will go seek it out. It comes from yonder way: some monster, some devil makes this noise, for it is no human voice, for certain." So forth he rides, and underneath a hill he finds a dragon fighting with a lion. "O! this is princely sport, indeed," said Guy; "fight on, that I may see who gets the day, and then I will set upon the conqueror." The dragon winds his crooked knotted tail about the lion's legs, to throw him down; but then the lion fastened on his scales, and nimbly did avoid the fall intended him. Then both with the utmost fury bite and tear, and so maintain a long and bloody fight. At last the lion fainted, turns aside, and looks about, as if he would be gone. "Nay, then," quoth Guy, "lion, I will take thy part, and execute my vengeance on this dragon." With that courageously to work he goes, and with the dragon carries on the fight, giving him blows with all his might and strength, and yet cannot penetrate his scaly sides. The monstrous beast displays his flaggy wings, and with most dreadful yelling at him comes; whose very looks might make a man afraid, so terrible seemed his devouring jaws; wide, gaping, grisly, like the mouth of hell; more terrible than pen or tongue can utter; his blazing eyes burning like living fire; and from his gorge sulphureous smoke he belched; aloft his speckled crest he mounted, higher than Guy could reach at length of weapon's stroke. Thus in most ireful mood he bore himself, crying as loud as watery billows roar. And then his mortal sting he stretched out, exceeding far the sharpest point of steel; then turns and winds his scaly tail about the horse's legs: with that, Guy hews upon him with his blade, and laid on him three men's strength at every stroke; one fatal blow he gave him in his side, from whence did issue streams of swarthy blood; the sword had made the passage wide and broad, so that like a flood the gore overspread the ground, which made the dragon turn to have forsook him. "Nay, then," quoth Guy, "thou hast not long to live; I see thou faintest, and ready art to fall." Then did he give him such a parting blow, that down the dragon came unto the ground; roaring and bellowing at such a rate, that the hideous sound did more affright the conqueror than did his fighting with him; so he rides away, and lets the monster lie. But looking back, he espies, behind his horse, the rescued lion following at his heels, which made Guy alight to engage with him likewise. But when the beast beheld his weapon drawn, he fawned upon him like a spaniel dog; and like that grateful lion which did save Andronicus, for pulling out a thorn, when by the laws he was condemned to be devoured by beasts upon the amphitheatre, the lion came, remembering his old kindness, and fawned upon him, and licked him, very kindly bearing, it seems, an old good turn in mind. Just so, this grateful lion dealt with him, for the same benefit which he had done, by saving him from the fierce and poisonous dragon. For though a lion is by nature cruel, as being a ravenous and devouring beast, yet, like a spaniel, he by his horse did run, and till he did again embark, stayed with him.

But the wind serving in a little time, Guy and his friend embarked again, and so pursued their voyage, and in Almain arrived in a short time; and there, according to his worth and merit, was entertained by the Emperor, who bid him kindly welcome into Christendom, and entertained him with a tournament, with kingly banquets, and with princely revelling; all striving to behold that mighty man, of whose great actions fame so loudly spoke; and of whose wondrous acts they had heard so much, and thought they could not do him too much honour.

But, taking leave of the Emperor and the rest, he travels to his old friend the Duke of Lovain, whom he had a particular respect for, and did above all others long to see. But, ere unto his journey's end he came, he met with an adventure by the way, and set a worthy wronged lady free, who forcibly was taken from her love, and he at the point of death, left sorely wounded. Of which take this following account.

The noble Terrey, a right valiant Earl, with his dear love, surnamed *Osile the Fair* (his precious and inestimable jewel), to take the air into the forest went, wherein a plot was laid to take away his life, that so another might enjoy his love. And on a sudden sixteen villains came upon the Earl and sadly wounded him: "Sirrah," said one, "thou hast a wench we claim; she must go with us; lie upon the ground, and if thou livest till thou canst see a passenger, beg him to make a grave to bury thee." Guy, finding Terrey in this wretched case, and hearing how his wife was ravished from him, administered what comfort he was able. He with the loss of blood looked pale and wan, and almost ready was to die indeed. "Come, courage, noble Earl," said Guy to him; "I will do my best to fetch thy love again, or else say, Guy is but a boasting coward." When Terrey heard the mention of that name, he straight revived, for of his worthy deeds fame had before sufficiently acquainted him. Then striving to arise from off the ground, he did his best endeavour to embrace him: "Thanks, gracious Heaven," quoth he, "with soul and heart, for sending such a man to right my wrongs."—"Which is the way," said Guy, "those villains went?" "The path by yonder oak," said woful Terrey. "I will follow them," said Guy, "and, by my knighthood, I will make each man come off by weeping cross." Scarce had he spoke, before he heard a shriek, which Terrey knew to be the fair Osile's. Away rid Guy, and, by that sound directed, he quickly found the barbarous villains out. Coming to them, "Wretched slaves," quoth he, "what is your design with this fair lady here? Enlarge her presently and set her free. You have done wrongs which you must dearly pay for: her husband wounded, and she used with violence, are crimes which all your lives can scarce atone for." With that they laughed, and said, "What fool is this, or rather madman, in his desperate mood, that fain by wilful death would get a name, and have the world report he hath been kind? Some frantic fit this fellow is surely in, that means to fight thus without fear or wit."—"If it be so," quoth Guy, "that fit is now on me, and you will find it will be a raging one." With that, Sir Guy, knitting his angry brow, bid the fair lady cease her pensive moans, "For you shall from these villains' hands be freed." Then, with a courage admirably bold, at every blow some one or other dies: which when the lady saw, she straight cried out: "O pity, worthy knight, these mortal wounds. It is a sight I can no longer bear; be not so bloody in revenging me. Upon my knees, I humbly do entreat thee; for it is to me a terrifying sight. O! with their lives thou takest mine away. If one more do die, my soul will faint and leave me. Thou worthily my honour hast defended, and hast enough revenged all my wrongs."

"Lady," said Guy, "at your request I cease. Depart, base rascals, all but two begone."—"But, villains," said he to the two remaining, "it was you that did this virtuous lady bind," and thereupon he gave each such a blow, having his sword put up within its scabbard, that to the ground they fell immediately. Then, rising from the ground, they thus excused it: "My lord, we did it to preserve her for your honour's use."

Then on his steed he let the lady ride, to seek her lord, whom she distressed left; and Guy became her guide unto the place; where, when they came, they found him dressed already; for in their absence there came by a hermit, which to his bleeding wounds did salve apply. Now Terrey and Osile abound in joy, and gratefully to Guy do all things give. "Be thou," said they, "renowned in life and death, whom while we live and breathe we will always honour."

"Nay, here's my hand," quoth Terrey, "worthy Guy,
To fight for thee, I will be proud to die."

CHAPTER X.

How Guy and Heraud travelled with Earl Terrey, and hearing his father was besieged by Duke Otton, went to relieve him ; and how Guy killed Duke Otton in single combat, and raised the siege.

THE light had now surrendered its dominion, and darkness ruled in all the lower world, when Earl Terrey, Guy, and fair Osile, wanting a guide through the unfrequented woods, heard the affrighting noise, on every side, of savage beasts that thirst for human blood. On every side a watchful eye they cast, lest on a sudden they should be surprised. At length they did espy two armed men, who listened to those cries as well as they, each having in his hand his naked sword. But, as they came nearer, Guy quickly knew the one of them was his dear friend Sir Heraud, and the other was as dear a friend of Terrey's, who by embracing did their gladness show. And when the Earl demanded of his cousin, what brought him to that lonely desert place? " My lord," said he, " I have unpleasing news, which yet in duty I am bound to tell : thy noble father is at this time besieged in his strong castle by Duke Otton's power, who hath protested by a solemn vow, that he about his ears will pull it down. And in revenge that thou hast got his love, he swears thy father's life shall not escape."

" His love ! " quoth Terrey, " speak, my fair Osile, acquaint this worthy man with thy soul's thought. Did I persuade thee ever to break thy faith, or been an instigator unto aught that is un-righteous in the sight of Heaven ? " " Never," said she ; " thou hast been truly just in all thy words, and all thy actions too : that wretch, indeed, pretended that he loved me, and would have forced my love away from thee. But to my dying day I will be thine : thou shalt enjoy me all the hours I live ; and when I alter this determination, may I be held accursed by God and man."

" Spoke like a virtuous lady," Guy replied ; " be ever constant, and thou needest not fear : nothing can lay a blemish on thy honour, whilst thou on love's foundation firmly standest. It is for love I range the world about, and every hour expose my life to dangers, and though an unknown stranger, am love's exile. But wherefore, Terrey, are thy looks so sad ? Thou has thy love in person to embrace; but mine, alas ! is far off as England, and for some years I have not seen her face."

"My lord," said Terrey, "know you not my grief, and heard this messenger relate the cause? My father is in distress, and wants some succour; and I should be a rebel to the laws of nature, not to sympathise with him, making his trouble a just cause of sorrow."

"If that be all," said Guy, "thou art to blame to spend so much as one poor sigh thereon. My name is enough to terrify Duke Otton. Let him but hear I come, and he will be gone. Something that passed between us is the reason of it: in France he felt my sword, but did not like it. Since that he laid a plot against my life by villains that surprised me in a wood; which treachery with vengeance I repaid: and who ever knew a traitor's end prove good? A curse is always the concomitant of base and wicked actions, in which the actors will be sure to suffer, as did Perillus first in his brazen bull. I will go with thee to relieve thy father; for the oppressed I have vowed to right. And reason now does much more strongly move it, since mine own wrongs urge me as well as thine. Therefore with speed let us hasten to the place, preventing mischief ere it run too far. Take time by the forelock, for he is bald behind, and good proves best when it is soonest done. Go then, with filial joy, like brave Æneas, and fetch thine old Anchises out of Troy."

"Courageous knight," quoth Terrey, "thy bold heart, I do perceive, can with no fear be daunted : thou art composed of Mars's element, and made of powerful limbs, to manage arms ; my melancholy thou hast banished quite, and with strong hope armed me instead of it."

This said, in haste away they post themselves, and in a short time came unto the castle where proud Duke Otton and all his forces lay, relying much upon his well paid soldiers ; but when his Captains of Guy's coming knew, they fled by night, and never bid farewell. This was discouragement unto the soldiers, to find their Captains had deserted them. But yet Duke Otton solemnly protested, though each man in the castle were a Guy, he would not basely quit his enterprise; "For though life is dear," said he, "yet honour is dearer."

"Terrey," quoth Guy, "we must not now be tedious. For my experience oft hath been my tutor, and taught me, that when an advantage offers, and gives me an occasion to begin, the enemy's own fear subdues himself, to which our force being added soon completes our victory. We will not make our prison in this place, as long as there is field room to be got. And since the Duke has no respect for me, it is my desire alone to combat him. But if you will not leave this castle here, I will leave you all, and go myself alone." And with these words, Heraud and he were going to depart, which, when the castle soldiers did perceive, giving a shout said they, "Thou art our general, and wheresoever thou goest we will follow thee: thy honourable steps we will not leave, let fortune use us as she pleases."

Thus, full of courage, they all march along, giving the onset, fearless of their enemies, making those multitudes that seemed invincible to fly before their brave victorious foes, leaving the most part slaughtered in the field. But when the Duke beheld his flying soldiers, "Perish," said he, "base villains! here I will die! Where is this Englishman that haunts my coast, and thus pursueth me from place to place? I challenge him to leave the army, and meet me face to face, that we may have an end of all old grudges."

"Agreed," quoth Guy, "proud foe, I give consent. Repent thy wrongs, and make thy conscience clear; for thou hast lived to see thy honour lost, which worthy men do hold most dear of all things. The noble-minded brand that man with shame, that lets his name and honour die before him." Then they towards each other did approach, and with great violence they lances broke; which being done, they took their swords in hand, and fought until they had spent great store of blood; for envy did the Duke's keen weapon whet, and on Guy's sword revenge did set an edge. At length, through loss of blood, the Duke fell down, and dying cried, "Farewell, vain world, farewell : by fortune's angry frown I am betrayed ; by sad experience now, I tell the world there is nothing constant that the earth contains ; death brings the proudest monarchs to their graves, and lays them level with the humblest swain. Bewitching vanities seduce and blind us ; and greatness only tends to make us proud, making our sad catastrophe the greater. There is no peace like to a happy ending : my dying hour yields more repenting grace than in my life I ever could attain to." His immortal soul did with these words depart, and left the breathless body where it dwelt, while woful passions did Guy's heart afflict, now wishing Otton were again alive (for true humility still shows compassion, to see the afflicted overborne with woes). Guy sheathed his sword, and said, "Remain thou there, until on England's happy shore I land ; for love of Phælice I will shed no more blood ; I have from her been too long away : now I will return my wages to receive."

Then mourning over poor Duke Otton's fate, he gave his breathless body to his friends ; and then he to the castle back returned, accompanied by Heraud his true friend ; where with great joy they were received of all, especially by Terrey and Osile, and the old Earl their father, as those that had by much the greater interest in what Guy's martial prowess had achieved. But after he had staid two days to rest himself, being almost tired with their extreme kindness, Heraud and he took leave, and so departed, carrying their prayers and their good wishes with them.

> Thus to be doing good was still Guy's lot ;
> Others the profit, he the honour got.
> Where'er he came, he set th' oppressed free,
> And to the prisoners he gave liberty :
> But was the scourge of wicked tyrants still,
> Not sparing those whom he found doing ill.

CHAPTER XI.

How Guy and Heraud, after having parted from Earl Terrey, met with a monstrous boar, which Guy killed: how he was entertained by the Dukes of Lovain and Lorrain, and afterwards returned into England : how he killed a dreadful dragon in Northumberland, and of the honour done him by the King, and his reception by fair Phælice.

GUY and his friend having thus taken their leave of Terrey and the fair Osile, as we have already said, bending their course towards their native land, resolved to see Duke Lovain in their way. But as they rode through a desert place, dark and obscured by the thick shady trees, which hardly would admit the sun to enter, they on a sudden met the hugest boar that ever mortal eye had yet beheld. "Although," said Guy to Heraud, "I intended to draw my sword no more till I saw England, and laid it down at my fair Phælice's feet, yet such a monster is sufficient warrant to draw it once again, lest it should live to be a plague to all the country near it. And, therefore, private keep thyself at a distance, and give me leave to encounter it alone." This said, away went Guy, and met the boar as he was hastening to him full of rage, which Guy perceiving, stood upon his guard, that so he might avoid his dreadful tusks ; then on his swinish head so hard he laid, that dead he left him who had many slain, for from that wood scarce any man came back, which was the cause it was so unfrequented. The monster being dead, Guy cut his head off, huge as it was, and put it on his spear, and carried it unto Duke Lovain's court. The very monster's head appeared so terrible, it frighted people as they rode along, although they then were sure it could not hurt them.

Guy being come into Duke Lovain's court, did there present him with the monster's head, which had destroyed so many of his subjects.

"Guy," said the Duke, "I have had large experience of your great kindness, and your love to me : and this last valiant act that you have done, in killing this prodigious monstrous boar, which has of late made such exceeding havoc of my subjects, and of all passengers that came that way, surpasses all the rest, and makes me still much more indebted to you." But to declare the welcome that he gave him with all his warlike trumpets, drums, and clarions, and all his nobles coming to congratulate Guy's safe return, with all the entertainments that were made him; and how the Duke of Lorrain too came thither, on notice given of Guy's arrival there, that so he might embrace that matchless man, of whom fame had such wondrous things declared; I say, should I relate all this at large, it would swell this little book into a volume. Suffice it therefore here to let you know Guy so much longed to be with his fair Phælice that he was weary of the honours done him, and begged they would let him now return to England, which, after having treated him ten days, they did consent to, and forthwith ordered one of their best ships to be new rigged and fitted up for Guy to sail to England in; and then, accompanying him to the seaside, "Go," said the Dukes, "and prosper, thou brave Englishman, the most renowned worthy of the world. Thrice happy is the land that gave thee birth, and much more happy is thy fairest Phælice, who must embrace the hero in her arms. May victory attend upon thy side, and may thy brows be with fresh laurels crowned."

Guy having given them his hearty thanks for all the undeserved honours paid him, straight hoisted sail, and having a fair wind, in four days' time arrived on English ground; the noise of which soon reached King Athelstan, who then at York his royal palace kept. Thither, being commanded by the King, he forthwith went to pay his duty and allegiance to him. The King received them (for Heraud was with Guy wherever he went) with so much joy and goodness that nothing could be more; welcoming them with such kind of words as these:

"Welcome to me, renowned martial man, my princely love upon you I bestow. I in your fortunate success rejoice, for fame has loudly told us all your story. Guy, thou hast laid a heavy hand, I hear, on Pagan infidels, and with thy sword has sent them home to the dark vaults where unbelievers dwell. Devouring beasts thou also hast destroyed, which have the terror been of human creatures; yet, worthy man, I think thou never didst slay, of all those monsters terrible and wild, a creature that is more cruel than there is one that at this day destroys whatever he meets, no farther off than is Northumberland, which is a dreadful dragon that haunts there. I speak not this to animate thee on, and hazard thy life at setting foot on shore; for divers have endeavoured to destroy this wicked beast, and perished in the attempt. No, Guy, I speak only to show thy happiness, which has exceeded that of other men, by freeing of them from their fears and dangers."

"Dread lord," said Guy, "as I am an English knight, faithful to God, and loyal to my king, I am resolved to go and see this dragon, and try whether my sword cannot work upon him; for I already have a dragon killed, with whom a lion first I found engaged, and whom he had also like to have overcome; but heaven my arm so strengthened that I soon overcame his power, and I will do this." Then, taking his humble leave, away he rides unto Northumberland to find the dragon, having a dozen knights to be his guides, who brought him where the dragon kept his den, feasting himself with nought but human flesh. "Now it is enough," said Guy, "do you stand off, and give me leave to find this hydra's head. He that has fed so much on human flesh, shall never more devour a man again; but, gentlemen, if here you please to stay, you of our battle may spectator be."

Then going to the cave, the dragon espied him, and forth he starts with lofty speckled breast; of form most dreadful; which when Guy beheld, into its rest he forthwith puts his lance, then spurs his horse, and to the dragon makes, encountering each the other with such fury as shook the very ground under them. Then Guy recoils and turns about his horse, and comes upon him with redoubled might: the dragon meets him with resistless force, and, like a reed, bit his strong lance in two. "Nay, then," said Guy, "if you are good at biting, I have a tool to pick your teeth withal;" and drew his never-failing flaming sword, and on him fell with furious blows so fierce, that many wide and bloody wounds he made. At which the dragon yawned, like hell's wide mouth, roaring aloud with a hideous noise, and with his claws he rent and tore the ground. Impatient of the smart he underwent, he with his wings would raise his body up, but Guy, with a bold stroke, so cooled his courage, that to distend his wings he wanted strength; and, with a few strokes more, Guy brought him down upon the ground, all wallowing in his blood, and from his mouth a fiery flake proceeded, whilst Guy with all his might was severing his monstrous head from his more monstrous body, which when he had done, "Now, bloody fiend," said he, "thou hast thy deserved recompence for all the human blood which thou hast shed. And now upon this broken piece of spear unto the King I will bear thy monstrous head, which will by him, I am sure, be well accepted."

The joyful knights then went and took a view of that same fearful creature without fear, which was indeed of strange and ugly hue; all wondering how it was possible to escape those teeth and claws so dreadful, sharp, and long. And when they had fixed the head upon a spear, and took measure of the body's length unto the King, who had removed his court from York to Lincoln, they repair with speed where he with some impatience waited their return; who in his arms embraced the warlike Guy, congratulating him on his victory: then, looking on the dragon's fearful head, "Heaven shield," said he, "and save me from all harm! Why, here is a face may well outface the devil. What staring eyes of burning glass be these, that might, alive, two flaming beacons seem! What scales of harness arm the crooked nose! and teeth more strong and sharp than those of steel! And also that gaping mouth and forked tongue may, even dead, make all the living fear, but more rejoice that thou hast overcome it. Victorious knight, thy actions we admire, and place thee highly in our royal favour: throughout the spacious orb thy fame shall spread more lofty than the *primum mobile.* To the succeeding age of the world thy victories shall be transmitted down; for I will have the monster's picture drawn on cloth of Arras, curiously wrought, which I in Warwick Castle will have placed, there to remain and tell to after ages that worthy Guy, a man of matchless strength and equal courage, destroyed a dragon thirty foot in length. And on this castle wall we will place his head, there to remain till length of time consume it. And, nobles all, make a triumphant festival, and give our knight the honour that he merits."

While thus at Lincoln Guy was entertained and feasted by the King in royal manner, he one day took an opportunity to tell the King the cause of his adventures, and that he did it for the love of Phælice, Earl Roband's only daughter; and then besought his royal majesty to intercede for him unto the Earl, who yet knew nothing of their loves; and that he would give consent unto their marriage.

The King assured him that he would not only use his interest with the Earl her father, to obtain his consent, but would himself honour their nuptials with his royal presence; with which Guy was well pleased, and humbly thanked his majesty.

Now all Guy's thoughts were taken up with Phælice, to whom he was preparing to be gone; but Phælice hearing that he was at Lincoln, and how he had been in Northumberland, and killed a dragon there, began to be impatient at his stay. And thereupon she came herself to Lincoln, and happily surprised her Guy as he was ready to depart for Warwick: with Juno's kind embrace, and Venus's kiss, Phælice embraced her long expected lover; and Guy returned it with that eagerness, which in the wars of Mars he used to show, glad that he now has Phælice in his arms: but after the first transports were a little over, Phælice, to chide her lover, thus begins: " Forgetful love, and too, too slow," said she, " I fear thou didst not mind the honest friend. What! seek a dragon ere thou lookest for me! and hazard life, yet neither come nor send to know if I remained in happy state. Some jealous woman would, perhaps, suppose she had been slighted, but I have no such thoughts; not but I wish, I must confess indeed, I had been the first that thou hadst seen on shore; but thou art welcome to thy Phælice now, and shalt no more unto the wars go forth, but lie within my peaceful arms at home. No, thou hast fought, my dear, too much already. For war's stern face has stole thy smiles away; but love will change thy countenance again, and make thy looks such as I saw them first, when I first chose and gave my heart to thee."

"Ah, Phælice!" Guy replied to her again, "what toils have I gone through for love of thee! and canst thou doubt that ever Guy should slight thee? No, first the sun shall cease to give us light, and all the stars shall leave their shining orbs, before one thought shall wander from my Phælice. I have learned the art of war enough already, now in Love's school I will take new lessons out, and doubt not but to be a good proficient in that more easy and delightful exercise. I have already made a friend, my Phælice, whose powerful intercession to thy father shall gain me his consent to marry thee; and when I tell thee it is the King himself, I doubt not but you will be of my opinion."

"His intercession," Phælice then replied, "will be, no doubt, effectual with my father; but I believe your merits are so great, you will have no need of any intercessor; for I am sure my father speaks of you as one for whom he has the utmost value."

"Why, then," said Guy, and smiled, "let us to Warwick, a place I love the best in all the world, because it is the place that brought up thee, and there I first was with thy beauty blessed. I love the castle and the castle ground, for there, my Phælice, thy face I first saw. Let us haste, my love, to that delightful seat, and seal those vows we have to each other made; I long, methinks at church to say these words, *I Guy take Phælice to my wedded wife;* and to hear immediate reply, *And I take Guy to be my wedded husband.*"

To which Phælice, with an air that showed how well she was pleased, made reply:

> "Though now our satisfaction's very great,
> Yet until then our joys can't be complete;
> There's pleasure in the ways that to it tend,
> But Hymen's joys must always crown the end."

CHAPTER XII.

How Guy and Phælice were married; with an account of their splendid wedding; how Guy soon after vowed a pilgrimage, and travelled into the Holy Land, &c.

GUY and fair Phælice having both agreed with speed to consummate their mutual joys, and tie that knot at Hymen's sacred temple, that only death can loose, first went to wait upon the King and Queen, and humbly to invite them to their wedding, which they agreed on such a day: then took their leaves, and thence repaired to Warwick.   Earl Roband had received letters from the King, letting him know that Guy was then in England, and that for love of his fair beauteous daughter, he had undertook the dreadful toils of war ; and was coming now to Warwick to ask his consent, and then to celebrate his nuptials there.   Earl Roband, overjoyed at this good news, immediately went forth to meet his new elected son-in-law.

Guy, seeing that the Earl was coming towards him, alighted from his horse, and low on the ground he bowed himself, but the good Earl soon raised him with his hand, and tenderly embraced him in his arms, with all the expression of true love and friendship. Guy then informed him of his love to Phælice, begging his pardon for his great presumption, and humbly asking his consent to marry her: to whom Earl Roband made this kind reply: "My daughter, worthy Guy, I freely give thee, nor is there anything on this side heaven I have more desired than such a husband for her ; that when in the annals of succeeding ages thy wondrous story shall at large be told, my daughter may be mentioned as thy wife, and that Earl Roband also was her father; and that from thee, and from my daughter Phælice, so numerous an issue may proceed as may in time fill all the world with heroes." Guy humbly thanked him for his consent, and told him, "The greatest honour he could boast of was to have such an Earl to be his father, and such a lady for his wife as Phælice."

Then Phælice being called, was asked if she was willing to have

Guy to be her husband: who, with a virgin blush, declared her satisfaction. The next thing now was the happy day in which their nuptials were to be consummated.

And now the long-expected day is come, in which these lovers must complete their happiness; and all the honours Hymen can dispense, he freely gives to grace the wedding-feast, for royal Athelstan and his fair Queen, to grace this nuptial, in their pomp appeared: the nobles likewise, in their richest robes, with worthy knights and gentlemen, besides ladies of honour, strive to outvie each other in honouring valiant Guy and his fair bride. There wanted nothing that could be procured to please the eye, or to content the mind; masks, midnight revels, tilts, and tournaments, with stately shows, and acting ancient stories, and banquets proper for such royal guests. The tables were with such great plenty stored that neither fish nor flesh was wanting; and bowls of nectar crowned their entertainment. Nor was the choicest music wanting there, while healths were drank to the fair bride.

Ten days this wedding-feast was celebrated, and the country round the better for it, for good Earl Roband never forgot the poor, and then the King and Queen, wishing all health and happiness to the new married couple, and the good Earl, that had so nobly treated them, returned again to Lincoln.

But as our lives are made of chequer work, and joy and mourning take their several turns, so this great joy was quickly after shadowed with a black cloud of sorrow; for hardly had the inconstant queen of night took her nocturnal ramble through the heavens (which journey usually she makes in eight and twenty days, or thereabouts), but good Earl Roband (Phælice's worthy father) resigns this life for immortality, and unto Guy bequeaths his whole estate; which filled them both with an unusual grief, in losing both a father and a friend. By his death, Guy became Earl of Warwick, confirmed therein by royal Athelstan; and all his land and lordships now are his, and he declared a nobleman of England.

But ah! how small a satisfaction it is that all the honours of the world can give us! For now Earl Guy, reflecting on past actions, can find no comfort in the sad reflection : he sees those things that gave him his renown were vain and wicked in the sight of Heaven.   Oft would he sit and meditate alone, on those vain steps that his rash youth had trod; then to himself with groans and grievous sighs would he cry out, " O, pardon me, just Heaven !   I have done nothing yet thy grace to purchase, but spent my time about a woman's face ; for beauty I have shed a world of blood, hating all others for one mortal creature.   How many days have I wasted for a wife, but for my sins never spent one weeping hour !   It is now high time repentance to begin : henceforth the remnant of my days I will spend in contrite sorrow for my former sins, that Heaven may pardon all the erring ways whereby fond flesh and blood deceived me.   Unto the world I will now go learn to die, let me be censured for it as men list ; I will please my Maker in whatever I can : ambitious pride hath been my youth's disease : I will teach age meekness ere my glass be run, and bid farewell to honour, wealth, and beauty ; I will go through hell itself to purchase heaven."

Phælice, perceiving he was melancholy, unto him came, and with him thus discoursed :—" My dearest lord, why are you so changed of late ?   Let me, as in your joys I share, so likewise in your sorrows bear a part.   If I have in anything offended you, let me know it, and I will instantly confess my fault, and make you satisfaction."

" No, my dear love," said Guy, " it is not with thee, it is with myself that I am discontented.   By the light of grace, I see the faults of nature : I am dead in sin, although I seem alive. Phælice, my sins, my countless sins appear, crying, ' Repent, and clear thy guilty conscience.'   I must deal with thee as Bavarus (a Prince of Rome) dealt with Sygunda his wife, who, from a deep impression that he felt solemnly vowed perpetual chastity. Entreating thee, even as thou lovest my soul, not to dissuade me from what I have done : hast thou not heard what Ethelfride did (a Christian woman), some time England's queen, who, once with child, did from her husband's bed absent herself for ever ?   And canst not thou, the phœnix of the realm, by imitation win immortal praise, leaving thy pure and spotless chastity to be admired by succeeding ages? I know thou canst; the greater part is divine, and will the soul's advantage much prefer. Thou didst procure, although I did excuse it, my pride, by conquests to obtain thy love. Heaven gave me valour, but I did abuse it; my heart and thoughts were too much elevated: I thought the crowns of kings were things inferior, and hardly worth accepting: but now I all such follies do contemn, resolving to become another man, and travel for the welfare of my soul; not as before, upon my horse in armour, but in a gown of grey, a palmer's weed, obscure my journey; for no leave I will take, but only leave my endless love to thee: here is my ring, receive this small memorial, and wear the same, to make thee think on me: let me have thine, which for thy sake I will keep, till with his cold hand death shall close my eyes."

When Phælice heard this strange surprising tale, judge, you that can, how much she wrung her hands, how much she sighed, how many tears she shed, yet wondrous meekly, contradicting nothing: for the devotion of that age was such, those were thought blessed who retired themselves, and whined away their days in solitude, leaving the world and its bewitching vanities.

And now he throws away his princely clothing, wherein he glittered with almost that splendour wherein the noonday sun to us appears: now his best habit was a homespun grey, such as employs the poor plain country people; a staff, a scrip, and in his hat a scollop shell, not to be known, nor in the least admired: and thus, with pensive heart and doleful tears, he leaves sweet England, and his fairest Phælice, who in her face a map of sorrow wears: all sad and mournful was her countenance, for she to all delight had bid farewell, since she from her beloved lord was parted thus.

Guy journeys on towards the Holy Land, where Jerusalem's fair city stood, in which our Saviour's head was crowned with thorns, without whose gate he shed for us his blood: to see his sepulchre was his design, the tomb that Joseph unto Jesus lent; with tedious miles he tired his weary feet, and through vast deserts passed a

2 B

thousand dangers. And whilst he thus pursuing was his way, he happened to meet with a most woful wight, a man that was no stranger to sorrow, for he had fifteen sons that were all captives, in slavish bondage and the extremest misery kept by a merciless and monstrous giant: which pressed their wretched father with that grief, that he was almost worn away to nothing; and being past all hopes to find relief, thus to himself bewailed his sad condition:

"Unhappy man, yea, thrice unhappy I, who court in vain the last of remedies: in vain I seek for death, which flies me still, though nothing else can ease the woes I feel! Ah! cruel tyrant, that of all my sons couldst not afford me one to comfort me, and with his hands to close my dying eyes! But out, alas! were they but happy there, I cared not, though I never saw them more! But oh, to think upon their miseries pierces my heart more than a thousand swords! And that which pierces deepest to my heart is this one thought, there they must still remain, and suffer without hope of remedy: this cutting thought is more than I can bear, and therefore thus I will end my wretched life." And as he spoke these words, he drew his sword, with an intent to sheath it in his bowels. But Guy, that listened to his sad complaint, stepped in in time, and happily prevented him. "Hold, father," said he, "yield not to despair; for you may live to see your sons at liberty: I have heard your sad complaint, and Heaven has sent me just in the nick of time to right your wrongs."

The melancholy man was much surprised to see a stranger in that lonely place ; then, looking steadfastly upon him, said, "Alas, poor pilgrim, I am beholden to thee, that to allay my cruel miseries wouldst flatter me to hope, when there is no room for it : my wrongs are grown so great they are past righting, and death alone is that which must relieve me."—"O, say not so," said Guy, "though I am a pilgrim, thou dost not know the strength that is in these arms, especially when Heaven invigorates them to fight in a just cause. Let me but know where thy sons are in captivity, and leave the rest to me."

"Know then, kind pilgrim," said the unhappy man, "since

you have a mind to understand my misery, that in yon castle, made impregnable as well by art as nature, there dwells one Amarat, of monstrous size, that is from the race of ancient giants sprung, who does support his great and bulky carcass only by feeding upon human flesh; and therefore seizes all that pass these woods, and, dead or living, bears them hence, into that cursed shambles of destruction, making no difference of either sex, but this, that with the women he satisfies his lust, and with the men his hunger. My only daughter, unadvisedly, as her ill fortune sure enough would have it, passing this way, was taken by the monster: this stirred the anger of my fifteen sons, who were resolved to rescue their poor sister, but in the vain attempt were taken prisoners; yet, for their sister's sake, their lives are spared, though they endure a thousand deaths for one."

"Your case," said Guy, "is sad, and I must pity you; but I am resolved to try what I can do, if you will but trust me with your sword and armour, to kill the tyrant, and redeem your children."

"Most willingly," replied the hopeless man, "would I contribute unto their release, but am afraid you will rather fall yourself into the tyrant's clutches, than redeem those that are there already; but, however, my sword and armour at your service are; and may you meet with the success that is answerable to your matchless courage." "Well," said Guy to him, "stay you, and pray, and doubt not my success against the tyrant."

Guy hereupon went up straight to the castle, his thoughts being employed to think what way he had best take to get the tyrant out; not doubting then but to overcome him easily. So going to the gate, he knocked thereat like one that would come in, and had some business of great consequence. The giant never was so roused before; for at his gate none used to knock so hard; he therefore takes his club and keys, and opening the gate goes out, staring about with watchful countenance: then seeing Guy, thus with disdain and anger he addresses him: "Sirrah," said he, "what business have you here? Have you a mind to feast the crows, and have your quarters hung upon these walls? For what else is it that you can expect? You might have heard that there is no ransom here for any one that falls into my clutches; but if you are ignorant, and know it not, this club that is in my hand shall teach you better."

Guy, nothing daunted with his bugbear words, replied again, "Why, how now! are you quarrelsome? You seem to be a very choleric person : but I have a weapon here shall match your club, and quickly bring you to a better temper." And so expecting no return again, he draws his sword, and with the same salutes him about the head, the shoulders, and sides, whilst his erected club did death proclaim ; striding like a Colossus over the Hellespont : but on the ground in vain he spent his strokes, for Guy was much too nimble for him still ; for, before he could heave his club again, Guy would be sure to give him the other stroke, for Guy for that advantage always watched : at length, through thirst, the giant feeble grew, and said to Guy, "As thou art of human kind, give leave that nature's wants may be supplied, and let me go and drink in yonder place : thou canst not yield to a request more small than to grant life a draught of poor cold water." "I grant thee leave," quoth Guy ; "go, drink thy fill ; pledge both the savage boar and the dragon too ; but never think again to drink cold water. Think, when thou drinkest, that now thou drinkest thy last." So to the spring he goes, and there his thirst he quenches with almost a tun of water. Guy was amazed to see him drink so much, and to the combat hastens him again : "Come, come," said he, "thou art long about thy liquor, thou wilt wrong the fish that in the river swim ; but I will see they shall have satisfaction, for with thy blood their wants shall be supplied." "Villain," quoth Amarat (for that is the name by which this monstrous giant must be called), "I crush thee in an instant ; thy life shall pay thy daring tongue's offence ; this club (which is about a hundredweight) shall my commission be to send thee packing : for ravens' diet thou shalt soon be dressed ; I'll break thy bones, as though they were but reeds." Incensed much by this bold Pagan's brags, which worthy Guy no longer could endure, he spends his blows on those supporting posts, which like to columns did his body bear. The giant for those wounds in choler grew, and desperately at Guy he threw his club, which did directly light upon his body, and threw him by its weight upon the ground; and ere Guy could recover from his fall, the giant got his club again in his fist, and struck at Guy another desperate blow; but missing Guy, stuck it fast into the ground. "'Traitor," quoth Guy, "thy falsehood I will repay; this act, basely to spill my blood." Says Amarat, "Against an enemy there is nothing base : I will murder any way; could I but poison into thy nostrils blow, thou soon shouldst see I would dispatch thee by it."—"'Tis well," said Guy, "thou openest thy black thoughts; thy beastly bulk is sure the dwelling of the devils. They are thy tenants whilst thou livest here, but when thou comest to hell they will be thy landlords. Vile miscreant, prepare thee for that place, the just reward of such inhuman monsters. But breathe thyself a time, while I go drink; for flaming Phœbus with his fiery eye, torments me so with heat, that I believe my thirst could scarce be quenched with an ocean. Thou knowest to thee I granted the same kindness." Quoth Amarat, "Thou hast no fool of me ; no, silly wretch, I have more wit than so : by all my gods I do rejoice to find that thirst constrains thee now; for all the treasure that the world can boast of, one drop of water shall not cool thy veins. Relieve my foe! and unto my own wrong refresh my adversary! why this would be a madman's part indeed! if thou imaginest this, thou art a child. No, fellow, I have known the world too long to be so simple ; now I know thy wants, I will not grant one minute's space of breathing." And with these words, heaving aloft his club into the air, he swings the same about, then rubs his temples, and his locks doth shake, and like the Cyclops in his pride he struts : "Sirrah," said he, " I heave a list to you, and the next blow I strike you will breathe your last ; for with this stroke you shall for ever perish. Take thou no care for drink, for never more a draught of water shall come near thy lips, but with thy blood I will soon carouse full merry : here is at thee with a butcher's downright blow, for it is thy blood that must assuage my fury."

"Infernal, false, obdurate fiend," said Guy, "thou seemest an imp of cruelty from hell: ungrateful monster, since thou hadst denied that thing to me wherein I used thee well, I will with my sword take the more deep revenge on thy accursed head, and quickly make thee shorter by so much. Now, thirst, farewell, I do disdain to drink, and therefore let the river keep its water, or let wild beasts be welcome thereunto, for with its pearly drops I will not meddle. Now, tyrant, know thy latest hour is come. For though perhaps you'll take the greeting ill, yet it is with a good will I give it you:" and thereupon he gave him such a blow as made the monster tumble on the ground. Then Guy set his foot upon the monster's breast, and from his shoulders did his head divide, which with a yawning mouth did widely gape; no dragon's jaws were ever larger seen, to open and to shut till life was gone: and then Guy took possession of the keys, and with them opened all the castle gates; where many woeful captives he set free, that had been long in misery confined, and had been tortured with great cruelties: and when he of their miseries inquired, each told a tale which from his eyes drew tears, and which they could not tell without sad sighs at the remembrance of their barbarous usage. There tender ladies in dark dungeons lay that in this desert wood had been surprised; and every day no other diet had than flesh of human creatures for their food: some with their lovers' bodies had been fed, burying their husbands' bodies in their wombs.

Now Guy bethinks him of the oppressed knight, with whom he left his pilgrim's gown and staff, and of his captive sons imprisoned here; and blames himself that first of all he had not released the wronged brethren from their woes: then on he goes, and, as he searched about, he grievous cries and lamentations heard, which, as a clue, led him to the fatal place; where finding an obscure and darksome gate, all strongly covered over with plates of iron, he looked amongst his keys, and there found one that soon unlocked and gave him entrance there. He was no sooner entered but he beheld the strangest sight that ever his eyes had seen: men that had there by slow degrees been famished, and could but just be said to be alive, looking like pictures which the painters draw when to our eyes they death would represent : of these some by the thumbs were hanged up, some by the heels, and others by the middle. With diligence he takes them from the walls, telling them they were now at liberty; which happy sound revived their drooping spirits. Then Guy to the perplexed knight, their father, repairs, and tells him what success he had against the inhuman keeper of that castle ; then bids him come, and there receive his sons : "Though poor and faint," said Guy, "yet they are alive ; accept of that, and seek to nourish them." The father's joy was scarce to be expressed ; but when he saw what skeletons they were, how like the living images of death, he scarce had strength to outlive that wretched sight. And the glad sons, seeing themselves at liberty, and their poor aged father still alive, were at a loss how to express their thanks to him that had so generously delivered them.

Guy then unto their father gave the keys, saying, "This castle do I give to thee, where tyranny has dwelt so many years; let it be now a place where pious pilgrims and weary travellers may find refreshment. Those tender ladies that were prisoners here, let them be sent away with ease and safety where they desire, when they have strength to travel; and always see you use wronged women well. Men may revenge the wrongs that they receive, but women have no strength to right themselves."   ·

The good old knight, surprised with joy and wonder, fell on the ground, and would have kissed Guy's feet. "Father," said Guy, "I pray forbear this homage ; no honour is due to me for what I have done; it was a stronger arm than mine that did it, and unto Him let all the praise be given. And now, I pray, exchange with me again : take you your coat of mail, and your strong sword; give me my staff, and my poor palmer's weed, for to the Holy Land my course is bent.

> Ambitious pride hath hurt me all it can,
> And now I'll mortify a sinful man."

CHAPTER XIII.

How Guy's departure out of England is taken; how he employed his time in his pilgrimage; how Phælice spent her time in his absence; and how, in his return, he routed Amanthus's army, and restored his old friend Earl Terrey to his lordships; and afterwards returned into England unknown.

How Guy turned pilgrim we before have told : but now it will be necessary to say something of what was said, both by the King and the nobility, of his so strange and sudden a departure : which was no sooner known at court, but both the King and the nobility were struck with admiration that Guy, who had so famous been for deeds of chivalry, and had performed so many mighty acts, all for love of Phælice, should so soon leave his fair and beauteous spouse for a toilsome solitary life : yet was his piety commended highly, who set a greater value on his soul, which by repentance he had refined from sin, than upon all the honour he had won, or glittering treasure that he was possessed of.

Now let us look on Guy, the man that sought to find out quarrels for his recreation ; who for his Phælice ranged the world about, delighting most in combats and alarms : but he, from his former mind estranged, shuns all occasions that may cause debate. In his own wrongs he vowed no blow to strike; nor injury, nor abuse should force him to it ; for he his natural temper hath subdued, and taken patience by the hand for his guide, to lead his thoughts where meekness keeps her residence.   No worldly joys can give his mind content : delights are gone, as though they never had been, and to repent is now his only care, for spending his youth in serving sin ; in contrite sorrow now he will pass his age, that little time to come which life shall borrow.   Sad were his looks, and pale was his complexion, his diet of the meanest, hard and spare : like a religious man he led his life, in a poor homely thin and threadbare habit; his dignities and honours were forgotten, nor did he the Warwick earldom now regard. Sometimes he would go and search into a grave, and there would find a rotten dead man's skull; and with the same would find a conference, examining at large each vanity, and then himself would answer for the head, as if the dead man answered for him self. "If thou hast been a monarch, where is thy crown? Or, who now stands in fear of thy stern looks?" "Death hath of my renown a conquest made, my golden sceptre he has taken from me, and now it is wielded by another hand; and I am now become so poor a thing, my poorest subjects envy not my place." "Perhaps thou hast been some counsellor of state, whose potent wit a mighty reason did rule; where is the policy of late thou hadst?" "Consumed and gone, like to an idle dream! I have not so much wit as will suffice to kill these worms that thus infest my coffin." "Perhaps thou wast some beauteous lady's face, for whose dear sake some have done strange exploits, even such as when the case was once my own, I for my dearest Phælice, have performed. Perhaps there was a skin about this skull fairer than that which Helen's was enclosed in; and on this scalp, bare and worm-eaten now, where nothing else is to be seen but bone, such yellow locks of hair were to be beheld, which for their beauty were esteemed like gold; and in those hollow caves two crystal eyes, and here such lips as love for kissing craves. But what is of all this beauty now become, so precious once in the esteem of men? By powerful death unto the dust it is turned, grown loath-some, filthy, and trodden under foot; and now there is only this poor picture left to tell the wise, All beauty is but vain." Such sad memorials he would oft prefer, of mortal frailty and the force of death, to teach the flesh how apt it is to mistake, and pass repentance off till it is too late: thus would he all things treat with such contempt that might seduce the soul from heavenly love.

Now for a while leave Guy to his own thoughts, and turn your eyes to another subject: to see new sorrows now look back to England; and to long absent years commit the other. Leave doleful Guy to cares and aged grief, and look how Phælice his poor lady fares; like to a widow all in black attire, she doth express her inward grief of heart. She of her chamber does a

prison make, and unto sorrow wholly is inclined. She that was
late the pride of the English court, with majesty will now consort
no longer; but lives like one that despises life and being, and
every day did die unto the world; seeing her folly with the eyes
of judgment, and noting well how fast false pleasures fly, leaving
more pain than they can cause delight. Her thoughts run after
her departed lord, and are in motion swifter far than he.
"Where is the place," said she, "can give him rest, that for his
pilgrimage hath thus forsaken me? Lament, my soul, under the
heavy burden, to think poor Guy remembers thee in tears.
Methinks he by some river side is sitting, and swells the waters
with his weeping eyes: methinks he often cries out, 'Phælice,
Phælice,' and echo through the skies does carry it; then rising
up, with might and main he runs, saying, 'Sweet echo, bring
my love again.' Then comes he to a cypress tree, and says,
'Sylvanus, this was once the lovely boy whom thou didst praise
for feature to the clouds, but here, alas! thy senseless joy is
transformed; it is nothing now but tree, and boughs, and leaves,
and made to wither as all beauties do.' And then, methinks, full
sadly down he sits, and on his bended knees his elbow stays,
with head on hand, saying, 'Farewell, vain honour, and all the
pleasures of my youthful days; my true repentance has displaced
you all; a happy end brings sinful souls to heaven.' Ah, worthy
man! that thus canst mortify thy rebel flesh to conquer Adam's
nature, and, that thou blessed eternity mightst gain, dost live
on earth but as a stranger in it; dead, though alive; and new-
born, though grown old; true, valiant Guy, that hast overcome
the devil. As thy advice was when thou didst go hence, that
I a vestal virgin's life should live; although, when I was a
maiden, by love's art thou didst persuade me to become a wife,
I vow by heaven, and Him that reigns above, to keep my thoughts
as truly chaste as thine: my beauty all I can I will obscure by
doleful lamentations, sighs, and tears; and will by abstinence
attain the way to overcome the force of sin's temptations. This
sentence very often I have read, 'A woman's chastity is virtue's
Queen.' Ceres and Bacchus I will shun with care; for they are

virtue's foes and vice's friends, and oft to a licentious life do lead ; but with sobriety I will still associate, and with spare diet take each day's repast : that soul thrives best that keeps the body bare. The courtly ornaments I wore of late in honour of King Athelstan's fair queen, even all those jewels and those robes of state, wherein to others I have appeared so glorious, shall with their pride and value now supply those naked poor that are about the streets ; the gold and silver I am now possessed of shall all employed be about good works. The purchase of eternal happiness is of all wealth most precious unto me : all that in want repair to Warwick Castle, and crave relief, shall there be sure to find it. For the halt, lame, and blind, I will prepare an hospital, which shall be well endowed ; and for the widow and the fatherless a special care I will be sure to take, that their necessities supplied may be ; and that young beginners may have wherewithal their calling to set up, I will take care : and for repairing of decayed highways, that travellers may better pass the roads, is also what I will take care about. These things I reckon to be the heavenly thrift, and laying treasure up where it cannot rust ; dispensing of the riches we receive, as each good steward is enjoined to do ; that after this short life is done, we may enjoy a life that is eternal. Farewell, vain world, of thee I take my leave, and of those things which thou dost most esteem ; thy shows are snares, deceitful are thy hopes, and only through false mirrors seemest fair. O, that in such disguise I could but travel (as once the kind Sulpitia did contrive in banishment to see her Lentulus) attending on my Guy, wherever he be ; or Hypsicratea like, in man's apparel, following her exiled king through love's desire : it would something ease my wounded heart of sorrow so to divide the burden which I bear, for where affection takes affliction's part in hard extremes, some comfort is expressed. And misery is more easy to abide when friends do with friends divide their crosses. But all in vain it is that I thus wish ; it nought avails, my woe is still the same ; though straying thoughts do wander here and there, my poor weak body must at home remain. Unto the Holy Land he is gone to travel, Heaven send me thither at my dying day. I will about my vows, and see them paid. The good that charity requires I will do; when grace persuades unto works of virtue, it is blessedness to further such desires; and while on earth I do remain a sinner, I will strive to please my God by living well."

In this resolve each day she spent her life, performing all those things she had proposed, and showed so great severity therein that she became the wonder of her sex, who were amazed, and even quite confounded, to see a lady so high born, so rich, and which is more, so rare a beauty too, pouring contempt upon all worldly pleasures; for she was deaf to all her friends' persuasions, nor unto any would she lend an ear that mentioned company or re-creation, or what she had determined sought to alter; but such as of compassion would discourse her, she would for blessed Jesus's sake relieve.

Meanwhile her wandering lord from land to land with weary steps repairs, to seek out places which pious pilgrims used to fre-quent; whilst age and grief, and mournful languishing, with silver hairs had crowned his hoary head, so that good Guy was changed exceedingly : for sorrow and sore travel gives a man a countenance more aged far than they who, with less cares, much longer time had lived; his old acquaintance in those foreign parts, that had his worthy actions seen before, and witness been of all his bold adventures, had lost Sir Guy, as one that had never lived: those that in armour knew his martial face did never expect him in a friar's weed.   Amongst the rest, to whom well known he had been, he met Earl Terrey, now a wandering exile, each unto other being grown strangers ; through sorrow, which the senses oft deceive, they had forgot that ever they saw each other, though Guy and Terrey had sworn brothers been.   But having to each other told their countries, and by what means they travellers became, and how one was a voluntary exile, but the other was constrained to be such : as they were parting with a kind adieu, "Oh, English-man," said Terrey, with a sigh, "I once had a friend, thy country-man, who righted me in my extremest wrongs, and was a champion in the cause of virtue, and was to every tyrant a sworn foe, for on oppression's neck he would set his foot : tell me, dear friend, hast thou not heard of Guy, that had a hand to help, a sword to fight in the behalf of all that were oppressed?" "I have," said Guy, "and knew him many years, he is Earl of Warwick now, and peer of England: what is thy name?" "My name," quoth he, "is Terrey, greater by birth than now my fortune makes me." "Terrey," quoth Guy, "I vow I will do thee right in what I can; my poor good-will esteem, for I too am a friend to the oppressed; and since thou lovest my friend, thy friend I will be. Direct me to the man that is thy foe, I will take thy part as far as strength will go; if Guy himself were here to join with us, he could but say, I will venture life for friends; and be assured, though simple I appear, I have oft had as good success as he." Terrey with hearty thanks requites his love, then brings him to his foe, whom he defies, and with his adverse champion bravely fights, who by a mortal wound dies at his feet. Yet it was, it seems, a man of matchless worth, who for that combat they had singled out. When this was done, the Earl demands his name; "Pardon," quoth Guy, "that were against my vow; to no man living I will my name reveal, for I have now both name and nature changed. Nature's corruption now my strife is to leave, and to receive a new regeneration.

> Farewell, my friend, if we on earth don't meet,
> In heaven hereafter we'll each other greet."

So he towards Judea's ground departs, to see Samaria and Galilee, places which Christian pilgrims much frequent, because their Saviour's choice was to be there. He to redeem our loss did suffer, even from the manger to the bloody cross. Much time Guy spent, and many years bestowed in travelling about from place to place, surveying each place in the Holy Land, that all his friends in England now supposed that he among the living was no more, for from all pilgrims that had back returned, of noble Guy no tidings could be heard: this put the world to silence, men were mute, because of Guy they knew not what for to say: that dreadful champion that when in bright armour struck such a terror wheresoever he came, was neither known nor feared in simple grey; but did endeavour all that ever he could never to be known to any mortal wight: for unto none would he disclose his name, nor tell to what country he belonged: his noble thoughts in his own breast concealed, his chief design was to remain obscure:

> Until by native love his mind was led,
> To lay his bones where he at first was bred.

CHAPTER XIV.

How Guy returned to England, which he found invaded by the Danes; and how he undertook to fight with Colbron, a Danish giant, whom he killed; upon which the Danish army was overthrown, and forced to fly the land. And how Guy afterwards took himself to a solitary cave, where he lived unknown.

As the most bright and glorious shining day will have a night of darkness to succeed, in which the earth will be wrapped up in clouds, and all the world be clothed in sable weeds, presenting us with drowsy heavy sleep, to keep the thoughts of death in memory, so youth the day of nature's strength and beauty, which had a splendour like the eye of heaven, must yield to fate, by the great law of nature, when length of years shall bring life's evening on. This cogitation dwelt in Guy's sage breast, and made him, when he was in Palestine, think of returning to his native country. He found himself to be well struck in years, and that his glass had but few sands to run, before the close of his declining days; and therefore he to England comes at last, there to be buried where he had been born; for this was all the cause that drew him back, to end his days there where they first began: that his poor body after all his toils, which through the world no resting-place had found, in English ground at last might safely rest.

Being arrived upon his native shore, his country in extreme distress he found; for in each place great store of armed troops against the foe was got in readiness. The King of Denmark to destroy the realm a mighty army had securely landed, which with incredible destruction marched, laying the country waste, and burning towns, and filling all the nation full of terror; which forced King Athelstan, for his security, with his small forces to retire to Winchester; which when the Danes once knew, they thither away, and with their warlike troops set down before it. But that was far too strong for them to take; their walls of stone were then invincible, nor had they cannon keys to let them in. The monk's invention was not then found out, of murdering men by wholesale with their gunpowder: a soldier then that would attain to honour, by manly strokes could only purchase it.

Beholding now how oft they were repulsed by those strong sallies that the English made, and that they were not like to take the city, they beat a parley, and therein proposed that they were willing to decide their quarrel by single combat, to save shedding blood, between a Dane and an Englishman; to which, when both sides had agreed, the Danes brought forth a mighty giant of a prodigious stature, demanding where the foxes all were hid; saying, "If there be one dare meet me here, that for his country will his valour show, let him come forth and try with me his manhood; or else the English are the worst of cowards. For craven cocks on their own dunghills will both crow and strike before they run and cry. Is English courage now become so low that none will fight? Are you so fearful grown? Then I pronounce you all faint-hearted fools, afraid to look upon a martial man. O what prodigious lies, in foreign lands, of these men's valour have I heard repeated! What great achievements have they oft performed, if lies be true! But they are sadly slandered; for in their feet their valour chiefly lies, for they with them can swiftly run away. They have an ancient proverb to instruct them, *That it is best sleeping in a whole skin.*" Thus did he vaunt in terms of high disdain; and threw down his gauntlet, saying, "There is my glove."

All this and more Guy unperceived had heard, and for his country's sake could bear no longer the insulting boast of this proud Danish monster: and therefore straightway goes unto the King, and thus, in pilgrim's weeds, addresses him: "Dread Lord, though in this simple habit hid, this proud insulting foe I beg to combat; for though I seem unfit for what I ask, I never attempted aught but what I did: and therefore doubt not but to free your kingdom from the invasion of injurious Danes, by overcoming this their boasted champion."

To whom the royal Athelstan replied, "Palmer, thou seemest to be a man of courage; but I fear for Colbron thou art much too weak: ah! I remember once I had a champion, upon whose head my crown I would have ventured: but valiant Guy, alas! is now no more. Had he been here, I had not been thus distressed."

To which Guy thus replied, "Great Athelstan, trust me for once, for though I am unknown, it is a just cause in which I do engage; and Heaven does still both favour and succeed the just side. I cannot see one brave an English king, but, aged as I am, my blood is fired, and nothing but his head shall be to me satisfaction for the affront."

At which bold speech of Guy's the King was amazed; and, wondering at the greatness of his spirit, said, "Palmer, I accept thee for my champion, and thou alone shalt be the man on whom I am resolved to venture England's crown." And thereupon ordered immediately that his own armour should be brought; which Guy, having received, soon put on; then girting his massy sword about him, came to the King, and of him took his leave; the King assuring him he did not doubt but Heaven, in whose great cause he was engaged now, would be his strong defence, and give him victory. "Amen," quoth Guy; and with great courage goes from Winchester's north gate unto Hide Mead, where he soon found that monster of a man, treading two yards of ground at every step.

"Art thou," the giant cried, "that mighty man on whom the King will venture England's crown? What, can he find for me no fitter match than this poor rascal in a threadbare coat? Where are all his worthy knights and champions now? A wretch so base as thou art I disdain."

"Giant," said Guy, "I matter not thy words, for hadst thou manhood, thus thou wouldst not rail, nor spend with blasts of

empty wind thy breath. A soldier's weapon best his tale can tell.
Thy destiny thou on my sword shall find, which, whilst thou hast
drops to bleed, will let thee blood: and thus I to chastise thee
will begin." And thereupon such blows he on him laid, that
Colbron never had felt the like before; who with his club waited
to meet his sword, intending to have broke it with one blow. But
Guy was well aware of his design, and by his own agility prevented
him; and therefore boldly he about him laid, until the lubbard's
breath was almost gone. For with a weighty club did Colborn
fight, which missing of his blow, fell on the ground, and the very
earth itself gave way, so ponderous were the strokes that he
designed. So long they held this wrathful furious fight that the
spectators knew not what to judge; though Guy on Colbron
still fresh wounds bestowed, as a presage of his ensuing victory;
and by his activity escaped the danger with which each blow of
Colbron's threatened him. At last, quoth Colbron, "Englishman,
forbear, and sue for mercy, ere I strike thee down." "Villain,"
quoth Guy, "thy coward's fear I scorn, I will have thy life, or it
my own shall cost. We will never part till one be conqueror;
the King hath ventured England on my head, and therefore I will
not yield an inch to thee, for all the wrath that Denmark ere
could boast: thou shalt find metal in these aged limbs; although
thy body bulkier be than mine, I have a heart bigger than thine
by odds. Think on thy ancient grandsire, Gogmagog, who was
at Dover fought by Corinæus, and by that worthy Briton overcome, though he with boldness like to thine had challenged him;
and as he then was served, so shalt thou now." And thereupon
Guy gave him such a stroke it made wide ruptures in the giant's
flesh, and very much provoked his furious choler, laying about
him with the utmost rage; meantime Guy managed both his parts
so well, which was to lay on a load upon his foe, and save himself
from his destructive blows, that he at length gave Colbron such
a wound that on the earth he tumbled in his gore; whilst with
his blood his soul departed hence, and in the sooty regions took
fresh quarters.

Forthwith a shout from out of the town was heard, that made

the welkin echo back the sound, which joyful was to every English heart, and brought as great a terror to the Danes, who with the utmost grief away departed.

King Athelstan then for his champion sent, to do him honour for this great exploit; who by the clergymen was first received with that solemnity his worth deserved; and next by all the nobles was embraced, and entertained with trumpets, drums, and other martial music. But Guy in these things took but little pleasure; refusing costly ornaments and jewels as things that he was out of love withal. To God he only gave the praise of all, blessing His name that thus had given him power to free his country from invading foes; and so entreats that he unknown might pass, to live where poverty regards not wealth, and be beholden to the help of none, and there, by stealth, sometime to view the world; *for true content doth bring so great a treasure, it makes the beggar richer than the king.* "With true content will I abide," said he, "in homely cottage free from all resort: for I have found within a monarch's court content can never long be made to dwell. No, there is ambition, pride, and envy there, and fawning flattery stepping still between." "Yet, gentle palmer," said the King, "I pray that thou at least wilt so far honour me, wherever thou resolvest to abide, as to acquaint me with thy name in private, which is the only boon I ask of thee. Tell me but who thou art, I will ask no more, and on my royal word I will conceal it."

"Why then," said he, "if it may please your majesty, I am your subject, Guy of Warwick named, that have for many years not seen your land, but been where youth by age and travel is tamed: yet there, dread prince, experience taught me wit, and of the follies of the world convinced me. And now I am returned to make my grave within that kingdom which first gave me life. Yet shall no creature else have the least notice of my arrival; no, not my dear wife, till sickness comes, such as does threaten death; then I will acquaint her of my last farewell."

The King thus having heard what Guy had said, went to him, and with joy in his arms embraced him, and with great admiration answers thus: "Most worthy Earl, preserver of thy country, it grieves my soul thou wilt not live with me. O would thy resolutions were to make, that my persuasions might prevent thy vow! But it is too late, they are grown ripe, I see, and thou art fixed in thy determination. Well, worthy man, in this I joy, however, that to thy native soil thou bringest thy bones; where standing monuments of thy great deeds shall last unto the world's remotest ages. In Warwick Castle shall thy sword be lodged, to witness to the world what thou hast been. And lest the future age should grow neglectful in the preserving of thy memory, the castle keeper shall receive a salary, which I myself will straightways settle on him, to keep thy sword in memory of thee. Thy armour likewise, and thy martial spear, which did thee service in thy high designs, shall all be carefully preserved there; that all such men as have distrustful thoughts may think (if from a truth it did not spring) a king would scorn to cheat his people so. And in thy chapel (distant thence a mile) a bone shall hang of that devouring beast, which did so long near Coventry remain, whose rib, by measure, was at least six foot, destroying many that did that way pass, until thy valiant arm the savage slew. By tradition it may down be handed, and unto those that thither come reported, this was Guy's armour, this his massy blade; these bones of murdering beasts which he overcame; and this the tomb wherein his corpse was safe deposited: this the true picture of his shape at length; and this the spear that of his strength did witness, for sure I hold it as a thing ungrateful (when thy remains shall mouldered be to dust) if none shall cause some muse to sing thy fame, and tell the worth of Guy, that English hero. Thy countrymen cannot so forgetful be, when out of sight to leave thee out of mind, when thou for them hast done such mighty things."

This said, in humble duty, wondrous meek, Guy, with a lowly reverence, left the King, to seek some solitary cave or den, which he unto his mansion house converted; and buried whilst alive he poorly lives, making his meat of wholesome herbs and roots. Sometimes he would repair to Warwick Castle, and crave an alms

at his dear lady's hands: who to pilgrims did more bounty show
than any lady in the land besides : and she would ask all palmers
that came there if they were ever in the Holy Land; or, if they
in their travels had seen an Englishman, lord of that noble castle,
who many years from hence had been away? "He was a knight
that never was conquered yet by any human power: I only fear
one cruel tyrant, who is called death; if he has met him, then,
my dearest lord, I never shall behold thy face again, until that
monster do as much for me, and so unite our hearts again together, which gracious Heaven grant: if Guy be dead, O let me
on the earth no longer stay." Thus often did he hear his wife
inquiring with deep complaints, from extreme passion flowing,
yet by no means would grant her kind request, nor yet bestow
one hopeful word of comfort; but yet would view her, as if his
heart would break; then, to prevent his speaking, turn away;
and so, even weeping, to his cell depart: there placing before his
eyes a dead man's head; saying, "With thee I will shortly come
to dwell, and therefore do despise this sinful flesh : my soul is
weary of a guest so bad, and therefore doth at rest desire to be.
My strength is from my feeble limbs departed, and sickness now
begins to gripe my heart : my happiness is now apace approaching,
and I am in hope my foe and I shall part. Long time, alas! I
have fed this adversary, by whom my soul hath been misled so
oft. To my dear Phælice I will send my ring, which I to keep
did promise for her sake. I now no longer will the time defer, for
fear lest death surprise me unawares. Methinks I feel his messenger
approach, and poor weak nature must be forced to yield."

Then called a herdsman as he passed by, and said, "Good
friend, one kindness I desire of thee, and hope thou wilt not
deny it me, for it is a matter that concerns me highly: it is thou
wilt repair to Warwick Castle, and for the Countess ask with
trusty care, and then into her hand this ring deliver, and say the
ancient pilgrim sent it her that lately at her gate with scrip did
stand, to beg an alms in blessed Jesus's name. And if she ask
thee where I may be found, direct her hither; she will well
reward thee."

"Sir," said the herdsman, "I shall be ashamed who never yet spake to a lady in my life: besides, I may perhaps come into trouble, to carry rings to the Earl of Warwick's countess. And then say I should lose it by the way, what would the Countess or yourself say to me?"

"Prithee," said Guy, "frame no such idle doubts, no prejudice can come to thee at all; the thing is honest about which thou goest, and none can call thee into question for it. A courteous ear the lady will give thee, and on my word you will receive no harm."

With that he goes and delivers the token to the Countess; which she receiving, was presently with admiration struck. "O friend," said she, "where is my husband's being?"

"Husband!" said he, "I nothing know of that. It was from an ancient beggar I received the ring, whose house I cannot well describe; for it is neither made of wood nor stone, but under ground he went into a hole. And in my conscience there alone he dwells, and never pays his landlord quarter's rent."

"Ah! it is my Guy," said she; "show me his cell, and for thy pains I will very well reward thee." And then ordering her steward to give the messenger a hundred marks for bringing her those welcome tidings, she straight went with him to the lonely cave, in which her lord led such a solitary life; but he, espying her, as weak and feeble as he was, went forth to meet her, and there her lord and she embraced each other, and wept a while ere they could speak a word: and after a good space that they had been silent, Guy first the doors of silence thus did break:

"Phælice," said he, "now take thy leave of Guy, who sent to thee, ere his sight decays: within thy arms I do entreat to die, and breathe my spirit hence from thy sweet soul. It is not long since to me thou gavest alms at Warwick's Castle gate; it is blessedness poor men's estate to pity. Look not so strange, my dear, lament not so. Ah! weep not, love, I do not want thy tears; for since my coming here I have plenty of tears of true remorse, conscience knows. Thou weepest not now, because I wept no more; but to behold me friendless, poor, and wretched.

My love, I have sought the place that I desire, though few
endeavour for eternal rest. The soul which unto heaven doth
aspire, and only seeks after celestial things, must leave the world
and all its fading joys, and all the vanities thereof detest: for
could we see it with a spiritual eye, we should discern it full of
nought but devils, that always lie in wait to ruin souls, and to that
end are always laying baits to trap and ensnare them. O Phælice!
I have spent (and then he wept) youth, nature's day, upon the
love of thee; and for my God have kept old rotten age, the night
of nature: Christ, my sin forgive; sorrow for this lies heavy on
my soul. O blessed Saviour! pardon my misdeeds, in that I
have destroyed so many men, even for one woman, to enjoy her
love. And therefore in this solitary cave, with God above I have
sought my peace to make; against whom I have been more misled by sin than all the hairs upon my head can number. The
other day, finding my body ill, and all the parts thereof with pain
oppressed, I did compose this will and testament to be the last I
ever ordain. Lo! here it is, and, if I can, I will read it, before I
cease to be a living man.

His last Will and Testament.

" EVEN in the name of Him whose mighty power did heaven and
earth and all things else create, as one that is this instant hour to
die, I do with an unfeigned heart and mind leave both the world
and everything therein. My soul I give to Him that gave it me;
receive it, Jesus, as in Thee I trust. I owe a debt of life that is
due to death, and when I have paid Him He can ask no more. It
is but a little breath, a very vapour, and I could wish He had it
long ago. But here is my comfort, whensoever He comes, it is
ready for Him, though He calls to-day. I owe the world that stock
of wealth it lent me when I at first began to traffic with it.
Less would have given nature more content: the world leaves me
naked, as I came into it; I ask but one poor sheet to wrap me in.
I do bequeath my numberless transgressions, my sins and evils,
they that are so many, that they exceed the bounds of all arith-

metic, those past, those present, all that are to come, to him that made them loads to burden me; Satan, receive them, for from thee they came. I give good thoughts, and every virtuous action, that every grace has guided me unto, to Him from whom proceedeth all that is good. For only evil I by nature do, being conceived, bred, and born in sin, and all my life has been most vile and vain. I give to sorrow all my sighs and tears, fetched from the bottom of a bleeding heart. I give to repentance, tears and watery eyes of a true convert, and unfeigned sighs. Let earth, or sea, a grave yield to my body; so Jesus to my soul grant room in heaven."

"Phælice, I faint, farewell, my loyal spouse : thy husband dies, assist me with thy prayers. I trust to meet thee in a better life, where tears from weeping eyes shall be wiped before the blessed Spirit ; come, in Jesus' name receive, and then convey my soul to heaven." With these last words death closed his eyes, and he to his Creator his blessed soul resigned, while mournful Phælice, well nigh dead with grief, to sorrow all her senses did abandon, and with her tears drowns her departed lord; beating her breast till breast and heart were sore, wringing her hands till she could no more strive. Then sighing said, "Ah ! cruel, cruel death, the dismal, doleful cause of all my sorrows, thou hast deprived me of my dearest lord. Since loathsome air my vital spirits draw, that thou, to recompense me for my loss, would strike that stroke which all my cares may kill : let me not see to-morrow's light, but make me cold as this dead carcass that before me lies; this true description of a mortal man :

Whose deeds of wonder, pass'd and gone before,
Hath left him now at death's dark prison door."

Kissing his face with a farewell of tears, she leaves the body for the grave to claim ; and from that place she bears as sad a soul as any of her sex on that occasion was ever known to do ;

her real grief soon sending her to her departed lord : living but
fifteen days after his death, and then, through extreme sorrow,
followed him.

THEIR EPITAPH.

UNDER this marble pile their lies a knight,
Whose great achievements oft perform'd in fight,
Has through earth's globe immortalised his name,
And given him a never-dying fame ;
For his great actions have perfumed the world,
Like incense upon sacred altars hurl'd.
To save his country he did his life expose,
'Gainst savage beasts, and far more savage foes ;
And in the height of all his valour's pride,
He always fought upon the justest side.
Nor in his youth more famed for war was he
Than in old age he was for piety ;
In pilgrimage to Palestine he went,
Upon himself imposing banishment :
All earthly pleasure he for heaven forsook,
And to a pilgrim's life himself betook.
Now here he rests in peace, and by his side
The fairest dame that ever made a bride ;
Who at so great a rate her lord did love
As none could equal but the bless'd above :
So bright their virtues were, when here alive,
Their names the world's great funeral shall survive.
All sure must know, by that which I have said,
That noble GUY and PHÆLICE here are laid.

THE
HISTORY OF FRIAR RUSH.

VII.

THE HISTORY OF FRIAR RUSH.

CHAPTER I.

How a Devil named Rush came to a Religious House to seek a service.

𝕿𝖍𝖊𝖗𝖊 𝖜𝖆𝖘 𝖘𝖔𝖒𝖊 𝖙𝖎𝖒𝖊 beyond the sea edified and founded a certain house and cloister of religious men, which house was founded at a great forest's side, for to maintain the service of Almighty God, and daily to pray for their benefactors and founders, and for the salvation of their own souls. This place, by reason of their founders and well-disposed people, which gave unto it largely of their goods and possessions, increased in riches, and every man had gold and silver at their will, and also of meat and drink they had great plenty; insomuch that they were so well at ease and had so much that they wist not what to do, they were so full of wantonness, whereby the service of Almighty God was not well maintained among them. For oftentimes they said neither matins nor evensong; and through their great negligence they forgot clean the charge that they were bound to when they entered into their religion, and they lived more like beasts without reason, than like men of good and holy conversation.

When the great Prince of Devils, which are the patrons of all vices, understood of the great misrule and vile living of these religious men, he consulted to keep them still in that state, and worse if it might be.

And these be the names of the devils :—Belphegor, who was Prince of Gluttony; Asmodeus, Prince of Lechery; and Beelzebub, Prince of Envy, who with many other devils assembled together, rejoiced for the misorder of these religious men. And as they were all assembled together with one accord, they chose a Devil to go and dwell among these religious men, for to maintain them the longer in their ungracious living. This Devil was put in raiment like an earthly creature, and went to a religious house, and there he stood at the gate a certain space all alone with a heavy countenance.

Then, within a while after, the Prior came unto the gate and espied Rush, the young man, standing there all alone.

Anon he said unto him, "What dost thou here, and what wouldst thou have?"

The young man with great reverence answered and said, "Sir, I am a poor young man and out of service, and fain would have a master. And, sir, if it please you to have me, I shall do you diligent service, and shall do so well that you and all your brethren and convent shall be glad of me; for I shall keep so well your secrets, that I trust to obtain at all times your good love and favour, and all theirs also."

And when the Prior had heard his words, he was moved with pity, and said, "Go into the kitchen to the Cook, and show him that I have sent thee thither, and bid him show thee what thou shalt do: for thou shalt be with him a certain season, till that some other better thing fall."

Then the young man made his reverence to the Prior, and thanked him, and forth he went to the kitchen, where he found the master Cook.

Anon he made reverence unto him, and said, "Sir, my master the Prior hath sent me hither unto you, and he commandeth you to show me what I shall do, for I must be here and help you."

The master Cook answered and said, "You be welcome." And anon he set him to such business as he had to do.

And thus the Devil became under Cook in the place that he was assigned unto by the Prince of Devils. And then he said (laughing to himself) as followeth:

"I am right glad that my purpose is come so well to pass, for now all mine intent is fulfilled, and I doubt not but all shall be ours. For I shall make such debate and strife among the Friars, that they shall never be at concord and peace. And I shall make them good staves wherewith the one shall beat well the other: and oftentimes they shall lie together by the ears, insomuch that there was never seen nor heard tell of such a rumour and discord in no cloister in the world. And I shall use myself so, that I shall be in great love and favour among them."

Then within four or five days after, it fortuned that the Prior came into the kitchen, and there he found the young man, to whom he said, "Where wast thou born, and what is thy name?"

The young man answered and said, "Sir, I was born very far hence, and Rush is my name."

Then said the Prior unto him, "Rush, canst thou couple hounds together?"

"Yea, sir," said Rush, "that I can do right well; and more than that, I can convey a fair woman into your chamber, and convey her home again so secretly, that no man shall spy it. And also I shall keep your counsel so secretly that it shall never be known."

And when the Prior heard Rush speak so, he was right glad of him, and said, "Rush, if thou canst do as thou hast said, I shall reward thee well for thy labour, and thou shalt be my most well-beloved servant; wherefore make an end of thy business, for soon thou shalt go a little way on a message for me." And so he departed and went to supper.

And when every man had supped, and Rush had done all his business in the kitchen, he came unto his master the Prior, and said, "Sir, what is your will with me?"

The Prior answered and said, "Here a little beside dwelleth a fair gentlewoman, the which I love very well, but I dare not discover my mind unto her myself. If thou canst find the means to bring her secretly unto me, I shall reward thee right well for thy labour and pain."

When Rush had heard the words of his master, and knew all

his mind, he answered and said, "Sir, be of good cheer, and let me alone with that matter."

And so departed Rush from his master, and went straight unto this gentlewoman's house. And when he was thither come, he found the gentlewoman sitting all alone. And when Rush was espied of her, he made unto her great courtesy, and with many reverences these words he said:

"Rest you merry, fair Mistress, the most fairest creature in the world. My Master greeteth you by me, desiring you to come and speak with him."

Then said the Gentlewoman to Rush, "Who is your Master, and what is his will with me?"

"Fair Mistress," said Rush, "I will show you. My Master is the Prior in a house of religion here beside, and he loveth you so well except that you come unto him I know he will be dead for sorrow."

And when the Gentlewoman had heard the words of Rush, she answered and said, "Fair Sir, it were great pity that the gentleman should die for my sake, and rather than he should so do for me, I will come to him, and show him all the courtesy that I can."

Rush was very glad of those comfortable words, and forth they went both together, till they came to the Prior's chamber. And when the Prior saw that she was come, he was the gladdest man in the world, and thanked Rush much for his labour and pain: and so the Prior received her into his chamber, and there he made her good cheer, and they had good meat and wine great plenty. And when the other friars perceived that Rush was such a privy fellow, and so well could keep counsel, they desired him to help them also, and so he did. They were so blinded with ignorance, that they never perceived that he was a very Devil, but every man had him in love and favour.

CHAPTER II.

How Friar Rush threw the master Cook into a kettle of water seething upon the fire, wherein he died.

IT befell upon a day that Rush went forth to sport him, and it was very late ere he came home again, and the master Cook was very angry with him that he was so long absent.

As soon as Rush was entered into the kitchen, the Cook began to chide, and said unto him, "Thou knave, where hast thou been so long?" and with a great staff he laid upon Rush and beat him sore.

And when Rush saw that the Cook was angry, and so far out of reason, and that he had beaten him sore, anon he began to wax very angry with the master Cook, and said unto him, "Thou villain, why hast thou beaten me thus? I will be revenged on thee." Suddenly he caught him in his arms, and threw him into a great kettle which was full of water seething upon the fire, and said, "Lie thou there, in the Devil's name : for now thou shalt neither fight nor chide no more with me :" and so Rush slew the master Cook.

Then when he had so done, he departed out of the kitchen, and went to the next town for his master. And in his absence certain of the friars came into the kitchen to speak with Rush, but they found nobody stirring therein, and some of them went to stand by the fireside, to tarry till Rush came in : for they thought he would not tarry long. And as they stood talking by the fireside, they spied a man in the kettle seething upon the fire. And anon they perceived that it was the master Cook, whereof they were greatly abashed. And with that, crying out, they went unto the Prior and showed him that the master Cook had drowned himself in a kettle seething upon the fire in the kitchen : for which tidings the Prior was right sorry.

In the mean season Rush came home, and anon the friars showed Rush of the great misfortune that was fallen on the master Cook in the kitchen, and he made as he had been sorry therefor, and had known nothing thereof, and he was in great love and favour with the Prior and all the friars, that they mistrusted him nothing for that deed, and so there was no more mention of the master Cook. Then the Prior commanded that Rush should be made Cook, and all the convent was right glad of that, and so he was himself also, for he thought his enterprises came well to pass after his mind, and as he would have it.

Thus Rush became master Cook in the kitchen, and dressed their meat marvellous well: for in the Lent, and in the Advent, both Fridays and also other days, he put bacon into their pottage-pot, the which made the pottage to savour well. And he dressed their meat so deliciously, that the Prior and all the friars had great marvel that he did it so well: in so much that they said he did much better than their other master Cook did, and that he was a more cunninger man in his occupation, and could do much better in his office. Thus Rush continued in that office the space of seven years, and did right well, and every man had him in love and favour.

Then it fortuned upon a day the Prior and his brethren were assembled together in a general council, and as they stood talking together, the Prior remembered Rush, and anon he said unto his brethren, "Friends, we have here Rush, which is our master Cook in our kitchen, and he is an old servant, and much diligent and true service he hath done to us, and he hath continued among us longer than any servant that ever we had: wherefore methink it reason that he were promoted into some other office, and made a Brother among us." Then all the whole convent with one voice said they were content it should so be.

So the Prior sent for Rush, and when he was come before him and all his brethren, the Prior said, "Rush, it is so; thou hast been here a long season, and we have found thee hitherto a true and diligent servant, wherefore we will that thou be promoted, and take upon thee an habit as we have, and to become a Brother among us."

Rush answered and said, "My Masters, I thank you all," and then the Prior gave Rush his habit, and put it on his back. And so Rush became a Brother in the place; nevertheless he kept his office still.

How Friar Rush made Truncheons for the Friars to fight withal.

WHEN Rush had on the habit of a Friar, and was a Brother in the place, he had more vacation days than he had before. And as a king or a great prince prepareth ordinances against their wars, in likewise did Friar Rush : for when all his business was done in the kitchen, and that he had leisure, he went and sat in the port of the utter gate, and there he was making of good big truncheons of oak. And he made them with hilts over the hand for slipping, of the which the other Friars had great marvel, and demanded of him wherefore he made those truncheons.

Rush answered and said, "Fair Sirs, I make them for this intent: that if there come any thieves hither for to rob us, and to spoil our place, yet shall we have weapons to defend us withal. And therefore I make them. And, moreover, when any need shall be, come to me and every man shall have one, and they shall be ready at your commandment." And then the Friars thanked him and so departed.

Then it fortuned upon a day, that the Prior and sub-Prior fell at discord, and were grievously angry, the one with the other, and would have fought together but only for shame; nevertheless, the anger abode still in their hearts. Within a while after, the noise spread abroad among the Friars that the Prior and the sub-Prior were fallen at discord, for the which they were angry in their minds. And they that loved the Prior took his part; and they that loved the sub-Prior took his part: and so they murmured among themselves.

Then they appointed in their minds to revenge their quarrels at one time or other; and so, to make a more surer way in fulfilling their malicious minds and angry hearts, every man after other went privately to Friar Rush to lend them staves, insomuch that there was not a Friar in the place but he had one; and they never went without their staves under their habit, and the one

2 D

knew not that the other had any, they kept them so secretly.   And
when Friar Rush had delivered all his staves he was right glad
in his heart, for he knew right well there should be a great fray
among them either one time or other.

So it fortuned afterward, as it is a common custom among
religious people at a high feast, to keep solemn service, and every
man to be at matins at midnight, and so upon a good night, all
the whole convent assembled together in the quier, and were
ready to begin matins; they tarried for nothing but for the
coming of the Prior.   Then anon the Prior came into the quier,
and sat him down in his place, and as he looked about him, he
espied that the sub-Prior was there present.   With that his heart
began to grudge of the old anger that was fallen between them
two, and he thought in his mind that he could never be revenged
in a better time, and suddenly he rose out of his place and went
to the sub-Prior, and with his fist he gave him a good buffet.
The sub-Prior, who was moved with the stroke, started unto the
Prior and gave him another buffet: and with that they went
freshly together by the ears.   And when the other Friars saw
that, every man rose out of their places and drew out their
truncheons, and together they went : who had been there should
have seen good buffets given on both parties.

When Friar Rush saw that they were fighting together, anon
he blew out all the candles and lamps that were burning in the
church, and left no manner of light therein whereby the one might
see the other : and when he had so done, he took his truncheon
in his hand, and went into the quier among the thickest of the
Friars, the which were fighting freshly without light, and there he
laid so lustily about, that many of them he felled to the ground,
and left them there for dead.   And when he had so done, he
stole his way from them, and as he went, he found standing in
the portal of the quier a great old desk.   And anon he took the
desk between both his hands and threw it over the portal into the
quier among all the Friars, and hurt many sore, in so much that
some had an arm broken and some a leg, and other some had
their noses clean pared from their faces, that the blood ran in

their mouths, and as for broken heads to the hard scalp were
no dainty, for every man had one, there escaped none free away.
Who had been there should have had a goodly pastime to see the
Friars creep about the quier, and instead of *Domine labia* they
cried out, "Alas and well away!"

Then when the fray was done and all the noise ceased, Rush
came in among them with a candle-light in his hand, and made
as he had known nothing thereof, and said to them, "Fie for
shame, Sirs! how fortuned this discord to fall among yourselves?
I see well now you regard not your honour, nor the good name
of your place. All the people shall say ye be not honest, nor
good religious men, the which words I would be loth to hear,
and I may not suffer our place so to fall in an evil name: wherefore, good Masters, I require you to set your hearts at rest, and put
the matter into my hands, and I shall do so much that all shall
be well, and you shall be good friends again, and no words shall
be spoken thereof." Then every man complained to him of their
great hurt. And he made semblance as he had been sorry therefor; and then they that could go went up to their cells, and
they that could not go did creep up as well as they could, and
laid them down in their beds, and there they lay till they were
whole again.

And in the space of three weeks and more God was evil served,
for in all that space they sung neither matins nor evensong, nor
never entered into the church, for it was suspended, and for shame
they durst never let it be known. And when they were all whole,
and every man upon his feet again, and might go about the house,
they brought again their staves to Friar Rush, and thanked him
much, and then Friar Rush said unto them, "Sirs, when ye
have need of them again, ye shall find them ready here at your
commandment," for which they gave him thanks, and departed. ·

When Friar Rush saw that they were gone, and that he had
all his staves again, he laughed unto himself and said, "I am
right joyful that mine enterprises be come so well to pass, for I
have done many mischievous deeds since I came first, and yet I
will do more before I depart hence. For I shall cause them to

be damned, and I shall bring their bodies and souls into the
burning fire of hell, there to remain world without end and of
me shall be spoken a thousand years hereafter."

How Friar Rush grimed the waggon with tar, and what cheer he made in the country.

ANOTHER time it fortuned that the Prior had a journey to ride
into the country about a little business that he had there to do,
and anon he called Rush his servant unto him and said, "Rush,
go thy way into the court, and take with thee a dishful of grease,
and grease well the wheels and axletrees of the waggon, and make
all things ready against to-morrow in the morning, for I must ride
forth to-morrow betimes."

Then Rush departed from his master, and went about his
business, and instead of grease, he took a great vessel full of tar,
and anointed the waggon all over with it, both within and without,
and especially in the place where the Prior should sit : and when
he had done, he returned to his master's chamber. Then the
Prior demanded of Rush if he had done as he commanded him.
"Yea, Sir," said Rush, "ye may ride when please you." And so
they went to their beds. Then on the morrow after, the Prior
and Rush his servant, with his other company, rose up very early
in the morning for to accomplish their journey, and forth they
went unto their waggon. And when the Prior was entered
therein, he perceived himself all to be berayed[1] and smeared,
and all his clothes were filed therewith : and then he said to
Rush, "Thou lewd fellow, what hast thou done to this waggon
that I am thus arrayed therein?"

Rush answered and said, "Sir, I have done nothing but as
you commanded me."

"That is not," said the Prior, "for I commanded thee to take
grease and grease but the wheels and the axletrees, and thou hast
taken tar and anointed it all over, both within and without. Why
hast thou done so?"

---

[1] *Berayed*, befouled.

"Sir," said Rush, "I understood you bade me do so."

And when the Prior saw there was no other remedy, he commanded his servants to make ready another waggon, and in the mean season the Prior went into his chamber and put on another habit, and came again and mounted into the waggon and went their way, and so long they rode that they came to their journey's end.

And when they were alighted at their lodging the Prior called for his supper, and anon everything was made ready, and the good man of the house and the Prior sat down to supper together and made good cheer; and then the Prior called for wine of the best, and anon he had his commandment. And when the good man of the house and the Prior had supped, Rush and his fellows sat down to the reversions that their masters had left. But they had no wine: wherefore Rush was very sad, and ever he mused by what policy he might get some wine. And anon he called the wife of the house and said, "Mistress, I pray you fill a bottle of wine for me and my fellows," and so she did: and when that was gone they called for another: and then they called for the third, and so ended their supper. Then on the morrow, when the Prior had done all his business, and was ready to return home again, he called for a reckoning. And anon the good wife came in and gave him a reckoning of all things, both horse meat and man's meat; and at last she reckoned three bottles of wine that Rush and his fellows had. And when the Prior heard that his servants had drunk so much wine, anon he began to wax very angry, and asked her who commanded her to fill in so much wine?

The wife answered and said, "Sir, Rush your servant commanded me to fill it in, and he said that you should pay therefor."

Then anon the Prior called for Rush, and said unto him, "Thou lewd knave, why hast thou drunk so much wine? Might no less than bottles serve thee and thy fellows?"

"Sir," said Rush, "we have not drunk so much, for your horses hath had two of the bottles."

"My horses!" said the Prior; "what should they do with wine?"

"Yes, Sir," said Rush, "your horses laboured sorer than we did, and were very weary, and they had nothing but hay and oats; wherefore, methought it needful to give them some good drink to their coarse meat to comfort their hearts withal, and to cause them to be the lustier, and to have the better courage to bring you homeward."

And when the Prior had heard that answer of Rush, and saw there was no remedy but patience, he paid for the wine, and all things that he had taken there, and so rode home in his waggon; and Friar Rush never went forth again with his master.

How the Prior made Friar Rush Sexton among the Friars, and how he charged him to give him knowledge how many Friars were absent from matins at midnight, and what they were.

WHEN the Prior was come home, he made Friar Rush sexton of the church, and his office was to ring the bell and to light the candles, and to call the Friars to matins at midnight; and also the Prior commanded Rush and charged him that he should take good heed that there were none of the Friars absent from matins, and if there were, to give him knowledge thereof. Then said Rush to his master, "Sir, all your commandment shall be fulfilled," and so they departed.

And within three or four nights after, Rush espied certain of the Friars that were absent, and he marked them well, and on the morrow after he presented them to the Prior. And anon the Prior caused them to come before him, and gave them a check for their being absent. In a little time Rush had presented them all, which caused the Prior to be greatly offended with them.

When they perceived that Rush had made such complaints against them, they had him in much disdain, but they could not amend it; for he had them in such great fear, that never after they durst be absent, but well was he that might be first in the quier. When Rush perceived the Friars had him in so great fear, he devised to do some mischievous thing among them; and upon a night, a little before he should ring to matins, he went and brake down the stairs of the dorter,[1] and when he had so done, he went and rung to matins, and lighted the lamps and candles in the church, and went into the dorter, and called up the Friars, and so came and sat at the stairs-foot as he was wont to do.

He had sitten there but a while, but anon there came one, who thought no hurt but to go soberly into the quier as he was wont to do, and when he came to the stairs down he fell, and had a marvellous great fall. Then said Rush, "Thou art one." Presently there came another, and likewise down he fell, and had a sore fall. "Thou art two," said Rush. Anon came the third Friar, which had a mighty great belly, and was a gross man, and he made great haste, for he feared that he should have been last, and when he came to the stairs down he fell on his fellows' necks, and he was so great and so heavy that almost he had mischieved his fellows that lay under him. "Thou makest three," said Rush. And with that there came seven or eight together, and down they fell all at once. "Softly, Masters, for shame," said Rush; "ye come too many at once. Ye were not wont to be so hasty, but now I perceive well ye would deceive me, and one would excuse the other, and therefore ye come so thick to blind me in my tale. How should I now give account to the Prior of them that be absent? Surely, I cannot tell, but now I see well ye be too subtle for me. I would some other man had my office," and made as though he had been very angry with them.

Then the Friars, such as could go, though it were to their pains, rose up again and limping went into the quier, and they that fell first and lay under were sore hurt and could not go, and specially the Friar with the great belly. Yet, nevertheless, they crept into the quier as well as they could. And when they were all assembled together in the quier, each of them complained to other of their great hurts, and so they began matins. Who had been there should have heard a heavy song and a sad, for they were not merry in their hearts, their pains were so great.

When matins was done they that could go went up again into

[1] *Dorter*, dormitory.

their lodgings, and they that could not go lay still in the quier all night.   On the morrow word was brought to the Prior of the great misfortune that was fallen among the Friars at midnight; for the which misfortune the Prior was greatly displeased and angry in his mind, and thought verily it was Rush's deed, for he had done divers evil turns before.

Then the Prior sent for Rush to come speak with him, and when he was come, the Prior said unto Rush, "How fell this misfortune to-night among the Friars, that they be so sore hurt?"

"Sir," said Rush, "I will show you.   It is not unknown unto you that when you put me first into this office ye commanded me to give you knowledge when any of my brethren were absent from matins, and so have I done divers times, whereby many of them have been shent and chidden by you, and for that cause they owe me evil will, and fain would have me out of this office, if they wist how.   And for to accomplish their desire, and to cause you to be displeased with me, I shall show you what they have done this night.   Sir, it is so, that when the time was come I rung to matins, and lighted candles, and made all things ready, and when I had so done I went into the dorter to every man's cell and called them up, then I went and stood at the stairfoot for to tell them as they came down, as I was accustomed to do, and to know who came to matins and who did not.   And for spite that I should not reckon them, they came all on a cluster, and for haste the one thrust the other down the stairs, and he that had the greatest belly had the hardest fall.   Now, if they hurt themselves, what might I do withal?"

And when the Prior had heard the words of Rush he wist not what to say, but for to void all tribulations and misfortunes that might fall in time to come, he put Rush out of his office and set him in the kitchen again.   And when he was there all alone, he laughed to himself and said, "This enterprise is well brought to pass, and I have made a good excuse thereof to the Prior; yea, will I do more ere I depart out of this place."

How Rush went forth a-sporting, and was late forth, and how in
his way coming home he found a cow, which cow he divided into
two parts ; the one half he took on his neck and carried it with
him, and the other half he left still. And how soon he had
made it ready for the Friars' suppers.

It befell upon a time that Rush, when all his business was done
in the kitchen, he would go forth into the country to sport him,
and to pass the time with good company. As he walked on his
way, his chance was to come into a village, which was two or three
miles from the place where he did dwell, and when he was entered
into the village he looked round about him in every corner to find
out some company to make merry withal.

At the last he espied an alehouse, and in he entered, and there
he found good fellows playing at cards, and drinking, and made
cheer. Then Rush made obeisance to them, and sat down
among them, and drank with the players, and afterwards he fell
to play, and was as merry as any man in the company. So long
he played and passed the time, that clean he had forgotten what
he had to do at home, and the day went fast away, and the night
approached.

Anon Rush looked up and perceived that it was almost night,
remembered himself that there was nothing ready at home for the
Prior's supper and convent, and it was almost supper time, wherefore he thought it was time to depart thence. So he paid for his
drink and took his leave, and homeward he went. And in his
way he found a fat cow grazing in the field, and suddenly he
divided her into two parts ; the one half he left lying there still,
and the other half he took on his neck and carried it home, and
quickly he made it ready. Some he put in the pot, and some
upon the spit, and he made a great fire and set on the pot, and
laid to the spit : and he made marvellous good pottage, and
roasted the meat very well, and he made such speed, that everything was ready by the hour accustomed to go to supper, whereof
the Prior and all the Friars had great marvel, that he had made
everything ready so soon, and was so well done ; for they knew

that it was late ere he came home. For some of the Friars had been in the kitchen a little before, and saw neither cook nor fire, nor anything prepared toward supper, wherefore they gave great praise to Rush, and said he was very quick in his office.

How a Farmer of the Prior's sought his Cow, and how he was desolated by the way homeward, and was fain to lie in a hollow tree; and of the vision that he had.

THERE was a poor husbandman, dwelling there beside, which was a farmer of the Prior's: the which poor man had a cow abroad in the fields, that was accustomed every night to come home at a certain hour, and never failed. And at the last a mischance fell unto her, for Friar Rush had slain her as she stood in the field, and so she failed of her coming home at her hour as she was wont to do.

And when the poor man saw that his cow came not home, he thought in his mind it was not well with her, so forth he went in an evening for to seek his cow, and so long he travelled about in the fields, that at the last he found the one half of his cow lying there. But the other half was clean gone, and she was so cleanly divided in two parts, that he imagined in his mind that it was not possible to be done but by man's hands, for if any wild beasts had done it they would have spoiled the flesh. So he returned homeward again, and ere he came at the half way, the night was so dark that he could not see which way he went, and so he went out of his way, and house could he find none. At the last he came to an hollow tree wherein he sat him down, thinking there to take his rest all night, and he had not sat there but a while, but anon there assembled a company of Devils, and among them they had a great principal master whose name was Lucifer, and he was the first that spake.

And the first that was called was a Devil, named Belzabub, and with a loud voice he said unto him, "Belzabub, what hast thou done for us?"

· Belzabub answered and said, "Sir, I have caused debate and strife to fall between brother and brother, insomuch the one hath slain the other."

"That is well done," said the master Devil, "thou shalt be well rewarded for thy labour."

Then forth he called another Devil, named Incubus, and demanded of him what he had done?

"Sir," said Incubus, "I have caused great debate and strife to fall between two lords, through the which they have had great wars, and many men have been slain."

Then said the master Devil, "Thou art a true servant to us, thou shalt be well rewarded for thy great labour and pain."

Then said the great master unto another Devil, named Norpell, "What hast thou done for us?"

"Sir," said Norpell, "I have been among players at the dice and cards, and I have caused them to swear many great oaths, and the one to slay the other: and also I have caused debate and strife to fall between man and wife, and caused the wife to cut her husband's throat."

"That was well done," said the master, "thou shalt be well rewarded for thy labour."

Then forth came another Devil named Downesnest, and said, "Sir, I have caused two old women to fight so sore together, and to beat each other about the head, that their eyes flew out."

"That was well done," said the master Devil, "with much thank thou shalt be rewarded for thy labour."

Then forth went Friar Rush freshly, and with a good courage, and said, "Sir, I am in a religious place, and I govern the prior and his convent as I will myself, and they have me in great love and favour; for I do them many great pleasures, and divers times I have caused debate and strife to fall among them, and I have made them staves, and caused them to fight stiffly together, and to break each other's heads, and their arms and legs, and yet will I do more among them ere I depart out of the place, for I shall make so great debate and strife among them that the one shall slay the other, then they shall come and dwell with us in hell, and burn in perpetual fire without end."

Then said the master Devil to Rush, "If thou have done as thou hast said, thou hast done well thy part, and I pray thee be diligent thyself about thy business, and stir them to sin, and specially to these three, that is to say, wrath, gluttony, and lechery, and briefly to make an end of thy enterprise, and slip it not: and when thou hast done, come home, and thou shalt be highly exalted and well rewarded for thy great labour and pain."

When Rush had told his tale, the great master Devil commanded every Devil to go his way and do the best he could; and thus they departed. Some went one way and some another, and thus they were scattered abroad in the world, to finish and make an end of their enterprises that they had taken in hand.

And when the poor husbandman which sat in the tree saw that all the Devils were departed and gone, he rejoiced in his heart and was right glad thereof, for as long as they were there, he was ever in great fear and dread. He was afraid that they should have seen him there, and ever he prayed unto Almighty God to be his guard, and save him from that foul and evil favoured company of devils, and to send him the light of the day that he were gone out of that place. For he was weary that he abode there so long, and oftentimes he looked up to see if he could perceive any light of the day whereby he might see to depart thence, for till then he durst not once stir out of that place, for he feared that they had been there still. Then within a while after, the day began to appear, and when he perceived that, anon he started up and looked round about him abroad in the fields, and when he perceived that there was nobody stirring, he thanked Almighty God that he was preserved out of that great jeopardy, and so departed.

How the Farmer which lay in the tree came unto the Prior on the morrow after, and tolde him the wordes that he had heard, and the words of Friar Rush, that he was a very devil.

As soon as the day began to appear the poor Farmer arose out of the tree, and took his way straight to the Prior, and he would never rest till he had spoken with him. And when he was come to his speech, anon he said: "Sir, this night hath fortuned to me a great adventure."

"How so?" said the Prior.

"Sir, yesternight late in the evening, I walked forth in the fields to seek a cow which I have missed this four or five days, and so long I wandered abroad till at the last I found the one half of my cow, but the other half was gone. And as I would have returned home again I was benighted so sore that I lost my way. Then I wist not whither to go, but spying a hollow tree, I sat me down, thinking there to take my rest till the day appeared again. And I had not sitten there but a while, but instantly there was assembled a great company of devils, which made a marvellous great noise, whereof I was sore afraid. They had among them a great master named Lucifer, who called all the rest to make a reckoning of all their service they had done since they departed out of hell. There I heard many marvellous tales. At the last forth came Friar Rush. Then said the great master Lucifer unto him, 'Rush, what hast thou done since thou departed out of hell?' and he answered that he had ruled you and all your convent, and caused you to chide and fight, and were never in unity and peace among yourselves. And he said he had caused you to live viciously, and yet he said he would do more ere he departed out of this place, for he will cause you to kill each other, and then you should be damned in hell, both body and soul. And so every devil departed and went about their business. Wherefore take heed, for he is a very devil."

And when the Prior had heard the words of the Farmer, he thanked him for his labour, and so they departed. The Farmer went home to his house, but the Prior was marvellously abashed at the words of the Farmer, and went into his chamber and was much grieved in his heart that he had so lewdly misordered himself against his Lord God. And with great contrition he kneeled down upon his knees, and asked Almighty God mercy and forgiveness for the great and grievous offences that he had committed and done against Him, and that he had so vilely misused the order of his religion. And when he had thus done he departed out of his chamber and went into the cloister, and caused all his brethren to come together. And when they were all assembled, the Prior told them every word as the husbandman had told him, and that Rush was a very devil and no earthly creature; at the which they were sore astonished, and were right sorry in their hearts that they had followed him so much in his mind, and done after his counsel, and were heavy in their hearts for their great and abominable sins that they had committed and done, and with great contrition they knelt down upon their knees and desired Almighty God for grace and pardon. Then the Prior caused every man to fall to contemplation and prayer.

Then forth they went and did the Prior's commandment, and briefly made them ready, and went to prayer all at once. And when they were come to the midst of their service the Prior departed out of the church and went to the kitchen, wherein he found Rush, who was there very busy. Then the Prior commanded him to stand still, and by virtue of Almighty God and of all the company of heaven, he conjured Rush into the likeness of a horse, and commanded him to go and stand at the gate in the same place that he stood in when he came thither first, and to stand there till service was done. So forth went Rush in the likeness of a horse, and stood at the gate as the Prior had commanded him.

And when service was done, the Prior and his brethren went to the gate to see what case Rush was in; and when they were come thither they found him standing in the likeness of a horse.

Then they demanded him to what intent he came into their place, and why he tarried there so long.

"Sirs," said Rush, "I came hither to cause you to do all mischief, as is aforesaid, and yet I would have done more ere I had gone hence; for I would have caused you to slay one another, and to be damned both body and soul."

· And when they had heard the words of Rush, every man held up his hands and thanked Almighty God that they had so well escaped that great misfortune.

Then Rush desired the Prior license to depart thence, and

promised that he would never more come there, nor do any man more hurt; upon that condition the Prior gave him leave to depart. Thus Rush departed from the place, and the Friars went to their cloister, and lived there solitary and chaste ever after, and served Almighty God better than ever they did before.

The Lamentation that Rush made when he was departed out of the house of Religion.

WHEN Rush was banished out of the house of Religion, and was turned into the same likeness that he was, then he wandered abroad in the world with an heavy heart, and these words he said: "Alas, alas, what shall I do? I wot not now whither to go, for all my seven years' labour is lost."

And as he wandered about, by fortune he met with his master Lucifer, but he would not have seen him by his will. Nevertheless his master espied him quickly, and said to him, "Rush, what tidings with thee?"

"Sir," said Rush, "I have lost all my labour that I have gone about this seven years."

"How so?" said his master.

"Sir, I shall show you," said Rush. "The last time that we were assembled together, there was a poor man lay in an old tree hard beside us, and he heard all that we said: and when we were departed, he arose and went unto the Prior and showed him all that we said, and specially the words that I had spoken, and so all my labour is lost, and I am banished that place."

"Well," said the master Devil to Rush, "thou shalt go some other way abroad, and look if thou canst find anything to do."

Then Rush walked about in the country, and long it was ere he could get any service: At last he fortuned to come unto a husbandman's house which lacked a servant, where he was entertained, but sore against the wife's consent. For this husbandman's wife was a very fair woman, and she loved well the parish Priest, and he loved her again, insomuch that oftentimes they made good cheer and banqueted together, and so continued and

kept company together a long time. Their meeting was so privy
and so secret that it was never known, and they, sure enough of
the good man, for he was accustomed every morning to rise early
and to go far into the field. And because his wife would prevent his coming home to dinner, she would always give him his
victuals in a bag with him, and a bottle full of drink, to the intent
he should tarry in the fields from morning to night. She would
not suffer him to keep a servant, or to have any manner of help :
for she was afraid that if they should have a servant, her secrets
should be known, and the goodman also feared that if he should
take a servant, that he would have but little lust to tarry there;
for the Devil himself could not endure the chiding and brawling
of that woman.

How Rush came to a Husbandman labouring in the field and desired to be entertained into his service.

RUSH travelling up and down, came to a Husbandman who was
labouring in the field, being all alone, and spake these words
unto him : "Rest you merry, sir, methinks you take great pains
to work so sore yourself; will it please you to entertain a servant?
I am a poor young man and am out of service, and I am very
willing to serve you if you please : and I trust to do you such
service, as shall be to your good content."

The husbandman answered him, and said : "Young man, I
would gladly give you entertainment, but my wife will never be
pleased with any servant that shall come into my house."

"Sir," said Rush, "let me alone, for I shall so work the matter,
that my dame shall be well pleased with me."

"Well," said the husbandman, "tarry with me till I have done
my business, and thou shalt go home with me."

When he. had finished his day's work, Rush went home with
him. They were no sooner come into the house, but the wife espying Rush, she began to gloom and to look marvellous angrily at
him : which the good man perceiving, he said unto her, "Dame,
I pray thee to be contented, thou knowest well enough that I

have more labour to do than I am able to make an end of alone, and therefore I have hired this young man to help me."

When his wife heard those words, she was more angry than before, and began to brawl and scold as if the Devil had been in her, and said unto him : " What a vengeance needest thou to take a servant ? thou art able enough thyself to do all the business that we have to do, and why should we take more charge upon us than we are able to bear ? but I now perceive thou art given to laziness, and hast little mind to work thyself."

When the good man heard her so highly displeased, he said, " Dame, I pray thee be contented, the young man is honest, and he hath promised me to be a good servant."

Yet for all these speeches she would not be pacified, but brawled still.

When Rush perceived her great impatience, he said unto her, " Dame, I pray you be contented, and be not angry with me, for you shall have no cause. My master hath hired me but for a while, upon a trial, and I trust, in that time, so to behave myself, as to give you both content. When my time cometh out, if you like my service you shall have it before any other whatsoever ; if not, I will be very well content to depart."

When the wife heard Rush speak so reasonably, she pacified herself, and said no more ; which caused the good man to be very glad, and so she set them to supper.

As they sat at meat, Rush demanded of his master what he should do the next day ? His master answered, " Thou must rise early and go to the field, and make an end of that which I was about this day." Which was a great day's work. So when they had supped they went to bed.

Early in the morning Rush arose and went to the field, and wrought so lustily, that he had done his work betimes ; for when his master came to bring him his breakfast, all his work was finished, whereat his master had great marvel. Then they sat down to breakfast, which being ended they went home, and did such things as were there to be done. When his dame saw that he had so soon ended his business, she thought that he was a profitable servant, and said little but let him alone.

In the evening Rush demanded of his master what he should do the next morrow? His master appointed him twice so much as he did the day before, which Rush refused not, but got up early in the morning, and went to the field, and about his work. So soon as his master was ready, he took his man's breakfast and came to the field, thinking to help Rush. He was no sooner come from his house but the Priest came to see his wife, and presently she made ready some good meat for them to be merry withal. And when the goodman came to the field, he found that Rush had done all that which he appointed, whereof he had great marvel. Then they sat down to breakfast, and as they sat together, Rush beheld his master's shoon, and perceived that for fault of greasing they were very hard. Then said Rush to his master, "Why are not your shoes better greased? I marvel that you can go in them, they be so hard; have you no more at home?"

"Yes," said his master, "I have another pair lying under a great chest at home in my chamber."

Then said Rush, "I will go home and grease them, that you may put them on to-morrow;" and so he walked homeward merrily and sung by the way. And when he approached near the house he sang out very loud. With that his dame looked out at the window, and perceived that it was her servant. She said unto the Priest, "Alas, what shall we do? our servant is come home, and my husband will not be long after." And with that she thrust the meat into the oven, and all that was upon the table.

"Where shall I hide me?" said the Priest.

"Go into the chamber, and creep under the great chest among the old shoon, and I shall cover you," and so he did.

And when Rush was come into the house his dame asked him why he came home so soon? Rush answered and said, "I have done all my business, and my master commanded me to come home and grease his shoon." Then he went into the chamber and looked under the chest, and there he found the Priest, and he took him by the heels and drew him out, and said, "Thou Priest, what dost thou here?" With that, the Priest held up his hands and cried him mercy, and desired him to save his honesty, and he would never more come there; and so Rush let him go for that once.

How Rush came home to make clean the stable, and how he found the Priest under the manger covered with straw.

WITHIN a while after this foresaid Priest thought once again to adventure himself and go to the husbandman's house. When he perceived that the goodman and Rush his servant was in the field a labouring, he went with all speed to the house, and when he was entered, the wife said he was welcome, and made ready a good dish of meat, and set it on the table before the Priest, then she drew drink and sat down beside him. They had not sitten there long, but anon Rush came singing homeward, and when she espied him she was abashed and wist not what to do, but thrust the meat into the oven as she did before.

Then said the Priest, "Where shall I hide me?"

"Come with me," said the wife, "into the stable, and creep under the manger, and I shall cover you with straw, and tarry there till he be gone again."

Then she turned again into the house, where she found Rush her servant, and anon she demanded of him why he came home so soon? Rush answered that he had done all his business, and he was come to make clean the stable. When the wife heard that, she was sorry in her heart, for she doubted that he would find the Priest again. Then forth went Rush into the stable, and took a great fork in his hand and began to shake up the straw: and when he came to the heap that the Priest lay in, the which seemed to him very great, yet nevertheless with his fork he took all up at once and bare it out of the door, and laid it on a great heap of muck that lay there. And with his fork he shaked the straw abroad, and when he had shaken out a little, anon he was aware of the Priest's gown. Then he said, "What a devil art thou?" and with his fork he turned the heap, and then he perceived that the Priest was come again. Then with his fork he gave him three or four good dry stripes and said, "Thou Priest, what dost thou here? Thou promised me the last day never more to come here, and now I see thou art a false Priest. But now I shall make an end of thee, and then shalt thou never deceive me more." And when the Priest heard him say so, he fell upon his knees and held up his hands, and prayed Rush to save his honour once again and he would never come there more, and if he did, then to do with him what he would.

Thus Rush let the Priest go the second time.

How Rush came home and found the Priest in the cheese-basket,
and how he trailed him about the town.

THEN within a fortnight or three weeks after, the Priest thought he was long absent from the husbandman's wife. And though it should cost him his life yet would he go thither once again. And on a day he perceiving the goodman was gone to the field, he took his way unto the house, and his wife quickly went and prepared good cheer for him, as she was wont to do; for they thought themselves sure enough for the time, but yet they were deceived. For when the goodman was come to the field, Rush had done all his business. Then they sat down and broke their fast with bread and cheese; and as they sat eating, Rush spied a hair in the cheese, and then he said to his master, "I trow my dame would poison us, or else she washeth not the basket that the cheese lieth in. Behold it is all full of hairs. I will go home and wash the basket and make it clean."

So leaving his master in the field and walking homewards, he sung merrily all the way. And when he approached near the house, the wife knew his voice and perceived that he was coming. Then wringing her hands she said unto the Priest, "Go hide you, or else you be but dead."

"Where shall I hide me?" said the Priest.

" Go up into the chamber and leap into the basket that hangeth out at the window, and I shall call you when he is gone again."

Then anon in came Rush, and she asked him why he came home so soon. Then said Rush, " I have done all my business in the field, and my master hath sent me home to wash your cheese-basket, for it is full of hairs." So he went into the chamber, and with his knife he cut the rope that the basket hung by, and down fell Priest and all into a great pool of water that was under the window. Then went he into the stable for a horse and rode into the pool, and took the rope that hung at the basket, and tying it to the horse's tail, rode through the pool three or four times. Then he rode through the town to cause the people to wonder at him, and so came home again. And all this while he made as though he had known nothing, but looking behind him, espied the Priest.

Then he alighted down and said unto him : " Thou shalt never more escape me, thy life is lost." With that the Priest held up his hands and said, " Here is a hundred pieces of gold : take them, and let me go."

So Rush took the gold and let the Priest go. And when his master came home he gave him the half of his money and bade him farewell, for he would go see the world.

How Rush became a servant to a Gentleman, and how the Devil was conjured out of the body of the Gentleman's daughter.

WHEN Rush was departed from the husbandman, he went abroad in the country to look if he could find any more adventures ; and so long he travelled about that at last he espied a gentleman's place, unto the which he took his way. And when he was come thither, as chance was, he found the gentleman walking up and down before his gate. And when Rush was appeared near unto him, he put off his bonnet and saluted him saying : " Rest you merry, good Gentleman."

" Welcome," said he.

" Sir," said Rush, " I am a poor young man and am out of service, and fain would I have a good master."

"What countryman art thou?" said the Gentleman; "and from whence comest thou?"

"Sir," said Rush, "I was born far hence, and many a mile have I gone to seek a good service, but none can I find."

"What canst thou do?" said the Gentleman; "and what is thy name?"

"Sir," said Rush, "I can do any manner of thing that shall please you to set me unto, and Rush is my name."

Then said the Gentleman unto him, "Rush, tarry here with me, and I will retain thee in my service."

When Rush heard the Gentleman speak so, he thanked him much and tarried there.

Then as the Gentleman and Rush went talking together, the Gentleman said unto him, "Rush, thou hast travelled far and gone through many strange countries: canst thou show me where to find any man can conjure a spirit out of a woman's body?"

"Sir," said Rush, "why ask you me that question?"

"I shall show thee," said the Gentleman. "I have a daughter which is a fair young woman, but she is sore troubled in her mind, and as I suppose she hath some Devil within her body."

"Sir," said Rush, "I pray you let me see her, and I trust speedily to find remedy for her."

Then the Gentleman brought Rush into the place and showed him his daughter. And when he saw her he knew what she had within her body: Anon he said unto the Gentleman, "Sir, there is remedy enough for this."

"Well," said the Gentleman, "if thou canst find me any that can help her thereof, I will reward him well for his labour, and thee also."

"Sir, I will show you what is to be done. There is a place of religion a forty or fifty miles hence, wherein I was a servant a long time, and the Prior is a cunning man in that science: and I doubt not, but if he were here even now, she should be holpen within this hour."

When the Gentleman heard the words of Rush, he rejoiced in his heart and was full glad of that good tidings.

And on the morrow after, the Gentleman sent his servant with his letters unto that house of religion, desiring the Prior to come and speak with him. When the Prior had read the Gentleman's letters, and knew for what cause he was sent for, he made him ready to ride with the messenger. Then forth they rode, and the next day they arrived at the Gentleman's place.

When the Gentleman understood that the Prior was come, he was glad and went to the gate, and with great reverence he received the Prior, and brought him into his place. Then the Gentleman commanded his servant to fill a cup of wine, that the Prior and he might drink together. And when they had drunk and refreshed themselves well, they walked forth into a fair garden, and they communed together of many things, and when they had finished all their communications, the Gentleman said unto the Prior : "Sir, the cause that you be come hither is this. It is so, that I have a young Gentlewoman to my daughter which is grievously vexed and troubled in her mind, and as I suppose she hath some wicked spirit in her body, and, sir, it was showed me by a servant of mine which was long servant in your place, that you could help her."

"Sir," said the Prior, "what is his name?"

The Gentleman said, "His name is Rush."

And when the Prior heard his name he knew him well enough, and said unto the Gentleman, "Sir, cause the gentlewoman to come before me, and I trust in Almighty God shortly to find a remedy for her."

When the Gentleman heard the Prior speak so, he was glad in his heart, and commanded in all haste to bring forth his daughter before the Prior : and when she was come into his presence, he commanded her to kneel down upon her knees, and also he commanded her father and her mother, and all the company that were there present, in likewise to kneel upon their knees, and pray unto Almighty God for the young Gentlewoman. And then he himself said certain prayers over her. Then he lifted up his hand and blessed her, and incontinent there flew a great Devil out of her mouth.

And the Prior bound the Devil so, that never after he came there. Thus was the young Gentlewoman restored to her right mind and health again.

Then the Gentleman would have given to the Prior a great sum of money for his labour, but he would take none, but said unto the Gentleman: "Sir, I have a new church in building, and I lack lead to cover the roof: and as it is informed me, this is a plentiful country thereof. Wherefore, sir, if it will please you to give me as much as shall serve me : I and my brethren shall be your daily beadsmen, and you shall be prayed for as long as the world endureth."

"Ye shall have as much as shall serve you," said the Gentleman ; "but how will ye do for the carriage?"

"Well enough," said the Prior.

Then the Gentleman brought him to a great heap of lead, and bade him take as much as would serve him. Presently the Prior called forth Rush and commanded him to take on his neck so much lead as would cover his church, and bear it home, and come again quickly. So Rush took the lead on his neck at once and carried it home, and he was there again within half an hour. Then the Prior took his leave of the Gentleman and departed, commanding Rush to bring him home also. Then Rush took him on his neck, and within one quarter of an hour he was at home. Then the Prior conjured Rush again into his own likeness, and commanded him to go into an old castle that stood far within the forest and never more to come out, but to remain there for ever. From which Devil, and all other Devils, defend us good Lord. Amen.

MORE OF THE HUNDRED MERRY TALES.

---><---

Of the ſkoler of oxford that prouyd by ſoupheſtry .ii. chekyns .iii.

A RYCH frankelyn in yᵉ contrey hauyngc by his wyfe but one chyld and no mo for the grete affeccyon that he had to his ſayde chylde founde hym at Oxford to ſcole by the ſpace of .ii. or .iii. yere. This yonge ſcoller in a vocacyon tyme for his dyſport came home to his fader.

It fortuned afterwarde in a nyght the fader yᵉ moder & the ſayde yonge ſcoller ſyttynge at ſupper hauynge before them no more mete but onely a cople of chykyns the fader ſayd this wyfe. Sone ſo it is that I haue ſpent moch money vpon the to fynde yᵉ to ſcole/ wherfore I haue grete deſyre to know what haſt lernyd. To whom yᵉ ſone anſwerde & ſayde. Fader I haue ſtudyed foueſtrye & by that ſcyence I can proue yᵗ theſe .ii. chykyns in yᵉ dyſh be thre chykyns. Mary ſayd yᵉ fader that wolde I ſayne ſe. The ſcoller toke one of yᵉ chykyns in his hand & ſayd. Lo here is one chykyn/ and incõtynent he toke both yᵉ chykyns in his hand ioyntly & ſayd here is .ii. chykyns and one & .ii. maketh .iii. Ergo here is .iii. chykyns. Then the fader toke one of the chykyns to hymſelfe and gaue another to his wyfe & ſayd thus. Lo I wyll haue one of yᵉ chykyns to my parte/ & thy moder ſhall haue another & bycauſe of thy good argument thou ſhalt haue yᵉ thyrde to thy ſupper/ for thou getteyſt no more mete here at this tyme/ whiche promyſe the fader kept & ſo the ſcoller went without his ſupper.

¶ By this tale men may fe that it is grete foly to put one to fcole to lerne any fubtyll fcyence whiche hath no naturall wytte.

Of the courtear that dyd caft the frere ouer the bote.

A COURTYER & a frere happenyd to mete togyder in a fery bote & in cōmunycacyon betwene them fell at wordys angry & dyf-pleafyd eche with other/ & fought & ftrogled togyder/ fo that at the laft yᵉ courtyer caft the frere ouer the bote/ fo was yᵉ frere drowned. The ferymā whiche had ben a man of warre the moft parte of his lyfe before and feynge the frere was fo drowned & gon fayd thus to the courtyer/ I befhrewe thy hart thou fholdeft haue taryed & foughte with hym a lande for nowe thou haft caufed me to lefe an halfpeny for my fare.

¶ By this tale a man may fe that he yᵗ is accoftumed in vycyous & cruel company fhall lofe that noble vertew to haue pyte & compaffyon vpon his neyghboure.

Of hym that aduenturyd body & fowle for hys prynce.

Two knyghtes there were whiche went to a ftondyng felde wᵗ theyr prynce. But one of them was cōfeffyd before he went/ but the other wēt into the felde w'out fhryft or repētaūce/ afterward this prīce wā yᵉ feld & had yᵉ vyctoryc yᵗ day/ wherfore he yᵗ was cōfeffyd came to yᵉ prīce & afkyd an offyce & fayd he had de-feruyd it for he had don good feruyce & aduētured that day as far as ony man in yᵉ felde/ to whŏ the other yᵗ was vncōfeffyd anfweryd and fayd nay by the mas I am more worthy to haue a rewarde than he/ for he aduenturyd but his body for your fake for he durft not go to yᵉ felde tyl he was cōfeffyd/ but as for me I dyd iupd both body lyfe & foule for your fake/ for I went to the felde without cōfeffyon or repentāce.

Of the frere that fayd dyrige for the hoggys fowle.

UPON a tyme certayn women in the countrey were appoynted to deryde and mokke a frere a lymytour that vfyd moche to vyfyth them. wherupon one of them a lytyll before that the frere came kylled an hog & for dyſport leyd it vnder the borde after the maner of a corſe and tolde the frere it was her good mā and deſyred hym to ſay dirige for his ſoule wherfore the frere and his felaw began Placebo and Dirige and ſo forth ſayd the ſeruyſe full deuowtly which the wyues ſo heryng/ coude not refrayne them ſelfe from lawghynge and wente in to a lytyll parler to lawgh more at theyr pleſure. Theſe frerys ſomwhat ſuſpeſted the cauſe and quykly or that yᵉ women were ware lokyd vnder the borde and ſpyed that it was an hog/ ſodenly toke it bytwene them and bare it homeward as faſt they myght. The women ſeyng that ran after the frere and cryed come agayn mayſter frere come agayne and let it allone/ nay by my fayth quod yᵉ frere he is a broder of oures and therfore he muſt nedys be buryed in our cloyſter/ and ſo the frerys gate the hog.

¶ By thys ye may ſe that they that vſe to deryde and mok other ſomtyme it tornyth to theyr one loſſe and damage.

Of maſter whyttyntons dreme.

SONE after one mayſter Whyttintō had bylded a colege on a nyght as he ſlept he dremyd that he ſad in his church & many folkys ther alſo/ & further he dremyd yᵗ he ſawe our lady in the ſame chyrch wᵗ a glas of goodly oyntement in her hand goynge to one aſkyng hym what he had done for her ſake/ whiche ſayd that he had ſayd our ladys ſauter euery day wherfore ſhe gaue hym a lytyll of the oyle. And anon ſhe went to another aſkyng hym what he had done for her ſake which ſayd that he had ſayd .ii. ladys ſauters euery day/ wherfore our lady gaue hym more of yᵉ oȳtement than ſhe gaue yᵉ other. This mayſter whyttentō then thought that when our lady ſholde come to hym ſhe wolde gyue hym all the hole glas bycauſe yᵗ he had bylded ſuch a gret colege & was very·glad in his mynd. But whē our lady cam to hym ſhe aſked hym what he had ſuffred for her ſake/ which wordys made hym gretly abaſhyd bycauſe he had nothyng to ſay for hym ſelfe/ & ſo he dremyd that for all the gret dede of byldyng of y⁰ fayd Colege he had no parte of y¹ goodly oynte-ment.

¶ By this ye may fe that to fuffer for goddys fake is more merytoryous than to gyue gret goodys.

Of the maltman of Colbroke.

A CERTAYNE maltman of colbroke whiche was a very couetous wreche and had no pleafure but onely to get money came to london to fell his malt and broughte with hym .iiii. capons & there refeyuyd .iiii. or .v. li. for malte and put it in a lytell purs tyed to his cote and after wente aboute the ftrettys to fell his capons whom a pollyng felowe that was a dycer and an vnthryft had efpyed and Imagyned how he myght begyle the man other of his capons or of his money and came to this maltman in the ftreet berynge thefe capons in his hande and afkyd hym how he wolde fell his capons and when he fhewyd hym the pryfe of them he bad hym go with hym to his mayfter and he wolde fhew them to his mayfter and he wolde caufe hym to haue money for them wherto he agreed.   This Poller wente to the cardynalls hat in lomberdys ftrete & when he came to the dore he toke the capons from the maltman and bad hym tary at the dore tyll he had fhewed his mayfter and he wolde come agayn to hym and brynge hym his money for them.   This poller when he had goten the capons wente in to the houfe and wente thorowe the other bak entre in to Cornhyll and foo toke the capons with hym/ and when this maltman had ftond there a good feafon he afkid one of the tauerners where the man was that had the Capons to fhewe to his mayfter/ mary quod the tauerner I can not tell the here is nother mayfter nor man in this houfe for this entre here is a comen hye way and gooth in to cornhyl/ I am fure he is gone a weye with thy capõs.   This maltman herynge that ran throwe the entre in to cornhyll and afkyd for a felowe in a tawny cote that had capons in his hand.   But no man coude tell hym whiche waye he was gone and foo the maltman lofte his capons and after wente in to his Inne all heuy and fade and toke his horfe to thentent to ryde home. This poller by that tyme had chaungyd hys rayment and borowyd a furryd gowne and came to the malt-man fyttynge on horfbak and fayd thus/ good man me thought I harde the inquire euyn now for one in a tawny cote that had ftolyn from the .iiii. capōs yf thou wylt gyue me a quart of wyne go with me and I fhall brynge yᵉ to a place where he fyttyth drynkyng with other felowes & had yᵉ capons in his hande. This maltman beynge glad therof graūtyd hym to gyue hym the wyne bycaufe he femyd to be an honeft man/ and went wᵗ hym vnto the dagger in chepe. This poller then fayd to hym go thy way ftreyght to thend of yᵗ long entre & there thou fhalt fe whether it be he or no & I wyl holde thy horfe here tyll thou come agayn. This maltman thynkyng to fynde the felow with his capōs wēt in & left his horfe with the other at the dore. And as foone as he was gon in to the houfe this poller lad the horfe awaye in to his owne lodgynge. This maltman inqueryd in the houfe for his felowe with the capons but no man coude tell hym no tydyngys of fuche man/ wherfore he came agayne to yᵉ dore all fad & lokyd for hym yᵗ had his hors to kepe/ & bycaufe he fawe hym not he afkyd dyuers there for hym/ & fome fayd they faw hym & fome fayde they faw hym not/ but no man coude tell whiche waye he was gone wherfore he wente home to his Inne more fad thā he was before/ wherfore his hoft gaue hym coūcell to get hym home & beware how he truftyd any men in londō. This maltman feynge none other cōfort went hys hy way homewarde.

This poller which lyngeryd alway there aboute the Inne hard tell that the maltman was goyng homewarde a fote apparelyd hym lyke a mannys prentyfe & gat a lytell boget ftuffyd full of ftones on his bake & wente before hym to charynge croffe & taryed tyll yᵉ maltman came/ & afkyd hym whether he wente whiche fayd to Colbroke. Mary quod yᵉ other I am glad therof for I muft goo to braynforde to my mayfter to bere hym money which I haue in my boget & I wolde be glad of cōpany. This maltman bycaufe of his owne money was glad of his cōpany/ & fo they agreed & wente togyder a whyle. At the laft this poller went fomwhat before to knyghtbryge & fat vpon yᵉ brydge & reftyd

hym with his boget on his bak/ & when he faw yᵉ maltmã almoſt
at hym he let his boget fall ouer yᵉ brydge in to ye water. & incontynent ſtart vp & ſayd to yᵉ maltman alas I haue let my bogct
fal in to yᵉ water & there is .xl. li. of money therin/ yf thou wylt
wade in to yᵉ water & go ſeke it & get it me agayne I ſhall gyue
yᵉ .xii. pence for thy labour/ this maltman hauynge pyte of his
loiſe & alſo glad to get the .xii. pence plukyd of his hoſe cote &
ſhyrt & wadyd into yᵉ water to ſeke for the boget. And in yᵉ
mene whyle this poller gote his clothis & cote wher to the purs
of money was tyde & lepte ouer the hedge & wente to weſt-
mynſter.

This maltman within a whyle after with grete payne & depe
wadynge founde yᵉ boget & came·out of the water & ſawe not his
felowe there & ſawe that his clothys & money were not there as
he left them ſuſpeċtyd yᵉ mater and openyd the boget and than
founde nothynge therin but ſtonys cryed out lyke a mad man and
ran all nakyd to london agayne and ſayde alas alas helpe or I
ſhall be ſtolen. For my capons be ſtolen. My hors is ſtolen.
My money and clothys be ſtolen and I ſhall be ſtolen myſelf.
And ſo ran aboute the ſtretys in london nakyd & mad cryenge
alway I ſhall be ſtole. I ſhall be ſtolen. And ſo contynuyd mad
durynge his lyfe & ſo dyed lyke a wretche to the vtter deſtruccyon
of hym ſelf & ſhame to all his kyn.

¶ By this tale ye may ſe that many a couctouſe wrech yᵗ louyd
his good better than god and ſettyth his mynde inordynatly theron by the ryghte iugment of god oftymes comyth to a myſerable
and ſhamfull ende.

PRINTED BY BALLANTYNE, HANSON AND CO.
EDINBURGH AND LONDON.

www.ingramcontent.com/pod-product-compliance
Lightning Source LLC
Chambersburg PA
CBHW030941110726
47900CB00004B/1084